Clerical Exams

4th Edition

Christi M. Heuer
Sharon S. Saronson, MSE

www.petersons.com/arco

ARCO
THOMSON LEARNING

Australia • Canada • Mexico • Singapore • Spain • United Kingdom • United States

ARCO
THOMSON LEARNING

An ARCO Book

ARCO is a registered trademark of Thomson Learning, Inc., and is used herein under license by Peterson's.

About Peterson's

Founded in 1966, Peterson's, a division of Thomson Learning, is the nation's largest and most respected provider of lifelong learning online resources, software, reference guides, and books. The Education Supersite[SM] at petersons.com—the Web's most heavily traveled education resource—has searchable databases and interactive tools for contacting U.S.-accredited institutions and programs. CollegeQuest® (CollegeQuest.com) offers a complete solution for every step of the college decision-making process. GradAdvantage™ (GradAdvantage.org), developed with Educational Testing Service, is the only electronic admissions service capable of sending official graduate test score reports with a candidate's online application. Peterson's serves more than 55 million education consumers annually.

Thomson Learning is among the world's leading providers of lifelong learning, serving the needs of individuals, learning institutions, and corporations with products and services for both traditional classrooms and for online learning. For more information about the products and services offered by Thomson Learning, please visit www.thomsonlearning.com. Headquartered in Stamford, Connecticut, with offices worldwide, Thomson Learning is part of The Thomson Corporation (www.thomson.com), a leading e-information and solutions company in the business, professional, and education marketplaces. The Corporation's common shares are listed on the Toronto and London stock exchanges.

An American BookWorks Corporation Project

For more information, contact Peterson's, 2000 Lenox Drive, Lawrenceville, NJ 08648; 800-338-3282; or find us on the World Wide Web at: www.petersons.com/about

Fourth Edition

ISBN 0-7689-0699-7

Printed in the United States of America

10 9 8 7 6 5 4 3 2 1 03 02 01

CONTENTS

WHAT THIS BOOK WILL DO FOR YOU

Arco Publishing has followed testing trends and methods ever since the firm was founded in 1937. We *specialize* in books that prepare people for tests. Based on this experience, we have prepared the best possible book to help *you* score high.

To write this book we carefully analyzed every detail surrounding the forthcoming examinations. Since there is such variation in exams, we cannot predict exactly what your exam will be like. *However*, after studying many announcements and many exams, we have written this book to prepare you for the most probable question types. The instructional chapters will prepare you for questions that you are likely to face. The model exams, while they are not actual exams, will give you excellent practice and preparation for your emergency communications exam. Other features of this book include details about:

- the job itself
- official and unofficial announcements concerning the examination
- all the previous examinations, although many not available to the public
- related examinations
- technical literature that explains and forecasts the examination

CAN YOU PREPARE YOURSELF FOR YOUR TEST?

You want to pass this test. That's why you bought this book. Used correctly, your "self-tutor" will show you what to expect and will give you a speedy brush-up on the subjects tested in your exam. Some of these are subjects not taught in schools at all. Even if your study time is very limited, you should:

- become familiar with the type of examination you will have
- improve your general examination-taking skill
- improve your skill in analyzing and answering questions involving reasoning, judgment, comparison, and evaluation
- improve your speed and skill in reading and understanding what you read—an important part of your ability to learn and an important part of most tests

This book will help you in the following ways:

Present every type of question you will get on the actual test. This will make you at ease with the test format.

Find your weaknesses. Once you know what subjects you're weak in, you can get right to work and concentrate on those areas. This kind of selective study yields maximum test results.

Give you confidence *now*. It will build your self-confidence while you are preparing for the test. As you proceed, it will prevent the kind of test anxiety that causes low test scores.

Stress the multiple-choice type of question because that's the kind you'll have on your test. You must not be satisfied with merely knowing the correct answer for each question. You must find out why the other choices are incorrect. This will help you remember a lot you thought you had forgotten.

After testing yourself, you may find that you are weak in a particular area. You should concentrate on improving your skills by using the specific practice sections in this book that apply to you.

HOW DO I USE THIS BOOK?

If you already know what type of career you wish to pursue, this book will help you prepare for any of the major exams. If you don't know what type of job you'd like to apply for, this book will also help you. Not only will you be able to prepare for your exam, but you will also find information here about various types of careers, and perhaps it will narrow down your choices. This book offers you an overview of the world of civil service, a brief introduction to federal, state, and city employers and their hiring requirements, and in-depth descriptions of a number of widely used examinations.

PART ONE

There are five parts to this book. Part One covers the major employment sectors: federal, state, municipal (city), and private Industry careers. There's more than enough for everyone here. Each sector has its own requirements and tests. However, as you will see, there are certain types of questions that will appear on most of these exams, regardless of the type of test you will take.

Also in this section is important information on test-taking techniques. This will give you guidelines to help you prepare for the actual test. Feeling anxious before you take a test is a normal reaction. We provide you with tips on feeling relaxed and comfortable with your exam so you can get a great test score.

PART TWO

Part Two is an overview of the various types of careers available. If you haven't already been in the field, you will be surprised by the number of different job opportunities there are as well as the varied jobs within an area. For example, did you know that there are almost 2,000 different job titles just within the United States Postal Service? This is just *one* federal agency.

If you are beginning your career or job shopping at this time, you should read this section carefully. It will help introduce you to the different jobs and the many opportunities that await you. We hope you will be inspired and excited and will be motivated to apply for, study for, and land one of those jobs. If this section helps you narrow your area of interest, you can then concentrate on the exams that will help you prepare for the job you want. If you are still wide open, give equal attention to each exam.

PART THREE

That leads us into Part Three of this book. In this section, we detail test-types and requirements. We've also given you a review section so that you can practice on a variety of different question types. We suggest you go through this chapter to get an idea of where your strengths lie and what weaknesses you'll have to deal with on the actual test.

We've also provided you with a variety of different types of tests that you will encounter in almost any job you apply for in the civil service, since there are certain basics that need to be covered. For example, in most tests, you will be asked to understand vocabulary and the use of grammar. Some tests will test your memory abilities and your ability for recall. Can you alphabetize easily and quickly? That's an area also covered on many of these tests.

PART FOUR

In Part Four, there are either real examinations, (official sample examinations) or others are model examinations closely patterned on the actual exams. Timing, level of difficulty, question styles, and scoring methods all conform closely to the examinations for which they are meant to prepare. And a special feature of this book is that all the correct answers are explained.

When you do take the sample exams, try to set aside the full measure of time to take the exam at one sitting. Time yourself accurately (a stopwatch or a kitchen timer will work well) and stop working when the time is up. If you have not completed all of the questions when the time expires, stop anyway. Check your answers against the provided correct answers and score your paper. Then continue with the remaining questions to get in all the practice you can. Carefully study all the answer explanations, even those for questions that you answered correctly. By reading all of the explanations, you can gain greater insight into methods of answering questions and the reasoning behind the correct choices.

One very important suggestion: We strongly believe that regardless of the test that you think you're planning to take—or the career path you want to follow—try to take *all* of the exams in this book. It may seem like a lot of extra work, but you never know where you may end up. You may think you're interested in a job with the local city government, and end up instead in a private company. Or the exam you were hoping to take is not being given for another year, but some other test is being given next month. It is always better to be prepared.

PART FIVE

Finally, Part Five contains civil service career information resources. Here you will find out how to go about looking for available jobs, as well as important addresses, phone numbers, and Internet websites that will help you pursue your career in civil service.

The most important thing is to *use* this book. By going through all of the sections and reading them, reviewing question types, and taking the practice exams, you will be using what you learned here to the best of your ability to succeed in your intended career path.

PART ONE

So You Want to Work for The Government

Government service is one of the nation's largest sources of employment. About one in every six employed persons in the United States is in some form of civilian government service. Of those government employees, five out of six workers are employed by state or local governments, and the remainder work for the federal government.

As you can see, government employees represent a significant portion of the nation's work force. They work in large cities, small towns, and remote and isolated places such as lighthouses and forest ranger stations, and a small number of federal employees work overseas. In this chapter, we will outline the various types of careers that are available in the federal, state, and local governments.

WHERE THE JOBS ARE: FEDERAL CIVILIAN EMPLOYMENT

The federal government is the nation's largest employer. It employs almost 3 million civilian workers in the United States and an additional 130,000 civilian workers—half of them U.S. citizens—in U.S. territories and foreign countries. The headquarters of most government departments and agencies are in the Washington, D.C., area, but only one out of eight federal employees works there.

Federal employees work in occupations that represent nearly every kind of job in private employment as well as some unique to the federal government such as regulatory inspectors, foreign service officers, and Internal Revenue agents. Most federal employees work for the executive branch of the government.

The executive branch includes the Office of the President, the cabinet departments, and about 100 independent agencies, commissions, and boards. This branch is responsible for activities such as administering federal laws, handling international relations, conserving natural resources, treating and rehabilitating disabled veterans, delivering the mail, conducting scientific research, maintaining the flow of supplies to the armed forces, and administering other programs to promote the health and welfare of the people of the United States.

The Department of Defense, which includes the Departments of the Army, Navy, and Air Force, is the largest department. It employs about one million civilian workers. The Departments of Agriculture, Health and Human Services, and the Treasury are also big employers. The two largest independent agencies are the U.S. Postal Service and the Veterans Administration.

There is also federal civilian employment available in the legislative branch, which includes Congress, the Government Printing Office, the General Accounting Office, and the Library of Congress. The judicial branch, the smallest employer, hires people for work within the court system.

WHITE-COLLAR OCCUPATIONS

Because of its wide range of responsibilities, the federal government employs white-collar workers in a great many occupational fields. About one of four of these are administrative and clerical workers.

General clerical workers are employed in all federal departments and agencies. These include office machine operators, secretaries, stenographers, clerk-typists, mail- and file-clerks, telephone operators, and workers in computer and related occupations. In addition, there are the half million postal clerks and mail carriers.

Many government workers are employed in engineering and related fields. The engineers represent virtually every branch and specialty of engineering. There are large numbers of technicians in areas such as engineering, electronics, surveying, and drafting. Nearly two-thirds of all engineers are in the Department of Defense.

Of the more than 120,000 workers employed in accounting and budgeting work, 35,000 are professional accountants or Internal Revenue officers. Among technician and administrative occupations are accounting technicians, tax accounting technicians, and budget administrators. There are also large numbers of clerks in specialized accounting work. Accounting workers are employed throughout the government, particularly in the Departments of Defense and the Treasury and in the General Accounting Office.

Many federal employees work in hospitals or in medical, dental, and public health activities. Three out of five are either professional nurses or nursing assistants. Other professional occupations in this field include physicians, dieticians, technologists, and physical therapists. Technician and aide jobs include medical technicians, medical laboratory aides, and dental assistants. Employees in this field work primarily for the Veterans Administration; others work for the Departments of Defense and Health and Human Services.

Other government workers are engaged in administrative work related to private business and industry. They arrange and monitor contracts with the private sector and purchase goods and services needed by the federal government. Administrative occupations include contract and procurement specialists, production control specialists, and Internal Revenue officers. Two out of three of these workers are employed by the Departments of Defense and Treasury.

Another large group works in jobs concerned with the purchase, cataloging, storage, and distribution of supplies for the federal government. This field includes many managerial and administrative positions such as supply management officers, purchasing officers, and inventory management specialists, as well as large numbers of specialized clerical positions. Most of these jobs are in the Department of Defense.

Throughout the federal government, many people are employed in the field of law. They fill professional positions, such as attorneys or law clerks, and administrative positions, such as passport and visa examiners or tax law specialists. There also are many clerical positions that involve examining claims.

The social sciences also employ many government employees. Economists are employed throughout the government; psychologists and social workers work primarily for the Veterans Administration; and foreign affairs and international relations specialists, for the Department of State. One third of the workers in this field are social insurance administrators employed largely in the Department of Health and Human Services.

About 50,000 biological and agricultural science workers are employed by the federal government, mostly in the Departments of Agriculture and Interior. Many of these work in forestry and soil conservation activities. Others administer farm assistance programs. The largest number are employed as biologists, forest and range fire controllers, soil conservationists, and forestry technicians.

The federal government employs another 50,000 people in investigative and inspection work. Large numbers of these are engaged in criminal investigation and health regulatory inspections, mostly in the Departments of Treasury, Justice, and Agriculture.

Physical sciences is another area of government employment. Three out of four workers in the physical sciences are employed by the Departments of Defense, Interior, and Commerce. Professional workers include chemists, physicists, meteorologists, cartographers, and geologists. Aides and technicians include physical science technicians, meteorological technicians, and cartography technicians.

And in the mathematics field are professional mathematicians and statisticians and mathematics technicians and statistical clerks. They are employed primarily by the Departments of Defense, Agriculture, Commerce, and Health and Human Services.

Entrance requirements for white-collar jobs vary widely. A college degree in a specified field or equivalent work experience is usually required for professional occupations such as physicists and engineers.

Entrants into administrative and managerial occupations usually are not required to have knowledge of a specialized field, but must instead indicate a potential for future development by having a degree from a 4-year college or responsible job experience. They usually begin as trainees and learn their duties on the job. Typical jobs in this group are budget analysts, claims examiners, purchasing specialists, administrative assistants, and personnel specialists.

Technician, clerical, and aide-assistant jobs have entry-level positions for people with a high school education or the equivalent. For many of these positions, no previous experience or training is required. The entry level position is usually that of trainee. Persons who have junior college or technical school training or those who have specialized skills may enter these occupations at higher levels. Typical jobs are engineering technicians, supply clerks, clerk-typists, and nursing assistants.

BLUE-COLLAR OCCUPATIONS

Blue-collar occupations—craft, operative, laborer, and some service jobs—provide full-time employment for more than half a million federal workers. The Department of Defense employs about three fourths of these workers in establishments such as naval shipyards, arsenals, the Air or Army depots, as well as on construction, harbor, flood control, irrigation, or reclamation projects. Others work for the Veterans Administration, U.S. Postal Service, General Services Administration, Department of the Interior, and Tennessee Valley Authority.

The largest single blue-collar group consists of manual laborers. Large numbers also are employed in machine tool and metal work, motor vehicle operation, warehousing, and food preparation and serving. The federal government employs a wide variety of individuals in maintenance and repair work, such as electrical and electronic equipment installation and repair, and in vehicle and industrial equipment maintenance and repair. All these fields require a range of skill levels and include a variety of occupations comparable to the private sector.

Although the federal government employs blue-collar workers in many different fields, about half are concentrated in a small number of occupations. The largest group, the skilled mechanics, works as air-conditioning, aircraft, automobile, truck, electronics, sheet-metal, and general maintenance mechanics. Another large number of craft workers is employed as painters, pipefitters, carpenters, electricians, and machinists. A similar number serves as warehouse workers, truck drivers, and general laborers. An additional group of workers is employed as janitors and food service workers.

ENTRANCE REQUIREMENTS

Persons with previous training in a skilled trade may apply for a position with the federal government at the journey level. Those with no previous training may apply for appointment to one of several apprenticeship programs. Apprenticeship programs generally last four years; trainees receive both classroom and on-the-job training. After completing this training, a person is eligible for a position at the journey level. There are also a number of positions which require little or no prior training or experience, including janitors, maintenance workers, messengers, and many others.

THE MERIT SYSTEM

More than nine out of ten jobs in the federal government are under a merit system. The Civil Service Act, administered by the U.S. Office of Personnel Management, covers six out of ten federal titles. This act was passed by Congress to ensure that federal employees are hired on the basis of individual merit and fitness. It provides for competitive examinations and the selection of new employees from among the most qualified applicants.

Some federal jobs are exempt from civil service requirements either by law or by action of the Office of Personnel Management. However, most of these positions are covered by separate merit systems of other agencies such as the Foreign Service of the Department of State, the Federal Bureau of Investigation, the Nuclear Regulatory Commission, and the Tennessee Valley Authority.

EARNINGS, ADVANCEMENT, AND WORKING CONDITIONS

Most federal civilian employees are paid according to one of three major pay systems: the **General Pay Schedule,** the **Wage System**, or the **Postal Service Schedule.**

GENERAL PAY SCHEDULE

More than half of all federal workers are paid under the General Schedule (GS), a pay scale for workers in professional, administrative, technical, and clerical jobs, and for workers such as guards and messengers. General Schedule jobs are classified by the U.S. Office of Personnel Management in one of fifteen grades, according to the difficulty of duties and responsibilities and the knowledge, experience, and skills required of the workers. GS pay rates are set by Congress and apply to government workers nationwide. They are reviewed annually to see whether they are comparable with salaries in private industry. They are generally subject to upwards adjustment for very high-cost-of-living regions. In low-cost areas, the GS pay scale may exceed that of most private-sector workers.

Most employees receive within-grade pay increases at one-, two-, or three-year intervals if their work is acceptable. Within-grade increases may also be given in recognition of high-quality service. Some managers and supervisors receive increases based on their job performance rather than on time in grade.

High school graduates who have no related work experience usually start in GS-2 jobs, but some who have special skills begin at grade GS-3. Graduates of 2-year colleges and technical schools often can begin at the GS-4 level. Most people with bachelor's degrees appointed to professional and administrative jobs such as statisticians, economists, writers and editors, budget analysts, accountants, and physicists, can enter at grades GS-5 or GS-7, depending on experience and academic record. Those who have a master's degree or Ph.D. or the equivalent education or experience may enter at the GS-9 or GS-11 level. Advancement to higher grades generally depends upon ability, work performance, and openings in jobs at higher grade levels.

GENERAL SCHEDULE
(Range of Salaries)
Effective as of January 1, 2001

GS Rating	Low	High
1	$14,244	$ 17,819
2	16,015	20,156
3	17,474	22,712
4	19,616	25,502
5	21,957	28,535
6	24,463	31,798
7	27,185	35,339
8	30,107	39,143
9	33,254	43,226
10	36,621	47,610
11	40,236	52,305
12	48,223	62,686
13	57,345	74,553
14	67,765	88,096
15	79,710	103,623

FEDERAL WAGE SYSTEM

About one quarter of federal civilian workers are paid according to the Federal Wage System. Under this system, craft, service, and manual workers are paid hourly rates established on the basis of "prevailing" rates paid by private employers for similar work in the same locations. As a result, the federal government wage rate for an occupation varies by locality. This commitment to meeting the local wage scale allows the federal wage earner to bring home a weekly paycheck comparable to that which he or she would earn in the private sector and to enjoy the benefits and security of a government job at the same time. The federal wage earner has the best of all possible worlds in this regard.

Federal government employees work a standard 40-hour week. Employees who are required to work overtime may receive premium rates for the additional time or compensatory time off at a later date. Most employees work eight hours a day, five days a week, Monday through Friday, but in some cases, the nature of the work requires a different workweek. Annual earnings for most full-time federal workers are not affected by seasonal factors.

Federal employees earn 13 days of annual (vacation) leave each year during their first three years of service; 20 days each year until the end of 15 years; after 15 years, 26 days each year. Workers who are members of military reserve organizations also are granted up to 15 days of paid military leave a year for training purposes. A federal worker who is laid off, though federal layoffs are uncommon, is entitled to unemployment compensation similar to that provided for employees in private industry.

Other benefits available to most federal employees include: a contributory retirement system, optional participation in low-cost group life and health insurance programs which are partly supported by the government (as the employer), and training programs to develop maximum job proficiency and help workers achieve their highest potential. These training programs may be conducted in government facilities or in private educational facilities at government expense.

WHERE THE JOBS ARE: STATE AND LOCAL GOVERNMENTS

State and local governments provide a very large and expanding source of job opportunities in a wide variety of occupational fields. About fifteen million people work for state and local government agencies; nearly three fourths of these work in units of local government such as counties, municipalities, towns, and school districts. The job distribution varies greatly from that in federal government service. Defense, international relations and commerce, immigration, and mail delivery are virtually non-existent in state and local governments. On the other hand, there is great emphasis on education, health, social services, transportation, construction, and sanitation.

EDUCATIONAL SERVICES

About one half of all jobs in state and local government are in educational services. Educational employees work in public schools, colleges, and various extension services. About half of all education workers are instructional personnel. School systems, colleges, and universities also employ administrative personnel, librarians, guidance counselors, nurses, dieticians, clerks, and maintenance workers.

HEALTH SERVICES

The next largest field of state and local government employment is health services. Those employed in health and hospital work include physicians, nurses, medical laboratory technicians, dieticians, kitchen and laundry workers, and hospital attendants. Social services make up another aspect of health and welfare. Unfortunately, the need for welfare and human services has been increasing greatly. As the need grows, the opportunities for social workers and their affiliated administrative and support staff also grows.

GOVERNMENT CONTROL/FINANCIAL ACTIVITIES

Another million workers work in the areas of general governmental control and financial activities. These include chief executives and their staffs, legislative representatives, and persons employed in the administration of justice, tax enforcement and other financial work, and general administration. These functions require the services of individuals such as lawyers, judges and other court officers, city managers, property assessors, budget analysts, stenographers, and clerks.

STREETS AND HIGHWAYS

The movement of people is of great concern to both state and local governments. Street and highway construction and maintenance are of major importance. Highway workers include civil engineers, surveyors, operators of construction machinery and equipment, truck drivers, concrete finishers, carpenters, construction laborers, and, where appropriate, snow removers. Toll collectors are relatively few in number, but they too are state or county employees or employees of independent authorities of the states or counties. Mass transportation within municipalities and between the cities and their outlying suburbs is also the province of local government. Maintaining vehicles, roadbeds and signaling systems, and staffing the vehicles themselves, requires a large and varied work force.

POLICE AND FIRE PROTECTION SERVICES

Police and fire protection is another large field of employment. Along with uniformed officers, these services include extensive administrative, clerical, maintenance, and custodial personnel.

MISCELLANEOUS STATE AND LOCAL OCCUPATIONS

Other state and local government employees work in a wide variety of activities, including local utilities (water in most areas, electricity in some); natural resources; parks and recreation; sanitation; corrections; local libraries; sewage disposal; and housing and urban renewal. These activities require workers in diverse occupations such as economists, electrical engineers, electricians, pipefitters, clerks, foresters, and bus drivers.

CLERICAL, ADMINISTRATIVE, MAINTENANCE, AND CUSTODIAL WORKERS

A large percentage of employment in most government agencies is made up of clerical, administrative, maintenance, and custodial workers. Among the workers involved in these activities are word processors, secretaries, data processors, computer specialists, office managers, fiscal and budget administrators, bookkeepers, accountants, carpenters, painters, plumbers, guards, and janitors. The list is endless.

Most positions in state and local governments are filled by residents of the state or locality. Many localities have residency requirements. Exceptions are generally made for persons with skills that are in special demand.

EARNINGS

Job conditions and earnings of state and local government employees vary widely, depending upon occupation and locality. Salary differences from state to state and even within some states tend to reflect differences in the general wage level and cost of living in the various localities.

As with the federal government, a majority of state and local government positions are filled through some type of formal civil service test; that is, personnel are hired and promoted on the basis of merit. State and local government workers have the same protections as federal government workers: they cannot be refused employment because of their race; they cannot be denied promotion because someone else made a greater political contribution; and they cannot be fired because the boss's son needs a job. Jobs tend to be classified according to job description and pegged to a salary schedule that is based upon the job classifications. Periodic performance reviews also are standard expectations. Nearly every group of employees has some sort of union or organization, but the functions and powers of these units vary greatly.

Since states and local entities are independent, the benefits packages they offer their employees can be quite different. Most state and local government employees are covered by retirement systems or by the federal social security program. Most have some sort of health coverage. They usually work a standard week of 40 hours or less with overtime pay or compensatory time benefits for additional hours of work.

PREPARING YOURSELF FOR THE CIVIL SERVICE EXAMINATION

Most federal, state, and municipal units have recruitment procedures for filling civil service positions. They have developed a number, of methods to make job opportunities known. Places where such information may be obtained include:

1. The offices of the State Employment Services. There are almost two thousand throughout the country. These offices are administered by the state in which they are located, with the financial assistance of the federal government. You will find the address of the one nearest you in your telephone book.
2. Your state Civil Service Commission. Address your inquiry to the capital city of your state.
3. Your city Civil Service Commission. It is sometimes called by another name, such as the Department of Personnel, but you will be able to identify it in your telephone directory under the listing of city departments.
4. Your municipal building and your local library.
5. Complete listings are carried by such newspapers as *The Chief-Leader* (published in New York City), as well as by other city and state-wide publications devoted to civil service employees. Many local newspapers run a section on regional civil service news.
6. State and local agencies looking for competent employees will contact schools, professional societies, veterans organizations, unions, and trade associations.
7. School boards and boards of education, which employ the greatest proportion of all state and local personnel, should be asked directly for information about job openings.

You will find more in-depth information at the end of this book.

THE FORMAT OF THE JOB ANNOUNCEMENT

When a position is open and a civil service examination is to be given for it, a job announcement is drawn up. This generally contains everything an applicant has to know about the job.

The announcement begins with the job title and salary. A typical announcement then describes the work, the location of the position, the education and experience requirements, the kind of examination to be given, and the system of rating. It may also have something to say about veteran preference and the age limit. It tells which application form is to be filled out, where to get the form, and where and when to file it.

Study the job announcement carefully. It will answer many of your questions and help you decide whether you like the position and are qualified for it. We have included sample job announcements in a later chapter.

There is no point in applying for a position and taking the examination if you do not want to work where the job is. The job may be in your community or hundreds of miles away at the other end of the state. If you are not willing to work where the job is, study other announcements that will give you an opportunity to work in a place of your choice. A civil service job close to your home has an additional advantage since local residents usually receive preference in appointments.

The words **Optional Fields**—sometimes just the word **Options**—may appear on the front page of the announcement. You then have a choice to apply for that particular position in which you are especially interested. This is because the duties of various positions are quite different even though they bear the same broad title. A public relations clerk, for example, does different work from a payroll clerk, although they are considered broadly in the same general area.

Not every announcement has options. But whether or not it has them, the precise duties are described in detail, usually under the heading, **Description of Work.** Make sure that these duties come within the range of your experience and ability.

Most job requirements give a **deadline for filing** an application. Others bear the words, **No Closing Date** at the top of the first page; this means that applications will be accepted until the needs of the agency are met. In some cases a public notice is issued when a certain number of applications has been received. No application mailed past the deadline date will be considered.

Every announcement has a detailed section on **education and experience requirements** for the particular job and for the optional fields. Make sure that in both education and experience you meet the minimum qualifications. If you do not meet the given standards for one job, there may be others open where you stand a better chance of making the grade.

If the job announcement does not mention **veteran preference,** it would be wise to inquire if there is such a provision in your state or municipality. There may be none or it may be limited to disabled veterans. In some jurisdictions, surviving spouses of disabled veterans are given preference. All such information can be obtained through the agency that issues the job announcement.

Applicants may be denied examinations and eligible candidates may be denied appointments for any of the following reasons:

- intentional false statements
- deception or fraud in examination or appointment
- use of intoxicating beverages to the extent that ability to perform the duties of the position is impaired
- criminal, infamous, dishonest, immoral, or notoriously disgraceful conduct

The announcement describes the **kind of test** given for the particular position. Please pay special attention to this section. It tells what areas are to be covered in the written test and lists the specific subjects on which questions will be asked. Sometimes sample questions are given.

Usually the announcement states whether the examination is to be **assembled** or **unassembled.** In an assembled examination applicants assemble in the same place at the same time to take a written or performance test. The unassembled examination is one where an applicant does not take a test; instead, he or she is rated on his or her education and experience and whatever records of past achievement the applicant is asked to provide.

In the competitive examination all applicants for a position compete with each other; the better the mark, the better the chance of being appointed. Also, competitive examinations are given to determine desirability for promotion among employees.

Civil service written tests are rated on a scale of 100, with 70 usually as the passing mark.

FILLING OUT THE APPLICATION FORM

Having studied the job announcement and having decided that you want the position and are qualified for it, your next step is to get an application form. The job announcement tells you where to send for it.

On the whole, civil service application forms differ little from state to state and locality to locality. The questions that have been worked out after years of experimentation are simple and direct, designed to elicit a maximal amount of information about you.

Many prospective civil service employees have failed to get a job because of slipshod, erroneous, incomplete, misleading, or untruthful answers. Give the application serious attention, for it is the first important step toward getting the job you want.

Here, along with some helpful comments, are the questions usually asked on the average application form, although not necessarily in this order.

- **Name of examination or kind of position applied for.** This information appears in large type on the first page of the job announcement.
- **Optional job** (if mentioned in the announcement). If you wish to apply for an option, simply copy the title from the announcement. If you are not interested in an option, write *None*.
- **Primary place of employment applied for.** The location of the position was probably contained in the announcement. You must consider whether you want to work there. The announcement may list more than one location where the job is open. If you would accept employment in any of the places, list them all; otherwise list the specific place or places where you would be willing to work.
- **Name and address.** Give in full, including your middle name if you have one, and your maiden name as well if you are a married woman.
- **Home and office phones.** If none, write *None*.
- **Legal or voting residence.** The state in which you vote is the one you list here.
- **Height without shoes, weight, sex.** Answer accurately.
- **Date of birth.** Give the exact day, month, and year.
- **Lowest grade or pay you will accept.** Although the salary is clearly stated in the job announcement, there may be a quicker opening in the same occupation but carrying less responsibility and thus a lower basic entrance salary. You will not be considered for a job paying less than the amount you give in answer to this question.
- **Will you accept temporary employment if offered you for (a) one month or less, (b) one to four months, (c) four to twelve months?** Temporary positions come up frequently and it is important to know whether you are available.
- **Will you accept less than full-time employment?** Part-time work comes up now and then. Consider whether you want to accept such a position while waiting for a full-time appointment.
- **Were you in active military service in the Armed Forces of the United States?** Veterans' preference, if given, is usually limited to active service during the following periods: 12/7/41–12/31/46; 6/27/50–1/31/55; 6/1/63–5/7/75; 6/1/83–12/1/87; 10/23/83–11/21/83; 12/20/89–1/3/90; 8/2/90 to end of Persian Gulf hostilities.
- **Do you claim disabled veterans credit?** If you do, you have to show proof of a war-incurred disability compensable by at least 10 percent. This is done through certification by the Veterans Administration.
- **Special qualifications and skills.** Even though not directly related to the position for which you are applying, information about licenses and certificates obtained for teacher, pilot, registered nurse, and so on, is requested. List your experience in the use of machines and equipment and whatever other skills you have acquired. Also list published writings, public speaking experience, membership in professional societies, and honors and fellowships received.

- **Education.** List your entire educational history, including all diplomas, degrees, and special courses taken in any accredited or armed forces school. Also give your credits toward a college or a graduate degree.
- **References.** The names of people who can give information about you, with their occupations and business and home address, are often requested.
- **Your health.** Questions are asked concerning your medical record. You are expected to have the physical and psychological capacity to perform the job for which you are applying. Standards vary, of course, depending on the requirements of the position. A physical handicap usually will not bar an applicant from a job he can perform adequately unless the safety of the public is involved.
- **Work history.** Considerable space is allotted on the form for the applicant to tell about all his past employment. Examiners check all such answers closely. Do not embellish or falsify your record. If you were ever fired, say so. It is better for you to state this openly than for the examiners to find out the truth from your former employer.

Following are samples of a New York City Application for Examination and a state application from Louisiana.

WHY PEOPLE CHOOSE GOVERNMENT SERVICE

There are many similarities between work in the private sector and work for the government. Within each occupation, the similarities of the daily duties far outweigh the differences in employers. Regardless of the nature of the employer—government, private business, nonprofit organization—typists type; doctors heal, teachers teach; electricians install wiring.

As was mentioned at the beginning of this chapter, one in six of employed persons in the United States is in government service. The five in six persons who are employed by nongovernmental employers all hope for just compensation for their work, for promotions when merited, and for fair and equal treatment with reference to their co-workers. They all hope that they will not be discriminated against for any non-job-related reasons, that they will not be fired capriciously, and that their opinions and suggestions will be taken seriously. In the great majority of cases, these expectations will be met.

But, in the private sector, there are no guarantees of employment practices. In government service these guarantees are a matter of policy and law. Each governmental jurisdiction has its own body of rules and procedures. In other words, not all government service is alike. The Federal Civil Service does serve as a model for all other governmental units.

NEW YORK CITY APPLICATION FOR EXAMINATION

DEPARTMENT OF CITYWIDE ADMINISTRATIVE SERVICES
DIVISION OF CITYWIDE PERSONNEL SERVICES
1 Centre Street, 14th floor New York, NY 10007

APPLICATION FOR EXAMINATION

(Directions for completing this application are on the *back* of this form. Additional information is on the Special Circumstances Sheet)

Download this form on-line: nyc.gov/html/dcas

FOLLOW DIRECTIONS ON BACK
Fill in all requested information clearly, accurately, and completely.

The City will only process applications with complete, correct, legible information which are accompanied by correct payment or waiver documentation.

All unprocessed applications will be returned to the applicant.

1. EXAM #: ☐☐☐☐

Check One: ☐ Open Competitive ☐ Promotion

2. EXAM TITLE: ________

3. SOCIAL SECURITY NUMBER: ☐☐☐ - ☐☐ - ☐☐☐☐

4. LAST NAME: ________

5. FIRST NAME: ________

6. MIDDLE INITIAL: ☐

7. MAILING ADDRESS: ________

8. APT. #: ☐☐☐☐

9. CITY OR TOWN: ________

10. STATE: ☐☐

11. ZIP CODE: ☐☐☐☐☐ - ☐☐☐☐

12. PHONE: ☐☐☐ - ☐☐☐ - ☐☐☐☐

13. OTHER NAMES USED IN CITY SERVICE: ________

Questions 14 & 15: Discrimination on the basis of sex, sexual orientation, race, creed, color, age, disability status, veteran status or religious observance is prohibited by law. The City of New York is an equal opportunity employer. The identifying information requested on this form is to be used to determine the representation of protected groups among applicants. This information is voluntary and will not be made available to individuals making hiring decisions.

14. RACE/ETHNICITY (Check One):
- ☐ White
- ☐ Black
- ☐ Hispanic
- ☐ American Indian/ Alaskan Native
- ☐ Asian/Pacific Islander

15. SEX (Check One):
- ☐ Male
- ☐ Female

16. ARE YOU EMPLOYED BY THE HEALTH AND HOSPITALS CORPORATION? (Check One) ☐ YES ☐ NO

17. CHECK ALL BOXES THAT APPLY TO YOU: (Directions for this section are found on the "Special Circumstances" Sheet)
- ☐ I AM A SABBATH OBSERVER AND WILL REQUEST AN ALTERNATE TEST DATE (Verification required. See Item A on Special Circumstances Sheet)
- ☐ I HAVE A DISABILITY AND WILL REQUEST SPECIAL ACCOMMODATIONS (Verification required. See item B on Special Circumstances Sheet).
- ☐ I CLAIM VETERANS' CREDIT (For qualifications see item C on Special Circumstances Sheet)
- ☐ I CLAIM DISABLED VETERANS' CREDIT (For qualifications see item C on Special Circumstances Sheet)

18. Your Signature: ________________ **Date:** ________

STATE OF LOUISIANA APPLICATION—page 1

SF10
(Page 1)
REV. 1/97

STATE PRE-EMPLOYMENT APPLICATION

STATE OF LOUISIANA
DEPARTMENT OF CIVIL SERVICE
P.O. Box 94111, Capitol Station
Baton Rouge, Louisiana 70804-9111

AN EQUAL OPPORTUNITY EMPLOYER

FOR OFFICE USE

Special ______
Promo ______
Action(s) ______
______
Session ______
Data Entry Completed ______

1. TEST LOCATION-Check only one.

Baton Rouge (3) (Weekday) ☐	New Orleans (6) (Weekday) ☐	Lafayette (4) (Sat. only) ☐	Shreveport (7) (Sat. only) ☐
☐	New Orleans (12) (Saturday) ☐	Lake Charles (5) (Sat. only) ☐	West Monroe (8) (Sat. only) ☐

2.Enter Name and Complete Address below.

3. Parish of Residence

4. Are you 18 or older? ☐ Yes ☐ No

5. Other names ever used on SF-10

NAME - First	Middle	Last
Mailing Address		
City	State	Zip Code

6. Social Security Number
(For identification purpose)

Work Telephone No.

Home Telephone No.

PRINT NAME → LAST → FIRST → MIDDLE

7. REGISTER TITLE(S) APPLIED FOR	FOR OFFICE USE SER	CD	REJ	GRD	TR	ADDITIONAL TITLES	FOR OFFICE USE SER	CD	REJ	GRD	TR

JS No.
V.P.
S.R.

ALL TITLES LISTED ABOVE MUST HAVE THE SAME SERIES NO.

8. JOB LOCATION AVAILABILITY - IMPORTANT: Read Item 9 on the Instruction Page before completing this item. Mark at least one (1), but no more than twenty (20) parishes.

☐ 01 Acadia	☐ 09 Caddo	☐ 17 E. Baton Rouge	☐ 25 Jackson	☐ 33 Madison	☐ 41 Red River	☐ 49 St. Landry	☐ 57 Vermillion
☐ 02 Allen	☐ 10 Calcasieu	☐ 18 E. Carroll	☐ 26 Jefferson	☐ 34 Morehouse	☐ 42 Richland	☐ 50 St. Martin	☐ 58 Vernon
☐ 03 Ascension	☐ 11 Caldwell	☐ 19 E. Feliciana	☐ 27 Jeff Davis	☐ 35 Natchitoches	☐ 43 Sabine	☐ 51 St. Mary	☐ 59 Washington
☐ 04	☐ 12 Cameron	☐ 20 Evangeline	☐ 28 Lafayette	☐ 36 Orleans	☐ 44 St. Bernard	☐ 52 St. Tammany	☐ 60 Webster
☐ 05 Avoyelles	☐ 13 Catahoula	☐ 21 Franklin	☐ 29 Lafourche	☐ 37 Ouachita	☐ 45 St. Charles	☐ 53 Tangipahoa	☐ 61 W. Baton Rouge
☐ 06 Beauregard	☐ 14 Claiborne	☐ 22 Grant	☐ 30 LaSalle	☐ 38 Plaquemines	☐ 46 St. Helena	☐ 54 Tensas	☐ 62 W. Carroll
☐ 07 Bienville	☐ 15 Concordia	☐ 23 Iberia	☐ 31 Lincoln	☐ 39 Pte. Coupee	☐ 47 St. James	☐ 55 Terrebonne	☐ 63 W. Feliciana
☐ 08 Bossier	☐ 16 DeSoto	☐ 24 Iberville	☐ 32 Livingston	☐ 40 Rapides	☐ 48 St. John	☐ 56 Union	☐ 64 Winn

9. ☐ Permanent ☐ Temporary—Type of employment you will accept
NOTE: Most Temporary Appointments are 3 - 12 months

10. ☐ YES ☐ NO Do you possess a valid driver's license?

11. ☐ YES ☐ NO Do you possess a valid commercial driver's license?

12. ☐ YES ☐ NO Are you currently holding or running for an elective public office?

13. ☐ YES ☐ NO Have you ever been on probation or sentenced to jail/prison as a result of a felony conviction or guilty plea?

14. ☐ YES ☐ NO Have you ever been fired from a job or resigned to avoid dismissal?

NOTE: If answers to Items 13 and/or 14 are "YES", you MUST complete Item 24 on Page 2 of this application

15. ☐ YES ☐ NO Are you claiming Veteran's Preference points on this application? (If "YES", see Item 20 on Page 2.)

The following information is collected to complete Equal Opportunity Reports required by law. You ARE NOT LEGALLY OBLIGATED to provide this information.

16. RACIAL/ETHNIC GROUP ______ 16A. DATE OF BIRTH ______ 17. SEX ☐ Male ☐ Female

I HAVE READ THE FOLLOWING STATEMENTS CAREFULLY BEFORE SIGNING THIS APPLICATION:

18. Date	Social Security No. (for verification)

19. Signature of Applicant

AUTHORITY TO RELEASE INFORMATION: I consent to the release of information concerning my capacity and/or all aspects of prior job performance by employers, educational institutions, law enforcement agencies, and other individuals and agencies to duly accredited investigators, personnel technicians, and other authorized employees of the state government for the purpose of determining my eligibility and suitability for employment.

I certify that all statements made on this application and any attached papers are true and complete to the best of my knowledge. I understand that information on this application may be subject to investigation and verification and that any misrepresentation or material omission may cause my application to be rejected, my name to be removed from the eligible register and/or subject me to dismissal from state service.

STATE OF LOUISIANA APPLICATION—page 2

20. ACTIVE MILITARY SERVICE/VETERAN'S PREFERENCE
See Item 10 on the Instruction Page to determine your eligibility for Veteran's Preference. If you are a first-time applicant or if you are claiming Veteran's Preference for the first time, required PROOF MUST BE ATTACHED to this application to have preference points added to your score.

List the dates (month and year) and branch for all ACTIVE DUTY military service. Was this service performed on an active, full-time basis with full pay and allowances? (Check YES or NO for each period of service.)

FROM	TO	BRANCH OF SERVICE	YES	NO

List all GRADES held and dates of each grade. Begin with the highest grade. IMPORTANT: Use E-, O-, or WO-grade.

FROM	TO	GRADE HELD	FROM	TO	GRADE HELD

21. TRAINING AND EDUCATION

Have you received a high school diploma or equivalency certificate? ☐ YES Date received ____ ☐ NO Highest grade completed ____

A. LIST *BUSINESS OR* TECHNICAL COLLEGES ATTENDED

NAME/LOCATION OF SCHOOL	Dates Attended (Month & Year) FROM	TO	Did You Graduate? YES	NO	TITLE OF PROGRAM	CLOCK HOURS PER WEEK

List any accounting practice sets completed: ____

B. LIST COLLEGES *OR* UNIVERSITIES ATTENDED (Include graduate or professional schools)

NAME OF COLLEGE OR UNIVERSITY/ CITY AND STATE	Dates Attended (Month & Year) FROM	TO	Total Credit Hours Earned Semester	Quarter	Type of Degree Earned	Major Field of Study	Date Degree Received (Month & Yr.)

C. MAJOR SUBJECTS

	CHIEF UNDERGRADUATE SUBJECTS (Show Major on Line 1.)	Total Credit Hours Earned Semester	Quarter	CHIEF GRADUATE SUBJECTS (Show Major on Line 1.)	Total Credit Hours Earned Semester or Qtr.	
1						
2						
3						

22. LICENSES AND CERTIFICATION

List any job-related licenses or certificates that you have (CPA, lawyer, registered nurse, etc.)

	TYPE OF LICENSE OR CERTIFICATE (Specify Which One)	DATE ORIGINALLY LICENSED/ CERTIFIED	EXPIRATIO N DATE	NAME AND ADDRESS OF LICENSING OR CERTIFYING AGENCY
1				
2				

23. TYPING SPEED ____ WPM

DICTATION SPEED ____ WPM

24. Explain a "YES" answer to Items 13 and/or 14 here. A "YES" ANSWER WILL NOT NECESSARILY BAR YOU FROM STATE EMPLOYMENT. WE WILL CONSIDER THE DATE, FACTS, AND CIRCUMSTANCES OF EACH INDIVIDUAL CASE. For Item 13, give the law enforcement authority (city police, sherrif, FBI, etc.), the offense, date of offense, place, and disposition of case.

____

____

Name ____

STATE OF LOUISIANA APPLICATION—page 3

Name ______________________________

25. WORK EXPERIENCE — IMPORTANT: Read Item 11 of Instruction Page carefully before completing these items. List all jobs and activities including military service, part-time employment, self-employment, and volunteer work. BEGIN with your FIRST job in Block A; END with your MOST RECENT or PRESENT job.

A EMPLOYER/COMPANY NAME		KIND OF BUSINESS	
STREET ADDRESS		YOUR OFFICIAL JOB TITLE	
CITY AND STATE		BEGINNING SALARY	ENDING SALARY
DATES OF EMPLOYMENT (MO/DA/YR) FROM	AVERAGE HOURS WORKED PER WEEK TO	REASON FOR LEAVING	NO. OF EMPLOYEES YOU DIRECTLY SUPERVISED
NAME/TITLE OF YOUR SUPERVISOR)		LIST JOB TITLES OF EMPLOYEES YOU DIRECTLY SUPERVISED	
NAME/TITLE OF PERSON WHO CAN VERIFY THIS EMPLOYMENT (IF OTHER THAN SUPERVISOR)			

DUTIES: List the major duties involved with job and give an approximate percentage of time spent on each duty.

% OF TIME	MAJOR DUTIES
100%	

B EMPLOYER/COMPANY NAME		KIND OF BUSINESS	
STREET ADDRESS		YOUR OFFICIAL JOB TITLE	
CITY AND STATE		BEGINNING SALARY	ENDING SALARY
DATES OF EMPLOYMENT (MO/DA/YR) FROM	AVERAGE HOURS WORKED PER WEEK TO	REASON FOR LEAVING	NO. OF EMPLOYEES YOU DIRECTLY SUPERVISED
NAME/TITLE OF YOUR SUPERVISOR)		LIST JOB TITLES OF EMPLOYEES YOU DIRECTLY SUPERVISED	
NAME/TITLE OF PERSON WHO CAN VERIFY THIS EMPLOYMENT (IF OTHER THAN SUPERVISOR)			

DUTIES: List the major duties involved with job and give an approximate percentage of time spent on each duty.

% OF TIME	MAJOR DUTIES

STATE OF LOUISIANA APPLICATION—page 4

100%

USE REVERSE SIDE OF THIS PAGE IF ADDITIONAL SPACE REQUIRED FOR WORK EXPERIENCE

Name ______________________

25. WORK EXPERIENCE (Continued)

C EMPLOYER/COMPANY NAME		KIND OF BUSINESS	
STREET ADDRESS		YOUR OFFICIAL JOB TITLE	
CITY AND STATE		BEGINNING SALARY	ENDING SALARY
DATES OF EMPLOYMENT (MO/DA/YR) FROM	AVERAGE HOURS WORKED PER WEEK TO	REASON FOR LEAVING	NO. OF EMPLOYEES YOU DIRECTLY SUPERVISED
NAME/TITLE OF YOUR SUPERVISOR		LIST JOB TITLES OF EMPLOYEES YOU DIRECTLY SUPERVISED	
NAME/TITLE OF PERSON WHO CAN VERIFY THIS EMPLOYMENT (IF OTHER THAN SUPERVISOR)			

DUTIES: List the major duties involved with job and give an approximate percentage of time spent on each duty.

% OF TIME	MAJOR DUTIES
100%	

D EMPLOYER/COMPANY NAME		KIND OF BUSINESS	
STREET ADDRESS		YOUR OFFICIAL JOB TITLE	
CITY AND STATE		BEGINNING SALARY	ENDING SALARY
DATES OF EMPLOYMENT (MO/DA/YR) FROM	AVERAGE HOURS WORKED PER WEEK TO	REASON FOR LEAVING	NO. OF EMPLOYEES YOU DIRECTLY SUPERVISED
NAME/TITLE OF YOUR SUPERVISOR)		LIST JOB TITLES OF EMPLOYEES YOU DIRECTLY SUPERVISED	
NAME/TITLE OF PERSON WHO CAN VERIFY THIS EMPLOYMENT (IF OTHER THAN SUPERVISOR)			

DUTIES: List the major duties involved with job and give an approximate percentage of time spent on each duty.

% OF TIME	MAJOR DUTIES

TEST-TAKING TECHNIQUES

Many factors enter into a test score. The most important factor should be ability to answer the questions, which in turn indicates the ability to learn and perform the duties of the job. Assuming that you have this ability, knowing what to expect on the exam and familiarity with techniques of effective test taking should give you the confidence you need to do your best on the exam.

There is no quick substitute for long-term study and development of your skills and abilities to prepare you for doing well on tests. However, there are some steps you can take to help you do the very best that you are prepared to do. Some of these steps are done before the test, and some are followed when you are taking the test. Knowing these steps is often called being "test-wise." Following these steps may help you feel more confident as you take the actual test.

"Test-wiseness" is a general term which simply means being familiar with some good procedures to follow when getting ready for and taking a test. The procedures fall into four major areas: (1) being prepared, (2) avoiding careless errors, (3) managing your time, and (4) guessing.

BE PREPARED

Don't make the test harder than it has to be by not preparing yourself. You are taking a very important step in preparation by reading this book and taking the sample tests which are included. This will help you to become familiar with the tests and the kinds of questions you will have to answer.

As you use this book, read the sample questions and directions for taking the test carefully. Then, when you take the sample tests, time yourself as you will be timed in the real test.

As you are working on the sample questions, don't look at the correct answers before you try to answer them on your own. This can fool you into thinking you understand a question when you really don't. Try it on your own first, then compare your answer with the one given. Remember, in a sample test, you are your own grader; you don't gain anything by pretending to understand something you really don't.

On the examination day assigned to you, allow the test itself to be the main attraction of the day. Do not squeeze it in between other activities. Be sure to bring admission card, identification, and pencils, as instructed. Prepare these the night before so that you are not flustered by a last-minute search. Arrive rested, relaxed, and on time. In fact, plan to arrive a little bit early. Leave plenty of time for traffic tie-ups or other complications that might upset you and interfere with your test performance.

In the test room, the examiner will hand out forms for you to fill out. He or she will give you the instructions that you must follow in taking the examination. The examiner will tell you how to fill in the grids on the forms. Time limits and timing signals will be explained. If you do not understand any of the examiner's instructions, ASK QUESTIONS. It would be ridiculous to score less than your best because of poor communication.

At the examination, you must follow instructions exactly. Fill in the grids on the forms carefully and accurately. Misgridding may lead to loss of veteran's credits to which you may be entitled or misaddressing of your test results. Do not begin until you are told to begin. Stop as soon as the examiner tells you to stop. Do not turn pages until you are told to do so. Do not go back to parts you have already completed. Any infraction of the rules is considered cheating. If you cheat, your test paper will not be scored, and you will not be eligible for appointment.

The answer sheet for most multiple-choice exams is machine scored. You cannot give any explanations to the machine, so you must fill out the answer sheet clearly and correctly.

HOW TO MARK YOUR ANSWER SHEET

1. Blacken your answer space firmly and completely. ● is the only correct way to mark the answer sheet. ◐, ⊗, ⊘, ⊘, and ⊘ are all unacceptable. The machine might not read them at all.
2. Mark only one answer for each question. If you mark more than one answer, you will be considered wrong, even if one of the answers is correct.
3. If you change your mind, you must erase your mark. Attempting to cross out an incorrect answer like this ● will not work. You must erase any incorrect answer completely. An incomplete erasure might be read as a second answer.
4. All of your answering should be in the form of blackened spaces. The machine cannot read English. Do not write any notes in the margins.
5. MOST IMPORTANT: Answer each question in the right place. Question 1 must be answered in space 1; question 52 in space 52. If you should skip an answer space and mark a series of answers in the wrong places, you must erase all those answers and do the questions over, marking your answers in the proper places. You cannot afford to use the limited time in this way. Therefore, as you answer *each* question, look at its number and check that you are marking your answer in the space with the same number.
6. For the typing tests, type steadily and carefully. Just don't rush, since that's when the errors occur. Keep in mind that each error subtracts 1 wpm from your final score.

AVOID CARELESS ERRORS

Don't reduce your score by making careless mistakes. Always read the instructions for each test section carefully, even when you think you already know what the directions are. It's why we stress throughout this book that it's important to fully understand the directions for these different question-types *before* you go into the actual exam. It will not only reduce errors, but it will save you time—time you will need for the questions.

What if you don't understand the directions? You will have risked getting the answers wrong for a whole test section. As an example, vocabulary questions can sometimes test synonyms (words which have similar meanings), and sometimes test antonyms (words with opposite meanings). You can easily see how a mistake in understanding in this case could make a whole set of answers incorrect.

If you have time, reread any complicated instructions after you do the first few questions to check that you really do understand them. Of course, whenever you are allowed to, ask the examiner to clarify anything you don't understand.

Other careless mistakes affect only the response to particular questions. This often happens with arithmetic questions, but can happen with other questions as well. This type of error, called a "response error," usually stems from a momentary lapse of concentration.

Example

> The question reads: "The capital of Massachusetts is . . . ." The answer is (D) Boston, and you mark (B) because "B" is the first letter of the word "Boston."

Example

> The question reads: "8 – 5 = ..." The answer is (A) 3, but you mark (C) thinking "third letter."

A common error in Reading Comprehension questions is bringing your own information into the subject. For example, you may encounter a passage that discusses a subject you know something about. While this can make the passage easier to read, it can also tempt you to rely on your own knowledge about the subject. You must rely on information within the passage for your answers—in fact, sometimes the "wrong answer" for the questions are based on true information about the subject *not* given in the passage. Since the test-makers are testing your reading ability, rather than your general knowledge of the subject, an answer based on information not contained in the passage is considered incorrect.

MANAGE YOUR TIME

Before you begin, take a moment to plan your progress through the test. Although you are usually not expected to finish all of the questions given on a test, you should at least get an idea of how much time you should spend on each question in order to answer them all. For example, if there are 60 questions to answer and you have 30 minutes, you will have about one-half minute to spend on each question.

Keep track of the time on your watch or the room clock, but do not fixate on the time remaining. Your task is to answer questions. Do not spend too much time on any one question. If you find yourself stuck, do not take the puzzler as a personal challenge. Either guess and mark the question in the question booklet or skip the question entirely, marking the question as a skip and taking care to skip the answer space on the answer sheet. If there is time at the end of the exam or exam part, you can return and give marked questions another try.

MULTIPLE-CHOICE QUESTIONS

Almost all of the tests given on civil service exams are multiple-choice format. This means that you normally have four or five answer choices. But it's not something that should be overwhelming. There is a basic technique to answering these types of questions. Once you've understood this technique, it will make your test-taking far less stressful.

First, there should only be one correct answer. Since these tests have been given time and again, and the test-developers have a sense of which questions work and which questions don't work, it will be rare that your choices will be ambiguous. They may be complex, and somewhat confusing, but there will still be only one right answer.

The first step is to look at the question, without looking at the answer choices. Now select the correct answer. That may sound somewhat simplistic, but it's usually the case that your first choice is the correct one. If you go back and change it, redo it again and again, it's more likely that you'll end up with the wrong answer. Thus, follow your instinct. Once you have come up with the answer, look at the answer choices. If your answer is one of the choices, you're probably correct. It's not 100 percent infallible, but it's a strong possibility that you've selected the right answer.

With math questions you should first solve the problem. If your answer is among the choices, you're probably correct. Don't ignore things like the proper function signs (adding, subtracting, multiplying, and dividing), negative and positive numbers, and so on.

But suppose you don't know the correct answer. You then use the "process of elimination." It's a time-honored technique for test-takers. There is always one correct answer. There is usually one answer choice that is totally incorrect—a "distracter." If you look at that choice and it seems highly unlikely, then eliminate it. Depending on the number of choices (four or five), you've just cut down the number of choices to make. Now weigh the other choices. They may seem incorrect or they may be correct. If they seem incorrect, eliminate them. You've now increased your odds at getting the correct answer.

In the end, you may be left with only two choices. At that point, it's just a matter of guessing. But with only two choices left, you now have a 50 percent chance of getting it right. With four choices, you only have a 25 percent chance, and with five choices, only a 20 percent chance at guessing correctly. That's why the process of elimination is important.

Test-Taking Tips

1. Get to the test center early. Make sure you give yourself plenty of extra time to get there, park your car, if necessary, and even grab a cup of coffee before the test.
2. Listen to the test monitors and follow their instructions carefully.
3. Read every word of the instructions. Read every word of every question.
4. Mark your answers by completely darkening the answer space of your choice. Do not use the test paper to work out your answers.
5. Mark only ONE answer for each question, even if you think that more than one answer is correct. You must choose only one. If you mark more than one answer, the scoring machine will consider you wrong.
6. If you change your mind, erase completely. Leave no doubt as to which answer you mean.
7. If your exam permits you to use scratch paper or the margins of the test booklet for figuring, don't forget to mark the answer on the answer sheet. Only the answer sheet is scored.
8. Check often to be sure that the question number matches the answer space, that you have not skipped a space by mistake.
9. Guess according to the guessing suggestions we have made.
10. Stay alert. Be careful not to mark a wrong answer just because you were not concentrating.
11. Do not panic. If you cannot finish any part before time is up, do not worry. If you are accurate, you can do well even without finishing. It is even possible to earn a scaled score of 100 without entirely finishing an exam part if you are very accurate. At any rate, do not let your performance on any one part affect your performance on any other part.
12. Check and recheck, time permitting. If you finish any part before time is up, use the remaining time to check that each question is answered in the right space and that there is only one answer for each question. Return to the difficult questions and rethink them.

SHOULD YOU GUESS?

You may be wondering whether or not it is wise to guess when you are not sure of an answer (even if you've reduced the odds to 50 percent) or whether it is better to skip the question when you are not certain. The wisdom of guessing depends on the scoring method for the particular examination part. If the scoring is "rights only," that is, one point for each correct answer and no subtraction for wrong answers, then by all means you should guess. Read the question and all of the answer choices carefully. Eliminate those answer choices that you are certain are wrong. Then guess from among the remaining choices. You cannot gain a point if you leave the answer space blank; you may gain a point with an educated guess or even with a lucky guess. In fact, it is foolish to leave any spaces blank on a test that counts "rights only." If it appears that you are about to run out of time before completing such an exam, mark all the remaining blanks with the same letter. According to the law of averages, you should get some portion of those questions right.

If the scoring method is *rights minus wrongs*, such as the address checking test found on Postal Clerk Exam 470, DO NOT GUESS. A wrong answer counts heavily against you. On this type of test, do not rush to fill answer spaces randomly at the end. Work as quickly as possible while concentrating on accuracy. Keep working carefully until time is called. Then stop and leave the remaining answer spaces blank.

In guessing the answers to multiple-choice questions, take a second to eliminate those answers that are obviously wrong, then quickly consider and guess from the remaining choices. The fewer choices from which you guess, the better the odds of guessing correctly. Once you have decided to make a guess, be it an educated guess or a wild stab, do it right away and move on; don't keep thinking about it and wasting time. You should always mark the test questions at which you guess so that you can return later.

For those questions that are scored by subtracting a fraction of a point for each wrong answer, the decision as to whether or not to guess is really up to you.

A correct answer gives you one point; a skipped space gives you nothing at all, but costs you nothing except the chance of getting the answer right; a wrong answer costs you 1/4 point. If you are really uncomfortable with guessing, you may skip a question, BUT you must then remember to skip its answer space as well. The risk of losing your place if you skip questions is so great that we advise you to guess even if you are not sure of the answer. Our suggestion is that you answer every question in order, even if you have to guess. It is better to lose a few 1/4 points for wrong guesses than to lose valuable seconds figuring where you started marking answers in the wrong place, erasing, and re-marking answers. On the other hand, do not mark random answers at the end. Work steadily until time is up.

One of the questions you should ask in the testing room is what scoring method will be used on your particular exam. You can then guide your guessing procedure accordingly.

SCORING

If your exam is a short-answer exam such as those often used by companies in the private sector, your answers will be graded by a personnel officer trained in grading test questions. If you blackened spaces on the separate answer sheet accompanying a multiple-choice exam, your answer sheet will be machine scanned or will be hand scored using a punched card stencil. Then a raw score will be calculated using the scoring formula that applies to that test or test portion—rights only, rights minus wrongs, or rights minus a fraction of wrongs. Raw scores on test parts are then added together for a total raw score.

A raw score is *not* a final score. The raw score is not the score that finds its way onto an eligibility list. The civil service testing authority, Postal Service, or other testing body converts raw scores to a scaled score according to an unpublicized formula of its own. The scaling formula allows for slight differences in difficulty of questions from one form of the exam to another and allows for equating the scores of all candidates. Regardless of the number of questions and possible different weights of different parts of the exam, most civil service clerical test scores are reported on a scale of 1 to 10. The entire process of conversion from raw to scaled score is confidential information. The score you receive is not your number right, is not your raw score, and, despite being on a scale of 1 to 100, is not a percentage. It is a scaled score. If you are entitled to veterans' service points, these are added to your passing scaled score to boost your rank on the eligibility list. Veterans' points are added only to passing scores. A failing score cannot be brought to passing level by adding veterans' points. The score earned plus veterans' service points, if any, is the score that finds its place on the rank order eligibility list. Highest scores go to the top of the list.

PART TWO

Clerical Careers

Clerical work offers the proverbial "foot in the door" to thousands of occupations in government and in the private sector. Clerical work, in its own right, is clean and pleasant. Best of all, entry-level clerical work can open numerous different paths upwards to supervisory and administrative work or to other totally nonclerical jobs within the organization.

Clerical work is an ideal entry point at which young people can begin their careers and mature adults can reenter the job market after years of absence. There also is opportunity for career change into less physically strenuous office work for those whose earlier work demanded greater strength and stamina. Clerical work thus lends itself to those seeking semiretirement as well.

An alert clerical worker is in an ideal position to learn about the operations of the place in which he or she is employed. If the workplace is a government office, the clerical worker learns the functions of the office, the services delivered, the chain of command, the daily operations, and the ultimate mission of that office and the agency of which it is a unit. If the workplace is an office of an organization that provides a service to the public, the clerical worker's learning beyond the job at hand is similar to that of the government clerical worker. If the organization produces a product, then the clerical worker learns about the product itself, the business of producing and distributing the product, and advertising, marketing, and sales. Constant exposure to the business of the office, whatever it may be, allows the clerical worker to absorb knowledge while carrying out assigned duties. The job itself provides the education and background for moving ahead.

From a clerical job in government, a natural progression might be into higher-level, more complex clerical work with ever greater responsibility, or growth might be into different aspects of office work, or promotion might entail taking on supervisory duties with an eventual role in the ranks of administration.

A clerical job in the private sector opens even more avenues for growth and diversification of work. As the clerical worker grows more familiar with the firm, he or she may grow in any of the directions of the clerical worker in government, or may go into manufacturing itself, into the business aspects of the company, or out into the field as a member of the sales force. A clerical worker in one business tends to be exposed to many other businesses in the course of daily work. The clerical worker in one field may find that the business of a client or customer offers greater fulfillment and may move upward by moving to another company altogether.

Under the umbrella term "clerical work," there are hundreds of different jobs. There are filing jobs, typing jobs, stock-taking jobs, tabulating jobs, distribution jobs, bookkeeping jobs, data entry jobs, word processing jobs, statistical jobs, stenographic jobs—and the list goes on and on.

As varied as the types of jobs is the nature of employers. The Federal Government offers a wide range of clerical employment; so do state, county, and municipal governments. The U.S. Postal Service, an independent agency of the Federal Government, employs many clerical workers for processing and distributing mail. And jobs with private employers are too numerous to be categorized.

The U.S. Postal Service deserves an extra word. You may never have thought of the Postal Service in terms of a clerical career or any career. Indeed, your image of the Postal Service may be limited to your local letter carrier. However, the Postal Service is a good employer, and it affords excellent flexibility in terms of changing careers within the agency.

Employees of the Postal Service are federal employees who enjoy the very generous benefits offered by the government. These benefits include an automatic raise at least once a year, regular cost-of-living adjustments, liberal paid vacation and sick leave, life insurance, hospitalization, and the opportunity to join a credit union. At the same time, the operation of the Postal Service is businesslike and independent of politics. A postal worker's job is secure even though administrations may change. An examination system is used to fill vacancies. The examination system provides opportunities for those who are able and motivated to enter the Postal Service and to advance within it.

Since postal employment is so popular, entry is very competitive. In some parts of the country, certain exams are given as seldom as once every three years. The resulting list is used to fill vacancies as they occur during the next three years. An individual who has been employed by the Postal Service for at least a year may ask to take the exam for any position and, if properly qualified, may fill a vacancy ahead of a person whose name is on the regular list. (The supervisor does not need to grant the request to take a special exam to fill a vacancy, but such permission is usually given to employees with good performance records who have served an adequate period in their current positions.) It is even possible to change careers within the Postal Service. A distribution clerk might take an exam to enter personnel work; a mark-up clerk might aspire to a position as postal inspector. If the exam for the precise position that you want will not be administered for some time, it might be worthwhile to take the exam for another position in hopes of entering the Postal Service and then moving from within. There is never a fee for applying for a postal examination, so if you want to work for the Postal Service, take every exam for which you are qualified.

Salaries, hours, and some other working conditions as well are subject to frequent change. The postal workers have a very effective union that bargains for them and gains increasingly better conditions. At the time of your employment, you should make your own inquiry as to salary, hours, and other conditions as they apply to you. Job descriptions and requirements are less subject to change

ABOUT THE JOBS AND HOW TO QUALIFY FOR THEM

FEDERAL CLERICAL JOBS

Jobs in more than sixty different clerical fields are filled using the Federal Clerical Examination. These jobs, like many other jobs in the Federal Government, are in the General Schedule (or GS), which assigns different "grades" to jobs which have different levels of responsibility or require different levels of experience or education.

There are jobs at various grade levels in each clerical field. Generally, all you need to qualify for jobs at the entry grades is to have graduated from high school (or some have previous job experience). Some of the occupations at the entry level also require specific skills, such as typing or shorthand.

As you gain experience, you become eligible for promotion to higher level, more specialized clerical and administrative jobs. You can also enter the Federal Government for the first time at these higher grade levels if you already have the specialized experience or additional education these jobs require.

Except for the clerk-stenographer, the entry level for clerical jobs is GS-2, and initial hires are usually made at either GS-2 or GS-3. The entry level for clerk-stenographers is GS-3, and initial hires are usually made at GS-3 or GS-4. Appointment at the higher grade levels is made for applicants who have appropriate experience or education above the high school level. Experience from summer jobs and part-time jobs is often appropriate. Therefore, many applicants are eligible for entry at the higher grades without additional education.

SALARIES

In Part I of this book, you can find a basic pay scale table under the General Schedule (GS). Keep in mind that GS pay is adjusted by geography, and most of the jobs pay a higher salary. The exact pay information is available when there is a job announcement. These are just general guidelines.

Following are descriptions of some of the jobs in the clerical field.

CLERK-TYPIST

Most hiring at the entry level in the clerical field is done for clerk-typist positions, which combine clerical work with typing duties. Thousands of these clerk-typist positions are filled each year, particularly in areas where a number of federal agencies are located. Vacancies are constantly occurring in these positions as employees are promoted to higher-graded positions, transfer to other jobs, or leave for other reasons.

CLERK-STENOGRAPHER

Clerk-stenographer jobs combine clerical tasks with both dictation and typing duties. There are usually many job openings in areas where there are large concentrations of Federal employees, and many opportunities for movement into higher grades.

OFFICE AUTOMATION CLERK

Office automation clerks and assistants operate personal computers to perform word processing tasks, desktop publishing, database management, financial spreadsheets, electronic bulletin boards, etc. This work can also be carried out on mainframe computers through telecommunications equipment. This occupation is new, and office automation clerks are taking the place of clerk-typists in many organizations.

DATA TRANSCRIBER

The job title "data transcriber" covers positions which involve the input or recording of different types of data into data processing files. Several thousand entry-level data transcribers are usually hired each year, and the number of jobs in the field is increasing as more use is made of automated systems.

CLERK

The title "clerk" covers many specific positions in which typing, stenographic, or data entry skills either are not required or are not an important part of the job. (In a few cases, one of these skills is important, in which case it is included in the job title.) Opportunities at the entry level in these fields are more limited than for typist, stenographer, and data transcriber jobs because more of these positions require specialized experience or training. However, entry-level opportunities do exist in some fields, as described below.

There are thousands of general clerks, such as mail and file clerks and miscellaneous clerks, who perform a variety of typical office and record-keeping tasks. Most of these jobs are filled at the lower entry levels. There are also many entry-level openings for sales store checkers. These clerks work in a variety of store-like situations usually on military bases or in agency supply stores.

There are a variety of clerical jobs, such as the calculating machine operator, which involve the use of some type of office machine. Many of these jobs are filled at the entry level, although they often require special skills and training and have additional selection requirements specific to each job. There are several hundred of these office machine operator types of jobs.

Jobs in the following fields are usually above the entry level. However, some entry-level jobs are available. There are many jobs in the personnel field, supporting the professional personnel staff. There are good opportunities for advancement to technical and administrative jobs in this field. There are opportunities in the fields of supply, transportation, and stock control. Most of these positions exist in military and supply agencies. Finally, there are clerical positions in accounting, payroll, and fiscal work. For example, payroll clerks keep records and do other work related to issuing paychecks, and cash processing clerks handle and track cash disbursements.

JOB BENEFITS

Salaries for federal employees under the General Schedule are set to reflect non-Federal pay levels in similar occupations. Periodic pay increases are made for competent employees. Promotions, which are based on increases in responsibility and demonstration of increased experience and skill, result in more significant salary increases.

Paydays occur every two weeks. Deductions are made for federal, state, and local taxes as required, as well as a percentage of salary for retirement purposes. (New federal employees are covered under a combined Social Security and supplemental retirement program. This retirement system gives workers flexibility to move between private industry and federal employment without losing basic retirement benefits.)

Group health insurance and life insurance are available at reduced rates since the government pays part of the cost. Vacation benefits begin at thirteen working days a year for most new employees who are working full time, and increase as length of experience increases. Most full-time employees also earn thirteen days of sick leave with pay each year, regardless of their length of service.

Training for increased responsibility is often provided on the job, and employees are encouraged to continue their own training activities. In addition, the Government sponsors some formal training courses and sometimes pays for outside training which is directly related to improving job performance.

POSTAL CLERKS

Even within the Postal Service, the title "clerk" is used to designate a number of different functions. One group of clerks comprises window clerks, distribution clerks, machine-operating distribution clerks, and mark-up clerks. These clerks, all of whom directly handle mail in one way or another, are all chosen by virtue of their scores on Postal Examination 470, the Postal Clerk and Carrier Exam. Mark-up clerk candidates must also qualify on a computer-administered alpha-numeric typing test designated as Examination 715. The other group of clerks in the Postal Service perform more traditional clerical functions. These are the clerk-typists and clerk-stenographers. All candidates for these clerical positions must compete on Examination 710, which is a test of clerical aptitude and verbal abilities. In addition, they must qualify on Examination 712, a typing test which is administered on a computer. Candidates for the position of clerk-stenographer must also earn qualifying scores on Examination 711, the stenography test.

POSTAL CLERK—DUTIES OF THE JOB

People are most familiar with the window clerk who sits behind the counter in post office lobbies selling stamps or accepting parcel post. However, the majority of postal clerks are distribution clerks who sort incoming and outgoing mail in workrooms. Only in a small post office does a clerk do both kinds of work.

When mail arrives at the post office, it is dumped on long tables where distribution clerks and mail handlers separate it into groups of letters, parcel post, and magazines and newspapers. Clerks feed letters into stamp-canceling machines and cancel the rest by hand. The mail is then taken to other sections of the post office to be sorted by destination. Clerks first separate the mail into primary destination categories: mail for the local area, for each nearby state, for groups of distant states, and for some of the largest cities. This primary distribution is followed by one or more secondary distributions. For example, local mail is combined with mail coming in from other cities and is sorted according to street and number. In post offices with electronic mail-sorting machines, clerks simply push a button corresponding to the letter's destination, and the letter drops into the proper slot.

The clerks at post office windows provide a variety of services in addition to selling stamps and money orders. They weigh packages to determine postage and check to see if their size, shape, and condition are satisfactory for mailing. Clerks also register and insure mail and answer questions about postage rates, mailing restrictions, and other postal matters. Occasionally they may help a customer file a claim for a damaged package. In large post offices a window clerk may provide only one or two of these services and be called a registry, stamp, or money order clerk.

Working conditions of clerks differ according to the specific work assignments and the amount and kind of labor-saving machinery in the post office. In small post offices, clerks must carry heavy mail sacks from one part of the building to another and sort the mail by hand. In large post offices, chutes and conveyors move the mail, and much of the sorting is done by machine. In either case, clerks are on their feet most of the time, reaching for sacks of mail, placing packages and bundles into sacks while sorting, and walking around the workroom.

Distribution clerks may become bored with the routine of sorting mail unless they enjoy trying to improve their speed and accuracy. They also may have to work at night, because most large post offices process mail around the clock.

A window clerk, on the other hand, has a greater variety of duties, has frequent contact with the public, generally has a less strenuous job, and never has to work a night shift.

New clerks are trained on the job. Most clerks begin with simple tasks to learn regional groupings of states, cities, and ZIP codes. To help clerks learn these groupings, many post offices offer classroom instruction. A good memory, good coordination, and the ability to read rapidly and accurately are important. These traits are measured by performance on Exam 470.

Distribution clerks work closely with other clerks, frequently under the tension and strain of meeting deadlines. Window clerks must be tactful when dealing with the public, especially when answering questions or receiving complaints.

DISTRIBUTION CLERK, MACHINE—DUTIES OF THE JOB

Distribution clerks work indoors. Often clerks must handle sacks of mail weighing as much as 70 pounds. They sort mail and distribute it by using a complicated scheme that must be memorized. Machine distribution clerks must learn computer codes for the automatic routing of mail. Clerks may be on their feet all day. They also have to stretch, reach, and throw mail. The work of the distribution clerk is more routine than that of other postal clerks; however, the starting salary is higher. Distribution clerks begin at postal pay level six while other clerks and carriers begin at level five. Increasing automation within the postal service has made the job of the distribution clerk quite secure.

Although the amount of mail post offices handle is expected to grow as both the population and the number of businesses grow, modernization of post offices and installation of new equipment will increase the amount of mail each clerk can handle. For example, machines that semiautomatically mark destination codes on envelopes are now being introduced. These codes can be read by computer-controlled letter-sorting machines, which automatically drop each letter into the proper slot: for its destination. With this system, clerks read addresses only once, at the time they are coded, instead of several times, as they do now. Eventually this equipment will be installed in all large post offices.

Applicants must be physically able to perform the duties described. Any physical condition that causes the applicant to be a hazard to him/herself or to others will be a disqualification for appointment.

The distant vision for clerk positions must test at least 20/30 (Snellen) in one eye (glasses are permitted). Some distribution clerk positions may be filled by the deaf.

A physical examination, drug test, and psychological interview are required before appointment.

Letter-sorting machine operator applicants must take Exam 470.

MARK-UP CLERK, AUTOMATED—DUTIES OF THE JOB

The mark-up clerk, automated, operates an electro-mechanical machine to process mail that is classified as "undeliverable as addressed." In doing this, the mark-up clerk operates the keyboard of a computer terminal to enter data into and extract it from several databases including change of address, mailer's database, and address-correction file. The mark-up clerk must select the correct program and operating mode for each application, must affix labels to mail either manually or with mechanical devices, and must prepare forms for address-correction services. Other duties may include distribution of processed mark-ups to appropriate separations for further handling, operation of a photocopy machine, and other job-related tasks in support of primary duties.

QUALIFICATION REQUIREMENTS

An applicant for a mark-up clerk position must have had either six months of clerical or office-machine-operating experience or have completed high school or have had a full academic year (36 weeks) of business school. The record of experience and training must show ability to use reference materials and manuals; ability to perform effectively under pressure; ability to operate any office equipment appropriate to the position; ability to work with others; and ability to read, understand, and apply certain regulations and procedures commonly used in processing mail that is undeliverable as addressed.

For appointment, a mark-up clerk must be 18 years old, or 16 years old if a high school graduate. An applicant who will reach his or her eighteenth birthday within two years from the date of the exam may participate. A mark-up clerk must be able to read, without strain, printed material the size of typewritten characters and must have 20/40 (Snellen) vision in one eye. Glasses are permitted. In addition, the applicant must pass a computer-administered alpha-numeric typing test. Candidates with high scores on the competitive exam, Exam 470, and with the requisite experience are called to the alpha-numeric typing test, Exam 715, individually as openings occur and hiring is likely. The exam is administered on a personal computer with its numeric keyboard disabled so that the candidate must use only the main keyboard. The Postal Service does not distribute sample questions for Exam 715, but the instructions at the test site are very clear and ample time is allowed for preparation. The alpha-numeric typing test is not a competitive test. The candidate need only pass to qualify.

CLERK-TYPIST—DUTIES OF THE JOB

A clerk-typist types records, letters, memorandums, reports, and other materials from handwritten and other drafts or from a dictating machine. He or she sets up the material typed in accordance with the prescribed format and assembles it for initialing, signing, routing, and dispatch. The clerk-typist also cuts mimeograph stencils and masters for duplication by other processes. The miscellaneous office clerical duties of the position include making up file folders, keeping them in the prescribed order, and filing in them; making and keeping routine office records; composing routine memorandums and letters relating to the business of the office, such as acknowledgments and transmittals; examining incoming and outgoing mail of the office, routing it to the appropriate persons, and controlling the time allowed for preparation of replies to incoming correspondence; receipting and delivering salary checks and filling out various personnel forms; acting as receptionist and furnishing routine information over the telephone; relieving other office personnel in their absence; operating office machines such as the mimeograph, comptometer, and adding machine.

The applicant for a position as clerk-typist must have had one year of office experience or four years of high school business courses or 36 weeks of business or secretarial school. The applicant must also show that he or she has enough of the skills, abilities, and knowledge to read and understand instructions; perform basic arithmetic computations; maintain accurate records; prepare reports and correspondence if required; and operate office machines such as calculators, adding machines, duplicators, and the like. The applicant for a clerk-typist position must pass a test of clerical abilities, Exam 710, and a "plain copy" typing test, Exam 712, administered on a personal computer, with a speed of 45 wpm and good accuracy.

CLERK-STENOGRAPHER—DUTIES OF THE JOB

The clerk-stenographer performs all of the functions of the clerk-typist. In addition, the clerk-stenographer takes dictation, in shorthand or on a shorthand writing machine, of letters, memorandums, reports, and other materials given by the supervisor of the office and other employees. He or she then transcribes it on the typewriter, or word processor, setting up the material transcribed in accordance with prescribed format and assembling it for required initialing, signing, routing, and dispatch. In consideration of the extra training and skill required in the taking of dictation, the clerk-stenographer is rated at salary level five, rather than at the salary level four of the clerk-typist.

The applicant for the position of clerk-stenographer must meet all the requirements of the applicant for clerk-typist in terms of education or experience and in terms of skills, abilities, and knowledge. In addition to passing the test of clerical ability, Exam 710, and the computer-administered plain-copy typing test, Exam 712, the clerk-stenographer applicant must also pass the stenography test, Exam 711.

CLERICAL JOBS WITH THE STATE

Following the lead of the Federal Government, every state has instituted some form of civil service or merit-based hiring procedure. In matters of internal hiring, each state has complete autonomy; no higher authority tells a state which positions must be filled by examination or which examination to use. However, in the interests of efficiency and fairness in hiring, nearly all states fill clerical positions through civil service examinations.

In addition to administering examinations to fill job vacancies in state government, many states offer their testing services to counties and municipalities as well. Thus, a person qualifying on a state-administered clerical examination may, if he or she wishes, have name and ranking listed on any number of eligibility rosters in counties or towns in which the person might be willing to work. In other states, state testing is only for state positions, and counties and municipalities have their own individual arrangements or independent systems.

As testing arrangements may vary from state to state, so procedures and the tests themselves may also vary. In general, state-administered clerical tests will test the skills and abilities needed for specific jobs or families of jobs. Where applicable, typing and stenographic tests are part of the testing package. Since budgetary restraints limit available state personnel, most state examinations are of the multiple-choice variety for easy scoring.

Because of the variety in state examinations, we cannot give you the precise information you need for *your* exam in *your* state. However, the following excerpts from a Pennsylvania announcement are illustrative.

COUNTY CLERICAL EMPLOYMENT

In some states, county subdivisions serve as convenient geographical and political units but have relatively little operational governmental function. In such states, county clerical testing is limited to selection of personnel to staff county offices, most often health departments and court systems. In those states, the bulk of nonmunicipal government services are distributed between the state itself and townships, towns, or boroughs. Where the state is the main coordinating body, the state may test and compile eligibility lists for its constituent local governments.

Other states have vested a great deal of power and autonomy in their counties. The counties operate and administer their own highway systems, police divisions, hospitals, educational units, prisons, and recreational areas. Where the counties deliver so many services, they also tend to offer support and assistance to local governments within their borders. Thus, strong counties tend to assume the testing function for county-wide employment at various levels. A single clerical exam administered by a county might be used to establish eligibility lists for towns, incorporated villages, school districts, and library districts within that county. Applicants taking county exams can specify which local entities they would like to be considered for and can have their names placed on a number of lists on the basis of one exam score.

Counties also have a great deal of discretion in test development and in choosing which tests to administer. Any given county may decide at any time to purchase an examination from a commercial test developer, to utilize a state-developed exam, or to join a consortium of neighboring counties and have an examination specially developed according to the specifications of the cooperating counties. The county may also change its examination from administration to administration, searching out the best vehicle for choosing the most productive employees.

COMMONWEALTH OF PENNSYLVANIA STATE CIVIL SERVICE COMMISSION

Announces Examinations for

CLERICAL AND SECRETARIAL POSITIONS IN STATE AND LOCAL GOVERNMENT

Exam No.	Job Title	Job Code	Pay Schedule and Range
	State Government		
1.	Clerk Typist 1	00210	S2
2.	Clerk Typist 2	00220	S3
3.	Clerk Stenographer 1	00410	S2
4.	Clerk Stenographer 2	00420	S3
	Local Government		
5.	Clerk Typist 1	L0031	*
6.	Clerk Typist 2	L0032	*
7.	Clerk Stenographer 1	L0021	*
8.	Clerk Stenographer 2	L0022	*

* Local government salaries vary. Contact the Personnel Office of the local government program where you are interested in working for specific information.

APPLICATIONS WILL BE ACCEPTED UNTIL FURTHER NOTICE.
IN ITEM 2 OF YOUR "APPLICATION FOR EMPLOYMENT/PROMOTION," LIST THE SPECIFIC STATE AND/OR LOCAL JOB TITLES FOR WHICH YOU ARE WILLING TO ACCEPT EMPLOYMENT.

SPECIAL NOTE

In Harrisburg, Philadelphia, and Pittsburgh you may take the typing test on either a typewriter or an IBM personal computer. You do not need any previous computer experience to take the computer version of the test. If you want to take the test on a personal computer, write "PC" on your application in Item 2.

Nature of Work

Typists compose and type documents, letters and memoranda. They also sort, file, check material, and provide information. Duties vary in complexity from limited (Clerk Typist 1) to moderate (Clerk Typist 2).

Stenographers take dictation and transcribe the notes. They also compose and type letters and memoranda, provide information, and sort and file materials.

continued

COMMONWEALTH OF PENNSYLVANIA STATE CIVIL SERVICE COMMISSION—*continued*

Job Requirements

You must be a Pennsylvania resident, of good moral character, and capable of performing the physical activities of the job.

Minimum Requirements: If you pass the tests you will be considered to have met the minimum requirements.

Job Opportunities

Opportunities for appointment depend on normal turnover due to retirements, promotions, transfers, resignations, and so forth.

State Government Positions

These positions are located throughout Pennsylvania. The majority of jobs are in the metropolitan areas of Harrisburg, Philadelphia, and Pittsburgh. It will be to your advantage to make yourself available for locations where clerical positions are concentrated. You may choose as many as 10 counties or as few as one. PLEASE DO NOT MAKE YOURSELF AVAILABLE FOR LOCATIONS IN WHICH YOU ARE NOT WILLING TO WORK. ENTRY HIRES ARE MADE AT BOTH THE CLERK TYPIST 1 AND CLERK TYPIST 2 LEVELS. THEREFORE, YOU ARE ENCOURAGED TO APPLY FOR BOTH JOB TITLES.

There is a continuing need for bilingual (English and Spanish) typists and stenographers in the Philadelphia area. Individuals hired for these positions provide information and assistance to Spanish-speaking clients. Individuals possessing the required bilingual skills are encouraged to apply.

For the most recent information on job opportunities in State Government, contact either the personnel office of the state facility in your area or the agency personnel office located in Harrisburg.

Summer Positions

The Department of Environmental Resources will have approximately ten (10) seasonal Clerk Typist 1 positions available at State Parks throughout Pennsylvania. These jobs last from either the beginning of April or June to Labor Day or the beginning of October. Individuals hired for these jobs will be placed on leave without pay status during the winter months and have the right to return to the job the following year without retaking the clerical test. They also will have the opportunity to be considered for permanent employment if it becomes available.

Local Government Positions

Agencies using these classes include: City and County Housing Authorities, Job Training Partnership Act Sponsors, Pennsylvania Emergency Management Agency Offices, Area Agency on Aging Offices, County Mental Health/Mental Retardation Offices, County Children and Youth Offices and County Drug and Alcohol Abuse Centers. For most recent information on job opportunities, contact the personnel office where you are interested in working.

Variations of exam subjects and formats are greatest among law enforcement and correctional examinations. Subjects of clerical examinations are more limited by the nature of clerical work itself. There are just so many dimensions along which to test, just so many relevant predictors of clerical success. Even so, there are differences in approach according to job descriptions and from county to county.

For example, Westchester County in New York administers an examination for the entry-level job title "jr. typist." This is a two-part examination testing only typing speed and accuracy and spelling. Rank-order certification is made on the basis of this 90-question, 10-minute spelling test and five-minute plain-paper-copy typing test. With this certification, applicants may seek employment with local governments, school districts, and libraries throughout the county. The hiring bodies may, of course, require candidates to demonstrate other skills and abilities as well.

For a somewhat higher-level job title, that of "senior clerk-typist," Suffolk County of New York administers a much more comprehensive exam. The job description reads:

> DUTIES: Performs a wide variety of difficult and responsible clerical and typing functions requiring the application of independent judgment and clerical knowledge. Checks the accuracy and completeness of documents, applications, legal instruments, payment claims of vendors and contract claims. Composes routine letters and transcribes from dictating machine or types from rough copy of such items as reports, letters, statements, tabulations, vouchers, and legal documents. Keeps perpetual inventory and consumption records. May supervise a small number of clerical personnel engaged in routine clerical duties. Does related work as required.

CLERICAL EMPLOYMENT IN THE COURTS

The job title "court clerk" is generally not a title filled by entry-level clerical workers. The court clerk is usually a senior employee of the court with a number of years of service as a court officer and considerable legal knowledge. The court clerk does, indeed, perform many clerical duties, but these duties are only secondary to administrative and even paralegal responsibilities. Where the court clerk position is a promotional one, the clerical-type exams will have been passed at earlier stages of employment testing. The court clerk exam will be a test of legal knowledge.

In those areas where "court clerk" is the title applied to any clerical worker in the court system, the court clerk exam will, of course, be more typical of clerical examinations. More often, clerical workers in the courts fill job titles like "file clerk," "office clerk," and "clerk-typist." In the Unified Court System of New York, which staffs state and municipal courts, a typical job designation is "senior office typist." In announcing the opening of this job title, the Unified Court System of New York published the following job description:

> Senior Office Typists work with a limited degree of independence on a variety of office clerical and keyboarding tasks, as supervisors of small clerical sub-units, at public counters as information clerks, and perform other related duties.

MUNICIPAL CLERICAL POSITIONS

If you were not aware of this fact before, you most certainly now are convinced that clerical positions appear at every governmental level and in every locality. Big cities are no exception. Most big cities operate their own civil service systems, develop and administer their own examinations, and maintain their own eligibility lists. The job titles can be simple and all-inclusive, or they can be highly specialized, as in New York City. The following list comprises some of the clerical positions filled through the tests of the Personnel Department in the city of New York.

- Account Clerk
- Cashier
- Chief Clerk
- Chief Office Assistant
- Clerical Aide
- Clerk
- Clerk, Community Action Activities
- Clerk, Income Maintenance
- Clerk to the Board
- College Aide
- College Assistant
- College Office Assistant
- College Secretarial Assistant
- Committee Clerk
- Communications Clerk
- Computer Aide
- Computer Operator
- Deputy Chief Clerk
- Deputy City Clerk
- Document Clerk
- Legislative Clerical Assistant
- Legislative Clerk
- Legislative Stenographer
- Legislative Typist
- Medical Clerk
- Office Aide
- Office Aide (Typing Positions)
- Office Appliance Operator
- Office Assistant
- Office Associate
- Office Machine Associate
- Police Administrative Aide
- Property Clerk
- Public Records Aide
- Railroad Clerk
- Secretary
- Senior Clerk
- Senior Legislative Clerical Assistant
- Senior Legislative Clerk
- Senior Office Appliance Operator
- Senior Satisfaction Clerk

The city of New York tends to administer a separate exam for each job title as the list of eligibles for that title is exhausted or expires. But the exams used to test for similar positions are very similar to each other. Numbers of questions, timing, subjects tested, and proportion of questions on each subject vary little from exam to exam. Only the words and figures change.

The office aide exam in the second part of this book is an actual office aide examination given by the city of New York some years ago. Some question styles have changed over the years. Some new styles have been introduced; old, discredited question styles have been discarded. If you are taking a New York City exam, it will be similar, but not exactly the same as this. If your exam is for a city other than New York, you can expect less similarity.

Another city's exam may look more like a federal or state exam. Whatever the format, however, clerical skills are clerical skills, and much of the subject matter will be the same. Emphasis and question form may differ, but the ability you must demonstrate is the ability to perform clerical duties.

Do not ignore the municipal office aide exam in the second part of the book just because you are not taking a New York City exam. This exam will give you good practice in taking a varied exam that is not divided into discrete segments. Any test-taking practice will help in preparation for the exam you will take.

Following is a *typical* municipal notice of examination from New York City for a Clerical Associate. It is NOT a current notice.

THE CITY OF NEW YORK
DEPARTMENT OF
CITYWIDE ADMINSTRATIVE SERVICES

NOTICE OF EXAMINATION
CLERICAL ASSOCIATE

Exam. No. 0038
(For City Agencies Only)

WHAT THE JOB INVOLVES: At Assignment Level I: Clerical Associates, under supervision, with a limited latitude for independent judgment, perform clerical work in relation to records, files, invoices, and reports using alphabetical and numerical procedures including data/control coding; perform ordinary mathematical calculations; operate a telephone call directory or switchboard; perform clerical operations in an assigned area, such as the filing of material and the searching of files for material difficult to locate; prepare reports requiring the selection of data from simple records or statistics; check records for accuracy of information and for conformity with established policy and procedures; perform data entry and retrieval using a video display terminal or other automated office systems; maintain related library files; may perform incidental typing.

(This is a brief description of what you might do in this position and does not include all the duties of this position.)

THE SALARY: The current minimum salary is $19,642 per annum. This rate is subject to change. There are four assignment levels within this class of positions. Appointments to the higher assignment level(s) are made at the discretion of the agency:

HOW TO APPLY: If you believe you meet the requirements in the "How to Qualify" section, refer to the "Required Forms" section below for the form(s) that you must fill out. Return all completed form(s) and the application fee to DCAS Applications Section, 1 Centre Street, 14th floor, New York, NY 10007 by mail only. Applications will not be accepted in person.

HOW TO QUALIFY:

Education and Experience Requirements: By the last day of the Application Period you must have:

1. A four-year high school diploma or its educational equivalent; and
2. One year of full-time satisfactory clerical experience.

You may be given the test before we check your qualifications.

Skills Requirement: You will be required to meet the skill requirement of keyboard familiarity by demonstrating the ability to type accurately at a minimum speed of 100 keystrokes (20 words) per minute after errors are deducted. You must meet this requirement in order to be considered for appointment.

Residency Requirement: You must be a City resident within ninety days of the date you are appointed to this position if the appointing agency requires City residency and:

1. You begin City service as a result of this examination; or
2. You are currently a City employee and you began City service on or after September 1, 1986.

Since some agencies do not require City residency, consult the appointing agency's personnel office at the time of the appointment interview to find out if City residency is required. If you are required to be a City resident, you must maintain City residency as a condition of employment.

English Requirement: Candidates must be able to understand and be understood in English.

Proof of Identity: Under the Immigration Reform and Control Act of 1986, you must be able to prove your identity and your right to obtain employment in the United States prior to employment with the City of New York.

continued

THE CITY OF NEW YORK DEPARTMENT OF CITYWIDE ADMINSTRATIVE SERVICES—*continued*

REQUIRED FORM(S)

1. Application for Examination: Make sure that you follow all instructions included with your application form, including payment of fee. Save a copy of the instructions for future reference.
2. Education and Experience Test Paper: Write your social security number, the examination title and number in the box at the top right side of the cover page. Fill out Sections A.1 and B. This form must be filled out completely and in detail for you to receive your proper rating. Keep a copy of your completed Education and Experience Test Paper for your records.
3. Foreign Education Fact Sheet (Required only if you need credit for your foreign education to meet the education and experience requirements): If you were educated outside the United States, you must have your foreign education evaluated to determine its equivalence to education obtained in the United States. The services that are approved to make this evaluation are listed on the Foreign Education Fact Sheet included with your application packet. When you contact the evaluation service, ask for a "document-by-document" (general) evaluation of your foreign education. You must have one of these services submit its evaluation of your foreign education directly to the Department of Citywide Administrative Services no later than eight weeks from the last date for applying for this examination.

THE TEST: You will be given a multiple-choice test. Your score on this test will be used to determine your place on an eligible list. You must achieve a score of at least 70 percent to pass the test. The multiple-choice test may include questions on English language usage, reading comprehension, number facility, alphabetical and numerical filing, proofreading (matching), and other related areas.

You will also be given a qualifying practical typing test to determine if you meet the skill requirement of keyboard familiarity. In order to pass this test you must be able to type accurately at a minimum speed of 100 keystrokes (20 words) per minute after errors are deducted.

ADMISSION CARD: You should receive an Admission Card in the mail about 10 days before the date of the test. If you do not receive an Admission Card at least 4 days before the test date, you must go to the Examining Service Section, 1 Centre Street, 14th floor, Manhattan, to obtain a duplicate card.

THE TEST RESULTS: If you meet the education and experience requirements and pass both the multiple-choice test and the qualifying practical typing test, your name will be placed in score order on an eligible list and you will be given a list number. You will be notified by mail of your test results. You must pass the qualifying practical typing test in addition to meeting all other requirements and conditions in order for you to be considered for appointment when your name is reached on the eligible list.

ADDITIONAL INFORMATION

List Termination: The eligible list resulting from this examination will be terminated one year from the date it is established, unless extended by the Commissioner.

Promotion Test: A promotion examination for this title is being held for eligible City employees. The names appearing on the promotion list will be considered first in filling vacancies.

This examination is for all City agencies and not for the Health and Hospitals Corporation (HHC). If you would like to apply for Clerical Associate in HHC you must submit a separate application and fee for Exam. No. 0039 from November 1, 20____ through November 21, 20____.

SPECIAL TEST ACCOMMODATIONS: If you plan to request special testing accommodations due to disability or an alternate test date due to your religious belief, follow the instructions included with the "Application for Examination. "

CLERICAL JOBS IN THE PRIVATE SECTOR

Civil service testing, that is, testing for positions in the public sector, is standardized and uniform within each governmental jurisdiction. Testing in the private sector, by contrast, is highly individualized. A private employer has the option to test or not to test, to devise tailor-made tests for positions within the company, or to purchase ready-made exams from a commercial test publisher.

Most often a small, private employer will rely on school records, recommendations, personal interview, and, if relevant, typing and stenography tests. Large corporations often screen applicants with clerical tests of their own devising so as to avoid the time and effort of checking references and interviewing applicants who are unqualified in terms of skills and abilities.

Within the private sector, most clerical exams are administered by employment agencies—both temporary agencies and agencies that specialize in placing permanent employees. The agencies gain and maintain their reputations by sending qualified prospects to their clients. One way for an agency to verify the competence of people seeking employment is by testing their skills.

PART THREE

Civil Service Tests for Clerical Jobs

CIVIL SERVICE TEST REQUIREMENTS

ABOUT CIVIL SERVICE TESTS

Before we discuss the different types of tests you might encounter, following is some general information about Civil Service Tests. To be considered for most Civil Service jobs, especially entry level, applicants are required to take a test. Test grades are used to place applicants on job referral lists, often called "registers." These lists or "registers" of successful applicants are then sent by Civil Service to those agencies with vacancies to fill. The agency then contacts the highest scoring applicants for job interviews.

What are the Civil Service tests like? Different kinds of tests are given for different types of jobs. Most Civil Service tests are "paper-and-pencil" multiple-choice exams. Those applying for typing, word processing, and secretarial jobs also take a typing skills test, usually on a PC. Except for typing skills tests, most of these tests are not speed tests.

The tests are usually graded by computer. All questions on a test are valued equally; no question counts more than any other. Passing grades range from 70–99. The number of questions you must answer correctly to be considered passing depends on the kind of test you're taking. But on most tests you must answer 60–70 percent of the questions correctly in order to pass.

The typing skills test given to secretarial job applicants is graded for both speed and accuracy. To pass the skills test you must type at least 40 wpm, after penalties for errors. You would normally subtract 1 wpm for each error. The faster and more accurately you type, the higher your score will be. The results of this test combined with your multiple-choice test score determines your final grade.

It takes about two weeks for you to receive your grade, and once that grade is issued to you, your name goes on the "register" to be referred for vacancies. Your grade notice will tell you when your grade expires, which is usually about a year. Permanent state employee grades do not expire, but if there is a significant change in the test, the grade will be cancelled.

If you want to retake the test, you must wait six months, except for those tests specifically exempt from this rule. You should be cautious, however, If you retake the test, your new score will replace the old score, regardless of which grade is higher.

FEDERAL TESTING

EXAM SELECTION PROCEDURE

HOW AND WHERE TO APPLY

Examinations for clerical jobs are given directly by the individual federal agencies when-ever they are ready to hire. Sometimes examinations will be announced and given for all clerical occupations at one time, and sometimes separate examinations for specific jobs are announced. Clerical examinations are given frequently because of the large number of available jobs.

Information about applying for these and other federal jobs is provided by federal Job Information Centers throughout the country. These centers are listed in local telephone directories under "U.S. Government." You may also directly contact the personnel offices of federal agencies located in your area to find out if they are in the process of hiring and where they suggest you take the examination.

SELECTION REQUIREMENTS

Selection requirements for the clerical occupations in the Federal Government are based on studies of the training, experience, and skills required for successful job performance at the different grade levels. Job applicants must meet the education or experience require-ments, show evidence of having the required skills, and, for entry at GS-2 through 4 (GS-3 through 5 for clerk-stenographers), pass a job-related written test.

RATINGS

Applicants who meet the minimum experience and education requirements and skill levels are given numerical ratings based on their written test scores. Applicants must pass the written test in order to receive a rating. Qualified veterans of the military service have additional points added to their qualifying ratings.

WRITTEN TESTS

The written tests for clerical occupations measure the verbal and clerical skills needed for success in these jobs. In general, the same written test battery is used for all clerical jobs except data transcriber and sales store checker. This battery consists of two tests: a Verbal Tasks Test and a Clerical Tasks Test. Data transcriber and sales store checker applicants take only the Clerical Tasks Test. (There are other situations with other test requirements. These generally occur when a particular agency is testing applicants for clerical jobs located only in its offices, or for seasonal rather than permanent positions. For example, the Internal Revenue Service hires many seasonal clerical employees and uses a modified test for those positions.)

Because of these possible differences in requirements, you should check the specific examination announcement for each position in which you are interested to confirm the test battery you will have to take.

As long as a modified examination was not used, once you have passed the written test you do not have to take it again to apply for other clerical jobs. Nor do you have to reestablish that you meet the minimum experience or education requirements or have the required skills. (However, your rating can expire after a certain period of time; this will be shown on the rating form.)

Any questions you have about the tests you need to take, how your rating can be used, and whether it has expired can be answered by the Federal Job Information Center serving your area.

SKILL REQUIREMENTS

- When a job requires typing skill, you must be able to type accurately at 40 words per minute.
- When dictation skill is required, you must be able to transcribe dictation accurately at 80 words per minute. GS-2 data transcribers must be able to type accurately at 20 words per minute, and GS-3 and 4 data transcribers must be able to type accurately at 25 words per minute.
- Stenographer applicants may use any system of taking and transcribing dictation they wish.

Skill requirements may be measured in several different ways. The most frequently used method is the proficiency certificate. These certificates may be issued by schools and other authorized training organizations and by some state employment services. If this method is used, applicants are told where they can obtain a certificate if they do not already have one. Applicants with proficiency certificates usually do not have to take further tests to demonstrate their skill levels.

Another method which is sometimes used is self-certification by applicants. In this process, an applicant signs a statement that he or she meets the skill requirements for the job. Agencies usually require applicants who have self-certified their skills to take a performance test before they are hired.

APPLICANTS WITH DISABILITIES

Persons with disabilities are encouraged to apply for positions in the Federal Government. There are Selective Placement Specialists in OPM offices and in the agencies in your area who are responsible for helping applicants with disabilities to take advantage of the available employment opportunities.

Applicants must be physically and mentally able to perform the essential functions of the job for which they apply. Federal agencies must make reasonable accommodation to the known physical and mental limitations of a qualified applicant, including during the test process. Many test batteries have been modified for visually disabled, motor disabled, deaf, and learning disabled applicants. If you have one or more disabilities, you should state the nature of your disability on your test application card so that special testing arrangements can be made.

The Federal Clerical Examination consists of two separately timed sections, a Verbal Tasks Test and a Clerical Tasks Test.

THE VERBAL TASKS TEST

WHAT THE TEST IS ABOUT

The Verbal Tasks Test includes questions in such areas as spelling, meaning, and relationship of words; recognition of sentences which are grammatically correct; and reading, understanding, and using written material.

These test tasks relate to a variety of job tasks, such as proofreading and correcting typed copy, using instruction manuals, organizing new files of related materials, and carrying out written instructions.

There are 85 questions—25 on word meaning, 20 on word relationships, 20 on spelling, 10 on grammar, and 10 on reading. There are a few questions of each type on each page of the test. For each question, you will select the best answer from among a set of suggested answers.

HOW THE TEST IS ADMINISTERED

Each applicant is given a copy of the test booklet with sample questions and an answer sheet. Three minutes are allowed to study the directions and answer the sample questions. The separate answer sheet is then used for recording answers to the test. Exactly 35 minutes are allowed for the test.

Here are official directions and sample questions. You may allow yourself more than three minutes to study these now since you are not actually in a testing situation.

Directions: Study the sample questions carefully. Each question has four suggested answers. Decide which one is the best answer. Find the question number on the Sample Answer Sheet. Show your answer to the question by darkening completely the space corresponding to the letter that is the same as the letter of your answer. Keep your mark within the space. If you have to erase a mark, be sure to erase it completely. Darken only one answer for each question. Do NOT darken space (E) for any question.

1. *Previous* means most nearly

(A) abandoned
(B) former
(C) timely
(D) younger

2. Just as the procedure of a collection department must be clear-cut and definite, the steps being taken with the sureness of a skilled chess player, so the various paragraphs of a collection letter must show clear organization, giving evidence of a mind that, from the beginning, has had a specific end in view.

The paragraph best supports the statement that a collection letter should always

(A) show a spirit of sportsmanship
(B) be divided into several paragraphs
(C) be brief, but courteous
(D) be carefully planned

3. Decide which sentence is preferable with respect to grammar and usage suitable for a formal letter or report.

(A) They do not ordinarily present these kind of reports in detail like this.
(B) A report of this kind is not hardly ever given in such detail as this one.
(C) This report is more detailed than what such reports ordinarily are.
(D) A report of this kind is not ordinarily presented in this much detail.

4. Find the correct spelling of the word and darken the proper answer space. If no suggested spelling is correct, darken space D.

(A) athalete
(B) athelete
(C) athlete
(D) none of these

5. SPEEDOMETER is related to POINTER as WATCH is related to

(A) case
(B) hands
(C) dial
(D) numerals

Sample Answer Sheet

1. Ⓐ Ⓑ Ⓒ Ⓓ Ⓔ	4. Ⓐ Ⓑ Ⓒ Ⓓ Ⓔ
2. Ⓐ Ⓑ Ⓒ Ⓓ Ⓔ	5. Ⓐ Ⓑ Ⓒ Ⓓ Ⓔ
3. Ⓐ Ⓑ Ⓒ Ⓓ Ⓔ	

The correct answers for questions 1–5 are:

1. (B) **2.** (D) **3.** (D) **4.** (C) **5.** (B)

EXPLANATIONS

Sample Question 1. Word meaning questions consist of one given word followed by four different words labeled (A), (B), (C), and (D). You are to select the word which has the closest meaning to the word given in the question. It may help if you remember you are looking for the best match among the choices given, but not necessarily a perfect match.

Answering these questions depends upon your knowledge of vocabulary, but there are some steps you can take if you do not recognize the correct answer immediately.

- If you have a general idea about what the given word means, but are having trouble choosing an answer, try using the word in a short sentence. Then, substitute each of the answer choices in the same sentence to see which one seems best to fit the sentence.
- Try to break the given word into parts to see if the suffix (ending) or the prefix (beginning) of the word gives a clue about its meaning.

You could have used the above procedure to answer sample question 1. The correct answer to this question is choice (B), "former." If you did not know the meaning of "previous," but you remembered that the prefix "pre" usually means "before," you could have used that clue to help you to select choice (B) as the correct answer.

Sample Question 2. The reading questions consist of a paragraph followed by four statements. You read the paragraph first and then select the one statement which is based on information given in the paragraph.

- Do not worry if you are unfamiliar with the subject discussed in the paragraph. You do not need to have any knowledge about the subject of the paragraph since the answer to the question is always given in the paragraph itself.
- Do not worry about whether the correct statement, or any of the incorrect statements, are true. The important thing is that the correct answer is the only statement which says the same thing as is said in the paragraph. Some of the other statements may be true, but they are not based on the content of the paragraph.

- To select the correct statement, first eliminate choices which clearly conflict with the paragraph. Then, if you still have two or more choices, look for the specific section of the paragraph which covers the information given in each one of the choices.
- Compare the facts given carefully, until you can eliminate the remaining incorrect choices.

For sample question 2, choice (D) is correct because it is the only choice which states the basic point made in the paragraph. Choice (A) is meant to draw attention if you did not read the paragraph carefully and remembered only that chess, which is similar to a sport, was mentioned. Choice (B) would draw attention because the word "paragraphs" was mentioned, but the reading paragraph did not specify that a collection letter should have any particular number of paragraphs. Similarly, the reading paragraph did not say anything about being brief or courteous, so choice (C) is incorrect.

Sample Question 3. Grammar questions give four versions of a single sentence. Each sentence tries to express the same thought, but only one of them is grammatically correct.

- Most of the incorrect sentences are obviously poorly constructed.
- Others have such errors as using singular verbs with plural nouns.
- In the more difficult questions, you must pay attention to smaller details, like the misuse of punctuation, which can make a sentence very difficult to understand.

To answer these questions, first eliminate the sentences you are sure are incorrect. Then compare the remaining ones until you can choose one as being more correct than the others.

- It is possible that one sentence will seem to be correct because it uses the same informal grammar that people often use when talking. However, this type of sentence structure is not suitable for writing.

In sample question 3, choice (D) is correct. The major errors in the other choices are: choice (A) uses the plurals "these" and "reports" with the singular "kind"; choice (B) uses "not hardly ever" instead of the preferable "never"; and choice (C) inappropriately inserts "what" into the sentence.

Sample Question 4. Spelling questions give three spellings of a common word, labeled (A), (B), and (C). Each question also offers the option of "none of these" as choice (D). You must decide which one of the three given spellings is correct, or that none of them is correct.

- Sometimes it helps to answer these questions by looking away from the given choices and writing the word yourself on the margin of your test booklet. Then check to see if the spelling you believe is correct is given as one of the choices.

In sample question 4, choice (C) is correct.

Sample Question 5. Word relationship questions give two words which are related in some way, and then give the first word of a second word relationship which you are to complete. You are given four choices of words to complete that relationship. The correct choice is the word which completes that relationship in the way most similar to the relationship in the first pair of words.

To answer these questions, look at the first pair of words and decide what the relationship between the words is. Then choose the answer that best completes that relationship for the second pair of words.

- Remember that the correct answer is chosen because it completes an analogous relationship, not because it is on the same subject as the first pair of words.

Sample question 5 would be answered this way. Consider what a pointer is used for on a speedometer. It is used to indicate speed at a particular moment. A watch uses hands, choice (B), for the same general function, that is, to indicate something at a particular moment. In this case, the indication is of time. Choice (A) is incorrect because the watch case has nothing to do with this function. Choices (C) and (D) are wrong because although the dial and the numerals have to do with indicating the time, they do not perform the specific function of indicating something at any one particular moment.

THE CLERICAL TASKS TEST

WHAT THE TEST IS ABOUT

The Clerical Tasks Test is a test of speed and accuracy on four clerical tasks. There are 120 questions given with a short time limit. The test contains 30 questions on name and number checking, 30 on arranging names in correct alphabetical order, 30 on simple arithmetic, and 30 on inspecting groups of letters and numbers. The questions are arranged in groups or cycles of five questions of each type.

HOW THE TEST IS ADMINISTERED

Each applicant is given a copy of the test booklet with sample questions and an answer sheet. Ten minutes are allowed to study the directions and answer the sample questions printed on the two pages.

The separate answer sheet is then used for recording answers to the test. Exactly 15 minutes are allowed for this test.

HOW TO ANSWER THE TEST QUESTIONS

Directions for answering all four of the types of questions on the Clerical Tasks Test are given with the sample questions. Additional specific information on how to answer each type of question is given below. Look first at the sample questions on the test and then study the information here until you can understand how to answer the questions. (Do not limit yourself to the ten minutes allowed in the actual test situation.)

The Clerical Tasks Test is planned as a test of speed in carrying out these relatively simple clerical tasks. This means you should work quickly through the test. However, the test is also planned to measure accuracy, and there is a penalty for wrong answers in the total test score. This means you need to be careful as you work and that wild guessing is not a good idea. However, do not be so concerned about accuracy that you do the test more slowly than you should. Remember that both speed and accuracy are important to achieve a good score.

The different question types in this test appear on each page of the test. You may find it easier to answer all questions of one type that appear in the test rather than switching from one question type to another. This is perfectly acceptable, but extra caution should be taken to darken your answers in the right place on the answer sheet.

Directions: This test contains four kinds of questions. There are some of each kind of question on each page in the booklet. The time limit for the test will be announced by the examiner.

Study the sample questions carefully. Each question has five suggested answers. Decide which one is the best answer. Find the question number on the Sample Answer Sheet. Show your answer to the question by darkening completely the space that is lettered the same as the letter of your answer. Keep your mark within the space. If you have to erase a mark, be sure to erase it completely. Darken only one answer for each question.

In each line across the page there are three names or numbers that are very similar. Compare the three names or numbers and decide which ones are exactly alike. On the Sample Answer Sheet darken answer:

(A) if **ALL THREE** names or numbers are exactly **ALIKE**
(B) if only the **FIRST** and **SECOND** names or numbers are exactly **ALIKE**
(C) if only the **FIRST** and **THIRD** names or numbers are exactly **ALIKE**
(D) if only the **SECOND** and **THIRD** names or numbers are exactly **ALIKE**
(E) if **ALL THREE** names or numbers are **DIFFERENT**

1.	Davis Hazen	David Hozen	David Hazen
2.	Lois Appel	Lois Appel	Lois Apfel
3.	June Allan	Jane Allan	Jane Allan
4.	10235	10235	10235
5.	32614	32164	32614

If you finish the sample questions before you are told to turn to the test, it will be to your advantage to study the code given above for (A), (B), (C), (D), and (E). This code is repeated on every page.

In the next group of sample questions, there is a name in a box at the left, and four other names in alphabetical order at the right. Find the correct location for the boxed name so that it will be in alphabetical order with the others, and mark the letter of that location as your answer.

6. Jones, Jane

(A) →
Goodyear, G. L.
(B) →
Haddon, Harry
(C) →
Jackson, Mary
(D) →
Jenkins, William
(E) →

7. Kessler, Neilson

(A) →
Kessel, Carl
(B) →
Kessinger, D. J.
(C) →
Kessler, Karl
(D) →
Kessner, Lewis
(E) →

Sample Answer Sheet

1. Ⓐ Ⓑ Ⓒ Ⓓ Ⓔ
2. Ⓐ Ⓑ Ⓒ Ⓓ Ⓔ
3. Ⓐ Ⓑ Ⓒ Ⓓ Ⓔ
4. Ⓐ Ⓑ Ⓒ Ⓓ Ⓔ
5. Ⓐ Ⓑ Ⓒ Ⓓ Ⓔ
6. Ⓐ Ⓑ Ⓒ Ⓓ Ⓔ
7. Ⓐ Ⓑ Ⓒ Ⓓ Ⓔ

The correct answers for questions 1–7 are:

1. (E) 2. (B) 3. (D) 4. (A) 5. (C) 6. (E) 7. (D)

In the following questions, solve each problem and find your answer among the list of suggested answers for that question. Darken the Sample Answer Sheet (A), (B), (C), or (D) for the answer you obtained; or if your answer is not among these, darken (E) for that question.

8. Add: 22 +33

(A) 44
(B) 45
(C) 54
(D) 55
(E) none of these

9. Subtract: 24 − 3

(A) 20
(B) 21
(C) 27
(D) 29
(E) none of these

10. Multiply: 25 × 5

(A) 100
(B) 115
(C) 125
(D) 135
(E) none of these

11. Divide: 6)126

(A) 20
(B) 22
(C) 24
(D) 26
(E) none of these

There is one set of suggested answers for the next group of sample questions. Do not try to memorize these answers, because there will be a different set on each page in the test.

To find the answer to a question, find which suggested answer contains numbers and letters all of which appear in the question. If no suggested answer fits, darken (E) for that question.

12. 8 N K 9 G T 4 6
13. T 9 7 Z 6 L 3 K
14. Z 7 G K 3 9 8 N
15. 3 K 9 4 6 G Z L
16. Z N 7 3 8 K T 9

Suggested Answers
(A) = 7, 9, G, K
(B) = 8, 9, T, Z
(C) = 6, 7, K, Z
(D) = 6, S, G, T
(E) = none of these

Sample Answer Sheet

8. Ⓐ Ⓑ Ⓒ Ⓓ Ⓔ
9. Ⓐ Ⓑ Ⓒ Ⓓ Ⓔ
10. Ⓐ Ⓑ Ⓒ Ⓓ Ⓔ
11. Ⓐ Ⓑ Ⓒ Ⓓ Ⓔ
12. Ⓐ Ⓑ Ⓒ Ⓓ Ⓔ
13. Ⓐ Ⓑ Ⓒ Ⓓ Ⓔ
14. Ⓐ Ⓑ Ⓒ Ⓓ Ⓔ
15. Ⓐ Ⓑ Ⓒ Ⓓ Ⓔ
16. Ⓐ Ⓑ Ⓒ Ⓓ Ⓔ

The correct answers for questions 8–16 are:

8. (D) **9.** (B) **10.** (C) **11.** (E) **12.** (D) **13.** (C) **14.** (A) **15.** (E) **16.** (B)

EXPLANATIONS

Sample Questions 1–5. Memorizing the answer choices for this question type may be helpful in increasing your speed. In these questions, you are to compare three names or numbers and decide which ones are exactly alike. You then select your answer from a set of choices which describe whether all of them, some of them, or none of them are alike. These choices are labeled (A), (B), (C), (D), and (E) and are given at the top of the first page of the Sample Questions for the Clerical Tasks Test and are repeated on each page of the test booklet.

- These choices remain the same for all questions of this type in the test so if you memorize these choices you will not have to refer constantly back to them before choosing your answers.

Sample Questions 6–7. For the alphabetizing questions, remember that the most important rule for putting the names in order is to consider each letter in the complete last name in strict alphabetical order, exactly as it appears.

- This is true even when the name includes more than one capital letter (as in DeLong), or involves prefixes which are often spelled differently in different names (as in McDuff and MacDuff).
- Ignore punctuation, such as apostrophes and hyphens, that appear in a name (as in O'Hara).
- When two last names are identical in every way, then alphabetize according to the first and second names given, following the same rules.

Sample Questions 8–11. The key to the arithmetic questions is to avoid careless errors. Remember that the correct answer may not be included as one of the given alternatives. In this case you darken choice (E) on the answer sheet.

- Answers will always be exact (no decimal places), so if the answer you get is not exact, work the problem again.

Sample Questions 12–16. There are several different ways of approaching the letter and number inspection questions. You should use the method that works best for you.

One method is to work from the answer choices to the questions. Look at each answer choice and, one at a time, compare each letter or number it contains with the question until you can accept or reject it. Here is how you would use this method to answer Sample Question 12:

- Start by looking at the first number given in choice (A), which is a 7.
- Quickly scan question 12 for this number. Since it does not include a 7, choice (A) can be rejected.
- Next consider the first letter in choice (B), which is an 8. Scanning question 12 confirms that an 8 is present. Moving on to the next number in choice (B), the number 9, scanning of the question confirms its presence also, as well as the next letter in choice (B), the letter T. There is no Z, however, so choice (B) is then rejected.
- Using the same process of elimination for choice (C), no number 7 is found, and this choice is rejected.
- One by one, all of the letters and numbers in choice (D) are: found, so choice (D) is marked as correct on the separate answer sheet.
- If all the letters and numbers in choice (D) had not been found in question 12, then choice (E), "none of these," would have been marked as the correct answer.

You may be able to save time using this method by scanning for two of the letters or numbers given at one time.

Another method is to look at the particular question and quickly and lightly memorize all the numbers and letters it contains. Then, glance at each choice to select one which is a good possibility based on your memory.

- Carefully double-check this choice with each of the numbers and letters given in the question.
- If you use this method, be sure to spend only a few seconds memorizing the numbers and letters in the question, or you will waste too much time on one question.

Whichever method you choose, remember that any of the answer choices given may be used to answer more than one of the five questions included in the set on each page. Also, note that the letters and numbers given in the answer choices and questions do not have to be in the same order. Finally, unlike the situation with the answer choices given for the first five sample questions on the Clerical Tasks Test, the answer choices for these questions do not remain the same throughout the test. Therefore, it will not help you to memorize any of the answer choices given with these sample questions.

EXAM 470—SAMPLE QUESTIONS

MARK-UP CLERK POSITION TEST INSTRUCTIONS

During the test session for a mark-up clerk position, it will be your responsibility to pay close attention to what the examiner has to say and to follow all instructions. One of the purposes of the test is to see how quickly and accurately you can work. Therefore, each part of the test will be carefully timed. You will not START until you are told to do so. Also, when you are told to STOP, you must immediately STOP answering the questions. When you are told to work on a particular part of the examination, regardless of which part, you are to work on that part ONLY. If you finish a part before time is called, you may review your answers for that part, but you will not go on or back to any other part. Failure to follow ANY directions given to you by the examiner may be grounds for disqualification. Instructions read by the examiner are intended to ensure that each applicant has the same fair and objective opportunity to compete in the examination.

SAMPLE QUESTIONS

STUDY CAREFULLY BEFORE THE EXAMINATION.

The following questions are like the ones that will be on the test. Study these carefully. This will give you practice with the different kinds of questions and show you how to mark your answers.

PART A: ADDRESS CHECKING

In this part of the test, you will have to decide whether two addresses are alike or different. If the two addresses are exactly *Alike* in every way, darken choice (A) for the question. If the two addresses are *Different* in any way, darken choice (D) for the question.

Mark your answers to these sample questions on the Sample Answer Sheet below.

1.	2134 S 20th St	2134 S 20th St

Since the two addresses are exactly alike, mark choice (A) for question 1 on the Sample Answer Sheet.

2.	4608 N Warnock St	4806 N Warnock St
3.	1202 W Girard Dr	1202 W Girard Rd
4.	Chappaqua NY 10514	Chappaqua NY 10514
5.	2207 Markland Ave	2207 Markham Ave

Sample Answer Sheet

1. Ⓐ Ⓓ
2. Ⓐ Ⓓ
3. Ⓐ Ⓓ
4. Ⓐ Ⓓ
5. Ⓐ Ⓓ

The correct answers to questions 2–5 are:

2. (D) **3.** (D) **4.** (A) **5.** (D)

Your score on Part A of the actual test will be based on the number of wrong answers as well as on the number of right answers. Part A is scored right answers minus wrong answers. Random guessing should not help your score. For the Part A test, you will have six minutes to answer as many of the 95 questions as you can. It will be to your advantage to work as quickly and as accurately as possible. You will not be expected to be able to answer all the questions in the time allowed.

PART B: MEMORY FOR ADDRESSES

In this part of the test, you will have to memorize the locations (A), (B), (C), (D); or (E) of 25 addresses shown in five boxes, like those below. For example, "Sardis" is in Box (C), "6800–6999 Table" is in Box (B), and so forth. (The addresses in the actual test will be different.)

(A)	(B)	(C)	(D)	(E)
4700–5599 Table	6800–6999 Table	5600–6499 Table	6500–6799 Table	4400–4699 Table
Lismore	Kelford	Joel	Tatum	Ruskin
5600–6499 West	6500–6799 West	6800–6999 West	4400–4699 West	4700–5599 West
Hesper	Musella	Sardis	Porter	Nathan
4400–4699 Blake	5600–6499 Blake	6500–6799 Blake	4700–5599 Blake	6800–6999 Blake

Study the locations of the addresses for five minutes. As you study, silently repeat these to yourself. Then cover the boxes and try to answer the questions below. Mark your answers for each question by darkening the circle as was done for questions 1 and 2.

1. Musella
2. 4700–5599 Blake
3. 4700–5599 Table
4. Tatum
5. 4400–4699 Blake
6. Hesper
7. Kelford
8. Nathan
9. 6500–6799 Blake
10. Joel
11. 4400–4699 Blake
12. 6500–6799 West
13. Porter
14. 6800–6999 Blake

Sample Answer Sheet

1. Ⓐ ● Ⓒ Ⓓ Ⓔ
2. Ⓐ Ⓑ Ⓒ ● Ⓔ
3. Ⓐ Ⓑ Ⓒ Ⓓ Ⓔ
4. Ⓐ Ⓑ Ⓒ Ⓓ Ⓔ
5. Ⓐ Ⓑ Ⓒ Ⓓ Ⓔ
6. Ⓐ Ⓑ Ⓒ Ⓓ Ⓔ
7. Ⓐ Ⓑ Ⓒ Ⓓ Ⓔ
8. Ⓐ Ⓑ Ⓒ Ⓓ Ⓔ
9. Ⓐ Ⓑ Ⓒ Ⓓ Ⓔ
10. Ⓐ Ⓑ Ⓒ Ⓓ Ⓔ
11. Ⓐ Ⓑ Ⓒ Ⓓ Ⓔ
12. Ⓐ Ⓑ Ⓒ Ⓓ Ⓔ
13. Ⓐ Ⓑ Ⓒ Ⓓ Ⓔ
14. Ⓐ Ⓑ Ⓒ Ⓓ Ⓔ

The correct answers for questions 3–14 are:

3. (A) **5.** (A) **7.** (B) **9.** (C) **11.** (A) **13.** (D)
4. (D) **6.** (A) **8.** (E) **10.** (C) **12.** (B) **14.** (E)

During the examination, you will have three practice exercises to help you memorize the location of addresses shown in the five boxes. After the practice exercises, the actual test will be given. Part B is scored right answers minus one-fourth of the wrong answers. Random guessing should not help your score, but if you can eliminate one or more alternatives, it is to your advantage to guess. For the Part B test, you will have five minutes to answer as many of the 88 questions as you can. It will be to your advantage to work as quickly and as accurately as you can. You will not be expected to be able to answer all the questions in the time allowed.

PART C: NUMBER SERIES

For each *Number Series* question there is at the left a series of numbers that follow some definite order and at the right five sets of two numbers each. You are to look at the numbers in the series at the left and find out what order they follow. Then decide what the next two numbers in that series would be if the same order were continued. Darken your answers on the Sample Answer Sheet.

1. 1 2 3 4 5 6 7............ (A) 1 2 (B) 5 6 (C) 8 9 (D) 4 5 (E) 7 8

The numbers in this series are increasing by 1. If the series were continued for two more numbers, it would read: 1 2 3 4 5 6 7 8 9. Therefore the correct answer is 8 and 9 and you should have darkened (C) for question 1.

2. 15 14 13 12 11 10 9...... (A) 2 1 (B) 17 16 (C) 8 9 (D) 8 7 (E) 9 8

The numbers in this series are decreasing by 1. If the series were continued for two more numbers, it would read: 15 14 13 12 11 10 9 8 7. Therefore the correct answer is 8 and 7 and you should have darkened (D) for question 2.

3. 20 20 21 21 22 22 23 ..... (A) 23 23 (B) 23 24 (C) 19 19 (D) 22 23 (E) 21 22

Each number in this series is repeated and then increased by 1. If the series were continued for two more numbers, it would read: 20 20 21 21 22 22 23 23 24. Therefore the correct answer is 23 and 24 and you should have darkened (B) for question 3.

4. 17 3 17 4 17 5 17........ (A) 6 17 (B) 6 7 (C) 17 6 (D) 5 6 (E) 17 7

This series is the number 17 separated by numbers increasing by 1, beginning with the number 3. If the series were continued for two more numbers, it would read: 17 3 17 4 17 5 17 6 17. Therefore the correct answer is 6 and 17 and you should have darkened (A) for question 4.

5. 1 2 4 5 7 8 10............ (A) 11 12 (B) 12 14 (C) 10 13 (D) 12 13 (E) 11 13

The numbers in this series are increasing first by 1 (plus 1) and then by 2 (plus 2). If the series were continued for two more numbers, it would read: 1 2 4 5 7 8 10 (plus 1) 11 and (plus 2) 13. Therefore the correct answer is 11 and 13 and you should have darkened (E) for question 5.

Sample Answer Sheet

1. Ⓐ Ⓑ Ⓒ Ⓓ Ⓔ	**4.** Ⓐ Ⓑ Ⓒ Ⓓ Ⓔ
2. Ⓐ Ⓑ Ⓒ Ⓓ Ⓔ	**5.** Ⓐ Ⓑ Ⓒ Ⓓ Ⓔ
3. Ⓐ Ⓑ Ⓒ Ⓓ Ⓔ	

Now read and work sample questions 6–10 and darken your answers on the Sample Answer Sheet.

6. 21 21 20 20 19 19 18 .... (A) 18 18 (B) 18 17 (C) 17 18 (D) 17 17 (E) 18 19

7. 1 22 1 23 1 24 1 .... (A) 26 1 (B) 25 26 (C) 25 1 (D) 1 26 (E) 1 25

8. 1 20 3 19 5 18 7 .... (A) 8 9 (B) 8 17 (C) 17 10 (D) 17 9 (E) 9 18

9. 4 7 10 13 16 19 22......... (A) 23 26 (B) 25 27 (C) 25 26 (D) 25 28 (E) 24 27

10. 30 2 28 4 26 6 24 .... (A) 23 9 (B) 26 8 (C) 8 9 (D) 26 22 (E) 8 22

Sample Answer Sheet

6. Ⓐ Ⓑ Ⓒ Ⓓ Ⓔ **9.** Ⓐ Ⓑ Ⓒ Ⓓ Ⓔ
7. Ⓐ Ⓑ Ⓒ Ⓓ Ⓔ **10.** Ⓐ Ⓑ Ⓒ Ⓓ Ⓔ
8. Ⓐ Ⓑ Ⓒ Ⓓ Ⓔ

The correct answers to sample questions 6–10 are:

6. (B) **7.** (C) **8.** (D) **9.** (D) **10.** (E)

ANSWERS AND EXPLANATIONS

6. **The correct answer is (B).** Each number in the series repeats itself and then decreases by 1 or minus 1; 21 (repeat) 21 (minus 1) 20 (repeat) 20 (minus 1) 19 (repeat) 19 (minus 1) 18 (repeat) ? (minus 1) ?
7. **The correct answer is (C).** The number 1 is separated by numbers that begin with 22 and increase by 1; 1 22 1 (increase 22 by 1) 23 1 (increase 23 by 1) 24 1 (increase 24 by 1)?
8. **The correct answer is (D).** This is best explained by two alternating series-one series starts with 1 and increases by 2 or plus 2; the other series starts with 20 and decreases by 1 or minus 1.

   1 ^ 3 ^ 5 ^ 7 ^ ?

   20 19 18

9. **The correct answer is (D).** This series of numbers increases by 3 (plus 3) beginning with the first number—4 7 10 13 16 19 22 ? ?
10. **The correct answer is (E).** Look for two alternating series—one series starts with 30 and decreases by 2 (minus 2): the other series starts with 2 and increases by 2 (plus 2).

Now try questions 11–15.

11. 5 6 20 7 8 19 9.......... (A) 10 18 (B) 18 17 (C) 10 17 (D) 18 19 (E) 10 11

12. 4 6 9 11 14 16 19......... (A) 21 24 (B) 22 25 (C) 20 22 (D) 21 23 (E) 22 24

13. 8 8 1 10 10 3 12 .... (A) 13 13 (B) 12 5 (C) 12 4 (D) 13 5 (E) 4 12

14. 10 12 50 15 17 50 20 .... (A) 50 21 (B) 21 50 (C) 50 22 (D) 22 50 (E) 22 24

15. 20 21 23 24 27 28 32 33 38 39 .... (A) 45 46 (B) 45 52 (C) 44 45 (D) 44 49 (E) 40 46

Sample Answer Sheet

11. Ⓐ Ⓑ Ⓒ Ⓓ Ⓔ	**14.** Ⓐ Ⓑ Ⓒ Ⓓ Ⓔ
12. Ⓐ Ⓑ Ⓒ Ⓓ Ⓔ	**15.** Ⓐ Ⓑ Ⓒ Ⓓ Ⓔ
13. Ⓐ Ⓑ Ⓒ Ⓓ Ⓔ	

The correct answers to sample questions 11–15 are:

11. (A) **12.** (A) **13.** (B) **14.** (D) **15.** (A)

It will be to your advantage to answer every question in Part C that you can, since your score on this part of the test will be based on the number of questions that you answer correctly. Answer first those questions that are easiest for you. For the Part C test, you will have 20 minutes to answer as many of the 24 questions as you can.

PART D: ORAL DIRECTIONS

In this part of the test, you will be told to follow directions by writing in a test booklet and then on an answer sheet. The test booklet will have lines of material like the following five samples:

SAMPLE 1.	5 ____				
SAMPLE 2.	1	6	4	3	7
SAMPLE 3.	D	B	A	E	C
SAMPLE 4.	8 ____ (oval)	5 ____ (oval)	2 ____ (oval)	9 ____ (oval)	10 ____ (oval)
SAMPLE 5.	7 ____ (oval)	6 ____ (rectangle)	1 ____ (circle)	12 ____ (square)	

To practice this part of the test, tear out the page of instructions to be read. Then have somebody read the instructions to you while you follow them. When he or she tells you to darken the answer space on the Sample Answer Sheet, use the one on this page.

Your score for Part D will be based on the number of questions that you answer correctly. Therefore, if you are not sure of an answer, it will be to your advantage to guess. Part D will take about 25 minutes.

Sample Answer Sheet

1. Ⓐ Ⓑ Ⓒ Ⓓ Ⓔ	**5.** Ⓐ Ⓑ Ⓒ Ⓓ Ⓔ	**9.** Ⓐ Ⓑ Ⓒ Ⓓ Ⓔ
2. Ⓐ Ⓑ Ⓒ Ⓓ Ⓔ	**6.** Ⓐ Ⓑ Ⓒ Ⓓ Ⓔ	**10.** Ⓐ Ⓑ Ⓒ Ⓓ Ⓔ
3. Ⓐ Ⓑ Ⓒ Ⓓ Ⓔ	**7.** Ⓐ Ⓑ Ⓒ Ⓓ Ⓔ	**11.** Ⓐ Ⓑ Ⓒ Ⓓ Ⓔ
4. Ⓐ Ⓑ Ⓒ Ⓓ Ⓔ	**8.** Ⓐ Ⓑ Ⓒ Ⓓ Ⓔ	**12.** Ⓐ Ⓑ Ⓒ Ⓓ Ⓔ

INSTRUCTIONS TO BE READ FOR PART D—ORAL DIRECTIONS

(The words in parentheses should NOT be read aloud.)

You are to follow the instructions that I shall read to you. I cannot repeat them.

Look at the samples. Sample 1 has a number and a line beside it. On the line write A as in ace. **(Pause 2 seconds.)** Now, on the Sample Answer Sheet, find number 5 **(pause 2 seconds)** and darken the letter you just wrote on the line. **(Pause 2 seconds.)**

Look at Sample 2. (Pause slightly.) Draw a line under the third number. **(Pause 2 seconds.)** Now, on the Sample Answer Sheet, find the number under which you just drew a line and darken choice (B) as in boy. **(Pause 5 seconds.)**

Look at the letters in Sample 3. (Pause slightly.) Draw a line under the third letter in the line. **(Pause 2 seconds.)** Now, on your Sample Answer Sheet, find number 9 **(pause 2 seconds)** and darken the letter under which you drew a line. **(Pause 5 seconds.)**

Look at the five circles in Sample 4. (Pause slightly.) Each circle has a number and a line in it. Write D as in dog on the line in the last circle. **(Pause 2 seconds.)** Now, on the Sample Answer Sheet, darken the number-letter combination that is in the circle you just wrote in. **(Pause 5 seconds.)**

Look at Sample 5. (Pause slightly.) There are two circles and two boxes of different sizes with numbers in them. **(Pause slightly.)** If 4 is more than 2 and if 5 is less than 3, write A as in ace in the smaller circle. **(Pause slightly.)** Otherwise write choice (C) as in car in the larger box. **(Pause 2 seconds.)** Now, on the Sample Answer Sheet, darken the number-letter combination in the box or circle in which you just wrote. **(Pause 5 seconds.)**

Now look at the Sample Answer Sheet. (Pause slightly.) You should have darkened

4. (B) **5.** (A) **9.** (A) **10.** (D) **12.** (C)

(If the person preparing to take the examination made any mistakes, try to help him or her see why he or she made wrong marks.)

EXAM 710—SAMPLE QUESTIONS

CLERK-TYPIST AND CLERK-STENOGRAPHER

The following questions are samples of the types of questions that will be used on Examination 710. Study these questions carefully. Each question has several suggested answers. You are to decide which one is the *best answer*. Next, on the Sample Answer Sheet below, find the answer space that is numbered the same number as the question, then darken the space that is lettered the same as the answer you have selected.

CLERICAL APTITUDE: QUESTIONS 1 THROUGH 14

In questions 1 through 3, there is a name, number, or code in a box at the left and four other names, numbers, or codes in alphabetical or numerical order at the right. Find the correct space for the boxed name or number so that it will be in alphabetical and/or numerical order with the others and darken the letter of that answer space on your Sample Answer Sheet.

1. Roggen, Sam

(A) →
Rogers, Arthur L.
(B) →
Roghani, Fada
(C) →
Rogovin, H.T.
(D) →
Rogowski, Marie R.
(E) →

2. 05076012

(A) →
05076004
(B) →
05076007
(C) →
05076010
(D) →
05076021
(E) →

3. CBA—1875

(A) →
CAA—1720
(B) →
CAB—1819
(C) →
CAC—1804
(D) →
CAD—1402
(E) →

Sample Answer Sheet

1. Ⓐ Ⓑ Ⓒ Ⓓ Ⓔ
2. Ⓐ Ⓑ Ⓒ Ⓓ Ⓔ
3. Ⓐ Ⓑ Ⓒ Ⓓ Ⓔ

The correct answers for questions 1–3 are:

1. (B) **2.** (D) **3.** (E)

Questions 4 through 8 require you to compare names, addresses, or codes. In each line across the page there are three names, addresses, or codes that are very much alike. Compare the three and decide which ones are EXACTLY alike. On the Sample Answer Sheet, darken the answer choice:

(A) if **ALL THREE** names, addresses, or codes are exactly **ALIKE**
(B) if only the **FIRST** and **SECOND** names, addresses, or codes are exactly **ALIKE**
(C) if only the **FIRST** and **THIRD** names, addresses, or codes are exactly **ALIKE**
(D) if only the **SECOND** and **THIRD** names, addresses, or codes are exactly **ALIKE**
(E) if **ALL THREE** names, addresses, or codes are **DIFFERENT**

4.	Helene Bedell	Helene Beddell	Helene Beddell
5.	E T. Wedemeyer	F T. Wedemeyer	E T. Wedmeyer
6.	3214 W Beaumont St.	3214 Beaumount St.	3214 Beaumont St.
7.	BC 3105T-5	BC 3015T-5	BC 3105T-5
8.	4460327	4460327	4460327

For the next two questions, find the correct spelling of the word and darken the appropriate answer space on your Sample Answer Sheet. If none of the alternatives is correct, darken choice (D).

9. (A) accomodate
(B) acommodate
(C) accommadate
(D) none of the above

10. (A) manageble
(B) manageable
(C) manegeable
(D) none of the above

Sample Answer Sheet

4. Ⓐ Ⓑ Ⓒ Ⓓ Ⓔ
5. Ⓐ Ⓑ Ⓒ Ⓓ Ⓔ
6. Ⓐ Ⓑ Ⓒ Ⓓ Ⓔ
7. Ⓐ Ⓑ Ⓒ Ⓓ Ⓔ
8. Ⓐ Ⓑ Ⓒ Ⓓ Ⓔ
9. Ⓐ Ⓑ Ⓒ Ⓓ Ⓔ
10. Ⓐ Ⓑ Ⓒ Ⓓ Ⓔ

The correct answers for questions 4–10 are:

4. (D) **5.** (B) 6. (E) **7.** (C) **8.** (A) **9.** (D) **10.** (B)

For questions 11 through 14, perform the computation as indicated in the question and find the answer among the list of alternative responses. If the correct answer is not given among the choices, darken (E).

11. 32 + 26 =
(A) 69
(B) 59
(C) 58
(D) 54
(E) none of the above

12. 57 − 15 =
(A) 72
(B) 62
(C) 54
(D) 44
(E) none of the above

13. 23 × 7 =
(A) 164
(B) 161
(C) 154
(D) 141
(E) none of the above

14. 160/5 =
(A) 32
(B) 30
(C) 25
(D) 21
(E) none of the above

Sample Answer Sheet

11. Ⓐ Ⓑ Ⓒ Ⓓ Ⓔ **13.** Ⓐ Ⓑ Ⓒ Ⓓ Ⓔ
12. Ⓐ Ⓑ Ⓒ Ⓓ Ⓔ **14.** Ⓐ Ⓑ Ⓒ Ⓓ Ⓔ

The correct answers for questions 11–14 are:

11. (C) **12.** (E) **13.** (B) **14.** (A)

VERBAL ABILITIES: QUESTIONS 15 THROUGH 22

Questions 15 through 17 test your ability to follow instructions. Each question directs you to mark a specific number and letter combination on your Sample Answer Sheet. The questions require your total concentration because the answers that you are instructed to darken are, for the most part, NOT in numerical sequence (i.e., you would not use number 1 on your answer sheet to answer question 1; number 2 for question 2; etc.). Instead, you must darken the number and space specifically designated in each test question.

15. Look at the letters below. Draw a circle around the middle letter. Now, on your Sample Answer Sheet, find Number 16 and darken the space for the letter you just circled.

R C H

16. Draw a line under the number shown below that is more than 10 but less than 20. Find that number on your Sample Answer Sheet, and darken Space A.

5 9 17 22

17. Add the numbers 11 and 4 and write your answer on the blank line below. Now find this number on your Sample Answer Sheet and darken the space for the second letter in the alphabet.

______

Sample Answer Sheet

15. Ⓐ Ⓑ Ⓒ Ⓓ Ⓔ
16. Ⓐ Ⓑ Ⓒ Ⓓ Ⓔ
17. Ⓐ Ⓑ Ⓒ Ⓓ Ⓔ

The correct answers for questions 15–17 are:

15. (B) **16.** (C) **17.** (A)

Answer the remaining test questions on the Sample Answer Sheet in numerical sequence (i.e., Number 18 on the Sample Answer Sheet for question 18; number 19 for question 19, etc.).

Choose the sentence below that is most appropriate with respect to grammar, usage, and punctuation, so as to be suitable for a business letter or report and darken its letter on the Sample Answer Sheet.

18. (A) He should of responded to the letter by now.
(B) A response to the letter by the end of the week.
(C) The letter required his immediate response.
(D) A response by him to the letter is necessary.

Questions 19 and 20 consist of a sentence containing a word in boldface type. Choose the best meaning for the word in **boldface** type and darken its letter on the Sample Answer Sheet.

19. The payment was **authorized** yesterday. **Authorized** most nearly means

(A) expected
(B) approved
(C) refunded
(D) received

20. Please **delete** the second paragraph. **Delete** most nearly means

(A) type
(B) read
(C) edit
(D) omit

Sample Answer Sheet

18. Ⓐ Ⓑ ● Ⓓ Ⓔ
19. Ⓐ ● Ⓒ Ⓓ Ⓔ
20. Ⓐ Ⓑ Ⓒ ● Ⓔ

The correct answers for questions 18–20 are:

18. (C) **19.** (B) **20.** (D)

In questions 21 and 22 below, read each paragraph and answer the question that follows it by darkening the letter of the correct answer on the Sample Answer Sheet.

21. Window Clerks working for the Postal Service have direct financial responsibility for the selling of postage. In addition, they are expected to have a thorough knowledge concerning the acceptability of all material offered by customers for mailing. Any information provided to the public by these employees must be completely accurate.

The paragraph best supports the statement that Window Clerks

(A) must account for the stamps issued to them for sale.
(B) have had long training in other Postal Service jobs.
(C) must help sort mail to be delivered by carriers.
(D) inspect the contents of all packages offered for mailing.

22. The most efficient method for performing a task is not always easily determined. That which is economical in terms of time must be carefully distinguished from that which is economical in terms of expended energy. In short, the quickest method may require a degree of physical effort that may be neither essential nor desirable.

The paragraph best supports the statement that

(A) it is more efficient to perform a task slowly than rapidly.
(B) skill in performing a task should not be acquired at the expense of time.
(C) the most efficient execution of a task is not always the one done in the shortest time.
(D) energy and time cannot both be considered in the performance of a single task.

Sample Answer Sheet

21. Ⓐ Ⓑ Ⓒ Ⓓ Ⓔ
22. Ⓐ Ⓑ Ⓒ Ⓓ Ⓔ

The correct answers for questions 21 and 22 are:

21. (A) **22.** (C)

EXAM 711—SAMPLE QUESTIONS

This section discusses the stenography test for clerk-stenographer.

Only stenographer competitors take a stenography test. The sample below shows the length of material dictated. Sit down with your pencil and notebook, and hand this book to a friend. Have that person dictate the passage to you so that you can see how well prepared you are to take dictation at the rate of 80 words a minute. Each pair of lines is dictated in 10 seconds. Your friend should dictate periods, but not commas, and should read the exercise with the expression that the punctuation indicates.

Exactly on a minute start dictating. Finish reading each line at the number of seconds indicated below.

I realize that this practice dictation	
is not a part of the examination	10 sec.
proper and is not to be scored. (Period)	
When making a study of the private	20 sec.
pension structure and its influence on	
turnover, the most striking feature is its	30 sec.
youth. (Period) As has been shown, the time	
of greatest growth began just a few years	40 sec.
ago. (Period) The influence that this	
growth has had on the labor market and	50 sec.
worker attitudes is hard to assess,	
partly because the effects have not yet fully	1 min.
evolved and many are still in the	
growing stage. (Period) Even so, most pension	10 sec.
plans began with much more limited gains	
than they give now. (Period) For example,	20 sec.
as private plans mature they grant	
a larger profit and a greater range of gains to	30 sec.
more workers and thereby become more	
important. (Period) Plans that protect accrued pension	40 sec.
credits are rather new and are being	
revised in the light of past trends. (Period)	50 sec.
As informal and formal information on pension	
plans spreads, the workers become more	2 min.
aware of the plans and their provisions	
increase. (Period) Their impact on employee attitudes	10 sec.
and decisions will no doubt become	
stronger. (Period) Each year, more and more workers	20 sec.
will be retiring with a private pension,	
and their firsthand knowledge of the benefits to	30 sec.
be gained from private pensions will spread	
to still active workers. (Period) Thus, workers	40 sec.
may less often view pensions as just	
another part of the security package	50 sec.
based on service and more often	
see them as unique benefits. (Period)	3 min.

This transcript and word list for part of the above dictation are similar to those each competitor will receive for the dictation test. Many words have been omitted from the transcript. Compare your notes with it. When you come to a blank space in the transcript, decide what word (or words) belongs there. Look for the missing word in the word list. Notice what letter (A), (B), (C), or (D) is printed beside the word. Write that letter in the blank. Choice (B) is written in blank 1 to show how you are to record your choice. Write (E) if the exact answer is not in the word list. You may also write the word (or words) or the shorthand for it, if you wish. The same choice may belong in more than one blank.

ALPHABETIC WORD LIST

Write (E) if the answer is not listed.

a — (D)	make — (A)
attitudes — (C)	making — (B)
be — (B)	market — (B)
been — (C)	markets — (D)
began — (D)	marking — (D)
being — (A)	never — (B)
completely — (A)	not — (D)
examination — (A)	over — (C)
examine — (B)	part — (C)
examining — (D)	partly — (D)
feat — (A)	pension — (C)
feature — (C)	practical — (C)
full — (B)	practice — (B)
fully — (D)	private — (D)
greater — (D)	proper — (C)
grow — (B)	section — (D)
growing — (C)	so — (B)
had — (D)	still — (A)
has — (C)	structure — (D)
has been — (B)	structured — (B)
has had — (A)	to — (D)
has made — (A)	to be — (C)
in — (C)	trial — (A)
in part — (B)	turn — (D)
influence — (A)	turnover — (B)
labor — (C)	values — (A)
main — (B)	yet — (C)

TRANSCRIPT

I realize that this __B__ (1) dictation is _____ (2) a _____ (3) of the _____ (4) _____ (5) and is _____ (6) _____ (7) scored.

When _____ (8) a _____ (9) of the _____ (10) _____ (11) _____ (12) and its _____ (13) on _____ (14), the most striking _____ (15) is its youth. As _____ (16) shown, the time of _____ (17) growth began just a few years ago. The _____ (18) that this growth _____ (19) on the labor _____ (20) and worker _____ (21) is hard to assess, _____ (22) because the effects have not yet _____ (23) evolved and many are _____ (24) in the _____ (25) stage. . . .

(For the next sentences there would be another word list, if the entire sample dictation were transcribed.)

You will be given an answer sheet like the sample that follows, on which your answers can be scored by machine. Each number on the answer sheet stands for the blank with the same number in the transcript. Darken the space for the letter that is the same as the letter you wrote in the transcript. If you have not finished writing letters in the blanks in the transcript, or if you wish to make sure you have lettered them correctly, you may continue to use your notes after you begin marking the answer sheet.

Sample Answer Sheet

1. Ⓐ Ⓑ Ⓒ Ⓓ Ⓔ	8. Ⓐ Ⓑ Ⓒ Ⓓ Ⓔ	14. Ⓐ Ⓑ Ⓒ Ⓓ Ⓔ	20. Ⓐ Ⓑ Ⓒ Ⓓ Ⓔ
2. Ⓐ Ⓑ Ⓒ Ⓓ Ⓔ	9. Ⓐ Ⓑ Ⓒ Ⓓ Ⓔ	15. Ⓐ Ⓑ Ⓒ Ⓓ Ⓔ	21. Ⓐ Ⓑ Ⓒ Ⓓ Ⓔ
3. Ⓐ Ⓑ Ⓒ Ⓓ Ⓔ	10. Ⓐ Ⓑ Ⓒ Ⓓ Ⓔ	16. Ⓐ Ⓑ Ⓒ Ⓓ Ⓔ	22. Ⓐ Ⓑ Ⓒ Ⓓ Ⓔ
4. Ⓐ Ⓑ Ⓒ Ⓓ Ⓔ	11. Ⓐ Ⓑ Ⓒ Ⓓ Ⓔ	17. Ⓐ Ⓑ Ⓒ Ⓓ Ⓔ	23. Ⓐ Ⓑ Ⓒ Ⓓ Ⓔ
5. Ⓐ Ⓑ Ⓒ Ⓓ Ⓔ	12. Ⓐ Ⓑ Ⓒ Ⓓ Ⓔ	18. Ⓐ Ⓑ Ⓒ Ⓓ Ⓔ	24. Ⓐ Ⓑ Ⓒ Ⓓ Ⓔ
6. Ⓐ Ⓑ Ⓒ Ⓓ Ⓔ	13. Ⓐ Ⓑ Ⓒ Ⓓ Ⓔ	19. Ⓐ Ⓑ Ⓒ Ⓓ Ⓔ	25. Ⓐ Ⓑ Ⓒ Ⓓ Ⓔ
7. Ⓐ Ⓑ Ⓒ Ⓓ Ⓔ			

The correct answers for questions 1–25 are:

1. (B)	6. (D)	11. (C)	16. (B)	21. (C)
2. (D)	7. (C)	12. (D)	17. (E)	22. (D)
3. (C)	8. (B)	13. (A)	18. (A)	23. (D)
4. (A)	9. (E)	14. (B)	19. (A)	24. (A)
5. (C)	10. (D)	15. (C)	20. (B)	25. (C)

EXAM 712—SAMPLE QUESTIONS

THE TYPING TEST

A mastery of good typing skills is a basic prerequisite for all three postal positions that require typing: clerk-typist, clerk-stenographer, and mark-up clerk (automated). A high score on the written exam is not enough. While the score on the written exam determines your position on the list, your name cannot find its way onto the list at all unless you first demonstrate that your typing proficiency satisfies the speed and accuracy requirements mandated for the work position involved.

Assuming that you already know how to type, the best preparation for the Clerk-Typist and Clerk-Stenographer Typing Test, or indeed for any typing test, is typing. You may choose any material at all and practice copying it line for line, exactly as you see it. As on the actual typing test, spell, capitalize, punctuate, and begin and end lines exactly as they appear on the page being copied. The actual basic speed required on typing tests varies from 35 wpm to 50 wpm depending on the job itself. Once the minimum speed is met, accuracy counts even more than speed. Try to balance yourself so as to meet speed requirements while maintaining a very high level of accuracy.

If you are taking a typing exam in hopes of becoming a clerk-typist or clerk-stenographer with the U.S. Postal Service, you will take your test on a computer. If your typing test is being administered by a federal, state, county, or municipal entity or by a private employer, it may be administered on a computer or on a standard typewriter. Sometimes you are given the option of using a manual or electronic typewriter; you may even be permitted to bring your own typewriter if you wish. If you feel especially comfortable with your own typewriter and if it is easily portable, ask about this possibility. If you are taking your typing test on a typewriter that is being supplied, you will get a chance to turn the typewriter on and off and to check the preset margins and tabs to be sure they are accurate. You should not need to make any adjustments on a typewriter that is supplied.

The proctor will then distribute a practice exercise. For a postal position, the practice exercise should look very familiar. It is exactly the same exercise that appears on the sample question sheet that came with the yellow card telling you of your testing appointment. You should have already had lots of practice typing that paragraph. At any rate, in any typing test situation, the proctor will give you five minutes to practice copying a paragraph. This is a chance to limber up your fingers and to gain familiarity with the testing keyboard. This practice exercise will not count. If you have been practicing on a standard typewriter, the proctor will collect the papers and throw them into the wastebasket.

The following is a typical test exercise, though NOT the actual test exercise that you will be given. Follow instructions exactly, and practice, practice, practice. Words-per-minute points are marked on the test exercise for your guidance. Try to keep your typing error-free; if you make errors, try to increase your speed. Use an accurate signal timer or have a friend or relative time you.

Space, paragraph, spell, punctuate, capitalize, and begin and end each line precisely as shown in the exercise.

You will have exactly five minutes in which to make repeated copies of the test exercise itself on the paper that will be given to you. Each time you complete the exercise, simply double-space once and begin again. If you fill up one side of the paper, turn it over and continue typing on the other side. Keep on typing until told to stop.

Keep in mind that you must meet minimum standards in both speed and accuracy and that, above these standards, accuracy is twice as important as speed.

This is an example of the type of material which will be presented to
you as the actual typewriting examination. Each competitor will be
required to typewrite the practice material exactly as it appears on the
copy. You are to space, capitalize, punctuate, spell, and begin and end
each line exactly as it is presented in the copy. Each time you reach
the end of the paragraph you should begin again and continue to
practice typing the practice paragraph on scratch paper until the
examiner tells you to stop. You are advised that it is more important
to type accurately than to type rapidly.

Directions: In the examination you will have five minutes in which to make copies of the test exercise, keeping in mind that your eligibility will depend on accuracy as well as speed. When you complete the exercise, simply double space and begin again.

TEST EXERCISE

	1st typing of exercise	2nd typing of exercise
Because they have often learned to know types of archi-	______	52 wpm
tecture by decoration, casual observers sometimes fail to	______	54
realize that the significant part of a structure is not the	______	56
ornamentation but the body itself. Architecture, because	______	59
of its close contact with human lives, is peculiarly and	______	61
intimately governed by climate. For instance, a home built	______	64
for comfort in the cold and snow of the northern areas of	______	66
this country would be unbearably warm in a country with	______	68
weather such as that of Cuba. A Cuban house, with its open	______	71
court, would prove impossible to heat in a northern winter.	______	73
Since the purpose of architecture is the construction of	______	76
shelters in which human beings may carry on their numerous	______	78
activities, the designer must consider not only climatic con-	______	80
ditions, but also the function of a building. Thus, although	______	______
the climate of a certain locality requires that an auditorium	______	______
and a hospital have several features in common, the purposes	______	______
for which they will be used demand some difference in struc-	40 wpm	
ture. For centuries builders have first complied with these	42	______
two requirements and later added whatever ornamentation they	44	______
wished. Logically, we should see as mere additions, not as	47	______
basic parts, the details by which we identify architecture.	49	______

EACH TIME YOU REACH THIS POINT, DOUBLE-SPACE ONCE AND BEGIN AGAIN.

EXAM 715—SAMPLE QUESTIONS

ALPHA-NUMERIC TYPING TEST

MARK-UP CLERK, AUTOMATED

The Postal Service does not issue official sample questions for Exam 715.

Exam 715, the typing test for Mark-up Clerk applicants, is quite different from an ordinary typing test. You will take this test by private appointment, and all interaction will be between you and a computer. Do not be frightened. Even if you have had no experience whatsoever with computers, this is not an intimidating test. The computer is user-friendly and is very specific in spelling out directions. And, unless you are a typing whiz, the typing test itself is probably easier than a plain paper copying test.

As Exam 715 begins, the computer screen explains to you which buttons you will be using and what each does. You need to use very few buttons—letters, numbers, "return," "delete," and "lock caps." You will get a chance to use these and to become familiar with their operation as you fill in basic name and social security number types of information. A test administrator remains in the room to answer questions.

The computer then explains the typing task of the exam itself. A letter-number code appears on the upper right screen; you are to copy it, then press the return button to bring the next code to the screen. That's it. The codes all consist of four letters and three numbers, such as TYHO346 or BZIP801. The faster you type, the more codes you have an opportunity to copy. In the explanation phase of the exam, you will have 15 seconds in which to copy five codes. The computer will tell you how many you copied correctly.

After the explanation phase comes a practice session. You will be allowed five minutes to copy as many codes as you can correctly, again one at a time. The five-minute practice session does not count. This is your chance to experiment with looking at your fingers or at the screen; with memorizing each code to be typed, or with staring at the code while typing; with typing as fast as you can, not even looking at the screen to see if you are typing correctly; or with checking to make sure you are copying correctly and repairing errors before continuing.

Be aware that an error that has been corrected on the computer is not counted as an error. Since accuracy is so important and since correction is so easy on the computer, it is worthwhile to correct errors. Unless you are extremely inaccurate; you will not lose much time correcting errors and will gain valuable points through accuracy.

Here is a suggested approach:

1. Look at the code and quickly memorize it; four letters and three numbers should pose no problem for such a short-term task.
2. Type in the code, looking at the center of the screen where the letters and numbers that you are typing appear.
3. Delete and retype if you spot an error.
4. Hit the return button and do the same for the next code.

The five-minute practice period should allow you to establish a rhythm for this process. When the five minutes are up, your score will flash on the screen. A score of 14 is required for passing. If you have scored 14 or higher, approach the actual test with confidence. If your score is lower than 14, be reassured that it will not be counted. Remember that you used the first few minutes of the practice period to perfect your system. You now have five minutes to use the system with which you have become comfortable. Your second score, the score that does count, will be higher.

The actual test session is exactly like the practice session, with different codes of course. At the end of the five-minute test, your final score will appear on the screen. You will know instantly whether you have passed or failed; whether you are eligible or ineligible. If you are eligible, you can expect to be called for an employment interview sometime in the near future.

PRACTICE EXERCISE

Directions: Use the following letter-number codes to test your ability to record them accurately into a computer. Starting from the top left column, try to memorize each letter-number code, type it using your keyboard and press return. Go on to the next code.

RJKF566	BVEI155	GKZP876
YTMN068	FUQS478	EDBJ582
FULD727	JMGE610	OLDE751
TTHU950	SQWP0I0	LEAP274
NORT707	BDEY851	PHYX593
FLIO015	CZDT874	BLDV592
OYJX055	FTTD123	KHTP805
GYKN094	RHVZ417	IFWK173
WEST301	TGIF629	YCWI142
DRHK967	PDQD157	OLZT809
AVNB893	EAST383	VMHW649
RKBY775	GSAP013	HTCQ858
LGBU919	UQFP180	JFTA862

STATE TESTING

The Clerical examination is made up of 3 parts: a written test, typing test and a stenographic test. All applicants must take a written and a typing test. The written test will be weighted 50 percent and the typing test will be weighted 50 percent. Applicants for Clerk Stenographer 1 and 2 must also pass a stenographic test. The stenographic test will not be weighted as part of the final score.

You must pass all parts of the test to be considered for employment.

Any part of the test may be cancelled by the Commission, and the weight added to the remaining part.

WRITTEN TEST

The written test will consist of a 12-minute Name and Number Checking speed test, and a 1 1/2-hour clerical abilities test which will cover the subject areas below.

Subject Matter Areas	Number of Questions
Name and Number Checking	65
Sorting File Material	10
Alphabetizing	15
Taking Telephone Messages	15
Capitalization/Punctuation/Grammar	15
Effective Expression	10
Spelling	25
Arithmetic Operations	15
TOTAL	170

TYPING TEST

The typing performance test will consist of a 5-minute practice exercise followed by the actual test, which will have a 5-minute time limit. A score of 40 words per minute, after deduction for errors, must be achieved in order to pass the typing performance test. Applicants may provide their own typewriters for the typing test.

STENOGRAPHIC TEST

The stenographic test will consist of a practice exercise followed by the actual test. Dictation will be given at the rate of 80 words per minute. Applicants will have time to transcribe their notes. Applicants for Clerk Stenographer 1 must not have more than 10 percent errors on the stenographic test. Applicants for Clerk Stenographer 2 must not have more than 5 percent errors on the test. Any stenographic system including the use of a shorthand machine is acceptable. Applicants who wish to use shorthand machines must provide their own.

TEST RESULTS

Employment and promotion lists will be established. You will be notified in writing of your test results.

If you take the test and want to take it again, you may be retested 6 months after the date of your last examination. You must retake all parts of the examination. A new application is required for a retest.

LOCAL TESTING

SCOPE OF THE EXAMINATION

The examination for this title will consist of two parts: (I) a written test; and (II) a qualifying typing performance test.

I. The *Written test* will cover knowledge, skills, and/or abilities in such areas as:

1. Office practices;
2. English usage;
3. Reading comprehension;
4. Arithmetic reasoning;
5. Record keeping.

II. *Typing Test*—Straight-copy typing test rated for speed and accuracy at 35 words per minute on a personal computer. (Candidates will not be permitted to bring their own typewriters.)

There is so much variation in county clerical examinations that a sample exam might prove misleading. The best preparation for a county clerical examination, and indeed for any clerical examination, is thorough grounding in basic clerical skills and practice with many different kinds of exams.

Straight-copy typing tests, on the other hand, are all alike. Only the speed and error standards and requirements may vary. The chapter entitled "The Typing Test" specifically addresses the typing test for the Postal Clerk-Typist Exam. However, your own exam, for whatever typing-inclusive clerical position, will be very similar to it.

CLERICAL EMPLOYMENT TESTS FOR COURT-RELATED POSITIONS

The following is a description of the types of questions you might be asked.

The written examination will be multiple-choice and will assess the following:

1. **Spelling**
   These questions are designed to test a candidate's ability to spell words that office clerical employees encounter in their daily work.
2. **Knowledge of English Grammar and Usage, Punctuation, and Sentence Structure**
   These questions are designed to test a candidate's knowledge of the basic rules of English grammar, usage, punctuation, and sentence structure.
3. **Clerical Checking**
   These questions are designed to test a candidate's ability to identify differences among sets of written materials which are almost alike. Candidates are presented with sets of information containing names, numbers, codes, etc., and must determine how the sets may differ.
4. **Office Record Keeping**
   These questions are designed to test a candidate's ability to read, combine, and manipulate written information organized from several different sources. Candidates are presented with different types of tables which contain names, numbers, codes, etc., and must combine and reorganize the information to answer questions. All of the information required to answer the questions is provided in the tables; candidates are not required to have any special knowledge relating to the information provided.
5. **Reading, Understanding, and Interpreting Written Material**
   These questions are designed to test how well candidates can understand what they have read. Candidates are provided with short written passages from which some words have been removed. Candidates are required to select from four alternatives the word that best fits in each of the spaces.

KEYBOARDING TEST

Candidates will be notified when to appear for the performance examination. Only candidates who obtain a passing score on the written examination will be invited to participate in the performance examination(s).

All candidates who are successful on the above written exam will be called to take a qualifying performance test in keyboarding (typing) which will be held after the written examination date. Candidates will be required to type an exact copy of a selection at the rate of 45 words per minute. This is a five-minute test of accuracy and speed of keyboarding from straight copy.

Electric in-place typewriters and paper are available at all test sites. You may bring your own typewriter, whether electric or manual. If you bring an electric typewriter, you must bring an extension cord at least 10 feet long.

The sample examination for senior office typist, New York Unified Court System, in Part Two of this book is based upon the most recent administration of this exam. In some ways it is similar to many other clerical examinations; in some ways it is unique and intriguing. This exam introduces some new question styles and formats. It will be very much worth your time to try your hand at these questions. You want to prepare yourself for whatever type of question may appear on your exam. In a field of competent applicants, familiarity with question styles can give you the competitive edge, a higher score, and an offer of employment.

CLERICAL TESTING IN THE PRIVATE SECTOR

Since private sector testing is not organized or regulated, there is no one battery of tests and no one format that can be described. However, common sense dictates that prospective clerical workers are likely to be tested for ability in some of the following areas:

- Reading Comprehension
- Spelling
- Ability to Follow Directions
- Clerical Speed and Accuracy
- Proofreading
- Typing
- Vocabulary
- Simple Arithmetic Calculations
- Grammar and English Usage
- Interpreting Tables and Charts
- Stenography
- Computer Literacy

As the subjects for examination may vary, so the means for testing may vary as well. Some employers may administer tests entirely by computer. The applicant demonstrates subject matter mastery and competence at the computer at the same time. Since use of the computer is so central to so much clerical work—data entry, word processing, information retrieval, etc.—testing by computer is highly appropriate and is becoming more and more prevalent.

Most often the testing assumes some sort of combination form. Part of the exam is paper and pencil, either multiple choice or short answer, and part is typewriter- or computer-based.

The most significant difference between public and private sector testing is the nature of the competition. In a public sector Civil Service test, you compete against the entire population taking that test and strive for a high competitive rating. In a private sector testing situation, you are proving your own skills as an individual. While you may well be competing against other applicants for the same opening, your test performance only proves your competence for the work at hand. The competition is based on many personal factors of which clerical skill is only one aspect. Obviously you must have the skills and be able to prove yourself, but you do not face the same pressure to earn a high score on a private sector exam.

The best preparation for a private sector exam, as for a civil service exam, is competence in the subject areas and practice in the skills areas. If you can gain experience on a number of different typewriter models and with a number of computer programs you are more likely to find yourself being tested on a familiar machine. Familiarity leads to self-confidence and better performance.

The private sector clerical examination in the second part of this book is typical of that given by a number of large employment agencies that specialize in placement of clerical workers on both temporary and permanent bases. It is not an actual exam. Your exam may be quite different. Practice with this exam, however, will give you exposure to the non-multiple-choice exam style often favored by private sector employers.

In this section you have had a brief overview of the types of questions and tests that you might encounter when you go to take a clerical exam. One very important aspect of taking a test that we must continue to stress—understand the directions. Since most tests are timed, it is in your best interest to focus on the questions when taking the test. It becomes easier if you understand what the questions are asking, and you don't have to waste too much time trying to interpret what is being asked of you.

In the following chapter, you will find dozens of different types of questions, covering three major skill areas: Verbal, Mathematics, and Clerical. Take your time to work the questions through this chapter, and check your answers carefully. You might find that some of your problems arise from a lack of understanding what was asked of you. Reread and learn the directions and instructions. You find this to be extremely helpful when taking any exam in the future.

TEST REVIEW

In the following section we have provided an overall review of the three major types of questions you will probably encounter: Verbal, Basic Mathematics, and Clerical Skills. Regardless of the test you will take, you will likely have to answer some, if not all, of these types of questions.

We recommend that you go through each section and answer all of the questions. It might make it easier if you set up your own study plan. Perhaps you can set aside one part of a day for each section. You will quickly find out what types of questions will give you the most difficulty. Make sure you check your answers and read through the explanations. This should help you understand the material better, especially if you're having some difficulty with some of the questions.

As we've said several times throughout this book, it doesn't matter what job you'll be applying for, or what test you will be taking. Try to take the time to not only work through the review material, but also try to take as many of the different tests throughout the book as you can.

Although the exams described in this book are for different jobs and job descriptions, the tests are all essentially similar. For the most part, they consist of verbal tests, memory tests, alphabetization, clerical skills, mathematical ability, and so on. It is extremely important for you to take the sample exams in this book that pertain to the jobs for which you plan to apply. However, it is equally beneficial to take some of the other exams, since these will help you expand your knowledge, and give you additional practice. The higher you score on these exams, the greater are your chances for increasing your score on your specific exam. If you don't do as well as you expected, perhaps you need more review.

This section is a compilation of the various types of questions you will encounter. Although the questions will appear to be different, they will be testing similar skills. Take the time to go through these mini-tests, answer the questions to the best of your ability, and then check your answers. If you have problems with any of them, go back and study the answers. If you still have difficulty, perhaps you need some outside help.

VERBAL REVIEW

SPELLING

In this section of the test you will encounter several different forms of the same type of test—each asking if you can identify a misspelled word.

Directions: In each of the following groups, there is one misspelled word. Write the letter of that word on the line provided.

1. _____
(A) refferee
(B) eligible
(C) excitement
(D) reign

2. _____
(A) eighth
(B) acheivement
(C) aching
(D) readiness

3. _____
(A) imune
(B) orator
(C) ascertain
(D) pierce

4. _____
(A) wield
(B) gradually
(C) tumbleing
(D) philosophical

5. _____
(A) superior
(B) traffic
(C) interminable
(D) admittence

6. _____
(A) standardize
(B) peaceable
(C) fatigue
(D) involvment

7. _____
(A) arbitrary
(B) blemish
(C) testamony
(D) deprivation

8. _____
(A) apparently
(B) demolition
(C) resturant
(D) visibility

9. _____
(A) vacancy
(B) incredible
(C) minature
(D) interpreter

10. _____
(A) allottment
(B) baggage
(C) equitable
(D) colossal

Directions: In the following section, some words are spelled correctly and some are misspelled. If a word is spelled correctly, write the letter "C" on the line to the right. If a word is misspelled, write the correct spelling.

11. enrolement ________
12. grease ________
13. goalkeeper ________
14. qualitey ________
15. disatisfied ________
16. whisle ________
17. abundant ________
18. intellectuel ________
19. antena ________
20. cieling ________
21. controlled ________
22. disgise ________
23. physicain ________
24. noticable ________
25. nineteenth ________
26. consciousness ________
27. renounce ________
28. enamies ________
29. allergick ________
30. spagetti ________
31. apalogy ________
32. concerning ________
33. pianoes ________
34. celabration ________
35. license ________
36. privilege ________
37. sophmore ________
38. acheiving ________
39. lonliness ________
40. surroundings ________
41. prarie ________
42. legitamate ________
43. secretarial ________
44. dissagreeable ________
45. coincidence ________
46. concientious ________
47. comparision ________
48. salaries ________
49. creditted ________
50. forthcoming ________

VOCABULARY

Directions: Read each sentence carefully. Circle the letter of the word in the answer choices which best defines the italicized word in the sentence.

1. A *jubilant* sound came from the meeting room.
   (A) muffled
   (B) strange
   (C) loud
   (D) joyful

2. The rare plant was found growing in a *gorge*.
   (A) forest
   (B) canyon
   (C) cave
   (D) meadow

3. The reporter's comments *incensed* the politician.
   (A) angered
   (B) hurt
   (C) discouraged
   (D) puzzled

4. The young flight attendant showed *fortitude* during the crisis.

(A) quiet desperation
(B) patient courage
(C) careless disregard
(D) uncontrolled fear

5. The witness responded *languidly* to questions from the prosecutor.

(A) angrily
(B) abruptly
(C) weakly
(D) rudely

6. The family stayed in a *rustic* cabin.

(A) cozy
(B) simple
(C) neglected
(D) cheap

7. The visitor was surprised by his *affluent* surroundings.

(A) noisy
(B) dusty
(C) rich
(D) cheerful

8. Some of the workers expected to be *furloughed* soon.

(A) laid off
(B) transferred
(C) fired
(D) promoted

9. After a number of weeks, their hopes began to *materialize*.

(A) become more complex
(B) dissolve into confusion
(C) assume greater importance
(D) become actual fact

10. The new administration wanted to *consolidate* several assistance programs.

(A) create
(B) change
(C) cancel
(D) combine

11. *Potent* means most nearly

(A) healthy.
(B) predictable.
(C) effective.
(D) pleasant.

12. *Kernel* means most nearly

(A) core.
(B) radius.
(C) circumference.
(D) shape.

13. *Ratification* means most nearly
(A) limitation.
(B) confirmation.
(C) reaction.
(D) quotation.

14. *Intuition* means most nearly
(A) payment.
(B) faith.
(C) introduction.
(D) insight.

15. *Droves* means most nearly
(A) noisy groups.
(B) large numbers.
(C) organized clubs.
(D) enthusiastic teams.

16. *Concur* means most nearly
(A) offer.
(B) begin.
(C) concentrate.
(D) agree.

17. *Whet* means most nearly
(A) satisfy.
(B) test.
(C) stimulate.
(D) clarify.

18. *Quaint* means most nearly
(A) picturesque.
(B) famous.
(C) rural.
(D) ancient.

19. *Obnoxious* means most nearly
(A) ridiculous.
(B) obstinate.
(C) noisy.
(D) offensive.

20. *Incompatible* means most nearly
(A) in disagreement.
(B) incomplete.
(C) not logical.
(D) unacceptable.

LANGUAGE: GRAMMAR, PUNCTUATION, AND USAGE

Directions: Some of the following sentences are correct as written. Others contain an error of grammar, punctuation, or capitalization. On the lines beside each sentence, rewrite the sentence correctly. If the sentence contains no error, write "Correct as written."

1. It is always a pleasure for we boys to visit the firehouse.

   1. ______________________

2. The magician waved his hands so skillful that the audience was completely mystified.

   2. ______________________

3. Do not hand in the report until your certain that it is complete.

   3. ______________________

4. I fear that it is you who are mistaken.

   4. ______________________

5. Mailing a letter a few days early; is better than running the risk of its arriving late.

   5. ______________________

6. She is more capable than any other Woman in the office.

   6. ______________________

7. Mother would not let Mary and I attend the hockey game.

   7. ______________________

8. They're not the only ones to be blamed for the incident.

   8. ______________________

9. We intended to be gone before Tuesday.

   9. ______________________

10. I'm not certain that your's is the best solution. **10.** ____________________

11. Mary and Tanya waited breathlessly, each woman hoping she had passed the exam. **11.** ____________________

12. It was us girls who swept the gym floor after the dance. **12.** ____________________

13. Henderson the President of the Board, is also a resident of the building. **13.** ____________________

14. If you had been more patient, you might not have tore it. **14.** ____________________

15. I would like to visit these cities; Boston, Chicago, and Houston. **15.** ____________________

Directions: Circle the letter of the sentence that is grammatically correct.

16. (A) Steaming energetically, she took the teakettle off the burner.
(B) Energetically steaming, she took the teakettle off the burner.
(C) When it steamed energetically, she took the teakettle off the burner.
(D) Because of steaming energetically, she took the teakettle off the burner.

17. (A) By the time the skiers had set out for the resort, snow began to fall, coating the slopes with an inch of new powder.
(B) By the time the skiers had set out for the resort, snow had begun to fall, coating the slopes with an inch of new powder.
(C) By the time the skiers had set out for the resort, it began to snow, coating the slopes with an inch of new powder.
(D) By the time the skiers had set out for the resort, the snow started, coating the slopes with an inch of new powder.

18. (A) If he was our teacher, I would learn much more.
(B) Had he been our teacher, I would learn much more.
(C) If he was teaching us, I would learn much more.
(D) If he were our teacher, I would learn much more.

19. (A) Mary is lying the folded laundry on the bed, you should straighten the closets.
(B) While Mary is lying the folded laundry on the bed, you should straighten the closets.
(C) While Mary is laying the folded laundry on the bed, you should straighten the closets.
(D) When Mary is lying the folded laundry on the bed, you should straighten the closets.

20. (A) John's excuse is much better than the other person who didn't arrive on time.
(B) John's excuse is much better than the excuse of the other person who didn't arrive on time.
(C) John's excuse is much better than the one of the other person who didn't arrive on time.
(D) John's excuse is better than the other person who didn't arrive on time.

ANALOGIES

There are several distinct patterns in which analogies are written, using either words or symbols. For example, the following are three forms of the same analogy.

1. MAN is related to BOY as WOMAN is related to GIRL
2. MAN : BOY :: WOMAN : GIRL
3. MAN : BOY as WOMAN : GIRL

In all cases, an analogy shows a relationship. Discover the relationship between the terms in the first set and that relationship will be repeated in the second set. In the above analogy, MAN and BOY are related because one is the adult male and the other the young male of the human species. Similarly, WOMAN is the adult female and GIRL is the young female. Note that both pairs mention the adult first, and the young second. One pair is male, the other female. It is the adult:young relationship that is important rather than the male:female.

> **Directions:** Complete the analogy by circling the letter of the term that best completes the pair.

1. GLASSES is related to READING as FORK is related to

(A) picking
(B) eating
(C) snacking
(D) walking

2. DESPISE is related to ABHOR as SHUN is related to

(A) crave
(B) avoid
(C) exalt
(D) baffle

3. CONVERSE is related to SPEAK as DEBATE is related to

(A) tirade
(B) humor
(C) embroil
(D) argue

4. HOLD is related to RETAIN as FORSAKE is related to

(A) abandon
(B) force
(C) cherish
(D) encourage

5. I is related to WE as ME is related to

(A) you
(B) he
(C) us
(D) she

6. BARK is related to TREE as SKIN is related to

(A) burn
(B) pore
(C) cover
(D) man

7. MUSICIAN is related to SCORE as ACTOR is related to

(A) cue
(B) part
(C) play
(D) script

8. POLE : FLAG :: MAST :

(A) canoe
(B) boat
(C) sail
(D) sloop

9. .50 is related to 1/2 as .25 is related to

(A) 1/4
(B) 25/100
(C) 2.5%
(D) 25%

10. FLOWERS : VASE :: MILK :

(A) cup
(B) pitcher
(C) cow
(D) udder

11. SHIP is related to DOCK as PLANE is related to

(A) ordinary
(B) rocket
(C) hangar
(D) closet

12. SUBMARINE is related to FISH as AIRPLANE is related to

(A) bird
(B) dock
(C) propeller
(D) jet

13. PASTA is related to SAUCE as EGGS is related to

(A) chicken
(B) bacon
(C) boiled
(D) shells

14. CATERPILLAR : BUTTERFLY :: TADPOLE :

(A) snake
(B) frog
(C) worm
(D) turtle

15. HOOD is related to HEAD as CARPET is related to

(A) floor
(B) room
(C) rug
(D) wool

Directions: Circle the correct set of answers that will complete the analogy.

16. NEEDLE : SEW ::

(A) pencil : paper
(B) radio: electricity
(C) picture: color
(D) towel : dry

17. FAST : HUNGER ::

(A) camp : fire
(B) jog : fatigue
(C) sing : voice
(D) tight : choke

18. STONE : RING ::

(A) catch : bracelet
(B) earring : hang
(C) face : watch
(D) mask : hat

19. APPETIZER : DESSERT ::

(A) hat : shoes
(B) introduction : epilogue
(C) right : left
(D) step : stair

20. PRESS : BUTTON ::

(A) oak : acorn
(B) east : plate
(C) perish : starve
(D) plunge : knife

READING COMPREHENSION

One of the major keys to success in almost all fields of endeavor, especially in a clerical job, is the ability to read material and understand what you have read. Whether reading the directions on a test, understanding an office manual, or simply reading a newspaper or magazine for pleasure, the greater your reading comprehension, the more success you will have in whatever you attempt. The following paragraphs and questions will test your skills.

1. Only the female spider spins a web. She uses this web to trap food and as her home. She makes her web out of fine silk threads. This silk is a kind of protein and is made by glands inside the female spider's body. It takes a lot of time and energy for the spider to secrete the silk threads and connect them together to make her web.

The paragraph best supports the statement that in creating a web

(A) the female spider needs the support of her mate.
(B) a lot of labor is required.
(C) in order to make the web shine, it requires a lot of water.
(D) the spider needs sunlight in order to work.

2. Money is printed on a special kind of paper. This paper is made only for the purpose of printing money and no other use is allowed. The special paper is made of linen and cotton, which make it strong. The exact proportions of linen and cotton are kept secret. This makes the bills hard to reproduce.

   The paragraph best supports the statement that the government

   (A) is worried that the ink on printed money will fade.
   (B) tries to use different fabrics to create different bills.
   (C) is concerned about forgery.
   (D) is concerned that printed money will eventually tear.

3. Lithography is the art of drawing with a greasy substance, usually crayon, on a stone, metal, or paper surface, and then printing. It is based on the fact that the surface attracts grease and the grease is repelled by water. It is the most direct of all graphic arts, for in practicing it the artist first sees the exact value of each line that he draws and then has his or her drawing reproduced so accurately that it may truly be said to have been multiplied. Etchings involve a process in which a drawing is engraved on a metal plate; a woodcut is a drawing carved in wood. For both of these processes the artist must wait for a print to estimate his or her work fairly.

   The paragraph best supports the statement that the advantage of lithography as a means of reproducing drawings is that it

   (A) is quicker and neater than other methods.
   (B) gives faithful reproductions.
   (C) requires no special materials.
   (D) is less expensive than other methods.

4. It is believed that voice training may contribute to personality development and to improved social adjustment. First of all, it has been fairly well established that people tend to become what they believe others think them to be. When people react more favorably toward us because our voices convey the idea that we are friendly, competent, and interesting, there is a strong tendency for us to develop those qualities in our personality. A good voice, then, like good clothes, can do much for an ego that otherwise might tend to droop.

   This paragraph best supports the statement that a good voice

   (A) is more important than looking good.
   (B) can contribute greatly to a feeling of poise.
   (C) makes others unconscious of our faults.
   (D) is not as important as wearing good clothes.

5. A lighthouse gives navigators the ship's location, and warns them away from rocks and shoals that can damage the ship. At night, each lighthouse emits flashes of light. These flashes may be long or short, and are combined in a series unique to that lighthouse. No other lighthouse uses the same pattern, and because each sequence is distinctive, navigators can determine the ship's position.

   This paragraph best supports the statement that the light from each lighthouse

   (A) is different for each ship that passes.
   (B) is the same throughout the world.
   (C) cannot be seen in a fog.
   (D) can be easily identified by its types of flashes.

Directions: Base your answers to questions 6–10 on the information in the following passage.

In an experiment, several people were put in an airtight room. The air soon became warm and moist. The amount of carbon dioxide increased, and the amount of oxygen decreased. Everyone felt very uncomfortable. Then, without letting in any fresh air, an electric fan was turned on. Almost as soon as the air was set in motion, everyone became comfortable again.

This, and many other experiments, show that the moisture, temperature, and movement of indoor air are of more importance than the amount of oxygen or carbon dioxide that it contains. Air that contains little more than the usual amount of carbon dioxide is not dangerous to breathe. Air that contains a little less than the usual amount of oxygen is not dangerous to breathe.

Without proper ventilation, the air of a room in winter may become as dry as that of the Sahara Desert. In very dry air, the temperature must be 80 degrees Fahrenheit or more before we feel comfortably warm. Dry air causes the skin and the linings of the nose, throat, and air tubes to become dry. When this happens, germs are able to break through these linings very easily.

6. When several people were kept in an airtight room, the

(A) oxygen increased; carbon dioxide decreased.
(B) oxygen decreased; the air became dry.
(C) carbon dioxide increased; oxygen decreased.
(D) air became cool and dry.

7. Without proper ventilation, the air in a room

(A) becomes dangerous.
(B) becomes 80° Fahrenheit.
(C) becomes a desert.
(D) becomes dry.

8. According to this article, what made the people comfortable again?

(A) moving the air
(B) reducing the oxygen
(C) increasing the temperature
(D) increasing carbon dioxide

9. We become more susceptible to germs when the linings of our nose and throat are

(A) moist
(B) hot
(C) cost
(D) dry

10. The best title for this selection might be

(A) "Stopping Germs."
(B) "Oxygen and Carbon Dioxide."
(C) "Pollution."
(D) "Indoor Air."

Directions: Base your answers to questions 11–15 only on the information in the following passage.

The earth rotates as it travels around the sun, and the sun therefore appears to move across the sky. This rotation of the earth causes a difference in time in different places around the world. Within the United States, including the mainland and its coastal areas, there are six major time zones: Pacific Standard Time, Mountain Standard Time, Central Standard Time, Eastern Standard Time, Alaska Standard Time, and Hawaii Standard Time. Small parts of Alaska fall within two other time zones: the extreme western border of Alaska falls within the Bering Standard Time Zone, and the extreme northeastern tip falls within the Yukon Time Zone.

The time zones on the United States mainland each differ by one hour. When it is 4:00 in the Pacific Standard Time Zone, it is 5:00 in the Mountain Standard Time Zone, 6:00 in the Central Standard Time Zone, and 7:00 in the Eastern Standard Time Zone.

11. The earth

(A) travels around the sun.
(B) appears to move across the sky.
(C) causes differences in time.
(D) All of the above.

12. The best title for this selection would be

(A) "Time Zones in the United States."
(B) "The Rotation of the Earth."
(C) "How to Tell Time."
(D) "The Movement of the Sun."

13. In the United States there are

(A) four major time zones.
(B) six major time zones.
(C) two major time zones.
(D) five major time zones.

14. The time variance from zone to zone is

(A) six hours.
(B) four hours.
(C) one hour.
(D) three hours.

15. If it is 3:00 PM in the Pacific Standard Time Zone, what time would it be in the Eastern Standard Time Zone?

(A) 2:00 PM
(B) 4:00 PM
(C) 5:00 PM
(D) 6:00 PM

READING, UNDERSTANDING, AND INTERPRETING WRITTEN MATERIAL

The passage below contains several numbered blanks. Below the passage are listed sets of words numbered to match the blanks. Read the passage once quickly to get the overall idea, then read the passage through a second time more slowly. Choose the word from each set that makes the most sense both in the sentence and the total paragraph. Circle the letter of the correct answer.

Pear trees were first ______ (1) in areas of North America that tend to be ______ (2). Such climates ______ (3) the bacterial disease, which usually begins in the pear tree's blossoms. The first ______ (4) are usually ______ (5) after a spring rain. Flowers ______ (6) and turn black, while leaves become black and scorched-looking. The ______ (7) is called "fire blight." That is because of the tree's ______ (8). The tree looks as though it has been burned. Once it reaches a blossom, the bacteria ______ (9) through the flower into the tree, ______ (10) tree tissue.

1. (A) dug
   (B) planted
   (C) bought
   (D) lost

2. (A) wild
   (B) empty
   (C) damp
   (D) hearty

3. (A) stop
   (B) hinder
   (C) encourage
   (D) kill

4. (A) symptoms
   (B) death
   (C) size
   (D) grapes

5. (A) wasted
   (B) removed
   (C) helped
   (D) noticed

6. (A) wither
   (B) empty
   (C) blossom
   (D) explode

7. (A) plant
   (B) disease
   (C) pear
   (D) flower

8. (A) size
   (B) appearance
   (C) strength
   (D) position

9. (A) falls
   (B) twists
   (C) leaves
   (D) penetrates

10. (A) helping
    (B) killing
    (C) soiling
    (D) filling

Bread was a ______ (11) food staple in ancient times. The earliest ______ (12) were made, it is thought, from roasted ______ (13) mixed with ______ (14) to create a ______ (15) that could be spread on hot stone. After a while, a hard ______ (16) would form. This product, known as flat bread, was a precursor of the ______ (17). Although flat breads are still eaten in many places, most Western cultures prefer raised, or leavened, breads made light and fluffy through the use of ______ (18). When added to wheat flour mixed with water, yeast causes ______ (19) to form. Elastic proteins within the flour trap these gases. Consequently, the mixture ______ (20).

11. (A) poor
(B) common
(C) unpleasant
(D) foreign

12. (A) breads
(B) stones
(C) drinks
(D) papers

13. (A) chicken
(B) powder
(C) grains
(D) tomatoes

14. (A) ink
(B) cocoa
(C) water
(D) leaves

15. (A) paste
(B) drink
(C) cone
(D) dinner

16. (A) seed
(B) sheet
(C) point
(D) ball

17. (A) roll
(B) cake
(C) cookie
(D) tortilla

18. (A) seeds
(B) yeast
(C) cinnamon
(D) pepper

19. (A) poison
(B) flakes
(C) gases
(D) lumps

20. (A) cools
(B) dries
(C) melts
(D) swells

CORRECT ANSWERS—VERBAL REVIEW

SPELLING

1. **The correct answer is (A).** refferee should be referee
2. **The correct answer is (B).** acheivement should be achievement
3. **The correct answer is (A).** imune should be immune
4. **The correct answer is (C).** tumbleing should be tumbling
5. **The correct answer is (D).** admittence should be admittance
6. **The correct answer is (D).** involvment should be involvement
7. **The correct answer is (C).** testamony should be testimony
8. **The correct answer is (D).** resturant should be restaurant
9. **The correct answer is (D).** minature should be miniature
10. **The correct answer is (A).** allottment should be allotment
11. The correct spelling is: enrollment
12. Correct as written.
13. Correct as written.
14. The correct spelling is: quality
15. The correct spelling is: dissatisfied
16. The correct spelling is: whistle
17. Correct as written.
18. The correct spelling is: intellectual
19. The correct spelling is: antenna
20. The correct spelling is: ceiling
21. Correct as written.
22. The correct spelling is: disguise
23. The correct spelling is: physician
24. The correct spelling is: noticeable
25. Correct as written.
26. The correct spelling is: consciousness
27. Correct as written.
28. The correct spelling is: enemies
29. The correct spelling is: allergic
30. The correct spelling is: spaghetti
31. The correct spelling is: apology
32. Correct as written.
33. The correct spelling is: pianos
34. The correct spelling is: celebration
35. Correct as written.
36. Correct as written.
37. The correct spelling is: sophomore
38. The correct spelling is: achieving
39. The correct spelling is: loneliness
40. Correct as written.
41. The correct spelling is: prairie
42. The correct spelling is: legitimate
43. Correct as written.
44. The correct spelling is: disagreeable
45. Correct as written.
46. The correct spelling is: conscientious
47. The correct spelling is: comparison
48. Correct as written.
49. The correct spelling is: credited
50. Correct as written.

VOCABULARY

1. **The correct answer is (D).** joyful
2. **The correct answer is (B).** canyon
3. **The correct answer is (A).** angered
4. **The correct answer is (B).** patient courage
5. **The correct answer is (C).** weakly
6. **The correct answer is (B).** simple
7. **The correct answer is (C).** rich
8. **The correct answer is (A).** laid off
9. **The correct answer is (D).** become actual fact
10. **The correct answer is (D).** combine
11. **The correct answer is (C).** effective
12. **The correct answer is (A).** core
13. **The correct answer is (B).** confirmation
14. **The correct answer is (D).** insight
15. **The correct answer is (B).** large numbers
16. **The correct answer is (D).** agree
17. **The correct answer is (C).** stimulate
18. **The correct answer is (A).** picturesque
19. **The correct answer is (D).** offensive
20. **The correct answer is (A).** in disagreement

LANGUAGE: GRAMMAR, PUNCTUATION, AND USAGE

1. It is always a pleasure for us boys to visit the firehouse. Use the objective case (us) rather than the nominative case (we). The word us is the object of the preposition for.
2. The magician waved his hands so skillfully that the audience was completely mystified. Skillful is an adjective, however in this sentence the word is used as an adverb. Therefore, it needs an "ly."
3. Do not hand in the report until you're certain that it is complete. The contraction, you're, means "you are," which is correct in this sentence. The spelling, "your" is a possessive pronoun.
4. Correct as written.
5. Mailing a letter a few days early is better than running the risk of its arriving late. This is one complete thought. No semi-colon is needed.
6. She is more capable than any other woman in the office is. Woman should not be capitalized. It is not a proper noun. Because we are comparing the capability of "she" to all the other women, we need to include the word "is."
7. Mother would not let Mary and me attend the hockey game. Use the objective case (me) rather than the nominative case (I).
8. Correct as written.
9. Correct as written.
10. I'm not certain that yours is the best solution. Yours is a possessive pronoun, no apostrophe is needed
11. Correct as written.
12. It was we girls who swept the gym floor after the dance. Use nominative case (we) rather than objective case (us). The word we is the subject of the verb, swept.
13. Henderson, the president of the board, is also a resident of the building. The appositive, the president of the board, refers to Henderson and must be set off by commas. President of the board is not capitalized because we do not know specifically what board he is president of.
14. If you had been more patient, you might not have torn it. The present perfect tense using have and the past participle (torn) are needed because this is an action that occurred sometime in the past.
15. I would like to visit these cities: Boston, Chicago, and Houston. Use a colon, not a semi-colon, when writing a list of items.

16. **The correct answer is (C).** All the other sentences have dangling participles, which indicate that "she" is the one "steaming energetically," rather than the teakettle.
17. **The correct answer is (B).** The verb forms agree. Choices (A), (C), and (D) are incorrect because each of the sentences has two conflicting verb forms.
18. The words, If I were indicates the correct use of the subjunctive. In the other answer choices, the two verb forms that are used are neither in the same tense nor express the subjunctive correctly.
19. **The correct answer is (C).** It indicates that Mary and the reader should be doing different tasks at the same time. Choices (A), (B), and (D) use the incorrect verb, lie instead of lay. In addition, choice (A) should have a semi-colon separating the two clauses.
20. **The correct answer is (B).** It compares the two excuses. Choices (A), (C), and (D) compare an excuse with a person.

ANALOGIES

1. **The correct answer is (B).** eating. The relationship is—object:use.
2. **The correct answer is (B).** avoid. The relationship is—synonyms.
3. **The correct answer is (D).** argue. The relationship is—synonyms.
4. **The correct answer is (A).** abandon. The relationship is—synonyms.
5. **The correct answer is (C).** us. The relationship is—singular:plural.
6. **The correct answer is (D).** man. The relationship is—part:whole.
7. **The correct answer is (D).** script. The relationship is—person in a profession:tool/object used.
8. **The correct answer is (C).** sail. The relationship is—a whole:object that is part of the whole.
9. **The correct answer is (A).** 1/4. The relationship is—mathematical ratio.
10. **The correct answer is (C).** pitcher. The relationship is—object:container.
11. **The correct answer is (C).** hanger. The relationship is—vehicle:housing.
12. **The correct answer is (A).** bird. The relationship is—manmade:nature
13. **The correct answer is (B).** bacon. The relationship is—food:complement.
14. **The correct answer is (B).** frog. The relationship is—young:adult.
15. **The correct answer is (A).** floor. The relationship is—covering:object used to cover.
16. **The correct answer is (D).** towel:dry. The relationship is—object:use.
17. **The correct answer is (B).** jog:fatigue. The relationship is—cause:effect.
18. **The correct answer is (C).** face:watch. The relationship is—part of a whole:whole.
19. **The correct answer is (B).** introduction:epilogue. The relationship is—start:finish.
20. **The correct answer is (D).** plunge:knife. The relationship is—way to use:object used.

READING COMPREHENSION

1. **The correct answer is (B).** a lot of labor is required.
2. **The correct answer is (C).** is concerned about forgery.
3. **The correct answer is (B).** gives faithful reproductions.
4. **The correct answer is (B).** can contribute greatly to a feeling of poise.
5. **The correct answer is (D).** can be easily identified by its types of flashes.
6. **The correct answer is (C).** carbon dioxide increased; oxygen decreased.
7. **The correct answer is (D).** becomes dry.
8. **The correct answer is (A).** moving the air.
9. **The correct answer is (D).** dry.
10. **The correct answer is (D).** "Indoor Air"
11. **The correct answer is (A).** travels around the sun.
12. **The correct answer is (A).** "Time Zones in the United States."
13. **The correct answer is (B).** six major time zones.
14. **The correct answer is (C).** one hour
15. **The correct answer is (D).** 6:00 PM

READING, UNDERSTANDING, AND INTERPRETING WRITTEN MATERIAL

Pear trees were first **planted** (1) in areas of North America that tend to be **damp** (2). Such climates **encourage** (3) the bacterial disease, which usually begins in the pear tree's blossoms. The first **symptoms** (4) are usually **noticed** (5) after a spring rain. Flowers **wither** (6) and turn black, while leaves become black and scorched-looking. The **disease** (7) is called "fire blight." That is because of the tree's **appearance** (8). The tree looks as though it has been burned. Once it reaches a comparison blossom, the bacteria **penetrates** (9) through the flower into the tree, **killing** (10) tree tissue.

1. **The correct answer is (B).** planted
2. **The correct answer is (C).** damp
3. **The correct answer is (C).** encourage
4. **The correct answer is (A).** symptoms
5. **The correct answer is (D).** noticed
6. **The correct answer is (A).** wither
7. **The correct answer is (B).** disease
8. **The correct answer is (B).** appearance
9. **The correct answer is (D).** penetrates
10. **The correct answer is (B).** killing

Bread was a **common** (11) food staple in ancient times. The earliest **breads** (12) were made, it is thought, from roasted **grains** (13) mixed with **water** (14) to create a **paste** (15) that could be spread on hot stone. After a while, a hard **sheet** (16) would form. This product, known as flat bread, was a precursor of the **tortilla** (17). Although flat breads are still eaten in many places, most Western cultures prefer raised, or leavened, breads made light and fluffy through the use of **yeast** (18). When added to wheat flour mixed with water, yeast causes **gases** (19) to form. Elastic proteins within the flour trap these gases. Consequently, the mixture **swells** (20).

11. **The correct answer is (B).** common
12. **The correct answer is (A).** breads
13. **The correct answer is (C).** grains
14. **The correct answer is (C).** water
15. **The correct answer is (A).** paste
16. **The correct answer is (B).** sheet
17. **The correct answer is (D).** tortilla
18. **The correct answer is (B).** yeast
19. **The correct answer is (C).** gases
20. **The correct answer is (D).** swells

BASIC MATHEMATICS REVIEW

COMPUTATIONS

Directions: Perform the computation as indicated in the question and find the answer among the list of alternative responses. If the correct answer is not given among the choices, circle (E).

1. $50 + 20$

(A) 77
(B) 50
(C) 70
(D) 30
(E) none of these

2. $25 - 5$

(A) 20
(B) 30
(C) 25
(D) 27
(E) none of these

3. 11×4

(A) 15
(B) 44
(C) 34
(D) 41
(E) none of these

4. $3\overline{)24}$

(A) 8
(B) 7
(C) 6
(D) 27
(E) none of these

5. 15×3

(A) 15
(B) 45
(C) 30
(D) 18
(E) none of these

6. $16 + 6$

(A) 26
(B) 20
(C) 24
(D) 23
(E) none of these

7. $9\overline{)81}$

(A) 90
(B) 81
(C) 9
(D) 8
(E) none of these

8. $\begin{array}{r} 19 \\ -\ 18 \\ \hline \end{array}$

(A) 9
(B) 37
(C) 1
(D) 2
(E) none of these

9. $\begin{array}{r} 43 \\ +\ 12 \\ \hline \end{array}$

(A) 31
(B) 53
(C) 55
(D) 35
(E) none of these

10. $\begin{array}{r} 77 \\ -\ 45 \\ \hline \end{array}$

(A)22
(B) 31
(C) 33
(D) 32
(E) none of these

11. $\begin{array}{r} 23 \\ \times\ 7 \\ \hline \end{array}$

(A) 161
(B) 30
(C) 141
(D) 210
(E) none of these

12. $5\overline{)75}$

(A) 20
(B) 17
(C) 15
(D) 25
(E) none of these

13. $\begin{array}{r} 96 \\ -\ 14 \\ \hline \end{array}$

(A) 110
(B) 83
(C) 81
(D) 72
(E) none of these

14. $\begin{array}{r} 56 \\ +\ 29 \\ \hline \end{array}$

(A) 85
(B) 76
(C) 77
(D) 87
(E) none of these

15. $\begin{array}{r} 45 \\ \times\ 4 \\ \hline \end{array}$

(A) 165
(B) 180
(C) 160
(D) 49
(E) none of these

16. $3\overline{)54}$

(A) 51
(B) 17
(C) 18
(D) 54
(E) none of these

17. $\begin{array}{r} 13 \\ \times\ 11 \\ \hline \end{array}$

(A) 24
(B) 130
(C) 143
(D) 131
(E) none of these

18. $\begin{array}{r} 31 \\ -\ 19 \\ \hline \end{array}$

(A) 22
(B) 12
(C) 28
(D) 50
(E) none of these

19. $\begin{array}{r} 84 \\ +\ 69 \\ \hline \end{array}$

(A) 143
(B) 151
(C) 154
(D) 145
(E) none of these

20. $5\overline{)65}$

(A) 14
(B) 13
(C) 70
(D) 60
(E) none of these

21. $\begin{array}{r} 33 \\ +\ 44 \\ \hline \end{array}$

(A) 11
(B) 55
(C) 70
(D) 77
(E) none of these

22. $\begin{array}{r} 34 \\ \times\ 2 \\ \hline \end{array}$

(A) 36
(B) 32
(C) 86
(D) 68
(E) none of these

23. $9\overline{)189}$

(A) 91
(B) 198
(C) 12
(D) 21
(E) none of these

24. $\begin{array}{r} 51 \\ -\ 33 \\ \hline \end{array}$

(A) 22
(B) 28
(C) 84
(D) 12
(E) none of these

25. $10\overline{)250}$

(A) 2
(B) 75
(C) 50
(D) 25
(E) none of these

26. $\begin{array}{r} 35 \\ +\ 16 \\ \hline \end{array}$

(A) 21
(B) 51
(C) 19
(D) 41
(E) none of these

27. $\begin{array}{r} 108 \\ -\ \ 38 \\ \hline \end{array}$

(A) 70
(B) 69
(C) 60
(D) 78
(E) none of these

28. $\begin{array}{r} 15 \\ \times\ 13 \\ \hline \end{array}$

(A) 28
(B) 195
(C) 2
(D) 150
(E) none of these

29. $\begin{array}{r} 16 \\ \times\ 8 \\ \hline \end{array}$

(A) 48
(B) 228
(C) 128
(D) 24
(E) none of these

30. $\begin{array}{r} 38 \\ -\ 29 \\ \hline \end{array}$

(A) 67
(B) 11
(C) 8
(D) 12
(E) none of these

31. $7\overline{)91}$

(A) 12
(B) 14
(C) 84
(D) 13
(E) none of these

32. $\begin{array}{r} 86 \\ +\ 24 \\ \hline \end{array}$

(A) 110
(B) 62
(C) 100
(D) 114
(E) none of these

33. $\begin{array}{r} 74 \\ +\ 18 \\ \hline \end{array}$

(A) 92
(B) 82
(C) 56
(D) 66
(E) none of these

34. $\begin{array}{r} 100 \\ -\ \ 39 \\ \hline \end{array}$

(A) 71
(B) 61
(C) 69
(D) 79
(E) none of these

35. $4\overline{)292}$

(A) 78
(B) 72
(C) 73
(D) 76
(E) none of these

36. $\begin{array}{r} 20 \\ \times\ 17 \\ \hline \end{array}$

(A) 314
(B) 240
(C) 430
(D) 217
(E) none of these

37. $\begin{array}{r} 82 \\ -\ 29 \\ \hline \end{array}$

(A) 101
(B) 67
(C) 111
(D) 53
(E) none of these

38. $\begin{array}{r} 51 \\ +\ 48 \\ \hline \end{array}$

(A) 99
(B) 90
(C) 109
(D) 97
(E) none of these

39. $\begin{array}{r} 37 \\ \times\ 8 \\ \hline \end{array}$

(A) 247
(B) 296
(C) 563
(D) 246
(E) none of these

40. $9\overline{)369}$

(A) 378
(B) 41
(C) 36
(D) 69
(E) none of these

NUMBER SERIES

Number series questions consist of a series of numbers that follow some definite order. The numbers progress from left to right according to some rule. For example, a simple series such as 1 2 3 4 . . . consists of merely adding 1 to the previous number. The next number in the series would then be 5, since 4 + 1 = 5. The next would be 6, and so on.

Directions: Study each series in the questions below, and choose the answer pair that continues the series according to the pattern established. Circle the correct pattern on the page.

1. 2 4 6 8 10 12 .... (A) 13 (B) 14 (C) 15 (D) 16 (E) 17

2. 27 24 21 18 15 12 .... (A) 11 (B) 10 (C) 9 (D) 8 (E) 7

3. 7 5 14 10 21 15 28 20 ... (A) 25 (B) 30 (C) 35 (D) 40 (E) 26

4. 15 21 28 36 45 55 .... (A) 65 (B) 66 (C) 67 (D) 68 (E) 69

5. 21 9 24 9 27 9 30 9...... (A) 9 (B) 27 (C) 36 (D) 33 (E) 32

6. 3 6 4 8 6 12 10.......... (A) 20 (B) 18 (C) 16 (D) 24 (E) 28

7. 1 1 2 3 5 8 13........... (A) 1 (B) 23 (C) 18 (D) 19 (E) 21

8. 100 91 82 73 64......... (A) 63 (B) 56 (C) 45 (D) 53 (E) 55

9. 24 24 20 20 16 16 12 .... (A) 8 (B) 12 (C) 10 (D) 16 (E) 9

10. 3 4 6 9 13 18............ (A) 24 (B) 23 (C) 26 (D) 31 (E) 27

11. 8 9 16 17 32 33 .... (A) 56 (B) 64 (C) 65 (D) 66 (E) 55

12. 5 7 10 14 15 21 20 28.... (A) 25 (B) 26 (C) 35 (D) 30 (E) 32

13. 64 2 32 4 16 8 8 .... (A) 4 (B) 32 (C) 8 (D) 16 (E) 12

14. 42 42 50 34 58 26 66 .... (A) 74 (B) 34 (C) 46 (D) 18 (E) 40

15. 15 16 14 15 13 14 12 13 . (A) 16 (B) 15 (C) 14 (D) 12 (E) 11

16. 1 2 6 24 120 720 .... (A) 840 (B) 873 (C) 1000 (D) 4940 (E) 5040

17. 50 100 40 80 30 60 20 ... (A) 10 (B) 20 (C) 30 (D) 40 (E) 50

18. 77 67 57 60 63 53 43 46 . (A) 56 (B) 46 (C) 51 (D) 43 (E) 49

19. 4 5 8 13 20 29 .... (A) 39 (B) 49 (C) 38 (D) 40 (E) 45

20. 32 12 42 22 52 32........ (A) 42 (B) 32 (C) 72 (D) 62 (E) 22

21. 10 11 13 16 20 25........ (A) 24 (B) 30 (C) 31 (D) 29 (E) 32

22. 5 12 10 17 20 27......... (A) 40 (B) 54 (C) 44 (D) 47 (E) 36

23. 6 7 8 6 8 9 6 9 10......... (A) 11 (B) 6 (C) 12 (D) 8 (E) 10

24. 14 17 15 15 17 13 20 11 . (A) 9 (B) 20 (C) 24 (D) 23 (E) 17

25. 99 9 89 18 78 27 66 36 .. (A) 45 (B) 53 (C) 46 (D) 54 (E) 55

CORRECT ANSWERS—BASIC MATHEMATICS REVIEW

COMPUTATIONS

1. The correct answer is (C).

$$\begin{array}{r} 50 \\ +\ 20 \\ \hline 70 \end{array}$$

2. The correct answer is (A).

$$\begin{array}{r} 25 \\ -\ \ 5 \\ \hline 70 \end{array}$$

3. The correct answer is (B).

$$\begin{array}{r} 11 \\ \times\ \ 4 \\ \hline 44 \end{array}$$

4. The correct answer is (A).

$$\begin{array}{r} 8 \\ 3\overline{)24} \end{array}$$

5. The correct answer is (B).

$$\begin{array}{r} 13 \\ \times\ \ 3 \\ \hline 45 \end{array}$$

6. The correct answer is (E).

$$\begin{array}{r} 16 \\ +\ \ 6 \\ \hline 22 \end{array}$$

7. The correct answer is (C).

$$\begin{array}{r} 9 \\ 9\overline{)81} \end{array}$$

8. The correct answer is (C).

$$\begin{array}{r} 19 \\ -\ 18 \\ \hline 1 \end{array}$$

9. The correct answer is (C).

$$\begin{array}{r} 43 \\ +\ 12 \\ \hline 55 \end{array}$$

10. The correct answer is (D).

$$\begin{array}{r} 77 \\ -\ 45 \\ \hline 32 \end{array}$$

11. The correct answer is (A).

$$\begin{array}{r} 23 \\ \times\ \ 7 \\ \hline 161 \end{array}$$

12. The correct answer is (C).

$$\begin{array}{r} 15 \\ 5\overline{)75} \end{array}$$

13. The correct answer is (E).

$$\begin{array}{r} 96 \\ -\ 14 \\ \hline 82 \end{array}$$

14. The correct answer is (A).

$$\begin{array}{r} 56 \\ +\ 29 \\ \hline 85 \end{array}$$

15. The correct answer is (B).

$$\begin{array}{r} 45 \\ \times\ \ 4 \\ \hline 180 \end{array}$$

16. The correct answer is (C).

$$\begin{array}{r} 18 \\ 3\overline{)54} \end{array}$$

17. The correct answer is (C).

$$\begin{array}{r} 13 \\ \times\ 11 \\ \hline 143 \end{array}$$

18. The correct answer is (B).

$$\begin{array}{r} 31 \\ \times\ 19 \\ \hline 12 \end{array}$$

19. The correct answer is (E).

$$\begin{array}{r} 84 \\ +\ 69 \\ \hline 153 \end{array}$$

20. The correct answer is (B).

$$\begin{array}{r} 13 \\ 5\overline{)65} \end{array}$$

21. The correct answer is (D).

$$\begin{array}{r} 33 \\ +\ 44 \\ \hline 77 \end{array}$$

22. The correct answer is (D).

$$\begin{array}{r} 34 \\ \times\ 2 \\ \hline 68 \end{array}$$

23. The correct answer is (D).

$$\begin{array}{r} 21 \\ 9\overline{)189} \end{array}$$

24. The correct answer is (E).

$$\begin{array}{r} 51 \\ -\ 33 \\ \hline 18 \end{array}$$

25. The correct answer is (D).

$$\begin{array}{r} 25 \\ 10\overline{)250} \end{array}$$

26. The correct answer is (B).

$$\begin{array}{r} 35 \\ +\ 16 \\ \hline 51 \end{array}$$

27. The correct answer is (A).

$$\begin{array}{r} 108 \\ -\ 38 \\ \hline 70 \end{array}$$

28. The correct answer is (B).

$$\begin{array}{r} 15 \\ \times\ 13 \\ \hline 195 \end{array}$$

29. The correct answer is (C).

$$\begin{array}{r} 16 \\ \times\ 8 \\ \hline 128 \end{array}$$

30. The correct answer is (E).

$$\begin{array}{r} 38 \\ -\ 29 \\ \hline 9 \end{array}$$

31. The correct answer is (D).

$$\begin{array}{r} 13 \\ 7\overline{)91} \end{array}$$

32. **The correct answer is (A).**

$$\begin{array}{r} 86 \\ +\ 24 \\ \hline 110 \end{array}$$

33. **The correct answer is (A).**

$$\begin{array}{r} 74 \\ +\ 18 \\ \hline 92 \end{array}$$

34. **The correct answer is (B).**

$$\begin{array}{r} 100 \\ -\ 39 \\ \hline 61 \end{array}$$

35. **The correct answer is (C).**

$$\begin{array}{r} 73 \\ 4\overline{)292} \end{array}$$

36. **The correct answer is (E).**

$$\begin{array}{r} 20 \\ \times\ 17 \\ \hline 340 \end{array}$$

37. **The correct answer is (D).**

$$\begin{array}{r} 82 \\ -\ 29 \\ \hline 57 \end{array}$$

38. **The correct answer is (A).**

$$\begin{array}{r} 51 \\ +\ 48 \\ \hline 99 \end{array}$$

39. **The correct answer is (B).**

$$\begin{array}{r} 37 \\ \times\ 8 \\ \hline 296 \end{array}$$

40. **The correct answer is (B).**

$$\begin{array}{r} 41 \\ 9\overline{)369} \end{array}$$

NUMBER SERIES

1. **The correct answer is (B).** In this series, each subsequent number is 2 more than the previous number. Therefore, the next number in the series is 12 + 2 or 14.
2. **The correct answer is (C).** In this series, each subsequent number is 3 less than the previous number. Therefore, the next number in the series is 12 – 3 or 9.
3. **The correct answer is (C).** This is an alternating series. The first series, beginning with 7, shows every other number as a multiple of 7. The second series, beginning with 5, shows every other number as a multiple of 5. The last number shown is 20, a multiple of 5. So the next number in the series must be a multiple of 7. Since the last multiple of 7 shown is 7 × 4 or 28, the next number in the series must be 7 × 5 or 35.
4. **The correct answer is (B).** To each subsequent number in this series, add one more than what was added to the previous number. Add 6 to 15 to get 21. Add 7 to 21 to get 28 . . . add 10 to 45 to get 55, and add 11 to 55 to get the next number in the series, 66.
5. **The correct answer is (D).** This is an alternating series. In the first series, beginning with 21, every other number is increased by 3. The second series, beginning with 9, shows every other number being 9. The last number shown is 9, so the next number must be 3 more than the second to last number shown, 30. Therefore, the next number is 30 + 3 or 33.
6. **The correct answer is (A).** The pattern in this series is to multiply by 2, then subtract 2. Since the last number shown in the series, 10, is 12 – 2, the next number must be 10 × 2 or 20.
7. **The correct answer is (E).** Each subsequent number in this series is the sum of the two previous numbers in the series. Therefore, the next number must be 8 + 13 or 21.

8. **The correct answer is (E).** In this series, each subsequent number is 9 less than the previous number. Therefore, the next number in the series is 64 – 9 or 55.
9. **The correct answer is (B).** In this series each number repeats itself, then decreases by 4. Since the last number in the series, 12, has not yet been repeated, the next number in the series must be 12.
10. **The correct answer is (A).** To each subsequent number in this series, add one more than what was added to the previous number. Add 1 to 3 to get 4. Add 2 to 4 to get 6 . . . add 5 to 13 to get 18, and add 6 to 18 to get the next number in the series, 24.
11. **The correct answer is (B).** This is an alternating series. The first series, beginning with 8, shows every other number multiplied by 2. The second series, beginning with 9, is one more than the number it follows. Since the last number shown in this series is 33, which is one more than the number it follows, 32, the next number must be 32 × 2 or 64.
12. **The correct answer is (A).** This is an alternating series. The first series, beginning with 5, shows every other number as a multiple of 5. The second series, beginning with 7, shows every other number as a multiple of 7. The last number shown is 28, a multiple of 7. So the next number in the series must be a multiple of 5. Since the last multiple of 5 shown is 5 × 4 or 20, the next number in the series must be 5 × 5 or 25.
13. **The correct answer is (D).** This is an alternating series. The first series, beginning with 64, shows every other number as half the size of previous number in this series. The second series, beginning with 2, shows every other number twice as large as the previous number in this series. The last number shown is 8. Look back to the alternating previous number in this series, 16. Since 8 is half the size of 16, the next number in the series must be twice as large as the alternating number it would follow, which is 8.Therefore, the next number in the series must be 8 × 2 or 16.
14. **The correct answer is (D).** This is an alternating series. In the first series, beginning with 42, every other number is increased by 8. The second series, beginning with the second 42, shows every other number being decreased by 8. The last number shown is 66, which is 8 more than 58. So the next number is 8 less than the number preceding 66. Therefore, the next number in this series is 26 – 8 or 18.
15. **The correct answer is (E).** The pattern in this series is to increase by 1, then subtract 2. Since the last number shown in the series, 13, is 12 + 1, the next number must be 13 – 2 or 11.
16. **The correct answer is (E).** The pattern in this series is to multiply each subsequent number by one more than the previous number. Multiply 1 × 2 to get 2. Multiply 2 × 3 to get 6 . . . 120 × 6 to get 720, and multiply 720 × 7 to get the next number in the series, 5040.
17. **The correct answer is (D).** This is an alternating series. In the first series, beginning with 50, every other number is decreased by 10. In the second series, beginning with the 100, every other number is decreased by 20. The last number shown is 20, which is 10 less than 30. So the next number must be 20 less than the number preceding 20. Therefore, the next number in this series is 60 – 20 or 40.
18. **The correct answer is (E).** The pattern in this series is to decrease by 10, decrease by 10, add 3, and add 3. The last numbers shown are 63 – 10 or 53, 53 – 10 or 43, and 43 + 3 or 46. So the next number must be 46 + 3 or 49.
19. **The correct answer is (D).** In this series, add consecutive odd numbers to each number in the series to get the next number. Add 1 + 4 to get 5. Add 3 + 5 to get 8 . . . add 9 + 20 to get 29 and add 29 + 11 to get the next number in the series, 40.
20. **The correct answer is (D).** The pattern in this series is to decrease by 20, then add 30. Since the last number shown in the series, 32, is 52 – 20, the next number must be 32 + 30 or 62.
21. **The correct answer is (C).** The pattern in this series is to add each subsequent number by one more than the previous number. Add 10 + 1 to get 11. Add 11 + 2 to get 13 . . . 20 + 5 to get 25, and add 25 + 6 to get the next number in the series, 31.

22. **The correct answer is (A).** This is an alternating series. The first series, beginning with 5, shows every other number multiplied by 2. The second series, beginning with 12, is seven more than the number it follows. Since the last number shown in this series is 27, which is seven more than the number it follows, 20, the next number must be 20 × 2 or 40.
23. **The correct answer is (B).** This is an alternating series made up of three separate series. The first series repeats the number 6. In the second series, beginning with 7, each subsequent number is increased by 1. In the third series, beginning with 8, each subsequent number is also increased by 1. Since the last two numbers shown in this series are increased by 1, the next number must be 6.
24. **The correct answer is (C).** This is an alternating series. In the first series, beginning with 14, add one more than what was added to the previous number in this series. Add 1 + 14 to get 15. Add 2 + 15 to get 17, and so forth. Every number in the second series, beginning with 17, is decreased by 2. The last number shown is 11, which is 13 – 2. So the next number in the series must be 20 + 4 or 24.
25. **The correct answer is (B).** This is an alternating series. In the first series, beginning with 99, each number is decreased by one more than the previous number in this series, starting with 10. Subtracting 99 – 10 results in 89, and subtracting 89 – 11 results in 78. In the second series, beginning with 9, each number is a multiple of 9. The last number shown, 36, is a multiple of 9, so the next number must belong to the first series. Since 66 results from 78 – 12, the next number in the series must be 66 – 13 or 53.

CLERICAL SKILLS REVIEW

Clerical skills are not the same as Verbal and Mathematical skills. They require a different type of thinking and approach to the questions. We've tried to give you an overview and typical practice questions that you might encounter on a clerical examination anywhere you live.

RECORD KEEPING

These questions involve organizing or collation of data from different sources, including scheduling, maintaining records, a completion of a table summarizing data using totals, subtotals, averages, and percents. A key component of these questions is interpretation of data. We've given you some typical questions.

Number of Test Applicants by Location and Test Results

	South Street Test Center		West Street Test Center	
Type of Test	Number of Applicants	Percent	Number of Applicants	Percent
Verbal	15	21	35	44
Mathematics	20	29	20	25
Reading	25	36	10	12
Typing	10	14	15	19
Totals	70	100	80	100

1. Which type of test has the least number applicants?

   (A) Verbal
   (B) Mathematics
   (C) Reading
   (D) Typing

2. Which two subjects get the most number of applicants?

   (A) Verbal and Mathematics
   (B) Mathematics and Reading
   (C) Reading and Verbal
   (D) Typing and Verbal

3. The average number of tests taken at the South Street Test Center was most nearly

   (A) 15
   (B) 17
   (C) 19
   (D) 21

Company	Ticker Symbol	52-week High	52-week Low	2/14 Close	2/21 Close	$ Change from Pervious Week
Apple Computer	AAPL	75.19	13.63	19.50	18.88	–0.62
AT&T	T	60.81	16.50	21.76	20.40	–1.36
BellSouth	BLS	53.50	34.94	41.31	41.56	0.25
Dell Computer	DELL	59.69	16.25	22.94	20.63	–2.31
IBM	IBM	134.94	80.06	115.10	107.51	–7.59
Intel	INTC	75.81	29.81	34.13	30.75	–3.38
Microsoft	MSFT	115.00	40.25	58.38	56.25	–2.13

4. Based on the Stock table above, which company had the highest stock price over a one-year period?

(A) Apple Computer
(B) Microsoft
(C) AT&T
(D) Intel

5. Which company had the greatest difference over a one-week period?

(A) Dell Computer
(B) IBM
(C) Intel
(D) Microsoft

6. Which company had the highest amount of profit over the previous week?

(A) IBM
(B) Intel
(C) Apple Computer
(D) BellSouth

7. Over the 52-week period given in this table, which company had the greatest amount of difference in the selling price of their stock?

(A) Apple Computer
(B) BellSouth
(C) IBM
(D) Intel

8. Over this same 52-week period, which company had the smallest amount of difference in the selling price of their stock?

(A) AT&T
(B) Dell Computer
(C) IBM
(D) Microsoft

COMPARISONS

There are a few different forms of these questions that will appear on one of the tests you might take. Try these different types of problems.

In the following questions, compare the names or numbers, and mark the answer, as follows:

(A) if **ALL THREE** names or numbers are exactly **ALIKE**
(B) if only the **FIRST** and **SECOND** names or numbers are exactly **ALIKE**
(C) if only the **FIRST** and **THIRD** names or numbers are exactly **ALIKE**
(D) if only the **SECOND** and **THIRD** names or numbers are exactly **ALIKE**
(E) if **ALL THREE** names or numbers are **DIFFERENT**

1.	7599877	75998772	7598977
2.	10405067	10405067	10405067
3.	R.O. Olaffson	R.O. Olafson	R.O. Olafsson
4.	Marian Martinsen	Marian Martinson	Marian Martinsen
5.	Yardley Armoury	Yardley Armoury	Yardlay Armoury
6.	Nester R. Heasherly	Nester R. Heasherly	Nester R. Heatherly
7.	Peter M. Smyth	Peter N. Smyth	Peter N. Smyth
8.	7-49811113	7-4981113	7-49811113
9.	Stewart Tyrolean Thwaite	Stewert Tyrolean Thwaite	Stewart Tyrolean Thwaite
10.	Parliamentarianism	Parliamentarianism	Parliamentarism

ALPHABETIZATION

In the following questions, find the correct place for the name on the left.

1. Lombardi, L.

(A) →
Lombardi, Joseph, F.
(B) →
Lombardi, Joseph, M.
(C) →
Lombardi, Joseph, P.
(D) →
Lombardi, Joseph R.
(E) →

2. Manners, Robert

(A) →
Manhim, Marcus
(B) →
Manley, James
(C) →
Mann, Peter
(D) →
Mannen, Philip
(E) →

3. Kuzniarski, John

(A)→
Kvasnak, Martin
(B) →
Kwashnak, Marlene
(C) →
Kydes, Christopher
(D) →
Kyle, Arlene
(E) →

4. Sessler, William

(A) →
Sese, Irene
Alicya
(C) →
Sessler, Wilson
(D) →
Sethi, Murtha
(E) →

5. Watts, Juliana

(A) →
Watson, Dale
(B) →
Wattenmaker, Kate
(C) →
Wattley, Carrie
(D) →
Waugh, Julia
(E) →

6. Allan

(A) →
DeMita, Allen
(B) →
DeMond, Albert
(C) →
DeMorgan, Alicia
(D) →
DeMott, Alice
(E) →

7. Wong, Francesca

(A) →
Won, Eun
(B) →
Wong, Chuen
(C) →
Wong, Fun
(D) →
Wong, G. P.
(E) →

8. Zandri, Peter

(A) →
Zamore, D.R.
(B) →
Zamore, Peter
(C) →
Zandri, Peter and Lynn
(D) →
Zandri, Stanley
(E) →

9. Rose, Brad

(A) →
Rosa, Gary
(B) →
Rosen, Ellis
(C) →
Rosenfeld, Thomas
(D) →
Rosenthal, Martin
(E) →

10. Center for Counseling

(A) →
Ridgefield Boys Club
(B) →
Ridgefield Car Wash
(C) →
Ridgefield Chamber of Commerce
(D) →
Ridgefield Cleaners
(E) →

ADDRESS CHECKING

This is a check of accuracy. How quickly can you read two addresses and determine if they are the same in every way, or different in any way? Let's practice these, and keep in mind that each question should take less than 4 seconds!

Directions: Each question consists of two addresses. If the two addresses are alike in EVERY way, mark (A) next to the question. If the two addresses are different in ANY way, mark (D) next to the question.

1.	12224 Hundred Acres Road	1224 Hundred Acres Road
2.	1901 Farm Field Ridge Rd.	1901 Farm Field Ridge Rd.
3.	43465 Old Pond Tpke	434465 Old Pond Tpke
4.	721 N.E. 216th Street	721 N.E. 215th Street
5.	Anchorage, AK 99516	Anchorage, AK 99156
6.	16 Westmorland Dr.	16 Westmoreland Dr.
7.	Williams, Eugene, OR 97403	Williams, Eugene, OR 97403
8.	4 Hawleyville Rd, Bemont	4 Haleyville Rd, Bemont
9.	65 Deer Run Hill, Vestal, NY 13850	65 Dear Run Hill, Vestal, NY 13850
10.	195 Barry Avenue, #10534	195 Barry Avenue, #15034
11.	390 West 1st, Tucson, AZ 85706	390 West 1st, Tuscon, AZ 85706
12.	2660 Woodley Road N.W.	2660 Wooley Road N.W.
13.	Albuquerque, NM 87123	Albuquerque, NM 81723
14.	R.E. Cornelious, 15 Delmare St.	R.E. Cornelius, 15 Delmare St.
15.	22 Twilight Lane, Bergenfield	22 Twilight Lane, Bergenfield
16.	Arturo DeLuca, 9 Benson Lane	Arturo DeLuca, 9 Bensen Lane
17.	27 Old Hattertown Road	27 Old Hatterstown Road
18.	1764-22 East Taligan Rd.	1764-22 East Taligan Dr.
19.	8510 Pan American Freeway NE	8501 Pan American Freeway NE
20.	106 Paseo de Corrales	106 Paseo de Corrales

MEMORY FOR ADDRESSES

The previous questions tested your ability to quickly compare addresses. Now you're asked to memorize and then recall them at a later time. This is a good time to test your reading comprehension skills first. As in any exam that you take in life, it is important to understand the directions. The directions for this section are somewhat complex. As such, you can spend altogether too much time reading them and trying to figure out what they mean, when you get to an actual exam. Here, however, you have the luxury of time, since this section is for review, and that means you can read and reread these directions until you clearly understand them. Don't begin working until you are 100 percent sure that you know what you have to do.

PRACTICE 1

The five boxes below are labeled (A), (B), (C), (D), and (E). In each box are three sets of number spans with names and two names that are not associated with numbers. As quickly as possible, try to memorize the box location of each name and number span. The position of a name or number span within its box is not important. You need only remember the letter of the box in which the item is to be found. You will use these names and numbers to answer the questions.

(A)	(B)	(C)	(D)	(E)
4300-4799 walk	8600-8999 walk	2600-2899 walk	7400-7999 walk	5200-5699 walk
Flutter	Sled	Swelling	Banner	Wolf
7400-7999 star	2600-2899 star	4300-4799 star	5200-5699 star	8600-8999 star
Tuba	Nail	Stand	Walker	Sink
8600-8999 horse	4300-4799 horse	7400-7999 horse	5200-5699 horse	2600-2899 horse

Directions: Next to each question, indicate the letter of the box in which each item that follows is to be found. Try to mark each item without looking back at the boxes. If, however, you get stuck, you may refer to the boxes. On the actual examination, you will not be able to look back.

1. Swelling
2. 5200-5699 walk
3. Flutter
4. 4300-4799 walk
5. 2600-2899 star
6. 8600-8999 walk
7. 5200-5699 star
8. 8600-8999 star
9. Sled
10. 7400-7999 star
11. 5200-5699 horse
12. Stand
13. 2600-2899 walk
14. Nail
15. Banner
16. 4300-4799 horse
17. Wolf
18. 8600-8999 star
19. Banner
20. Walker
21. 7400-7999 walk
22. 8600-8999 walk
23. Tuba
24. Stand
25. 4300-4799 star
26. 7400-7999 horse
27. 2600-2899 horse
28. Sink
29. 8600-8999 horse
30. Nail

PRACTICE 2

Let's try another round of these using the same boxes as before. By now you must have a better sense of recall. Of course, it helps to look for patterns—or create them yourself. For example, what about "I'm walking the star horse." You can then recall that those numbers with these three words (walk, star, horse) are in that order in each column. The top row is "walk," the second row is "star," and the bottom row is horse. Try to create others for both numbers and words.

(A)	(B)	(C)	(D)	(E)
4300-4799 walk	8600-8999 walk	2600-2899 walk	7400-7999 walk	5200-5699 walk
Flutter	Sled	Swelling	Banner	Wolf
7400-7999 star	2600-2899 star	4300-4799 star	5200-5699 star	8600-8999 star
Tuba	Nail	Stand	Walker	Sink
8600-8999 horse	4300-4799 horse	7400-7999 horse	5200-5699 horse	2600-2899 horse

1. 7400-7999 star
2. 4300-4799 star
3. Swelling
4. 4300-4799 walk
5. Flutter
6. 5200-5699 star
7. 8600-8999 walk
8. Wolf
9. 2600-2899 walk
10. Tuba
11. 2600-2899 star
12. Sled
13. Nail
14. 7400-7999 walk
15. Sink
16. 8600-8999 horse
17. 7400-7999 horse
18. Stand
19. Flutter
20. 8600-8999 star
21. Walker
22. 5200-5699 horse
23. 8600-8999 walk
24. Swelling
25. Banner
26. 2600-2899 horse
27. 2600-2899 star
28. Nail
29. 2600-2899 horse
30. 8600-8999 star
31. 7400-7999 star
32. 5200-5699 walk
33. 7400-7999 horse
34. Tuba
35. 8600-8999 horse
36. Sink
37. Sled
38. 5200-5699 horse
39. 4300-4799 horse
40. 4300-4799 walk
41. 8600-8999 star
42. Banner
43. 5200-5699 walk
44. 7400-7999 walk
45. Swelling
46. 4300-4799 horse
47. Tuba
48. 4300-4799 star
49. 2600-2899 walk
50. Banner

CORRECT ANSWERS—CLERICAL SKILLS REVIEW

RECORD KEEPING

1. **The correct answer is (D).** If you add each of the number of applicants in both test centers for each test, you will find that there are 25 applicants for the Typing test. Verbal is the highest with 50, Mathematics has 40, and Reading has 35.
2. **The correct answer is (A).** Again, if you add them across, you'll find that Verbal and Mathematics had the highest number of applicants.
3. **The correct answer is (B).** To find the answer, divide the total number of tests taken (70) by the number of subjects (4). 70 ÷ 4 = 17.5
4. **The correct answer is (B).** The highest price of the companies listed in the answer choices is Microsoft at $115.00. Although IBM had the highest price of the companies on the chart, the company was not included in the choices.
5. **The correct answer is (B).** The greatest difference was $7.59. Make sure you read the question carefully and answer only what is being asked.
6. **The correct answer is (D).** Only BellSouth had a profit. All of the other companies showed a loss.
7. **The correct answer is (A).** The price difference between the close of business on 2/21 from the 52 week high was $56.31. Although Microsoft had a difference of $58.75, it was not one of the answer choices. To find the difference, subtract the latest price given from the 52 week high.
8. **The correct answer is (C).** Of the four choices given, IBM had the smallest difference in price—$27.43.

COMPARISONS

1. **The correct answer is (B).** The third number reverses 998 to 989.
2. **The correct answer is (A).** All three names are exactly alike.
3. **The correct answer is (E).** The surname of each is spelled differently, the first with "ff" and one "s"; the second with one "f" and one "s" and the last with one "f" and "ss".
4. **The correct answer is (C).** The surname ends in "sen" in the first and third, and "son" in the second.
5. **The correct answer is (B).** Yardley ends in "ley" in the first two choices and "lay" in the last one.
6. **The correct answer is (B).** "Heasherly" is the same in the first two choices, but is spelled "Heatherly" in the third choice.
7. **The correct answer is (A).** All three names are exactly alike.
8. **The correct answer is (C).** The middle number is missing the number "1." The first and third choices contain four "1"s, and the middle only three.
9. **The correct answer is (C).** Stewart ends in "ert" in the middle choice. The first and third choices end in "art."
10. **The correct answer is (B).** The third choice is missing "ian" toward the end of the word.

ALPHABETIZATION

1. **The correct answer is (E).** Lombardi, Joseph, R.; Lombardi, L.
2. **The correct answer is (E).** Mann, Peter; Mannen, Philip; Manners, Robert
3. **The correct answer is (A).** Kuzniarski, John; Kvasnak, Martin
4. **The correct answer is (C).** Sessa, Alicya; Sessler, William; Sessler, Wilson
5. **The correct answer is (D).**Wattley, Carrie; Watts, Juliana; Waugh, Julia
6. **The correct answer is (B).** DeMita, Allen; DeMoll, Allan; DeMond, Albert
7. **The correct answer is (C).** Wong, Chuen; Wong, Francesca; Wong, Fun
8. **The correct answer is (C).** Zamore, Peter; Zandri, Peter; Zandri, Peter and Lynn
9. **The correct answer is (B).** Rosa, Gary; Rose, Brad; Rosen, Ellis
10. **The correct answer is (C).** Ridgefield Car Wash; Ridgefield Center for Counseling; Ridgefield Chamber of Commerce

ADDRESS CHECKING

1. **The correct answer is (D).** 12224 and 1224
2. **The correct answer is (A).** Both are exactly alike.
3. **The correct answer is (D).** The second choice has an extra "4."
4. **The correct answer is (D).** 216th Street and 215th Street
5. **The correct answer is (D).** The ZIP code in the second reverses the numbers 51 to 15.
6. **The correct answer is (D).** Westmorland and Westmoreland.
7. **The correct answer is (A).** Both are exactly alike.
8. **The correct answer is (D).** Hawleyville versus Haleyville. The second choice is missing the "w."
9. **The correct answer is (D).** The first word is different: Deer versus Dear.
10. **The correct answer is (D).** The ZIP codes are different: 10534 and 15034
11. **The correct answer is (D).** Tucson is spelled differently in the second choice. The letters "cs" are reversed in the second choice.
12. **The correct answer is (D).** Woodley versus Wooley. The second choice is missing the letter "d."
13. **The correct answer is (D).** ZIP code numbers are reversed: 871 versus 817.
14. **The correct answer is (D).** Corneliuous and Cornelius.
15. **The correct answer is (A).** Both are exactly alike.
16. **The correct answer is (D).** Bensen is spelled differently: Benson and Bensen.
17. **The correct answer is (D).** In the second column, "Hatterstown" has an "s" that is missing in the first column.
18. **The correct answer is (D).** The address is the first column is Taligan Rd. and in the second is Taligan Dr.
19. **The correct answer is (D).** The numerical address is different in each choice. The last two digits are reversed: 8510 and 8501.
20. **The correct answer is (A).** Both are exactly alike.

MEMORY FOR ADDRESSES

PRACTICE 1

1. **The correct answer is (C).**
2. **The correct answer is (E).**
3. **The correct answer is (A).**
4. **The correct answer is (A).**
5. **The correct answer is (B).**
6. **The correct answer is (E).**
7. **The correct answer is (D).**
8. **The correct answer is (E).**
9. **The correct answer is (B).**
10. **The correct answer is (A).**
11. **The correct answer is (D).**
12. **The correct answer is (C).**
13. **The correct answer is (C).**
14. **The correct answer is (B).**
15. **The correct answer is (D).**
16. **The correct answer is (B).**
17. **The correct answer is (E).**
18. **The correct answer is (E).**
19. **The correct answer is (D).**
20. **The correct answer is (D).**
21. **The correct answer is (D).**
22. **The correct answer is (B).**
23. **The correct answer is (A).**
24. **The correct answer is (C).**
25. **The correct answer is (C).**
26. **The correct answer is (C).**

27. The correct answer is (E).
28. The correct answer is (E).
29. The correct answer is (A).
30. The correct answer is (B).

PRACTICE 2

1. The correct answer is (A).
2. The correct answer is (C).
3. The correct answer is (C).
4. The correct answer is (A).
5. The correct answer is (A).
6. The correct answer is (D).
7. The correct answer is (B).
8. The correct answer is (E).
9. The correct answer is (C).
10. The correct answer is (A).
11. The correct answer is (B).
12. The correct answer is (B).
13. The correct answer is (B).
14. The correct answer is (D).
15. The correct answer is (E).
16. The correct answer is (A).
17. The correct answer is (C).
18. The correct answer is (C).
19. The correct answer is (A).
20. The correct answer is (E).
21. The correct answer is (D).
22. The correct answer is (D).
23. The correct answer is (B).
24. The correct answer is (C).
25. The correct answer is (D).
26. The correct answer is (E).
27. The correct answer is (B).
28. The correct answer is (B).
29. The correct answer is (E).
30. The correct answer is (E).
31. The correct answer is (A).
32. The correct answer is (E).
33. The correct answer is (C).
34. The correct answer is (A).
35. The correct answer is (A).
36. The correct answer is (E).
37. The correct answer is (B).
38. The correct answer is (D).
39. The correct answer is (B).
40. The correct answer is (A).
41. The correct answer is (E).
42. The correct answer is (D).
43. The correct answer is (E).
44. The correct answer is (D).
45. The correct answer is (C).
46. The correct answer is (B).
47. The correct answer is (A).
48. The correct answer is (C).
49. The correct answer is (C).
50. The correct answer is (D).

PART FOUR

Official Sample Exams

ANSWER SHEET

FEDERAL CLERICAL EXAMINATION

VERBAL TASKS TEST

1. Ⓐ Ⓑ Ⓒ Ⓓ Ⓔ	23. Ⓐ Ⓑ Ⓒ Ⓓ Ⓔ	44. Ⓐ Ⓑ Ⓒ Ⓓ Ⓔ	65. Ⓐ Ⓑ Ⓒ Ⓓ Ⓔ
2. Ⓐ Ⓑ Ⓒ Ⓓ Ⓔ	24. Ⓐ Ⓑ Ⓒ Ⓓ Ⓔ	45. Ⓐ Ⓑ Ⓒ Ⓓ Ⓔ	66. Ⓐ Ⓑ Ⓒ Ⓓ Ⓔ
3. Ⓐ Ⓑ Ⓒ Ⓓ Ⓔ	25. Ⓐ Ⓑ Ⓒ Ⓓ Ⓔ	46. Ⓐ Ⓑ Ⓒ Ⓓ Ⓔ	67. Ⓐ Ⓑ Ⓒ Ⓓ Ⓔ
4. Ⓐ Ⓑ Ⓒ Ⓓ Ⓔ	26. Ⓐ Ⓑ Ⓒ Ⓓ Ⓔ	47. Ⓐ Ⓑ Ⓒ Ⓓ Ⓔ	68. Ⓐ Ⓑ Ⓒ Ⓓ Ⓔ
5. Ⓐ Ⓑ Ⓒ Ⓓ Ⓔ	27. Ⓐ Ⓑ Ⓒ Ⓓ Ⓔ	48. Ⓐ Ⓑ Ⓒ Ⓓ Ⓔ	69. Ⓐ Ⓑ Ⓒ Ⓓ Ⓔ
6. Ⓐ Ⓑ Ⓒ Ⓓ Ⓔ	28. Ⓐ Ⓑ Ⓒ Ⓓ Ⓔ	49. Ⓐ Ⓑ Ⓒ Ⓓ Ⓔ	70. Ⓐ Ⓑ Ⓒ Ⓓ Ⓔ
7. Ⓐ Ⓑ Ⓒ Ⓓ Ⓔ	29. Ⓐ Ⓑ Ⓒ Ⓓ Ⓔ	50. Ⓐ Ⓑ Ⓒ Ⓓ Ⓔ	71. Ⓐ Ⓑ Ⓒ Ⓓ Ⓔ
8. Ⓐ Ⓑ Ⓒ Ⓓ Ⓔ	30. Ⓐ Ⓑ Ⓒ Ⓓ Ⓔ	51. Ⓐ Ⓑ Ⓒ Ⓓ Ⓔ	72. Ⓐ Ⓑ Ⓒ Ⓓ Ⓔ
9. Ⓐ Ⓑ Ⓒ Ⓓ Ⓔ	31. Ⓐ Ⓑ Ⓒ Ⓓ Ⓔ	52. Ⓐ Ⓑ Ⓒ Ⓓ Ⓔ	73. Ⓐ Ⓑ Ⓒ Ⓓ Ⓔ
10. Ⓐ Ⓑ Ⓒ Ⓓ Ⓔ	32. Ⓐ Ⓑ Ⓒ Ⓓ Ⓔ	53. Ⓐ Ⓑ Ⓒ Ⓓ Ⓔ	74. Ⓐ Ⓑ Ⓒ Ⓓ Ⓔ
11. Ⓐ Ⓑ Ⓒ Ⓓ Ⓔ	33. Ⓐ Ⓑ Ⓒ Ⓓ Ⓔ	54. Ⓐ Ⓑ Ⓒ Ⓓ Ⓔ	75. Ⓐ Ⓑ Ⓒ Ⓓ Ⓔ
12. Ⓐ Ⓑ Ⓒ Ⓓ Ⓔ	34. Ⓐ Ⓑ Ⓒ Ⓓ Ⓔ	55. Ⓐ Ⓑ Ⓒ Ⓓ Ⓔ	76. Ⓐ Ⓑ Ⓒ Ⓓ Ⓔ
13. Ⓐ Ⓑ Ⓒ Ⓓ Ⓔ	35. Ⓐ Ⓑ Ⓒ Ⓓ Ⓔ	56. Ⓐ Ⓑ Ⓒ Ⓓ Ⓔ	77. Ⓐ Ⓑ Ⓒ Ⓓ Ⓔ
14. Ⓐ Ⓑ Ⓒ Ⓓ Ⓔ	36. Ⓐ Ⓑ Ⓒ Ⓓ Ⓔ	57. Ⓐ Ⓑ Ⓒ Ⓓ Ⓔ	78. Ⓐ Ⓑ Ⓒ Ⓓ Ⓔ
15. Ⓐ Ⓑ Ⓒ Ⓓ Ⓔ	37. Ⓐ Ⓑ Ⓒ Ⓓ Ⓔ	58. Ⓐ Ⓑ Ⓒ Ⓓ Ⓔ	79. Ⓐ Ⓑ Ⓒ Ⓓ Ⓔ
16. Ⓐ Ⓑ Ⓒ Ⓓ Ⓔ	38. Ⓐ Ⓑ Ⓒ Ⓓ Ⓔ	59. Ⓐ Ⓑ Ⓒ Ⓓ Ⓔ	80. Ⓐ Ⓑ Ⓒ Ⓓ Ⓔ
17. Ⓐ Ⓑ Ⓒ Ⓓ Ⓔ	39. Ⓐ Ⓑ Ⓒ Ⓓ Ⓔ	60. Ⓐ Ⓑ Ⓒ Ⓓ Ⓔ	81. Ⓐ Ⓑ Ⓒ Ⓓ Ⓔ
18. Ⓐ Ⓑ Ⓒ Ⓓ Ⓔ	40. Ⓐ Ⓑ Ⓒ Ⓓ Ⓔ	61. Ⓐ Ⓑ Ⓒ Ⓓ Ⓔ	82. Ⓐ Ⓑ Ⓒ Ⓓ Ⓔ
19. Ⓐ Ⓑ Ⓒ Ⓓ Ⓔ	41. Ⓐ Ⓑ Ⓒ Ⓓ Ⓔ	62. Ⓐ Ⓑ Ⓒ Ⓓ Ⓔ	83. Ⓐ Ⓑ Ⓒ Ⓓ Ⓔ
20. Ⓐ Ⓑ Ⓒ Ⓓ Ⓔ	42. Ⓐ Ⓑ Ⓒ Ⓓ Ⓔ	63. Ⓐ Ⓑ Ⓒ Ⓓ Ⓔ	84. Ⓐ Ⓑ Ⓒ Ⓓ Ⓔ
21. Ⓐ Ⓑ Ⓒ Ⓓ Ⓔ	43. Ⓐ Ⓑ Ⓒ Ⓓ Ⓔ	64. Ⓐ Ⓑ Ⓒ Ⓓ Ⓔ	85. Ⓐ Ⓑ Ⓒ Ⓓ Ⓔ
22. Ⓐ Ⓑ Ⓒ Ⓓ Ⓔ			

The total raw score on this test consists of the total number of questions that are answered correctly. There is no penalty for wrong answers or correction made for guessing. However, no credit is given for any question with more than one answer marked.

My raw score ______________

ANSWER SHEET

CLERICAL TASKS TEST

1. Ⓐ Ⓑ Ⓒ Ⓓ Ⓔ	31. Ⓐ Ⓑ Ⓒ Ⓓ Ⓔ	61. Ⓐ Ⓑ Ⓒ Ⓓ Ⓔ	91. Ⓐ Ⓑ Ⓒ Ⓓ Ⓔ
2. Ⓐ Ⓑ Ⓒ Ⓓ Ⓔ	32. Ⓐ Ⓑ Ⓒ Ⓓ Ⓔ	62. Ⓐ Ⓑ Ⓒ Ⓓ Ⓔ	92. Ⓐ Ⓑ Ⓒ Ⓓ Ⓔ
3. Ⓐ Ⓑ Ⓒ Ⓓ Ⓔ	33. Ⓐ Ⓑ Ⓒ Ⓓ Ⓔ	63. Ⓐ Ⓑ Ⓒ Ⓓ Ⓔ	93. Ⓐ Ⓑ Ⓒ Ⓓ Ⓔ
4. Ⓐ Ⓑ Ⓒ Ⓓ Ⓔ	34. Ⓐ Ⓑ Ⓒ Ⓓ Ⓔ	64. Ⓐ Ⓑ Ⓒ Ⓓ Ⓔ	94. Ⓐ Ⓑ Ⓒ Ⓓ Ⓔ
5. Ⓐ Ⓑ Ⓒ Ⓓ Ⓔ	35. Ⓐ Ⓑ Ⓒ Ⓓ Ⓔ	65. Ⓐ Ⓑ Ⓒ Ⓓ Ⓔ	95. Ⓐ Ⓑ Ⓒ Ⓓ Ⓔ
6. Ⓐ Ⓑ Ⓒ Ⓓ Ⓔ	36. Ⓐ Ⓑ Ⓒ Ⓓ Ⓔ	66. Ⓐ Ⓑ Ⓒ Ⓓ Ⓔ	96. Ⓐ Ⓑ Ⓒ Ⓓ Ⓔ
7. Ⓐ Ⓑ Ⓒ Ⓓ Ⓔ	37. Ⓐ Ⓑ Ⓒ Ⓓ Ⓔ	67. Ⓐ Ⓑ Ⓒ Ⓓ Ⓔ	97. Ⓐ Ⓑ Ⓒ Ⓓ Ⓔ
8. Ⓐ Ⓑ Ⓒ Ⓓ Ⓔ	38. Ⓐ Ⓑ Ⓒ Ⓓ Ⓔ	68. Ⓐ Ⓑ Ⓒ Ⓓ Ⓔ	98. Ⓐ Ⓑ Ⓒ Ⓓ Ⓔ
9. Ⓐ Ⓑ Ⓒ Ⓓ Ⓔ	39. Ⓐ Ⓑ Ⓒ Ⓓ Ⓔ	69. Ⓐ Ⓑ Ⓒ Ⓓ Ⓔ	99. Ⓐ Ⓑ Ⓒ Ⓓ Ⓔ
10. Ⓐ Ⓑ Ⓒ Ⓓ Ⓔ	40. Ⓐ Ⓑ Ⓒ Ⓓ Ⓔ	70. Ⓐ Ⓑ Ⓒ Ⓓ Ⓔ	100. Ⓐ Ⓑ Ⓒ Ⓓ Ⓔ
11. Ⓐ Ⓑ Ⓒ Ⓓ Ⓔ	41. Ⓐ Ⓑ Ⓒ Ⓓ Ⓔ	71. Ⓐ Ⓑ Ⓒ Ⓓ Ⓔ	101. Ⓐ Ⓑ Ⓒ Ⓓ Ⓔ
12. Ⓐ Ⓑ Ⓒ Ⓓ Ⓔ	42. Ⓐ Ⓑ Ⓒ Ⓓ Ⓔ	72. Ⓐ Ⓑ Ⓒ Ⓓ Ⓔ	102. Ⓐ Ⓑ Ⓒ Ⓓ Ⓔ
13. Ⓐ Ⓑ Ⓒ Ⓓ Ⓔ	43. Ⓐ Ⓑ Ⓒ Ⓓ Ⓔ	73. Ⓐ Ⓑ Ⓒ Ⓓ Ⓔ	103. Ⓐ Ⓑ Ⓒ Ⓓ Ⓔ
14. Ⓐ Ⓑ Ⓒ Ⓓ Ⓔ	44. Ⓐ Ⓑ Ⓒ Ⓓ Ⓔ	74. Ⓐ Ⓑ Ⓒ Ⓓ Ⓔ	104. Ⓐ Ⓑ Ⓒ Ⓓ Ⓔ
15. Ⓐ Ⓑ Ⓒ Ⓓ Ⓔ	45. Ⓐ Ⓑ Ⓒ Ⓓ Ⓔ	75. Ⓐ Ⓑ Ⓒ Ⓓ Ⓔ	105. Ⓐ Ⓑ Ⓒ Ⓓ Ⓔ
16. Ⓐ Ⓑ Ⓒ Ⓓ Ⓔ	46. Ⓐ Ⓑ Ⓒ Ⓓ Ⓔ	76. Ⓐ Ⓑ Ⓒ Ⓓ Ⓔ	106. Ⓐ Ⓑ Ⓒ Ⓓ Ⓔ
17. Ⓐ Ⓑ Ⓒ Ⓓ Ⓔ	47. Ⓐ Ⓑ Ⓒ Ⓓ Ⓔ	77. Ⓐ Ⓑ Ⓒ Ⓓ Ⓔ	107. Ⓐ Ⓑ Ⓒ Ⓓ Ⓔ
18. Ⓐ Ⓑ Ⓒ Ⓓ Ⓔ	48. Ⓐ Ⓑ Ⓒ Ⓓ Ⓔ	78. Ⓐ Ⓑ Ⓒ Ⓓ Ⓔ	108. Ⓐ Ⓑ Ⓒ Ⓓ Ⓔ
19. Ⓐ Ⓑ Ⓒ Ⓓ Ⓔ	49. Ⓐ Ⓑ Ⓒ Ⓓ Ⓔ	79. Ⓐ Ⓑ Ⓒ Ⓓ Ⓔ	109. Ⓐ Ⓑ Ⓒ Ⓓ Ⓔ
20. Ⓐ Ⓑ Ⓒ Ⓓ Ⓔ	50. Ⓐ Ⓑ Ⓒ Ⓓ Ⓔ	80. Ⓐ Ⓑ Ⓒ Ⓓ Ⓔ	110. Ⓐ Ⓑ Ⓒ Ⓓ Ⓔ
21. Ⓐ Ⓑ Ⓒ Ⓓ Ⓔ	51. Ⓐ Ⓑ Ⓒ Ⓓ Ⓔ	81. Ⓐ Ⓑ Ⓒ Ⓓ Ⓔ	111. Ⓐ Ⓑ Ⓒ Ⓓ Ⓔ
22. Ⓐ Ⓑ Ⓒ Ⓓ Ⓔ	52. Ⓐ Ⓑ Ⓒ Ⓓ Ⓔ	82. Ⓐ Ⓑ Ⓒ Ⓓ Ⓔ	112. Ⓐ Ⓑ Ⓒ Ⓓ Ⓔ
23. Ⓐ Ⓑ Ⓒ Ⓓ Ⓔ	53. Ⓐ Ⓑ Ⓒ Ⓓ Ⓔ	83. Ⓐ Ⓑ Ⓒ Ⓓ Ⓔ	113. Ⓐ Ⓑ Ⓒ Ⓓ Ⓔ
24. Ⓐ Ⓑ Ⓒ Ⓓ Ⓔ	54. Ⓐ Ⓑ Ⓒ Ⓓ Ⓔ	84. Ⓐ Ⓑ Ⓒ Ⓓ Ⓔ	114. Ⓐ Ⓑ Ⓒ Ⓓ Ⓔ
25. Ⓐ Ⓑ Ⓒ Ⓓ Ⓔ	55. Ⓐ Ⓑ Ⓒ Ⓓ Ⓔ	85. Ⓐ Ⓑ Ⓒ Ⓓ Ⓔ	115. Ⓐ Ⓑ Ⓒ Ⓓ Ⓔ
26. Ⓐ Ⓑ Ⓒ Ⓓ Ⓔ	56. Ⓐ Ⓑ Ⓒ Ⓓ Ⓔ	86. Ⓐ Ⓑ Ⓒ Ⓓ Ⓔ	116. Ⓐ Ⓑ Ⓒ Ⓓ Ⓔ
27. Ⓐ Ⓑ Ⓒ Ⓓ Ⓔ	57. Ⓐ Ⓑ Ⓒ Ⓓ Ⓔ	87. Ⓐ Ⓑ Ⓒ Ⓓ Ⓔ	117. Ⓐ Ⓑ Ⓒ Ⓓ Ⓔ
28. Ⓐ Ⓑ Ⓒ Ⓓ Ⓔ	58. Ⓐ Ⓑ Ⓒ Ⓓ Ⓔ	89. Ⓐ Ⓑ Ⓒ Ⓓ Ⓔ	118. Ⓐ Ⓑ Ⓒ Ⓓ Ⓔ
29. Ⓐ Ⓑ Ⓒ Ⓓ Ⓔ	59. Ⓐ Ⓑ Ⓒ Ⓓ Ⓔ	90. Ⓐ Ⓑ Ⓒ Ⓓ Ⓔ	119. Ⓐ Ⓑ Ⓒ Ⓓ Ⓔ
30. Ⓐ Ⓑ Ⓒ Ⓓ Ⓔ	60. Ⓐ Ⓑ Ⓒ Ⓓ Ⓔ		120. Ⓐ Ⓑ Ⓒ Ⓓ Ⓔ

On this test there is a penalty for wrong answers. The total raw score on the test is the number of right answers minus one-fourth of the number of wrong answers. (Fractions of one-half or less are dropped.) First count the number of correct answers you have made. Do not count as correct any questions with more than one answer marked. Then count the number of incorrect answers. Omits are not counted as wrong answers, but double responses do count as wrong. Multiply the total number of incorrect answers by one-fourth. Subtract this number from the total number correct to get the test total score. For example, if you were to answer 89 questions correctly and 10 questions incorrectly, and you omitted 21 questions, your total score would be 87 (89 minus one-fourth of 10 equals 87).

89 questions correct, 10 questions incorrect

89
− 3 (10 ÷ 4 = 2.5 = 3)
87 Raw Score

Number Right	minus	Number Wrong	equals	Raw Score
____________	−	(____ ÷ 4)	=	____________

FEDERAL CLERICAL EXAMINATION

VERBAL TASKS TEST

Time: 35 Minutes—85 Questions

Directions: Read each question carefully. Select the best answer and darken the answer space of your choice on the answer sheet. Answers and Explanations are on page 150.

1. *Flexible* means most nearly

(A) breakable
(B) flammable
(C) pliable
(D) weak

2. *Option* means most nearly

(A) use
(B) choice
(C) value
(D) blame

3. To verify means most nearly to

(A) examine
(B) explain
(C) confirm
(D) guarantee

4. *Indolent* means most nearly

(A) moderate
(B) hopeless
(C) selfish
(D) lazy

5. *Respiration* means most nearly

(A) recovery
(B) breathing
(C) pulsation
(D) sweating

6. PLUMBER is related to WRENCH as PAINTER is related to

(A) brush
(B) pipe
(C) shop
(D) hammer

7. LETTER is related to MESSAGE as PACKAGE is related to

(A) sender
(B) merchandise
(C) insurance
(D) business

8. FOOD is related to HUNGER as SLEEP is related to
   (A) night
   (B) dream
   (C) weariness
   (D) rest

9. KEY is related to TYPEWRITER as DIAL is related to
   (A) sun
   (B) number
   (C) circle
   (D) telephone

10. (A) I think that they will promote whoever has the best record.
    (B) The firm would have liked to have promoted all employees with good records.
    (C) Such of them that have the best records have excellent prospects of promotion.
    (D) I feel sure they will give the promotion to whomever has the best record.

11. (A) The receptionist must answer courteously the questions of all them callers.
    (B) The receptionist must answer courteously the question what are asked by the callers.
    (C) There would have been no trouble if the receptionist had have always answered courteously.
    (D) The receptionist should answer courteously the questions of all callers.

12. (A) collapsible
    (B) collapseable
    (C) collapseble
    (D) none of these

13. (A) ambigeuous
    (B) ambigeous
    (C) ambiguous
    (D) none of these

14. (A) predesessor
    (B) predecesar
    (C) predecesser
    (D) none of these

15. (A) sanctioned
    (B) sancktioned
    (C) sanctionned
    (D) none of these

16. "Some fire-resistant buildings, although wholly constructed of materials that will not burn, may be completely gutted by the spread of fire through their contents by way of hallways and other openings. They may even suffer serious structural damage by the collapse of metal beams and columns."

    The quotation best supports the statement that some fire-resistant buildings
    (A) can be damaged seriously by fire.
    (B) have specially constructed halls and doors.
    (C) afford less protection to their contents than would ordinary buildings.
    (D) will burn readily.

17. Civilization started to move ahead more rapidly when people freed themselves of the shackles that restricted their search for the truth.

The paragraph best supports the statement that the progress of civilization

(A) came as a result of people's dislike for obstacles
(B) did not begin until restrictions on learning were removed
(C) has been aided by people's efforts to find the truth
(D) is based on continually increasing efforts

18. *Vigilant* means most nearly

(A) sensible
(B) watchful
(C) suspicious
(D) restless

19. *Incidental* means most nearly

(A) independent
(B) needless
(C) infrequent
(D) casual

20. *Conciliatory* means most nearly

(A) pacific
(B) contentious
(C) obligatory
(D) offensive

21. *Altercation* means most nearly

(A) defeat
(B) concurrence
(C) controversy
(D) vexation

22. *Irresolute* means most nearly

(A) wavering
(B) insubordinate
(C) impudent
(D) unobservant

23. DARKNESS is related to SUNLIGHT as STILLNESS is related to

(A) quiet
(B) moonlight
(C) sound
(D) dark

24. DESIGNED is related to INTENTION as ACCIDENTAL is related to

(A) purpose
(B) caution
(C) damage
(D) chance

25. ERROR is related to PRACTICE as SOUND is related to
(A) deafness
(B) noise
(C) muffler
(D) horn

26. RESEARCH is related to FINDINGS as TRAINING is related to
(A) skill
(B) tests
(C) supervision
(D) teaching

27. (A) If properly addressed, the letter will reach my mother and I.
(B) The letter had been addressed to myself and my mother.
(C) I believe the letter was addressed to either my mother or 1.
(D) My mother's name, as well as mine, was on the letter.

28. (A) The supervisors reprimanded the typists, whom she believed I had made careless errors.
(B) The typists would have corrected the errors had they of known that the supervisor would see the report.
(C) The errors in the typed reports were so numerous that they could hardly be overlooked.
(D) Many errors were found in the reports which they typed and could not disregard them.

29. (A) minieture
(B) minneature
(C) mineature
(D) none of these

30. (A) extemporaneous
(B) extempuraneus
(C) extemperaneous
(D) none of these

31. (A) problemmatical
(B) problematical
(C) problematicle
(D) none of these

32. (A) descendant
(B) decendant
(C) desendant
(D) none of these

33. The likelihood of America's exhausting its natural resources seems to be growing less. All kinds of waste are being reworked and new uses are constantly being found for almost everything. We are getting more use out of our goods and are making many new byproducts out of what was formerly thrown away.

The paragraph best supports the statement that we seem to be in less danger of exhausting our resources because
(A) economy is found to lie in the use of substitutes.
(B) more service is obtained from a given amount of material.
(C) we are allowing time for nature to restore them.
(D) supply and demand are better controlled.

34. Telegrams should be clear, concise, and brief. Omit all unnecessary words. The parts of speech most often used in telegrams are nouns, verbs, adjectives, and adverbs. If possible, do without pronouns, prepositions, articles, and copulative verbs. Use simple sentences, rather than complex or compound ones.

The paragraph best supports the statement that in writing telegrams one should always use

(A) common and simple words.
(B) only nouns, verbs, adjectives, and adverbs.
(C) incomplete sentences.
(D) only the words essential to the meaning.

35. To *counteract* means most nearly to

(A) undermine
(B) censure
(C) preserve
(D) neutralize

36. *Deferred* means most nearly

(A) reversed
(B) delayed
(C) considered
(D) forbidden

37. *Feasible* means most nearly

(A) capable
(B) justifiable
(C) practicable
(D) beneficial

38. To *encounter* means most nearly to

(A) meet(C) overcome
(B) recall
(D) retreat

39. *Innate* means most nearly

(A) eternal
(B) well-developed
(C) native
(D) prospective

40. STUDENT is related to TEACHER as DISCIPLE is related to

(A) follower
(B) master
(C) principal
(D) pupil

41. LECTURE is related to AUDITORIUM as EXPERIMENT is related to

(A) scientist (B) chemistry
(C) laboratory
(D) discovery

42. BODY is related to FOOD as ENGINE is related to

(A) wheels
(B) fuel
(C) motion
(D) smoke

43. SCHOOL is related to EDUCATION as THEATER is related to

(A) management
(B) stage
(C) recreation
(D) preparation

44. (A) Most all these statements have been supported by persons who are reliable and can be depended upon.
(B) The persons which have guaranteed these statements are reliable.
(C) Reliable persons guarantee the facts with regards to the truth of these statements.
(D) These statements can be depended on, for their truth has been guaranteed by reliable persons.

45. (A) The success of the book pleased both the publisher and authors.
(B) Both the publisher and they was pleased with the success of the book.
(C) Neither they or their publisher was disappointed with the success of the book.
(D) Their publisher was as pleased as they with the success of the book.

46. (A) extercate
(B) extracate
(C) extricate
(D) none of these

47. (A) hereditory
(B) hereditary
(C) hereditairy
(D) none of these

48. (A) auspiceous
(B) auspiseous
(C) auspicious
(D) none of these

49. (A) sequance
(B) sequence
(C) sequense
(D) none of these

50. The prevention of accidents makes it necessary not only that safety devices be used to guard exposed machinery but also that mechanics be instructed in safety rules which they must follow for their own protection, and that the lighting in the plant be adequate.

The paragraph best supports the statement that industrial accidents

(A) may be due to ignorance.
(B) are always avoidable.
(C) usually result from inadequate machinery.
(D) cannot be entirely overcome.

51. The English language is peculiarly rich in synonyms, and there is scarcely a language spoken that has not some representative in English speech. The spirit of the AngloSaxon race has subjugated these various elements to one idiom, making not a patch-work, but a composite language.

The paragraph best supports the statement that the English language

(A) has few idiomatic expressions.
(B) is difficult to translate.
(C) is used universally.
(D) has absorbed words from other languages.

52. *To acquiesce* means most nearly to

(A) assent
(B) acquire
(C) complete
(D) participate

53. *Unanimity* means most nearly

(A) emphasis
(B) namelessness
(C) harmony
(D) impartiality

54. *Precedent* means most nearly

(A) example
(B) theory
(C) law
(D) conformity

55. *Versatile* means most nearly

(A) broad-minded
(B) well-known
(C) up-to-date
(D) many-sided

56. *Authentic* means most nearly

(A) detailed
(B) reliable
(C) valuable
(D) practical

57. BIOGRAPHY is related to FACT as NOVEL is related to

(A) fiction
(B) literature
(C) narration
(D) book

58. COPY is related to CARBON PAPER as MOTION PICTURE is related to

(A) theater
(B) film
(C) duplicate
(D) television

59. EFFICIENCY is related to REWARD as CARELESSNESS is related to

(A) improvement
(B) disobedience
(C) reprimand
(D) repetition

60. ABUNDANT is related to CHEAP as SCARCE is related to

(A) ample
(B) costly
(C) inexpensive
(D) unobtainable

61. (A) Brown's & Company employees have recently received increases in salary.
(B) Brown & Company recently increased the salaries of all its employees.
(C) Recently Brown & Company has increased their employees' salaries.
(D) Brown & Company have recently increased the salaries of all its employees.

62. (A) In reviewing the typists' work reports, the job analyst found records of unusual typing speeds.
(B) It says in the job analyst's report that some employees type with great speed.
(C) The job analyst found that, in reviewing the typists' work reports, that some unusual typing speeds had been made.
(D) In the reports of typists' speeds, the job analyst found some records that are kind of unusual.

63. (A) oblitorate
(B) oblitterat
(C) obbliterate
(D) none of these

64. (A) diagnoesis
(B) diagnossis
(C) diagnosis
(D) none of these

65. (A) contenance
(B) countenance
(C) countinance
(D) none of these

66. (A) conceivably
(B) concieveably
(C) conceiveably
(D) none of these

67. Through advertising, manufacturers exercise a high degree of control over consumers' desires. However, the manufacturer assumes enormous risks in attempting to predict what consumers will want and in producing goods in quantity and distributing them in advance of final selection by the consumers.

The paragraph best supports the statement that manufacturers

(A) can eliminate the risk of overproduction by advertising.
(B) distribute goods directly to the consumers.
(C) must depend upon the final consumers for the success of their undertakings.
(D) can predict with great accuracy the success of any product they put on the market.

68. In the relations of humans to nature, the procuring of food and shelter is fundamental. With the migration of humans to various climates, ever new adjustments to the food supply and to the climate became necessary.

The paragraph best supports the statement that the means by which humans supply their material needs are

(A) accidental.
(B) varied.
(C) limited.
(D) inadequate.

69. *Strident* means most nearly

(A) swaggering
(B) domineering
(C) angry
(D) harsh

70. To *confine* means most nearly to

(A) hide
(B) restrict
(C) eliminate
(D) punish

71. To *accentuate* means most nearly to

(A) modify
(B) hasten
(C) sustain
(D) intensify

72. *Banal* means most nearly

(A) commonplace
(B) tranquil
(C) tranquil
(D) indifferent

73. *Incorrigible* means most nearly

(A) intolerable
(B) retarded
(C) irreformable
(D) brazen

74. POLICEMAN is related to ORDER as DOCTOR is related to

(A) physician
(B) hospital
(C) sickness
(D) health

75. ARTIST is related to EASEL as WEAVER is related to

(A) loom
(B) cloth
(C) threads
(D) spinner

76. CROWD is related to PERSONS as FLEET is related to
(A) expedition
(B) officers
(C) navy
(D) ships

77. CALENDAR is related to DATE as MAP is related to
(A) geography
(B) trip
(C) mileage
(D) vacation

78. (A) Since the report lacked the needed information, it was of no use to them.
(B) This report was useless to them because there were no needed information in the shortest time.
(C) Since the report did not contain the needed information, it was not real useful to them.
(D) Being that the report lacked the needed information, they could not use it.

79. (A) The company had hardly declared the dividend till the notices were prepared for mailing.
(B) They had no sooner declared the dividend when they sent the notices to the stockholders.
(C) No sooner had the dividend been declared than the notices were prepared for mailing.
(D) Scarcely had the dividend been declared than the notices were sent out.

80. (A) compitition
(B) competition
(C) competetion
(D) none of these

81. (A) occassion
(B) occasion
(C) ocassion
(D) none of these

82. (A) knowlege
(B) knolledge
(C) knowledge
(D) none of these

83. (A) deliborate
(B) deliberate
(C) delibrate
(D) none of these

84. What constitutes skill in any line of work is not always easy to determine; economy of time must be carefully distinguished from economy of energy as the quickest method may require the greatest expenditure of muscular effort, and may not be essential or at all desirable.

The paragraph best supports the statement that

(A) the most efficiently executed task is not always the one done in the shortest time.
(B) energy and time cannot both be conserved in performing a single task.
(C) a task is well done when it is performed in the shortest time.
(D) skill in performing a task should not be acquired at the expense of time.

85. It is difficult to distinguish between bookkeeping and accounting. In attempts to do so, bookkeeping is called the art, and accounting the science of recording business transactions. Bookkeeping gives the history of the business in a systematic manner; and accounting classifies, analyzes, and interprets the facts thus recorded.

The paragraph best supports the statement that

(A) accounting is less systematic than bookkeeping.
(B) accounting and bookkeeping are closely related.
(C) bookkeeping and accounting cannot be distinguished from one another.
(D) bookkeeping has been superseded by accounting.

END OF VERBAL TASKS TEST

If you finish before time is up, check your work on this part only. Do not turn to the next part until the signal is given.

CLERICAL TASKS TEST

Time: 15 Minutes—120 Questions

Answers and Explanations are on page 153.

In questions 1–5, compare the three names or numbers, and darken the answer space:

(A) if **ALL THREE** names or numbers are exactly **ALIKE**
(B) if only the **FIRST** and **SECOND** names or numbers are exactly **ALIKE**
(C) if only the **FIRST** and **THIRD** names or numbers are exactly **ALIKE**
(D) if only the **SECOND** and **THIRD** names or numbers are exactly **ALIKE**
(E) if **ALL THREE** names or numbers are **DIFFERENT**

1.	5261383	5261383	5261338
2.	8125690	8126690	8125609
3.	W. E. Johnston	W. E. Johnson	W. E. Johnson
4.	Vergil L. Muller	Vergil L. Muller	Vergil L. Muller
5.	Atherton R. Warde	Asheton R. Warde	Atherton P. Warde

In questions 6–10, find the correct place for the name in the box.

6. Hackett, Gerald

(A) →
Habert, James
(B) →
Hachett, J. J.
(C) →
Hachetts, K. Larson
(D) →
Hachettson, Leroy
(E) →

7. Margenroth, Alvin

(A) →
Margeroth, Albert
(B) →
Margestein, Dan
(C) →
Margestein, David
(D) →
Margue, Edgar
(E) →

8. Bobbitt, Olivier E

(A) →
Bobbitt, D. Olivier
(B) →
Bobbitt, Olive B.
(C) →
Bobbitt, Olivia H.
(D) →
Bobbitt, R. Olivia
(E) →

9. Mosely, Werner

(A) →
Mosely, Albert
(B) →
Mosley, Alvin
(C) →
Mosley, S. M.
(D) →
Mosley, Vinson, N.
(E) →

10. Youmuns, Frank L.

(A) →
Youmons, Frank G.
(B) →
Youmons, Frank H.
(C) →
Youmons, Frank K.
(D) →
Youmons, Frank M.
(E) →

11. Add: 43
+ 32

(A) 55
(B) 65
(C) 66
(D) 75
(E) none of these

12. Add: 43
+ 32

(A) 55
(B 65
(C 66
(D) 75
(E) none of these

12. Subtract: 83
− 4

(A) 73
(B) 79
(C) 80
(D) 89
(E) none of these

13. Multiply: 41
× 7

(A) 281
(B) 287
(C) 291
(D) 297
(E) none of these

14. Divide: 6)306

(A) 44
(B) 51
(C) 52
(D) 60
(E) none of these

15. Add: 37
+ 15

(A) 42
(B) 52
(C) 53
(D) 62
(E) none of these

For each question below, find which one of the suggested answers appears in that question.

16. 6 2 5 K 4 P T G	Suggested Answers	(A) = 4, 5, K, T
17. L 4 7 2 T 6 V K		(B) = 4, 7, G, K
18. 3 5 4 L 9 V T G		(C) = 2, 5, G, L
19. G 4 K 7 L 3 5 Z		(D) = 2, 7, L, T
20. 4 K 2 9 N 5 T G		(E) = none of these

In questions 21–25, compare the three names or numbers and darken the answer space:

(A) if **ALL THREE** names or numbers are exactly **ALIKE**
(B) if only the **FIRST** and **SECOND** names or numbers are exactly **ALIKE**
(C) if only the **FIRST** and **THIRD** names or numbers are exactly **ALIKE**
(D) if only the **SECOND** and **THIRD** names or numbers are exactly **ALIKE**
(E) if **ALL THREE** names or numbers are **DIFFERENT**

21.	2395890	2395890	2395890
22.	1926341	1926347	1926314
23.	E. Owens McVey	E. Owen McVey	E. Owen McVay
24.	Emily Neal Rouse	Emily Neal Rowse	Emily Neal Rowse
25.	H. Merritt Audubon	H. Merriott Audubon	H. Merritt Audubon

In questions 26–30, find the correct place for the name, in the box.

26. Watters, N. O.

(A) →
Waters, Charles L.
(B) →
Waterson, Nina R.
(C) →
Watson, Nora J.
(D) →
Wattwood, Paul A.
(E) →

27. Johnston, Edward

(A) →
Johnston, Edgar R.
(B) →
Johnston, Edmond
(C) →
Johnston, Edmund
(D) →
Johnstone, Edmund A.
(E) →

28. Rensch, Adeline

(A) →
Ramsay, Amos
(B) →
Remschel, Augusta
(C) →
Renshaw, Austin
(D) →
Rentzel, Becky
(E) →

29. Schnyder, Maurice

(A) →
Schneider, Martin
(B) →
Schneider, Mertens
(C) →
Schnyder, Newman
(D) →
Schreibner, Norman
(E) →

30. Freedenburg, C. Erma

(A) →
Freedenberg, Emerson
(B) →
Freedenberg, Erma
(C) →
Freedenberg, Erma E.
(D) →
Freedinberg, Erma F.
(E) →

31. Subtract: $68 - 47$

(A) 10
(B) 11
(C) 20
(D) 22
(E) none of these

32. Multiply: 50×8

(A) 400
(B) 408
(C) 450
(D) 458
(E) none of these

33. Divide: $9\overline{)180}$

(A) 20
(B) 29
(C) 30
(D) 39
(E) none of these

34. Add: $78 + 131$

(A) 131
(B) 140
(C) 141
(D) 151
(E) none of these

35. Subtract: $89 - 70$

(A) 9
(B) 18
(C) 19
(D) 29
(E) none of these

For each question below, find which one of the suggested answers appears in that question.

36. 9 G Z 3 L 4 6 N
37. L 5 N K 4 3 9 V
38. 8 2 V P 9 L Z 5
39. V P 9 Z 5 L 8 7
40. 5 T 8 N 2 9 V L

Suggested Answers
(A) = 4, 9, L, V
(B) = 4, 5, N, Z
(C) = 5, 8, L, Z
(D) = 8, 9, N, V
(E) = none of these

In questions 41–45, compare the three names or numbers, and darken the answer space:

(A) if **ALL THREE** names or numbers are exactly **ALIKE**
(B) if only the **FIRST** and **SECOND** names or numbers are exactly **ALIKE**
(C) if only the **FIRST** and **THIRD** names or numbers are exactly **ALIKE**
(D) if only the **SECOND** and **THIRD** names or numbers are exactly **ALIKE**
(E) if **ALL THREE** names or numbers are **DIFFERENT**

41.	6219354	6219354	6219354
42.	2312793	2312793	2312793
43.	1065407	1065407	1065047
44.	Francis Ransdell	Frances Ramsdell	Francis Ramsdell
45.	Cornelius Detwiler	Cornelius Detwiler	Cornelius Detwiler

In questions 46–50, find the correct place for the name in the box.

46. DeMattia, Jessica

(A) →
DeLong, Jesse
(B) →
DeMatteo, Jessie
(C) →
Derby, Jessie S.
(D) →
DeShazo, L. M.
(E) →

47. Theriault, Louis

(A) →
Therien,Annette
(B) →
Therien, Elaine
(C) →
Thibeault, Gerald
(D) →
Thiebeault, Pierre
(E) →

48. Gaston, M. Hubert

(A) →
Gaston, Dorothy M.
(B) →
Gaston, Henry N.
(C) →
Gaston, Isabel
(D) →
Gaston, M. Melvin
(E) →

49. SanMiguel, Carlos

(A) →
SanLuis, Juana
(B) →
Santilli, Laura
(C) →
Stinnett, Nellie
(D) →
Stoddard, Victor
(E) →

50. DeLaTour, Hall F.

(A) →
Delargy, Harold
(B) →
DeLathouder, Hilda
(C) →
Lathrop, Hillary
(D) →
LaTour, Hulbert E.
(E) →

51. Multiply: $\begin{array}{r} 62 \\ \times\ 5 \\ \hline \end{array}$

(A) 300
(B) 310
(C) 315
(D) 360
(E) none of these

52. Divide: $3\overline{)153}$

(A) 41
(B) 43
(C) 51
(D) 53
(E) none of these

53. Add: $\begin{array}{r} 47 \\ +\ 21 \\ \hline \end{array}$

(A) 58
(B) 59
(C) 67
(D) 68
(E) none of these

54. Subtract: $\begin{array}{r} 87 \\ -\ 42 \\ \hline \end{array}$

(A) 34
(B) 35
(C) 44
(D) 45
(E) none of these

55. Multiply: $\begin{array}{r} 37 \\ \times\ 3 \\ \hline \end{array}$

(A) 91
(B) 101
(C) 104
(D) 114
(E) none of these

For each question below, find which one of the suggested answer; appears in that question.

56.	N	5	4	7	T	K	3	Z	Suggested Answers	(A) = 3, 8, K, N
57.	8	5	3	V	L	2	Z	N		(B) = 5, 8, N, V
58.	7	2	5	N	9	K	L	V		(C) = 3, 9, V, Z
59.	9	8	L	2	5	Z	K	V		(D) = 5, 9, K, Z
60.	Z	6	5	V	9	3	P	N		(E) = none of these

In questions 61–65, compare the three names or number, and darken the answer space:

(A) if **ALL THREE** names or numbers are exactly **ALIKE**
(B) if only the **FIRST** and **SECOND** names or numbers are exactly **ALIKE**
(C) if only the **FIRST** and **THIRD** names or numbers are exactly **ALIKE**
(D) if only the **SECOND** and **THIRD** names or numbers are exactly **ALIKE**
(E) if **ALL THREE** names or numbers are **DIFFERENT**

61.	6452054	6452654	6452054
62.	8501268	8501268	8501286
63.	Ella Burk Newham	Ella Burk Newnham	Elena Burk Newnham
64.	Jno. K. Ravencroft	Jno. H. Ravencroft	Jno. H. Ravencraft
65.	Martin Wills Pullen	Martin Wills Pulen	Martin Wills Pullen

In questions 66–70, find the correct place for the name in the box.

66. O'Bannon, M. J.

(A) →
O'Beirne, B. B.
(B) →
Oberlin, E. L.
(C) →
Oberneir, L. P.
(D) →
O'Brian, S. F.
(E) →

67. Entsminger, Jacob

(A) →
Ensminger, J.
(B) →
Entsminger, J. A.
(C) →
Entsminger, Jack
(D) →
Entsminger, James
(E) →

68. Iacone, Pete R.

(A) →
Iacone, Pedro
(B) →
Iacone, Pedro M.
(C) →
Iacone, Peter F.
(D) →
Iascone, Peter W.
(E) →

Gladys

(A) →
Shepard, Dwight
(B) →
Shepard, F. H.
(C) →
Shephard, Louise
(D) →
Shepperd, Stella
(E) →

Melvin T.

(A) →
Thackston, Milton G.
(B) →
Thackston, Milton W.
(C) →
Thackston, Theodore
(D) →
Thackston, Thomas G.
(E) →

57

(A) 51
(B) 52
(C) 53
(D) 54
(E) none of these

(A) 75
(B) 84
(C) 85
(D) 95
(E) none of these

73. Subtract: $\begin{array}{r} 86 \\ -\ 57 \\ \hline \end{array}$

(A) 18
(B) 29
(C) 38
(D) 39
(E) none of these

74. Multiply: $\begin{array}{r} 68 \\ \times\ 4 \\ \hline \end{array}$

(A) 242
(B) 264
(C) 272
(D) 274
(E) none of these

75. Divide: $9\overline{)639}$

(A) 71
(B) 73
(C) 81
(D) 83
(E) none of these

For each question below, find which one of the suggested answers appears in that question.

76.	6	Z	T	N	8	7	4	V
77.	V	7	8	6	N	5	P	L
78.	N	7	P	V	8	4	2	L
79.	7	8	G	4	3	V	L	T
80.	4	8	G	2	T	N	6	L

Suggested Answers
- (A) = 2, 7, L, N
- (B) = 2, 8, T, V
- (C) = 6, 8, L, T
- (D) = 6, 7, N, V
- (E) = none of these

In questions 81–85, compare the three names or numbers, and darken the answer space:

(A) if **ALL THREE** names or numbers are exactly **ALIKE**
(B) if only the **FIRST** and **SECOND** names or numbers are exactly **ALIKE**
(C) if only the **FIRST** and **THIRD** names or numbers are exactly **ALIKE**
(D) if only the **SECOND** and **THIRD** names or numbers are exactly **ALIKE**
(E) if **ALL THREE** names or numbers are **DIFFERENT**

81.	3457988	3457986	3457986
82.	4695682	4695862	4695682
83.	Stricklund Kanedy	Stricklund Kanedy	Stricklund Kanedy
84.	Joy Harlor Witner	Joy Harloe Witner	Joy Harloe Witner
85.	R. M. O. Uberroth	R. M. O. Uberroth	R. N. O. Uberroth

In questions 86–90, find the correct place for the name in the box.

86. Dunlavey, M. Hilary

(A) →
Dunleavy, Hilary G.
(B) →
Dunleavy, Hilary K.
(C) →
Dunleavy, Hilary S.
(D) →
Dunleavy, Hilery W.
(E) →

87. Yarbrough, Maria

(A) →
Yabroudy, Margy
(B) →
Yarboro, Marie
(C) →
Yarborough, Marina
(D) →
Yarborough, Mary
(E) →

88. Prouty, Martha

(A) →
Proutey, Margaret
(B) →
Proutey, Maude
(C) →
Prouty, Myra
(D) →
Prouty, Naomi
(E) →

89. Pawlowicz, Ruth M.

(A) →
Pawalek, Edward
(B) →
Pawelek, Flora G.
(C) →
Pawlowski, Joan M.
(D) →
Pawtowski, Wanda
(E) →

90. Vanstory, George

(A) →
Vanover, Eva
(B) →
VanSwinderen, Floyd
(C) →
VanSyckle, Harry
(D) →
Vanture, Laurence
(E) →

91. Add: $\begin{array}{r} 28 \\ +35 \\ \hline \end{array}$

(A) 53
(B) 62
(C) 64
(D) 73
(E) none of these

92. Subtract: $\begin{array}{r} 78 \\ -69 \\ \hline \end{array}$

(A) 7
(B) 8
(C) 18
(D) 19
(E) none of these

93. Multiply: $\begin{array}{r} 86 \\ \times\ 6 \\ \hline \end{array}$

(A) 492
(B) 506
(C) 516
(D) 526
(E) none of these

94. Divide: $8\overline{)648}$

(A) 71
(B) 76
(C) 81
(D) 89
(E) none of these

95. Add: $\begin{array}{r} 97 \\ +34 \\ \hline \end{array}$

(A) 131
(B) 132
(C) 140
(D) 141
(E) none of these

For each question below, find which one of the suggested answers appears in that question.

96.	V 5 7 Z N 9 4 T	Suggested Answers	(A) = 2, 5, N, Z
97.	4 6 P T 2 N K 9		(B) = 4, 5, N, P
98.	6 4 N 2 P 8 Z K		(C) = 2, 9, P, T
99.	7 P 5 2 4 N K T		(D) = 4, 9, T, Z
100.	K T 8 5 4 N 2 P		(E) = none of these

In questions 101– 105, compare the three names or numbers, and darken the answer space:

(A) if **ALL THREE** names or numbers are exactly **ALIKE**
(B) if only the **FIRST** and **SECOND** names or numbers are exactly **ALIKE**
(C) if only the **FIRST** and **THIRD** names or numbers are exactly **ALIKE**
(D) if only the **SECOND** and **THIRD** names or numbers are exactly **ALIKE**
(E) if **ALL THREE** names or numbers are **DIFFERENT**

101.	1592514	159257	41592574
102.	2010202	2010202	2010220
103.	6177396	6177936	6177396
104.	Drusilla S. Ridgeley	Drusilla S. Ridgeley	Drusilla S. Ridgeley
105.	Andrei I. Toumantzev	Andrei I. Tourmantzev	Andrei I. Toumantzov

In questions 106–110, find the correct place for the name in the box.

106. Fitzsimmons, Hugh

(A) →
Fitts, Harold
(B) →
Fitzgerald, June
(C) →
FitzGibbon, Junius
(D) →
FitzSimons, Martin
(E) →

107. D'Amato, Vincent

(A) →
Daly, Steven
(B) →
D'Amboise, S. Vincent
(C) →
Daniel, Vail
(D) →
DeAlba, Valentina
(E) →

108. Schaeffer, Roger D.

(A) →
Schaffert, Evelyn M.
(B) →
Schaffner, Margaret M.
(C) →
Schafhirt, Milton G.
(D) →
Shafer, Richard E.
(E) →

109. White-Lewis, Cecil

(A) →
Whitelaw, Cordelia
(B) →
White-Leigh, Nancy
(C) →
Whitely, Rodney
(D) →
Whitlock, Warren
(E) →

110. VanDerHeggen, Don

(A) →
VanDemark, Doris
(B) →
Vandenberg, H. E.
(C) →
VanDercook, Marie
(D) →
vanderLinden, Robert
(E) →

111. Add: $\begin{array}{r} 75 \\ +\ 49 \\ \hline \end{array}$

(A) 124
(B) 125
(C) 134
(D) 225
(E) none of these

112. Subtract: $\begin{array}{r} 69 \\ -\ 45 \\ \hline \end{array}$

(A) 14
(B) 23
(C) 24
(D) 26
(E) none of these

113. Multiply: $\begin{array}{r} 36 \\ \times\ 8 \\ \hline \end{array}$

(A) 246
(B) 262
(C) 288
(D) 368
(E) none of these

114. Divide: $8\overline{)328}$

(A) 31
(B) 41
(C) 42
(D) 48
(E) none of these

115. Multiply: $\begin{array}{r} 58 \\ \times\ 9 \\ \hline \end{array}$

(A) 472
(B) 513
(C) 521
(D) 522
(E) none of these

For each question below, find which one of the suggested answers appears in that question.

116.	Z 3 N P G 5 4 2	Suggested Answers	(A) = 2, 3, G, N
117.	6 N 2 8 G 4 P T		(B) = 2, 6, N, T
118.	6 N 4 T V G 8 2		(C) = 3, 4, G, K
119.	T 3 P 4 N 8 G 2		(D) = 4, 6, K, T
120.	6 7 K G N 2 L 5		(E) = none of these

END OF CLERICAL TASKS TEST

CORRECT ANSWERS—FEDERAL CLERICAL EXAMINATION

VERBAL TASKS TEST

1. C	**16.** A	**30.** A	**44.** D	**58.** B	**72.** A
2. B	**17.** C	**31.** B	**45.** D	**59.** C	**73.** C
3. C	**18.** B	**32.** A	**46.** C	**60.** B	**74.** D
4. D	**19.** D	**33.** B	**47.** B	**61.** B	**75.** A
5. B	**20.** A	**34.** D	**48.** C	**62.** A	**76.** D
6. A	**21.** C	**35.** D	**49.** B	**63.** D	**77.** C
7. B	**22.** A	**36.** B	**50.** A	**64.** C	**78.** A
8. C	**23.** C	**37.** C	**51.** D	**65.** B	**79.** C
9. D	**24.** D	**38.** A	**52.** A	**66.** A	**80.** B
10. A	**25.** C	**39.** C	**53.** C	**67.** C	**81.** B
11. D	**26.** A	**40.** B	**54.** A	**68.** B	**82.** B
12. A	**27.** D	**41.** C	**55.** D	**69.** D	**83.** B
13. C	**28.** C	**42.** B	**56.** B	**70.** B	**84.** A
14. D	**29.** D	**43.** C	**57.** A	**71.** D	**85.** B
15. A					

CLERICAL TASKS TEST

1. B	**21.** A	**41.** A	**61.** C	**81.** D	**101.** D
2. E	**22.** E	**42.** A	**62.** B	**82.** C	**102.** B
3. D	**23.** E	**43.** B	**63.** E	**83.** A	**103.** C
4. A	**24.** D	**44.** E	**64.** E	**84.** D	**104.** A
5. E	**25.** C	**45.** A	**65.** C	**85.** B	**105.** E
6. E	**26.** D	**46.** C	**66.** A	**86.** A	**106.** D
7. A	**27.** D	**47.** A	**67.** D	**87.** E	**107.** B
8. D	**28.** C	**48.** D	**68.** C	**88.** C	**108.** A
9. B	**29.** C	**49.** B	**69.** D	**89.** C	**109.** C
10. E	**30.** D	**50.** C	**70.** E	**90.** B	**110.** D
11. D	**31.** E	**51.** B	**71.** A	**91.** E	**111.** A
12. B	**32.** A	**52.** C	**72.** C	**92.** E	**112.** C
12. B	**33.** A	**53.** D	**73.** B	**93.** C	**113.** C
14. B	**34.** C	**54.** D	**74.** C	**94.** C	**114.** B
15. B	**35.** C	**55.** E	**75.** A	**95.** A	**115.** D
16. A	**36.** E	**56.** E	**76.** D	**96.** D	**116.** A
17. D	**37.** A	**57.** B	**77.** D	**97.** C	**117.** B
18. E	**38.** C	**58.** E	**78.** A	**98.** E	**118.** B
19. B	**39.** C	**59.** D	**79.** E	**99.** B	**119.** A
20. A	**40.** D	**60.** C	**80.** C	**100.** B	**120.** E

ANSWERS AND EXPLANATIONS

VERBAL TASKS TEST

1. **The correct answer is (C).** FLEXIBLE means *adjustable* or *pliable.* An office which offers flexible hours may operate from 6 A.M. to 10 P.M.
2. **The correct answer is (B).** An OPTION is a *choice.* When you cast your vote, you are exercising your option.
3. **The correct answer is (C).** To VERIFY is to *check the accuracy of* or to *confirm.* A notary stamp verifies that the signature on the document is the signature of the person named.
4. **The correct answer is (D).** INDOLENT means *idle* or *lazy.* An indolent person is not likely to become a productive employee.
5. **The correct answer is (B).** RESPIRATION is *breathing.* Respiration is the process by which animals inhale and exhale air.
6. **The correct answer is (A).** A BRUSH is a tool of the PAINTER's trade as a WRENCH is a tool of the PLUMBER's trade.
7. **The correct answer is (B).** A PACKAGE transports MERCHANDISE just as a LETTER transmits a MESSAGE.
8. **The correct answer is (C).** SLEEP alleviates WEARINESS just as FOOD alleviates HUNGER.
9. **The correct answer is (D).** The DIAL is an input device of a TELEPHONE just as a KEY is an input device of a TYPEWRITER.
10. **The correct answer is (A).** *Whoever* is the subject of the phrase "whoever has the best record." Choices B and C are wordy and awkward.
11. **The correct answer is (D).** All the other choices contain obvious errors.
12. **The correct answer is (A).** The correct spelling is: collapsible.
13. **The correct answer is (C).** The correct spelling is: ambiguous.
14. **The correct answer is (D).** The correct spelling is: predecessor.
15. **The correct answer is (A).** The correct spelling is: sanctioned.
16. **The correct answer is (A).** The paragraph presents the problems of fire in fire-resistant buildings. It suggests that the contents of the buildings may burn even though the structural materials themselves do not, and the ensuing fire may even cause the collapse of the buildings. The paragraph does not compare the problem of fire in fire-resistant buildings with that of fire in ordinary buildings.
17. **The correct answer is (C).** The search for truth has speeded the progress of civilization. Choice B is incorrect in its statement that "civilization did not begin until. . . ." Civilization moved ahead slowly even before restrictions on learning were removed.
18. **The correct answer is (B).** VIGILANT means *alert* or *watchful.* A worker must remain vigilant to avoid accidents on the job.
19. **The correct answer is (D).** INCIDENTAL means *happening in connection with something else* or *casual.* Having the windshield washed is incidental to filling the gas tank and checking the oil.
20. **The correct answer is (A).** CONCILIATORY means *tending to reconcile* or *to make peace.* The apology was offered as a conciliatory gesture.
21. **The correct answer is (C).** An ALTERCATION is a *quarrel* or a *controversy.* The two drivers had an angry altercation as to who was at fault in the accident.
22. **The correct answer is (A).** IRRESOLUTE means *indecisive* or *wavering.* The couple was irresolute as to the choice of next summer's vacation.
23. **The correct answer is (C).** STILLNESS and SOUND are opposites, as are DARKNESS and SUNLIGHT.
24. **The correct answer is (D).** That which is ACCIDENTAL happens by CHANCE as that which is DESIGNED happens by INTENTION.

25. **The correct answer is (C).** A MUFFLER reduces SOUND as PRACTICE reduces ERRORs.
26. **The correct answer is (A).** The desired result of TRAINING is the development of SKILL as the desired result of RESEARCH is scientific FINDINGS.
27. **The correct answer is (D).** Choices A and C are incorrect in use of the subject form "I" instead of the object of the preposition "me." Choice B incorrectly uses the reflexive "myself." Only I can address a letter to myself.
28. **The correct answer is (C).** All the other choices are quite obviously incorrect.
29. **The correct answer is (D).** The correct spelling is: miniature.
30. **The correct answer is (A).** The correct spelling is: extemporaneous.
31. **The correct answer is (B).** The correct spelling is: problematical.
32. **The correct answer is (A).** The correct spelling of first choice is: descendant. An alternative spelling which is also correct is descendent. A correct spelling is offered among the choices, so choice (A) is the correct answer.
33. **The correct answer is (B).** In a word, we are preserving our natural resources through recycling.
34. **The correct answer is (D).** If you omit all unnecessary words, you use only the words essential to the meaning.
35. **The correct answer is (D).** To COUNTERACT is to *act directly against* or to *neutralize.* My father's vote for the Republican candidate always counteracts my mother's vote for the Democrat.
36. **The correct answer is (B).** DEFERRED means *postponed* or *delayed.* Because I had no money in the bank, I deferred paying my taxes until the due date.
37. **The correct answer is (C).** FEASIBLE means *possible* or *practicable.* It is not feasible for the 92-year-old woman to travel abroad.
38. **The correct answer is (A).** To ENCOUNTER is to *come upon* or to *meet.* If you encounter my brother at the ball game, please give my regards.
39. **The correct answer is (C).** INNATE means *existing naturally* or *native.* Some people argue that the maternal instinct is learned rather than innate.
40. **The correct answer is (B).** The DISCIPLE learns from a MASTER as a STUDENT learns from a TEACHER.
41. **The correct answer is (C).** In this analogy of place, an EXPERIMENT occurs in a LABORATORY as a LECTURE occurs in an AUDITORIUM.
42. **The correct answer is (B).** FUEL powers the ENGINE as FOOD powers the BODY
43. **The correct answer is (C).** RECREATION occurs in the THEATER as EDUCATION occurs in a SCHOOL.
44. **The correct answer is (D).** Choice A might state either "most" or "all" but not both; choice B should read "persons who"; choice C should read "with regard to. . . ."
45. **The correct answer is (D).** Choice (A) is incorrect because *both* can refer to only two, but the publisher and authors implies at least three; choice B requires the plural verb "were"; choice C requires the correlative construction "neither . . . nor."
46. **The correct answer is (C).** The correct spelling is: extricate.
47. **The correct answer is (B).** The correct spelling is: hereditary.
48. **The correct answer is (C).** The correct spelling is: auspicious.
49. **The correct answer is (B).** The correct spelling is: sequence.
50. **The correct answer is (A).** If instruction in safety rules will help to prevent accidents, some accidents must occur because of ignorance.
51. **The correct answer is (D).** The language that has some representative in English speech has had some of its words absorbed into English.
52. **The correct answer is (A).** To ACQUIESCE is to *give in* or to *assent.* I reluctantly will acquiesce to your request to stay out late with your friends.
53. **The correct answer is (C).** UNANIMITY is *complete agreement* or *harmony.* The plan had such widespread acceptance that the vote resulted in unanimity.

54. **The correct answer is (A).** A PRECEDENT is *an example that sets a standard.* After one employee was permitted to wear jeans in the office, a precedent had been set and soon others also dressed casually.
55. **The correct answer is (D).** VERSATILE means *adaptable* or *many-sided.* This versatile vacuum cleaner can be used indoors or out under both dry and wet conditions.
56. **The correct answer is (B).** AUTHENTIC means *genuine* or *reliable.* The painting attributed to Rembrandt was guaranteed to be authentic.
57. **The correct answer is (A).** The information and substance of a NOVEL is FICTION while the information and substance of BIOGRAPHY is FACT.
58. **The correct answer is (B).** FILM is the medium through which the action of a MOTION PICTURE is projected onto a screen; CARBON PAPER is the medium through which a COPY of words or drawings is transmitted from one piece of paper to another.
59. **The correct answer is (C).** CARELESSNESS earns a REPRIMAND as EFFICIENCY merits a REWARD.
60. **The correct answer is (B).** This analogy refers to the marketplace and the law of supply and demand. That which is SCARCE is likely to be COSTLY while that which is ABUNDANT will be CHEAP.
61. **The correct answer is (B).** In choice A the placement of the apostrophe is inappropriate; choices C and D use the plural, but there is only one company.
62. **The correct answer is (A).** Choices C and D are glaringly poor. Choice B is not incorrect, but choice A is far better.
63. **The correct answer is (D).** The correct spelling is: obliterate.
64. **The correct answer is (C).** The correct spelling is: diagnosis.
65. **The correct answer is (B).** The correct spelling is: countenance.
66. **The correct answer is (A).** The correct spelling is: conceivably.
67. **The correct answer is (C).** Since manufacturers are assuming risks in attempting to predict what consumers will want, their success depends on the ultimate purchases made by the consumers.
68. **The correct answer is (B).** Humans migrate to various climates and make adjustments to the food supply in each climate; obviously the means by which they supply their needs are varied.
69. **The correct answer is (D).** STRIDENT means *grating* or *harsh-sounding.* The sergeant barked out the orders in strident tones.
70. **The correct answer is (B).** To CONFINE is to *limit* or to *restrict.* If the child's illness is contagious, we must confine him to his home.
71. **The correct answer is (D).** To ACCENTUATE is to *stress, emphasize,* or *intensify.* Life is more pleasant when those we deal with accentuate the positive.
72. **The correct answer is (A).** BANAL means *insipid* or *commonplace.* His commentary was so banal that I had to stifle many yawns.
73. **The correct answer is (C).** One who is INCORRIGIBLE *cannot be changed or corrected;* the person is *irreformable.* Incorrigible offenders should be sentenced to prison for life.
74. **The correct answer is (D).** A DOCTOR promotes HEALTH as a POLICEMAN promotes ORDER.
75. **The correct answer is (A).** A WEAVER creates on a LOOM as an ARTIST creates on an EASEL.
76. **The correct answer is (D).** Many SHIPS make up the FLEET as many PERSONS make up a CROWD.
77. **The correct answer is (C).** MILEAGE is read from a MAP as the DATE is read from a CALENDAR.
78. **The correct answer is (A).** The other choices are quite clearly incorrect.
79. **The correct answer is (C).** Choices A and B use adverbs incorrectly; choice D is awkward and unidiomatic.
80. **The correct answer is (B).** The correct spelling is: competition.

81. **The correct answer is (B).** The correct spelling is: occasion.
82. **The correct answer is (C).** The correct spelling is: knowledge.
83. **The correct answer is (B).** The correct spelling is: deliberate.
84. **The correct answer is (A).** Time and effort cannot be equated. Efficiency must be measured in terms of results.
85. **The correct answer is (B).** The first sentence of the paragraph makes this statement.

CLERICAL TASKS TEST

1. **The correct answer is (B).** The last two digits of the third number are reversed.
2. **The correct answer is (E).** The middle digit of the second number is "6" while that of the first and third numbers is "5." The last two digits of the third number are reversed.
3. **The correct answer is (D).** The surname of the second and third names is "Johnson"; the surname of the first name is "Johnston."
4. **The correct answer is (A).** All three names are exactly alike.
5. **The correct answer is (E).** The middle initial of the third name differs from the other two. "Asheton" of the second name differs from "Atherton" of the other two.
6. **The correct answer is (E).** Hachettson; Hackett
7. **The correct answer is (A).** Margenroth; Margeroth
8. **The correct answer is (D).** Bobbitt, Olivia H.; Bobbitt, Olivier E.; Bobbitt, R. Olivia
9. **The correct answer is (B).** Mosely, Albert J.; Mosely, Werner; Mosley, Alvin
10. **The correct answer is (E).** Youmons; Youmuns
11. **The correct answer is (D).** $43 + 32 = 75$
12. **The correct answer is (B).** $83 - 4 = 79$
13. **The correct answer is (B).** $41 \times 7 = 287$
14. **The correct answer is (B).** $306 \div 6 = 51$
15. **The correct answer is (B).** $37 + 15 = 52$
16. **The correct answer is (A).** 6 2 5 **K** **4** P T G.
17. **The correct answer is (D).** L 4 **7** **2** **T** 6 V **K**. The answer cannot be choice (A) because question 17 contains no **5**; it cannot be choice (B) or choice (C) because question 17 contains no **G**.
18. **The correct answer is (E).** The answer cannot be choice (A) or choice (B) because question 18 contains no **K**; it cannot be choice (C) or choice (D) because question 18 contains no **2**.
19. **The correct answer is (B).** **G** **4** **K** **7** L 3 5 Z. The answer cannot be choice (A) because question 19 contains no T.
20. **The correct answer is (A).** **4** K 2 9 N **5** **T** G.
21. **The correct answer is (A).** All three numbers are exactly alike.
22. **The correct answer is (E).** The last two digits are, respectively, "41," "47," and "14."
23. **The correct answer is (E).** In the first name, the given name is "Owens" while in the other two it is "Owen." The surname of the second name is "McVey" while in the third name it is "McVay."

24. **The correct answer is (D).** In the second and third names, the surname is "Rowse"; in the first name it is "Rouse."
25. **The correct answer is (C).** In the second name the given name is "Merriott"; in the first and third it is "Merritt."
26. **The correct answer is (D).** Watson; Watters; Wattwood
27. **The correct answer is (D).** Johnston, Edmund; Johnston, Edward; Johnstone, Edmund A.
28. **The correct answer is (C).** Remschel; Rensch; Renshaw
29. **The correct answer is (C).** Schneider, Mertens; Schnyder, Maurice; Schnyder, Newman
30. **The correct answer is (D).** Freedenberg; Freedenburg; Freedinberg

31. **The correct answer is (E).**

$$\begin{array}{r} 68 \\ -\ 47 \\ \hline 21 \end{array}$$

32. **The correct answer is (A).**

$$\begin{array}{r} 50 \\ \times\ \ 8 \\ \hline 400 \end{array}$$

33. **The correct answer is (A).**

$$9\overline{)180}\ \ 9$$

34. **The correct answer is (C).**

$$\begin{array}{r} 78 \\ +\ 63 \\ \hline 141 \end{array}$$

35. **The correct answer is (C).**

$$\begin{array}{r} 89 \\ -\ 70 \\ \hline 75 \end{array}$$

36. **The correct answer is (E).** The answer cannot be choice (A) because question 36 contains no **V**; it cannot be choice (B) or choice (C) because question 36 contains no **5**; it cannot be choice (D) because question 36 contains no **8** or **V**.
37. **The correct answer is (A).** **L** 5 N K **4** 3 **9** **V**.
38. **The correct answer is (C).** **8** 2 V P 9 **L** **Z** **5**. The answer cannot be choice (A) or choice (B) because question 38 contains no **4**.
39. **The correct answer is (C).** V P 9 **Z** **5** **L** **8** 7. The answer cannot be choice (A) or choice (B) because question 39 contains no **4**.
40. **The correct answer is (D).** 5 T **8** **N** 2 **9** **V** L. The answer cannot be choice (A) or choice (B) because question 40 contains no **4**; it cannot be choice (C) because question 40 contains no **Z**.
41. **The correct answer is (A).** All three numbers are exactly alike.
42. **The correct answer is (A).** All three numbers are exactly alike.
43. **The correct answer is (B).** In the third number, the digits "40" are reversed to read "04."
44. **The correct answer is (E).** The first and third names have the same given name but different surnames. The second name has the same surname as the third, but the given name is different.
45. **The correct answer is (A).** All three names are exactly alike.
46. **The correct answer is (C).** DeMatteo; DeMattia; Derby
47. **The correct answer is (A).** Theriault; Therien
48. **The correct answer is (D).** Gaston, Isabel; Gaston, M. Hubert; Gaston, M. Melvin
49. **The correct answer is (B).** SanLuis; SanMiguel; Santilli
50. **The correct answer is (C).** DeLathouder; DeLaTour; Lathrop

51. The correct answer is (B).

$$\begin{array}{r} 62 \\ \times\ 5 \\ \hline 310 \end{array}$$

52. The correct answer is (C).

$$\begin{array}{r} 51 \\ 3\overline{)153} \end{array}$$

53. The correct answer is (D).

$$\begin{array}{r} 47 \\ +\ 21 \\ \hline 68 \end{array}$$

54. The correct answer is (D).

$$\begin{array}{r} 87 \\ -\ 42 \\ \hline 45 \end{array}$$

55. The correct answer is (E).

$$\begin{array}{r} 37 \\ \times\ 3 \\ \hline 111 \end{array}$$

56. The correct answer is (E). The answer cannot be choice (A) or choice (B) because question 56 contains no **8**; it cannot be choice (C) or choice (D) because question 56 contains no **9**.

57. The correct answer is (B). 8 5 3 **V** L 2 **Z N**. The answer cannot be choice (A) because question 57 contains no **K**.

58. The correct answer is (E). The answer cannot be choice (A) or choice (B) because question 58 contains no **8**; it cannot be choice (C) or choice (D) because question 58 contains no **Z**.

59. The correct answer is (D). 9 8 L 2 **5 Z K** V. The answer cannot be choice (A) or choice (C) because question 59 contains no **3**; it cannot be choice (B) because question 59 contains no **N**.

60. The correct answer is (C). Z 6 5 **V 9 3** P N. The answer cannot be choice (A) or choice (B) because question 60 contains no **8**.

61. The correct answer is (C). In the second number, the fifth digit differs from that in the other numbers.

62. The correct answer is (B). In the third number, the last two digits are reversed.

63. The correct answer is (E). The given name of the third name differs from that of the first two names; the surname of the first name is different from that of the second and third names.

64. The correct answer is (E). The middle initial of the first name differs from the middle initials of the other two; the surname of the third name differs from that of the first and second names.

65. The correct answer is (C). The surname of the second name is different from the surname of the first and third.

66. The correct answer is (A). O'Bannon; O'Beirne

67. The correct answer is (D). Entsminger, Jack; Entsminger, Jacob; Entsminger, James

68. The correct answer is (C). Iacone, Pedro M.; Iacone, Pete R.; Iacone, Peter F

69. The correct answer is (D). Shephard; Sheppard; Shepperd

70. The correct answer is (E). Thackston; Mackton

71. The correct answer is (A).

$$\begin{array}{r} 51 \\ 7\overline{)357} \end{array}$$

72. The correct answer is (C).

$$\begin{array}{r} 58 \\ +\ 27 \\ \hline 85 \end{array}$$

73. The correct answer is (B).

$$\begin{array}{r} 86 \\ -\ 57 \\ \hline 29 \end{array}$$

74. The correct answer is (C).

$$\begin{array}{r} 68 \\ \times\ \ 4 \\ \hline 272 \end{array}$$

75. The correct answer is (A).

$$9\overline{)639} = 71$$

76. The correct answer is (D). 6 Z T **N 8 7 4 V**. The answer cannot be choice (A) or choice (B) because question 76 contains no **2**; it cannot be choice (C) because question 76 contains no **L**.

77. The correct answer is (D). V 7 8 **6 N** 5 P L. The answer cannot be choice (A) or choice (B) because question 77 contains no **2**; it cannot be choice (C) because question 77 contains no **T**.

78. The correct answer is (A). N 7 P V 8 4 **2 L**.

79. The correct answer is (E). The answer cannot be choice (A) or choice (B) because question 79 contains no **2**; it cannot be choice (C) or choice (D) because question 79 contains no **6**.

80. The correct answer is (C). 4 **8** G 2 **T** N **6 L**. The answer cannot be (A) because question 80 contains no **7**; it cannot be (B) because question 80 contains no **V**.

81. The correct answer is (D). The last digit of the first number differs from the last digit of the second and third numbers.

82. The correct answer is (C). The fifth and sixth digits of the middle number are the reverse of the fifth and sixth digits of the first and third numbers.

83. The correct answer is (A). All three names are exactly alike.

84. The correct answer is (D). In the second and third names, the middle name is "Harloe"; in the first name, it is "Harlor."

85. The correct answer is (B). The central initial in the third name differs from the central initial in the first and second names.

86. The correct answer is (A). Dunlavey; Dunleavy

87. The correct answer is (E). Yarborough; Yarbrough

88. The correct answer is (C). Proutey, Maude; Prouty, Martha; Prouty, Myra

89. The correct answer is (C). Pawalek; Pawlowicz; Pawlowski

90. The correct answer is (B). Vanover; Vanstory; VanSwinderen

91. The correct answer is (E).

$$\begin{array}{r} 28 \\ +\ 35 \\ \hline 63 \end{array}$$

92. The correct answer is (E).

$$\begin{array}{r} 76 \\ -\ 69 \\ \hline 9 \end{array}$$

93. The correct answer is (C).

$$\begin{array}{r} 86 \\ \times\ \ 6 \\ \hline 516 \end{array}$$

94. The correct answer is (C).

$$8\overline{)648} = 81$$

95. The correct answer is (A).

$$\begin{array}{r} 97 \\ +\ 34 \\ \hline 131 \end{array}$$

96. The correct answer is (D). V 5 7 **Z** N **9 4 T**. The answer cannot be choice (A) or choice (C) because question 96 contains no **2**; it cannot be choice (B) because question 96 contains no **P**.

97. The correct answer is (C). 4 6 **P T 2** N **K 9**. The answer cannot be choice (A) or choice (B) because question 97 contains no **5**.

98. The correct answer is (E). The answer cannot be choice (A) or choice (B) because question 98 contains no **5**; it cannot be choice (C) or choice (D) because question 98 contains no **9**.

99. The correct answer is (B). 7 **P** 5 2 **4 N** K T. The answer cannot be choice (A) because question 99 contains no **Z**.

100. The correct answer is (B). **K** T 8 **5 4** N 2 **P**. The answer cannot be choice (A) because question 100 contains no Z.

101. The correct answer is (D). The next to the last digit of the first number differs from that of the other two numbers.

102. The correct answer is (B). The last two digits of the third number are reversed.

103. The correct answer is (C). The fifth and sixth digits of the second number are reversed.

104. The correct answer is (A). All three names are exactly alike.

105. The correct answer is (E). All three surnames are different.

106. The correct answer is (D). FitzGibbon; Fitzsimmons; FitzSimons

107. The correct answer is (B). Daly; D'Amato; D'Amboise

108. The correct answer is (A). Schaeffer; Schaffert

109. The correct answer is (C). White-Leigh; White-Lewis; Whitely

110. The correct answer is (D). VanDercook; VanDerHeggen; vanderLinden

111. The correct answer is (A).

$$\begin{array}{r} 75 \\ +\ 49 \\ \hline 124 \end{array}$$

112. The correct answer is (C).

$$\begin{array}{r} 69 \\ -\ 45 \\ \hline 24 \end{array}$$

113. The correct answer is (C).

$$\begin{array}{r} 36 \\ \times\ \ 8 \\ \hline 288 \end{array}$$

114. The correct answer is (B).

$$8\overline{)328}\ = 41$$

115. The correct answer is (D).

$$\begin{array}{r} 58 \\ \times\ \ 9 \\ \hline 522 \end{array}$$

116. The correct answer is (A).Z **3 N** P **G** 5 4 **2**.

117. The correct answer is (B).6 N **2** 8 G 4 P **T**. The answer cannot be choice (A) because question 117 contains no **3**.

118. The correct answer is (B).6 N 4 **T** V G 8 **2**. The answer cannot be choice (A) because question 118 contains no **3**.

119. The correct answer is (A).T **3** P 4 **N** 8 **G 2**.

120. The correct answer is (E). The answer cannot be choice (A) or choice (C) because question 120 contains no **3**; it cannot be choice (B) or choice (D) because question 120 contains no **T**.

ANSWER SHEET

U.S. POSTAL SERVICE CLERK, DISTRIBUTION CLERK (MACHINE) AND MARK-UP CLERK (AUTOMATED) EXAM

PART A—ADDRESS CHECKING

1. Ⓐ Ⓓ	**20.** Ⓐ Ⓓ	**39.** Ⓐ Ⓓ	**58.** Ⓐ Ⓓ	**77.** Ⓐ Ⓓ
2. Ⓐ Ⓓ	**21.** Ⓐ Ⓓ	**40.** Ⓐ Ⓓ	**59.** Ⓐ Ⓓ	**78.** Ⓐ Ⓓ
3. Ⓐ Ⓓ	**22.** Ⓐ Ⓓ	**41.** Ⓐ Ⓓ	**60.** Ⓐ Ⓓ	**79.** Ⓐ Ⓓ
4. Ⓐ Ⓓ	**23.** Ⓐ Ⓓ	**42.** Ⓐ Ⓓ	**61.** Ⓐ Ⓓ	**80.** Ⓐ Ⓓ
5. Ⓐ Ⓓ	**24.** Ⓐ Ⓓ	**43.** Ⓐ Ⓓ	**62.** Ⓐ Ⓓ	**81.** Ⓐ Ⓓ
6. Ⓐ Ⓓ	**25.** Ⓐ Ⓓ	**44.** Ⓐ Ⓓ	**63.** Ⓐ Ⓓ	**82.** Ⓐ Ⓓ
7. Ⓐ Ⓓ	**26.** Ⓐ Ⓓ	**45.** Ⓐ Ⓓ	**64.** Ⓐ Ⓓ	**83.** Ⓐ Ⓓ
8. Ⓐ Ⓓ	**27.** Ⓐ Ⓓ	**46.** Ⓐ Ⓓ	**65.** Ⓐ Ⓓ	**84.** Ⓐ Ⓓ
9. Ⓐ Ⓓ	**28.** Ⓐ Ⓓ	**47.** Ⓐ Ⓓ	**66.** Ⓐ Ⓓ	**85.** Ⓐ Ⓓ
10. Ⓐ Ⓓ	**29.** Ⓐ Ⓓ	**48.** Ⓐ Ⓓ	**67.** Ⓐ Ⓓ	**86.** Ⓐ Ⓓ
11. Ⓐ Ⓓ	**30.** Ⓐ Ⓓ	**49.** Ⓐ Ⓓ	**68.** Ⓐ Ⓓ	**87.** Ⓐ Ⓓ
12. Ⓐ Ⓓ	**31.** Ⓐ Ⓓ	**50.** Ⓐ Ⓓ	**69.** Ⓐ Ⓓ	**88.** Ⓐ Ⓓ
13. Ⓐ Ⓓ	**32.** Ⓐ Ⓓ	**51.** Ⓐ Ⓓ	**70.** Ⓐ Ⓓ	**89.** Ⓐ Ⓓ
14. Ⓐ Ⓓ	**33.** Ⓐ Ⓓ	**52.** Ⓐ Ⓓ	**71.** Ⓐ Ⓓ	**90.** Ⓐ Ⓓ
15. Ⓐ Ⓓ	**34.** Ⓐ Ⓓ	**53.** Ⓐ Ⓓ	**72.** Ⓐ Ⓓ	**91.** Ⓐ Ⓓ
16. Ⓐ Ⓓ	**35.** Ⓐ Ⓓ	**54.** Ⓐ Ⓓ	**73.** Ⓐ Ⓓ	**92.** Ⓐ Ⓓ
17. Ⓐ Ⓓ	**36.** Ⓐ Ⓓ	**55.** Ⓐ Ⓓ	**74.** Ⓐ Ⓓ	**93.** Ⓐ Ⓓ
18. Ⓐ Ⓓ	**37.** Ⓐ Ⓓ	**56.** Ⓐ Ⓓ	**75.** Ⓐ Ⓓ	**94.** Ⓐ Ⓓ
19. Ⓐ Ⓓ	**38.** Ⓐ Ⓓ	**57.** Ⓐ Ⓓ	**76.** Ⓐ Ⓓ	**95.** Ⓐ Ⓓ

ANSWER SHEET

PART B—MEMORY FOR ADDRESSES

1. Ⓐ Ⓑ Ⓒ Ⓓ Ⓔ	23. Ⓐ Ⓑ Ⓒ Ⓓ Ⓔ	45. Ⓐ Ⓑ Ⓒ Ⓓ Ⓔ	67. Ⓐ Ⓑ Ⓒ Ⓓ Ⓔ
2. Ⓐ Ⓑ Ⓒ Ⓓ Ⓔ	24. Ⓐ Ⓑ Ⓒ Ⓓ Ⓔ	46. Ⓐ Ⓑ Ⓒ Ⓓ Ⓔ	68. Ⓐ Ⓑ Ⓒ Ⓓ Ⓔ
3. Ⓐ Ⓑ Ⓒ Ⓓ Ⓔ	25. Ⓐ Ⓑ Ⓒ Ⓓ Ⓔ	47. Ⓐ Ⓑ Ⓒ Ⓓ Ⓔ	69. Ⓐ Ⓑ Ⓒ Ⓓ Ⓔ
4. Ⓐ Ⓑ Ⓒ Ⓓ Ⓔ	26. Ⓐ Ⓑ Ⓒ Ⓓ Ⓔ	48. Ⓐ Ⓑ Ⓒ Ⓓ Ⓔ	70. Ⓐ Ⓑ Ⓒ Ⓓ Ⓔ
5. Ⓐ Ⓑ Ⓒ Ⓓ Ⓔ	27. Ⓐ Ⓑ Ⓒ Ⓓ Ⓔ	49. Ⓐ Ⓑ Ⓒ Ⓓ Ⓔ	71. Ⓐ Ⓑ Ⓒ Ⓓ Ⓔ
6. Ⓐ Ⓑ Ⓒ Ⓓ Ⓔ	28. Ⓐ Ⓑ Ⓒ Ⓓ Ⓔ	50. Ⓐ Ⓑ Ⓒ Ⓓ Ⓔ	72. Ⓐ Ⓑ Ⓒ Ⓓ Ⓔ
7. Ⓐ Ⓑ Ⓒ Ⓓ Ⓔ	29. Ⓐ Ⓑ Ⓒ Ⓓ Ⓔ	51. Ⓐ Ⓑ Ⓒ Ⓓ Ⓔ	73. Ⓐ Ⓑ Ⓒ Ⓓ Ⓔ
8. Ⓐ Ⓑ Ⓒ Ⓓ Ⓔ	30. Ⓐ Ⓑ Ⓒ Ⓓ Ⓔ	52. Ⓐ Ⓑ Ⓒ Ⓓ Ⓔ	74. Ⓐ Ⓑ Ⓒ Ⓓ Ⓔ
9. Ⓐ Ⓑ Ⓒ Ⓓ Ⓔ	31. Ⓐ Ⓑ Ⓒ Ⓓ Ⓔ	53. Ⓐ Ⓑ Ⓒ Ⓓ Ⓔ	75. Ⓐ Ⓑ Ⓒ Ⓓ Ⓔ
10. Ⓐ Ⓑ Ⓒ Ⓓ Ⓔ	32. Ⓐ Ⓑ Ⓒ Ⓓ Ⓔ	54. Ⓐ Ⓑ Ⓒ Ⓓ Ⓔ	76. Ⓐ Ⓑ Ⓒ Ⓓ Ⓔ
11. Ⓐ Ⓑ Ⓒ Ⓓ Ⓔ	33. Ⓐ Ⓑ Ⓒ Ⓓ Ⓔ	55. Ⓐ Ⓑ Ⓒ Ⓓ Ⓔ	77. Ⓐ Ⓑ Ⓒ Ⓓ Ⓔ
12. Ⓐ Ⓑ Ⓒ Ⓓ Ⓔ	34. Ⓐ Ⓑ Ⓒ Ⓓ Ⓔ	56. Ⓐ Ⓑ Ⓒ Ⓓ Ⓔ	78. Ⓐ Ⓑ Ⓒ Ⓓ Ⓔ
13. Ⓐ Ⓑ Ⓒ Ⓓ Ⓔ	35. Ⓐ Ⓑ Ⓒ Ⓓ Ⓔ	57. Ⓐ Ⓑ Ⓒ Ⓓ Ⓔ	79. Ⓐ Ⓑ Ⓒ Ⓓ Ⓔ
14. Ⓐ Ⓑ Ⓒ Ⓓ Ⓔ	36. Ⓐ Ⓑ Ⓒ Ⓓ Ⓔ	58. Ⓐ Ⓑ Ⓒ Ⓓ Ⓔ	80. Ⓐ Ⓑ Ⓒ Ⓓ Ⓔ
15. Ⓐ Ⓑ Ⓒ Ⓓ Ⓔ	37. Ⓐ Ⓑ Ⓒ Ⓓ Ⓔ	59. Ⓐ Ⓑ Ⓒ Ⓓ Ⓔ	81. Ⓐ Ⓑ Ⓒ Ⓓ Ⓔ
16. Ⓐ Ⓑ Ⓒ Ⓓ Ⓔ	38. Ⓐ Ⓑ Ⓒ Ⓓ Ⓔ	60. Ⓐ Ⓑ Ⓒ Ⓓ Ⓔ	82. Ⓐ Ⓑ Ⓒ Ⓓ Ⓔ
17. Ⓐ Ⓑ Ⓒ Ⓓ Ⓔ	39. Ⓐ Ⓑ Ⓒ Ⓓ Ⓔ	61. Ⓐ Ⓑ Ⓒ Ⓓ Ⓔ	83. Ⓐ Ⓑ Ⓒ Ⓓ Ⓔ
18. Ⓐ Ⓑ Ⓒ Ⓓ Ⓔ	40. Ⓐ Ⓑ Ⓒ Ⓓ Ⓔ	62. Ⓐ Ⓑ Ⓒ Ⓓ Ⓔ	84. Ⓐ Ⓑ Ⓒ Ⓓ Ⓔ
19. Ⓐ Ⓑ Ⓒ Ⓓ Ⓔ	41. Ⓐ Ⓑ Ⓒ Ⓓ Ⓔ	63. Ⓐ Ⓑ Ⓒ Ⓓ Ⓔ	85. Ⓐ Ⓑ Ⓒ Ⓓ Ⓔ
20. Ⓐ Ⓑ Ⓒ Ⓓ Ⓔ	42. Ⓐ Ⓑ Ⓒ Ⓓ Ⓔ	64. Ⓐ Ⓑ Ⓒ Ⓓ Ⓔ	86. Ⓐ Ⓑ Ⓒ Ⓓ Ⓔ
21. Ⓐ Ⓑ Ⓒ Ⓓ Ⓔ	43. Ⓐ Ⓑ Ⓒ Ⓓ Ⓔ	65. Ⓐ Ⓑ Ⓒ Ⓓ Ⓔ	87. Ⓐ Ⓑ Ⓒ Ⓓ Ⓔ
22. Ⓐ Ⓑ Ⓒ Ⓓ Ⓔ	44. Ⓐ Ⓑ Ⓒ Ⓓ Ⓔ	66. Ⓐ Ⓑ Ⓒ Ⓓ Ⓔ	88. Ⓐ Ⓑ Ⓒ Ⓓ Ⓔ

PART C—NUMBER SERIES

1. Ⓐ Ⓑ Ⓒ Ⓓ Ⓔ	7. Ⓐ Ⓑ Ⓒ Ⓓ Ⓔ	13. Ⓐ Ⓑ Ⓒ Ⓓ Ⓔ	19. Ⓐ Ⓑ Ⓒ Ⓓ Ⓔ
2. Ⓐ Ⓑ Ⓒ Ⓓ Ⓔ	8. Ⓐ Ⓑ Ⓒ Ⓓ Ⓔ	14. Ⓐ Ⓑ Ⓒ Ⓓ Ⓔ	20. Ⓐ Ⓑ Ⓒ Ⓓ Ⓔ
3. Ⓐ Ⓑ Ⓒ Ⓓ Ⓔ	9. Ⓐ Ⓑ Ⓒ Ⓓ Ⓔ	15. Ⓐ Ⓑ Ⓒ Ⓓ Ⓔ	21. Ⓐ Ⓑ Ⓒ Ⓓ Ⓔ
4. Ⓐ Ⓑ Ⓒ Ⓓ Ⓔ	10. Ⓐ Ⓑ Ⓒ Ⓓ Ⓔ	16. Ⓐ Ⓑ Ⓒ Ⓓ Ⓔ	22. Ⓐ Ⓑ Ⓒ Ⓓ Ⓔ
5. Ⓐ Ⓑ Ⓒ Ⓓ Ⓔ	11. Ⓐ Ⓑ Ⓒ Ⓓ Ⓔ	17. Ⓐ Ⓑ Ⓒ Ⓓ Ⓔ	23. Ⓐ Ⓑ Ⓒ Ⓓ Ⓔ
6. Ⓐ Ⓑ Ⓒ Ⓓ Ⓔ	12. Ⓐ Ⓑ Ⓒ Ⓓ Ⓔ	18. Ⓐ Ⓑ Ⓒ Ⓓ Ⓔ	24. Ⓐ Ⓑ Ⓒ Ⓓ Ⓔ

ANSWER SHEET

PART D—FOLLOWING ORAL INSTRUCTIONS

1. Ⓐ Ⓑ Ⓒ Ⓓ Ⓔ	23. Ⓐ Ⓑ Ⓒ Ⓓ Ⓔ	45. Ⓐ Ⓑ Ⓒ Ⓓ Ⓔ	67. Ⓐ Ⓑ Ⓒ Ⓓ Ⓔ
2. Ⓐ Ⓑ Ⓒ Ⓓ Ⓔ	24. Ⓐ Ⓑ Ⓒ Ⓓ Ⓔ	46. Ⓐ Ⓑ Ⓒ Ⓓ Ⓔ	68. Ⓐ Ⓑ Ⓒ Ⓓ Ⓔ
3. Ⓐ Ⓑ Ⓒ Ⓓ Ⓔ	25. Ⓐ Ⓑ Ⓒ Ⓓ Ⓔ	47. Ⓐ Ⓑ Ⓒ Ⓓ Ⓔ	69. Ⓐ Ⓑ Ⓒ Ⓓ Ⓔ
4. Ⓐ Ⓑ Ⓒ Ⓓ Ⓔ	26. Ⓐ Ⓑ Ⓒ Ⓓ Ⓔ	48. Ⓐ Ⓑ Ⓒ Ⓓ Ⓔ	70. Ⓐ Ⓑ Ⓒ Ⓓ Ⓔ
5. Ⓐ Ⓑ Ⓒ Ⓓ Ⓔ	27. Ⓐ Ⓑ Ⓒ Ⓓ Ⓔ	49. Ⓐ Ⓑ Ⓒ Ⓓ Ⓔ	71. Ⓐ Ⓑ Ⓒ Ⓓ Ⓔ
6. Ⓐ Ⓑ Ⓒ Ⓓ Ⓔ	28. Ⓐ Ⓑ Ⓒ Ⓓ Ⓔ	50. Ⓐ Ⓑ Ⓒ Ⓓ Ⓔ	72. Ⓐ Ⓑ Ⓒ Ⓓ Ⓔ
7. Ⓐ Ⓑ Ⓒ Ⓓ Ⓔ	29. Ⓐ Ⓑ Ⓒ Ⓓ Ⓔ	51. Ⓐ Ⓑ Ⓒ Ⓓ Ⓔ	73. Ⓐ Ⓑ Ⓒ Ⓓ Ⓔ
8. Ⓐ Ⓑ Ⓒ Ⓓ Ⓔ	30. Ⓐ Ⓑ Ⓒ Ⓓ Ⓔ	52. Ⓐ Ⓑ Ⓒ Ⓓ Ⓔ	74. Ⓐ Ⓑ Ⓒ Ⓓ Ⓔ
9. Ⓐ Ⓑ Ⓒ Ⓓ Ⓔ	31. Ⓐ Ⓑ Ⓒ Ⓓ Ⓔ	53. Ⓐ Ⓑ Ⓒ Ⓓ Ⓔ	75. Ⓐ Ⓑ Ⓒ Ⓓ Ⓔ
10. Ⓐ Ⓑ Ⓒ Ⓓ Ⓔ	32. Ⓐ Ⓑ Ⓒ Ⓓ Ⓔ	54. Ⓐ Ⓑ Ⓒ Ⓓ Ⓔ	76. Ⓐ Ⓑ Ⓒ Ⓓ Ⓔ
11. Ⓐ Ⓑ Ⓒ Ⓓ Ⓔ	33. Ⓐ Ⓑ Ⓒ Ⓓ Ⓔ	55. Ⓐ Ⓑ Ⓒ Ⓓ Ⓔ	77. Ⓐ Ⓑ Ⓒ Ⓓ Ⓔ
12. Ⓐ Ⓑ Ⓒ Ⓓ Ⓔ	34. Ⓐ Ⓑ Ⓒ Ⓓ Ⓔ	56. Ⓐ Ⓑ Ⓒ Ⓓ Ⓔ	78. Ⓐ Ⓑ Ⓒ Ⓓ Ⓔ
13. Ⓐ Ⓑ Ⓒ Ⓓ Ⓔ	35. Ⓐ Ⓑ Ⓒ Ⓓ Ⓔ	57. Ⓐ Ⓑ Ⓒ Ⓓ Ⓔ	79. Ⓐ Ⓑ Ⓒ Ⓓ Ⓔ
14. Ⓐ Ⓑ Ⓒ Ⓓ Ⓔ	36. Ⓐ Ⓑ Ⓒ Ⓓ Ⓔ	58. Ⓐ Ⓑ Ⓒ Ⓓ Ⓔ	80. Ⓐ Ⓑ Ⓒ Ⓓ Ⓔ
15. Ⓐ Ⓑ Ⓒ Ⓓ Ⓔ	37. Ⓐ Ⓑ Ⓒ Ⓓ Ⓔ	59. Ⓐ Ⓑ Ⓒ Ⓓ Ⓔ	81. Ⓐ Ⓑ Ⓒ Ⓓ Ⓔ
16. Ⓐ Ⓑ Ⓒ Ⓓ Ⓔ	38. Ⓐ Ⓑ Ⓒ Ⓓ Ⓔ	60. Ⓐ Ⓑ Ⓒ Ⓓ Ⓔ	82. Ⓐ Ⓑ Ⓒ Ⓓ Ⓔ
17. Ⓐ Ⓑ Ⓒ Ⓓ Ⓔ	39. Ⓐ Ⓑ Ⓒ Ⓓ Ⓔ	61. Ⓐ Ⓑ Ⓒ Ⓓ Ⓔ	83. Ⓐ Ⓑ Ⓒ Ⓓ Ⓔ
18. Ⓐ Ⓑ Ⓒ Ⓓ Ⓔ	40. Ⓐ Ⓑ Ⓒ Ⓓ Ⓔ	62. Ⓐ Ⓑ Ⓒ Ⓓ Ⓔ	84. Ⓐ Ⓑ Ⓒ Ⓓ Ⓔ
19. Ⓐ Ⓑ Ⓒ Ⓓ Ⓔ	41. Ⓐ Ⓑ Ⓒ Ⓓ Ⓔ	63. Ⓐ Ⓑ Ⓒ Ⓓ Ⓔ	85. Ⓐ Ⓑ Ⓒ Ⓓ Ⓔ
20. Ⓐ Ⓑ Ⓒ Ⓓ Ⓔ	42. Ⓐ Ⓑ Ⓒ Ⓓ Ⓔ	64. Ⓐ Ⓑ Ⓒ Ⓓ Ⓔ	86. Ⓐ Ⓑ Ⓒ Ⓓ Ⓔ
21. Ⓐ Ⓑ Ⓒ Ⓓ Ⓔ	43. Ⓐ Ⓑ Ⓒ Ⓓ Ⓔ	65. Ⓐ Ⓑ Ⓒ Ⓓ Ⓔ	87. Ⓐ Ⓑ Ⓒ Ⓓ Ⓔ
22. Ⓐ Ⓑ Ⓒ Ⓓ Ⓔ	44. Ⓐ Ⓑ Ⓒ Ⓓ Ⓔ	66. Ⓐ Ⓑ Ⓒ Ⓓ Ⓔ	88. Ⓐ Ⓑ Ⓒ Ⓓ Ⓔ

SCORE SHEET

ADDRESS CHECKING

Your score on the Address Checking part is based upon the number of questions you answered correctly minus the number of questions you answered incorrectly. To determine your score, subtract the number of wrong answers from the number of correct answers.

Number Right	Minus	Number Wrong	=	Raw Score
____________	–	____________	=	____________

MEMORY FOR ADDRESSES

Your score on the Memory for Addresses part is based upon the number of questions you answered correctly minus one-fourth of the questions you answered incorrectly (number wrong divided by 4). Calculate this now:

Number Right	Minus	Number Wrong ÷ 4	=	Raw Score
____________	–	____________	=	____________

NUMBER SERIES

Your score on the Number Series part is based only on the number of questions you answered correctly. Wrong answers do not count against you.

Number Right	=	Raw Score
____________	=	____________

FOLLOWING ORAL INSTRUCTIONS

Your score on the Following Oral Instructions part is based only upon the number of questions you marked correctly on the answer sheet. The worksheet is not scored, and wrong answers on the answer sheet do not count against you.

Number Right	=	Raw Score
____________	=	____________

TOTAL SCORE

To find your total raw score, add together the raw scores for each section of the exam.

Address Checking Score ____________

\+

Memory for Addresses Score ____________

\+

Number Series Score ____________

\+

Following Oral Instructions Score ____________

=

____

Total Raw Score ____________

SELF EVALUATION CHART

Calculate your raw score for each test as shown above. Then check to see where your score falls on the scale from Poor to Excellent. Lightly shade in the boxes in which your scores fall.

Part	Excellent	Good	Average	Fair	Poor
Address Checking	80–95	65–79	50–64	35–49	1–34
Memory for Addresses	75–88	60–74	45–59	30–44	1–29
Number Series	21–24	18–20	14–17	11–13	1–10
Following Oral Instructions	27–31	23–26	19–22	14–18	1–13

U.S. POSTAL SERVICE CLERK, DISTRIBUTION CLERK (MACHINE) AND MARK-UP CLERK (AUTOMATED) EXAM

PART A—ADDRESS CHECKING

SAMPLE QUESTIONS

You will be allowed three minutes to read the directions and answer the five sample questions that follow. On the actual test, however, you will have only six minutes to answer 95 questions, so see how quickly you can compare addresses and still get the correct answer.

Directions: Each question consists of two addresses. If the two addresses are alike in **EVERY** way, darken answer space (A) on your answer sheet. If the two addresses are different in **ANY** way, darken answer space (D) on your answer sheet.

1.	Ft Collins CO 80523	Ft Collins CO 85023
2.	3626 Pennsylvania Ave NE	3626 Pennsylvania Ave NE
3.	2418 E 514th St	2418 E 515th St
4.	4437 Continental Tpke	4437 Continental Tpke
5.	682 Dunbarton Rd	682 Dunbarton Dr

Sample Answer Sheet

1. Ⓐ Ⓓ **4.** Ⓐ Ⓓ
2. Ⓐ Ⓓ **5.** Ⓐ Ⓓ
3. Ⓐ Ⓓ

Correct Answers

1. Ⓐ ● **4.** ● Ⓓ
2. ● Ⓓ **5.** Ⓐ ●
3. Ⓐ ●

PART A—ADDRESS CHECKING

6 Minutes—95 Questions

Directions: For each question, compare the address in the left column with the address in the right column. If the two addresses are **ALIKE IN EVERY WAY**, darken answer space (A) on your answer sheet. If the two addresses are **DIFFERENT IN ANY WAY**, darken answer space (D) on your answer sheet. Correct answers for this test are on page 185.

1.	1897 Smicksburg Rd	1897 Smithsburg Rd
2.	3609 E Paseo Aldeano	3909 E Paseo Aldeano
3.	11787 Ornamental Ln	1787 Ornamental Ln
4.	1096 Camino Grande E	1096 Camino Grande E
5.	2544 E Radcliff Ave	2544 E Redcliff Ave
6.	5796 E Narragansett Dr	5796 E Narragasett Dr
7.	12475 Ebbtide Way W	12475 Ebbtide Way W
8.	14396 N Via Armando	14396 S Via Armando
9.	2155 S Del Giorgio Rd	2155 S Del Giorgio Rd
10.	16550 Bainbridge Cir	165O5 Bainbridge Cir
11.	1826 Milneburg Rd	1826 Milneburg St
12.	Eureka KS 67045	Eureka KY 67045
13.	4010 Glenaddie Ave	4010 Glenaddie Ave
14.	13501 Stratford Rd	13501 Standford Rd
15.	3296 W 64th St	3296 E 64th St
16.	2201 Tennessee Cir	2201 Tennessee Cir
17.	1502 Avenue M NE	1502 Avenue N NE
18.	1096 SE Longrone Dr	1096 SE Longrone Dr
19.	1267 Darthmouth Ct	1267 Darthmont Ct
20.	825 Ophanage Rd	825 Ophanage Rd
21.	1754 Golden Springs Rd	1754 Golden Springs Road
22.	1015 Tallwoods Ln	1015 Tallwoods Ln
23.	1097 Lambada Dr	1097 Lambadd Dr
24.	Vredenburgh AL 36481	Verdenburgh AL 36481
25.	1800 Monticello Ave	1800 Monticello Ave
26.	1723 Yellowbird Ln	1723 Yellowbird Ct
27.	700 Valca Materials Rd	700 Valca Materials Rd
28.	1569 Ladywood Ln N	1569 Ladywood Ln W
29.	3256 Interurban Dr	3256 Interurban Dr
30.	1507 Haughton Cir	1507 Haughton Ct
31.	8971 Robertson Ave	8971 Robinson Ave
32.	3801 NE 49th Street	3801 NW 49th Street
33.	4102 Chalkville Rd	4102 Chalkview Rd
34.	1709 Ingersoll Cir	1709 Ingersoll Cir
35.	6800 N Nantucket Ln	6800 N Nantucket Ln
36.	12401 Tarrymore Dr	12401 Terrymore Dr
37.	1097 Huntsville Ave	1097 Huntsville Ave
38.	3566 Lornaridge Pl	3566 Lornaridge Pl
39.	2039 Klondike Ave SW	2039 Klondie Ave SW
40.	3267 Mayland Ln	3267 Maryland Ln
41.	12956 Strawberry Ln	12596 Strawberry Ln
42.	De Armanville AL 36257	De Armanville AL 36257
43.	6015 Anniston Dr	6015 Anneston Dr
44.	1525 E 90th St	1525 E 90th St

45.	1299 Chappaque Rd	1266 Chappaque Rd
46.	2156 Juliette Dr	2156 Juliaetta Dr
47.	999 N Hollingsworth St	999 S Hollingsworth St
48.	16901 Odum Crest Ln	19601 Odum Crest Ln
49.	9787 Zellmark Dr	9787 Zealmark Dr
50.	11103 NE Feasell Ave	11103 NE Feasell Ave
51.	51121 N Mattison Rd	51121 S Mattison Rd
52.	8326 Blackjack Ln	8326 Blackjack Blvd
53.	18765 Lagarde Ave	18765 Lagrande Ave
54.	11297 Gallatin Ln	11297 Gallatin Ln
55.	Wormleysburg PA 17043	Wormleysburg, PA 17043
56.	22371 N Sprague Ave	22371 S Sprague Ave
57.	15014 Warrior River Rd	15014 Warrior River Rd
58.	45721 Hucytown Plaza	45721 Hueytowne Plaza
59.	8973 Tedescki Dr	8793 Tedescki Dr
60.	12995 Raimond Muscoda Pl	12995 Raimont Muscoda Pl
61.	Phippsburg CO 80469	Phippsburg CA 80469
62.	52003 W 49th Ave	52003 W 46th Ave
63.	17201 Zenobia Cir	17210 Zenobia Cir
64.	4800 Garrison Cir	4800 Garrison Dr
65.	Los Angeles CA 90070	Los Angeles CA 90076
66.	14798 W 62nd Ave	14198 W 62nd Ave
67.	7191 E Eldridge Way	7191 E Eldridge Way
68.	1279 S Quintard Dr	1279 S Guintard Dr
69.	21899 Dellwood Ave	21899 Dillwood Ave
70.	7191 Zenophone Cir	7191 Zenohone Cir
71.	4301 Los Encinos Way	4301 Los Encinas Way
72.	19700 Ostronic Dr NW	19700 Ostronic Dr NE
73.	23291 Van Velsire Dr	23219 Van Velsire Dr
74.	547 Paradise Valley Rd	547 Paradise Valley Ct
75.	23167 Saltillo Ave	23167 SantilloAve
76.	43001 Mourning Dove Way	43001 Mourning Dove Way
77.	21183 Declaration Ave	21183 Declaration Ave
78.	10799 Via Sierra Ramal Ave	10799 Via Sierra Ramel Ave
79.	16567 Hermosillia Ct	16597 Hermosillia Ct
80.	Villamont VA 24178	Villamont VA24178
81.	18794 Villaboso Ave	18794 Villeboso Ave
82.	24136 Ranthom Ave	24136 Ranthon Ave
83.	13489 Golondrina Pl	13489 Golondrina St
84.	6598 Adamsville Ave	6598 Adamsville Ave
85.	12641 Indals Pl NE	12641 Indals Pl NW
86.	19701 SE 2nd Avenue	19701 NE 2nd Avenue
87.	22754 Cachalote Ln	22754 Cachalott Ln
88.	12341 Kingfisher Rd	12341 Kingsfisher Rd
89.	24168 Lorenzana Dr	24168 Lorenzano Dr
90.	32480 Blackfriar Rd	32480 Blackfriar Rd
91.	16355 Wheeler Dr	16355 Wheelen Dr
92.	5100 Magna Carta Rd	5100 Magna Certa Rd
93.	2341 N Federalist Pl	2341 N Federalist Pl
94.	22200 Timpangos Rd	22200 Timpangos Rd
95.	19704 Calderon Rd	19704 Calderon Rd

END OF ADDRESS CHECKING

PART B—MEMORY FOR ADDRESSES

SAMPLE QUESTIONS

The sample questions for this part are based upon the addresses in the five boxes below. Your task is to darken on your answer sheet the letter of the box in which each address belongs. You will have five minutes now to study the locations of the addresses. Then cover the boxes and try to mark the location of the sample questions. You may look back at the boxes if you cannot yet mark the address locations from memory.

The exam itself provides three practice sessions before the question set that really counts. Practice I and Practice III supply you with the boxes and permit you to refer to them if necessary. Practice II and the Memory for Addresses test itself do not permit you to look at the boxes. The test itself is based on memory.

(A)	(B)	(C)	(D)	(E)
8100–8399 Test	6800–6999 Test	7600–8099 Test	8400–8699 Test	7000–7599 Test
Pigeon	Vampire	Octopus	Ghost	Lever
7600–8099 City	7000–7599 City	8100–8399 City	6800–6999 City	8400–8699 City
Webb	Yak	Fleet	Hammer	Nougat
6800–6999 Mark	8400–8699 Mark	7000–7599 Mark	7600–8099 Mark	8100–8399 Mark

1. 7000–7599 Test
2. Octopus
3. Nougat
4. 8100–8399 Mark
5. 7000–7599 City
6. 8100–8399 City
7. Pigeon
8. 6800–6999 Mark
9. Vampire
10. Yak
11. 8400–8699 Test
12. 7600–8099 City
13. 7000–7599 Mark
14. Hammer

Sample Answer Sheet

1. Ⓐ Ⓑ Ⓒ Ⓓ Ⓔ
2. Ⓐ Ⓑ Ⓒ Ⓓ Ⓔ
3. Ⓐ Ⓑ Ⓒ Ⓓ Ⓔ
4. Ⓐ Ⓑ Ⓒ Ⓓ Ⓔ
5. Ⓐ Ⓑ Ⓒ Ⓓ Ⓔ
6. Ⓐ Ⓑ Ⓒ Ⓓ Ⓔ
7. Ⓐ Ⓑ Ⓒ Ⓓ Ⓔ
8. Ⓐ Ⓑ Ⓒ Ⓓ Ⓔ
9. Ⓐ Ⓑ Ⓒ Ⓓ Ⓔ
10. Ⓐ Ⓑ Ⓒ Ⓓ Ⓔ
11. Ⓐ Ⓑ Ⓒ Ⓓ Ⓔ
12. Ⓐ Ⓑ Ⓒ Ⓓ Ⓔ
13. Ⓐ Ⓑ Ⓒ Ⓓ Ⓔ
14. Ⓐ Ⓑ Ⓒ Ⓓ Ⓔ

Correct Answers

1. Ⓐ Ⓑ Ⓒ Ⓓ ●
2. Ⓐ Ⓑ ● Ⓓ Ⓔ
3. Ⓐ Ⓑ Ⓒ Ⓓ ●
4. Ⓐ Ⓑ Ⓒ Ⓓ ●
5. Ⓐ ● Ⓒ Ⓓ Ⓔ
6. Ⓐ Ⓑ ● Ⓓ Ⓔ
7. ● Ⓑ Ⓒ Ⓓ Ⓔ
8. ● Ⓑ Ⓒ Ⓓ Ⓔ
9. Ⓐ ● Ⓒ Ⓓ Ⓔ
10. Ⓐ Ⓑ Ⓒ Ⓓ Ⓔ
11. Ⓐ Ⓑ Ⓒ ● Ⓔ
12. ● Ⓑ Ⓒ Ⓓ Ⓔ
13. Ⓐ Ⓑ ● Ⓓ Ⓔ
14. Ⓐ Ⓑ Ⓒ ● Ⓔ

PRACTICE FOR MEMORY FOR ADDRESSES

Directions: The five boxes below are labelled (A), (B), (C), (D), and (E). In each box are three sets of number spans with names and two names that are not associated with numbers. In the next **THREE MINUTES,** you must try to memorize the box location of each name and number span. The position of a name or number span within its box is not important. You need only remember the letter of the box in which the item is to be found. You will use these names and numbers to answer three sets of practice questions that are NOT scored and one actual test that is scored. Correct answers are on page 186.

(A)	(B)	(C)	(D)	(E)
8100–8399 Test	6800–6999 Test	7600–8099 Test	8400–8699 Test	7000–7599 Test
Pigeon	Vampire	Octopus	Ghost	Lever
7600–8099 City	7000–7599 City	8100–8399 City	6800–6999 City	8400–8699 City
Webb	Yak	Fleet	Hammer	Nougat
6800–6999 Mark	8400–8699 Mark	7000–7599 Mark	7600–8099 Mark	8100–8399 Mark

PRACTICE I

Directions: Use the next **THREE MINUTES** to darken the answer space on the Practice I answer sheet the letter of the box in which each item that follows is to be found. Try to darken each answer choice without looking back at the boxes. If, however, you get stuck, you may refer to the boxes during this practice exercise. If you find that you must look at the boxes, try to memorize as you do so. This test is for practice only. It will not be scored.

1. 6800-6999 Test
2. 7000-7599 City
3. 8100-8399 Mark
4. Octopus
5. Webb
6. 7000-7599 Test
7. Nougat
8. 7600-8099 Mark
9. 7000-7599 City
10. Fleet
11. Hammer
12. 7000-7599 Mark
13. 7600-8099 City
14. 8400-8699 Test
15. 8400-8699 Mark
16. 7600-8099 City
17. Vampire
18. Lever
19. Ghost
20. 6800-6999 Mark
21. 8100-8399 City
22. 8400-8699 City
23. 8400-8699 Mark
24. Pigeon
25. Fleet
26. 8400-8699 Test
27. 7000-7599 Mark
28. 6800-6999 Test
29. 7600-8099 City
30. Yak
31. Nougat
32. 8100-8399 Test
33. 7000-7599 Test
34. Lever
35. 7000-7599 City
36. 7600-8099 Mark
37. Octopus
38. Webb
39. Hammer
40. 8100-8399 Mark
41. 7600-8099 Test
42. 6800-6999 City
43. 7600-8099 Test
44. Fleet
45. 6800-6999 Mark
46. 8100-8399 City
47. 8400-8699 City
48. 8400-8699 Mark
49. Yak
50. Vampire
51. 7000-7599 Test
52. 8100-8399 Mark
53. 8100-8399 Test
54. Ghost
55. Fleet
56. 6800-6999 Mark
57. 7000-7599 Mark
58. 7000-7599 City
59. Lever
60. Octopus
61. 7600-8099 Test
62. 8400-8699 Test
63. 7600-8099 City
64. Hammer
65. Pigeon
66. 7600-8099 Mark
67. 6800-6999 City
68. 6800-6999 Test
69. 8100-8399 City
70. Webb
71. Nougat
72. 7600-8099 Test
73. 8400-8699 City
74. 8400-8699 Mark
75. 8100-8399 Test
76. 7000-7599 City
77. 7000-7599 Mark
78. Hammer
79. Lever
80. Pigeon
81. 7600-8099 Test
82. 7000-7599 Test
83. 8100-8399 Mark
84. Vampire
85. Fleet
86. 7600-8099 City
87. 6800-6999 Mark
88. 8400-8699 City

ANSWER SHEET

PRACTICE I

1. Ⓐ Ⓑ Ⓒ Ⓓ Ⓔ	23. Ⓐ Ⓑ Ⓒ Ⓓ Ⓔ	45. Ⓐ Ⓑ Ⓒ Ⓓ Ⓔ	67. Ⓐ Ⓑ Ⓒ Ⓓ Ⓔ
2. Ⓐ Ⓑ Ⓒ Ⓓ Ⓔ	24. Ⓐ Ⓑ Ⓒ Ⓓ Ⓔ	46. Ⓐ Ⓑ Ⓒ Ⓓ Ⓔ	68. Ⓐ Ⓑ Ⓒ Ⓓ Ⓔ
3. Ⓐ Ⓑ Ⓒ Ⓓ Ⓔ	25. Ⓐ Ⓑ Ⓒ Ⓓ Ⓔ	47. Ⓐ Ⓑ Ⓒ Ⓓ Ⓔ	69. Ⓐ Ⓑ Ⓒ Ⓓ Ⓔ
4. Ⓐ Ⓑ Ⓒ Ⓓ Ⓔ	26. Ⓐ Ⓑ Ⓒ Ⓓ Ⓔ	48. Ⓐ Ⓑ Ⓒ Ⓓ Ⓔ	70. Ⓐ Ⓑ Ⓒ Ⓓ Ⓔ
5. Ⓐ Ⓑ Ⓒ Ⓓ Ⓔ	27. Ⓐ Ⓑ Ⓒ Ⓓ Ⓔ	49. Ⓐ Ⓑ Ⓒ Ⓓ Ⓔ	71. Ⓐ Ⓑ Ⓒ Ⓓ Ⓔ
6. Ⓐ Ⓑ Ⓒ Ⓓ Ⓔ	28. Ⓐ Ⓑ Ⓒ Ⓓ Ⓔ	50. Ⓐ Ⓑ Ⓒ Ⓓ Ⓔ	72. Ⓐ Ⓑ Ⓒ Ⓓ Ⓔ
7. Ⓐ Ⓑ Ⓒ Ⓓ Ⓔ	29. Ⓐ Ⓑ Ⓒ Ⓓ Ⓔ	51. Ⓐ Ⓑ Ⓒ Ⓓ Ⓔ	73. Ⓐ Ⓑ Ⓒ Ⓓ Ⓔ
8. Ⓐ Ⓑ Ⓒ Ⓓ Ⓔ	30. Ⓐ Ⓑ Ⓒ Ⓓ Ⓔ	52. Ⓐ Ⓑ Ⓒ Ⓓ Ⓔ	74. Ⓐ Ⓑ Ⓒ Ⓓ Ⓔ
9. Ⓐ Ⓑ Ⓒ Ⓓ Ⓔ	31. Ⓐ Ⓑ Ⓒ Ⓓ Ⓔ	53. Ⓐ Ⓑ Ⓒ Ⓓ Ⓔ	75. Ⓐ Ⓑ Ⓒ Ⓓ Ⓔ
10. Ⓐ Ⓑ Ⓒ Ⓓ Ⓔ	32. Ⓐ Ⓑ Ⓒ Ⓓ Ⓔ	54. Ⓐ Ⓑ Ⓒ Ⓓ Ⓔ	76. Ⓐ Ⓑ Ⓒ Ⓓ Ⓔ
11. Ⓐ Ⓑ Ⓒ Ⓓ Ⓔ	33. Ⓐ Ⓑ Ⓒ Ⓓ Ⓔ	55. Ⓐ Ⓑ Ⓒ Ⓓ Ⓔ	77. Ⓐ Ⓑ Ⓒ Ⓓ Ⓔ
12. Ⓐ Ⓑ Ⓒ Ⓓ Ⓔ	34. Ⓐ Ⓑ Ⓒ Ⓓ Ⓔ	56. Ⓐ Ⓑ Ⓒ Ⓓ Ⓔ	78. Ⓐ Ⓑ Ⓒ Ⓓ Ⓔ
13. Ⓐ Ⓑ Ⓒ Ⓓ Ⓔ	35. Ⓐ Ⓑ Ⓒ Ⓓ Ⓔ	57. Ⓐ Ⓑ Ⓒ Ⓓ Ⓔ	79. Ⓐ Ⓑ Ⓒ Ⓓ Ⓔ
14. Ⓐ Ⓑ Ⓒ Ⓓ Ⓔ	36. Ⓐ Ⓑ Ⓒ Ⓓ Ⓔ	58. Ⓐ Ⓑ Ⓒ Ⓓ Ⓔ	80. Ⓐ Ⓑ Ⓒ Ⓓ Ⓔ
15. Ⓐ Ⓑ Ⓒ Ⓓ Ⓔ	37. Ⓐ Ⓑ Ⓒ Ⓓ Ⓔ	59. Ⓐ Ⓑ Ⓒ Ⓓ Ⓔ	81. Ⓐ Ⓑ Ⓒ Ⓓ Ⓔ
16. Ⓐ Ⓑ Ⓒ Ⓓ Ⓔ	38. Ⓐ Ⓑ Ⓒ Ⓓ Ⓔ	60. Ⓐ Ⓑ Ⓒ Ⓓ Ⓔ	82. Ⓐ Ⓑ Ⓒ Ⓓ Ⓔ
17. Ⓐ Ⓑ Ⓒ Ⓓ Ⓔ	39. Ⓐ Ⓑ Ⓒ Ⓓ Ⓔ	61. Ⓐ Ⓑ Ⓒ Ⓓ Ⓔ	83. Ⓐ Ⓑ Ⓒ Ⓓ Ⓔ
18. Ⓐ Ⓑ Ⓒ Ⓓ Ⓔ	40. Ⓐ Ⓑ Ⓒ Ⓓ Ⓔ	62. Ⓐ Ⓑ Ⓒ Ⓓ Ⓔ	84. Ⓐ Ⓑ Ⓒ Ⓓ Ⓔ
19. Ⓐ Ⓑ Ⓒ Ⓓ Ⓔ	41. Ⓐ Ⓑ Ⓒ Ⓓ Ⓔ	63. Ⓐ Ⓑ Ⓒ Ⓓ Ⓔ	85. Ⓐ Ⓑ Ⓒ Ⓓ Ⓔ
20. Ⓐ Ⓑ Ⓒ Ⓓ Ⓔ	42. Ⓐ Ⓑ Ⓒ Ⓓ Ⓔ	64. Ⓐ Ⓑ Ⓒ Ⓓ Ⓔ	86. Ⓐ Ⓑ Ⓒ Ⓓ Ⓔ
21. Ⓐ Ⓑ Ⓒ Ⓓ Ⓔ	43. Ⓐ Ⓑ Ⓒ Ⓓ Ⓔ	65. Ⓐ Ⓑ Ⓒ Ⓓ Ⓔ	87. Ⓐ Ⓑ Ⓒ Ⓓ Ⓔ
22. Ⓐ Ⓑ Ⓒ Ⓓ Ⓔ	44. Ⓐ Ⓑ Ⓒ Ⓓ Ⓔ	66. Ⓐ Ⓑ Ⓒ Ⓓ Ⓔ	88. Ⓐ Ⓑ Ⓒ Ⓓ Ⓔ

PRACTICE II

Directions: The next 88 questions constitute another practice exercise. Darken your answers on the Practice II answer sheet. Again, the time limit is **THREE MINUTES.** This time, however, you must NOT look at the boxes while answering the questions. You must rely on your memory in marking the box location of each item. This practice test will not be scored.

1. 7000-7599 Mark
2. 6800-6999 City
3. 6800-6999 Test
4. Pigeon
5. Nougat
6. 8400-8699 Test
7. 7000-7599 City
8. 6800-6999 Mark
9. Hammer
10. Ghost
11. 7600-8099 City
12. 8100-8399 Mark
13. 7600-8099 Mark
14. 7600-8099 Test
15. Octopus
16. Webb
17. 8100-8399 City
18. 8400-8699 City
19. 6800-6999 Mark
20. Fleet
21. Lever
22. Yak
23. 8100-8399 Test
24. 7000-7599 Test
25. Vampire
26. Octopus
27. 6800-6999 Test
28. 6800-6999 City
29. 6800-6999 Mark
30. Lever
31. Nougat
32. 7000-7599 City
33. 8100-8399 Mark
34. 8100-8399 City
35. 8100-8399 Test
36. 8400-8699 Mark
37. Yak
38. Webb
39. 7600-8099 Test
40. 7000-7599 Mark
41. Fleet
42. 8400-8699 City
43. 7600-8099 City
44. 8400-8699 Test
45. Pigeon
46. Ghost
47. Hammer
48. 7600-8099 Mark
49. 7000-7599 Test
50. 8100-8399 Mark
51. 6800-6999 City
52. 7600-8099 Test
53. Lever
54. Hammer
55. 8100-8399 Test
56. 7000-7599 City
57. 7000-7599 Mark
58. Pigeon
59. Vampire
60. 8100-8399 City
61. 7600-8099 City
62. 7000-7599 Test
63. 6800-6999 Mark
64. Nougat
65. Yak
66. Webb
67. 8400-8699 Mark
68. 7600-8099 Mark
69. 8400-8699 City
70. 6800-6999 Test
71. Ghost
72. Octopus
73. Fleet
74. 8400-8699 Test
75. 7600-8099 Test
76. 6800-6999 Mark
77. 7600-8099 City
78. Nougat
79. Webb
80. 6800-6999 City
81. 6800-6999 Test
82. 7600-8099 Mark
83. Vampire
84. Octopus
85. 7000-7599 Test
86. 8100-8399 City
87. 6800-6999 Mark
88. 8100-8399 Test

PRACTICE ANSWER SHEET

PRACTICE II

1. Ⓐ Ⓑ Ⓒ Ⓓ Ⓔ
2. Ⓐ Ⓑ Ⓒ Ⓓ Ⓔ
3. Ⓐ Ⓑ Ⓒ Ⓓ Ⓔ
4. Ⓐ Ⓑ Ⓒ Ⓓ Ⓔ
5. Ⓐ Ⓑ Ⓒ Ⓓ Ⓔ
6. Ⓐ Ⓑ Ⓒ Ⓓ Ⓔ
7. Ⓐ Ⓑ Ⓒ Ⓓ Ⓔ
8. Ⓐ Ⓑ Ⓒ Ⓓ Ⓔ
9. Ⓐ Ⓑ Ⓒ Ⓓ Ⓔ
10. Ⓐ Ⓑ Ⓒ Ⓓ Ⓔ
11. Ⓐ Ⓑ Ⓒ Ⓓ Ⓔ
12. Ⓐ Ⓑ Ⓒ Ⓓ Ⓔ
13. Ⓐ Ⓑ Ⓒ Ⓓ Ⓔ
14. Ⓐ Ⓑ Ⓒ Ⓓ Ⓔ
15. Ⓐ Ⓑ Ⓒ Ⓓ Ⓔ
16. Ⓐ Ⓑ Ⓒ Ⓓ Ⓔ
17. Ⓐ Ⓑ Ⓒ Ⓓ Ⓔ
18. Ⓐ Ⓑ Ⓒ Ⓓ Ⓔ
19. Ⓐ Ⓑ Ⓒ Ⓓ Ⓔ
20. Ⓐ Ⓑ Ⓒ Ⓓ Ⓔ
21. Ⓐ Ⓑ Ⓒ Ⓓ Ⓔ
22. Ⓐ Ⓑ Ⓒ Ⓓ Ⓔ
23. Ⓐ Ⓑ Ⓒ Ⓓ Ⓔ
24. Ⓐ Ⓑ Ⓒ Ⓓ Ⓔ
25. Ⓐ Ⓑ Ⓒ Ⓓ Ⓔ
26. Ⓐ Ⓑ Ⓒ Ⓓ Ⓔ
27. Ⓐ Ⓑ Ⓒ Ⓓ Ⓔ
28. Ⓐ Ⓑ Ⓒ Ⓓ Ⓔ
29. Ⓐ Ⓑ Ⓒ Ⓓ Ⓔ
30. Ⓐ Ⓑ Ⓒ Ⓓ Ⓔ
31. Ⓐ Ⓑ Ⓒ Ⓓ Ⓔ
32. Ⓐ Ⓑ Ⓒ Ⓓ Ⓔ
33. Ⓐ Ⓑ Ⓒ Ⓓ Ⓔ
34. Ⓐ Ⓑ Ⓒ Ⓓ Ⓔ
35. Ⓐ Ⓑ Ⓒ Ⓓ Ⓔ
36. Ⓐ Ⓑ Ⓒ Ⓓ Ⓔ
37. Ⓐ Ⓑ Ⓒ Ⓓ Ⓔ
38. Ⓐ Ⓑ Ⓒ Ⓓ Ⓔ
39. Ⓐ Ⓑ Ⓒ Ⓓ Ⓔ
40. Ⓐ Ⓑ Ⓒ Ⓓ Ⓔ
41. Ⓐ Ⓑ Ⓒ Ⓓ Ⓔ
42. Ⓐ Ⓑ Ⓒ Ⓓ Ⓔ
43. Ⓐ Ⓑ Ⓒ Ⓓ Ⓔ
44. Ⓐ Ⓑ Ⓒ Ⓓ Ⓔ
45. Ⓐ Ⓑ Ⓒ Ⓓ Ⓔ
46. Ⓐ Ⓑ Ⓒ Ⓓ Ⓔ
47. Ⓐ Ⓑ Ⓒ Ⓓ Ⓔ
48. Ⓐ Ⓑ Ⓒ Ⓓ Ⓔ
49. Ⓐ Ⓑ Ⓒ Ⓓ Ⓔ
50. Ⓐ Ⓑ Ⓒ Ⓓ Ⓔ
51. Ⓐ Ⓑ Ⓒ Ⓓ Ⓔ
52. Ⓐ Ⓑ Ⓒ Ⓓ Ⓔ
53. Ⓐ Ⓑ Ⓒ Ⓓ Ⓔ
54. Ⓐ Ⓑ Ⓒ Ⓓ Ⓔ
55. Ⓐ Ⓑ Ⓒ Ⓓ Ⓔ
56. Ⓐ Ⓑ Ⓒ Ⓓ Ⓔ
57. Ⓐ Ⓑ Ⓒ Ⓓ Ⓔ
58. Ⓐ Ⓑ Ⓒ Ⓓ Ⓔ
59. Ⓐ Ⓑ Ⓒ Ⓓ Ⓔ
60. Ⓐ Ⓑ Ⓒ Ⓓ Ⓔ
61. Ⓐ Ⓑ Ⓒ Ⓓ Ⓔ
62. Ⓐ Ⓑ Ⓒ Ⓓ Ⓔ
63. Ⓐ Ⓑ Ⓒ Ⓓ Ⓔ
64. Ⓐ Ⓑ Ⓒ Ⓓ Ⓔ
65. Ⓐ Ⓑ Ⓒ Ⓓ Ⓔ
66. Ⓐ Ⓑ Ⓒ Ⓓ Ⓔ
67. Ⓐ Ⓑ Ⓒ Ⓓ Ⓔ
68. Ⓐ Ⓑ Ⓒ Ⓓ Ⓔ
69. Ⓐ Ⓑ Ⓒ Ⓓ Ⓔ
70. Ⓐ Ⓑ Ⓒ Ⓓ Ⓔ
71. Ⓐ Ⓑ Ⓒ Ⓓ Ⓔ
72. Ⓐ Ⓑ Ⓒ Ⓓ Ⓔ
73. Ⓐ Ⓑ Ⓒ Ⓓ Ⓔ
74. Ⓐ Ⓑ Ⓒ Ⓓ Ⓔ
75. Ⓐ Ⓑ Ⓒ Ⓓ Ⓔ
76. Ⓐ Ⓑ Ⓒ Ⓓ Ⓔ
77. Ⓐ Ⓑ Ⓒ Ⓓ Ⓔ
78. Ⓐ Ⓑ Ⓒ Ⓓ Ⓔ
79. Ⓐ Ⓑ Ⓒ Ⓓ Ⓔ
80. Ⓐ Ⓑ Ⓒ Ⓓ Ⓔ
81. Ⓐ Ⓑ Ⓒ Ⓓ Ⓔ
82. Ⓐ Ⓑ Ⓒ Ⓓ Ⓔ
83. Ⓐ Ⓑ Ⓒ Ⓓ Ⓔ
84. Ⓐ Ⓑ Ⓒ Ⓓ Ⓔ
85. Ⓐ Ⓑ Ⓒ Ⓓ Ⓔ
86. Ⓐ Ⓑ Ⓒ Ⓓ Ⓔ
87. Ⓐ Ⓑ Ⓒ Ⓓ Ⓔ
88. Ⓐ Ⓑ Ⓒ Ⓓ Ⓔ

PRACTICE III

Directions: The names and addresses are repeated for you in the boxes below. Each name and each number span is in the same box in which you found it in the original set. You will now be allowed **FIVE MINUTES** to study the locations again. Do your best to memorize the letter of the box in which each item is located. This is your last chance to see the boxes.

(A)	(B)	(C)	(D)	(E)
8100–8399 Test	6800–6999 Test	7600–8099 Test	8400–8699 Test	7000–7599 Test
Pigeon	Vampire	Octopus	Ghost	Lever
7600–8099 City	7000–7599 City	8100–8399 City	6800–6999 City	8400–8699 City
Webb	Yak	Fleet	Hammer	Nougat
6800–6999 Mark	8400–8699 Mark	7000–7599 Mark	7600–8099 Mark	8100–8399 Mark

Directions: This is your last practice test. Darken the answer space for the location of each of the 88 items on your answer sheet. You will have **FIVE MINUTES** to answer these questions. Do NOT look back at the boxes. This practice test will not be scored.

1. Fleet
2. Lever
3. 8400-8699 Test
4. 7000-7599 City
5. 6800-6999 Mark
6. Vampire
7. Pigeon
8. 8100-8399 Test
9. 8100-8399 Mark
10. 7000-7599 Test
11. 8100-8399 City
12. Octopus
13. Ghost
14. Yak
15. 6800-6999 City
16. 6800-6999 Test
17. 7600-8099 Mark
18. 7600-8099 City
19. Hammer
20. Nougat
21. 8400-8699 Mark
22. 8400-8699 City
23. 8400-8699 Test
24. 7000-7599 Mark
25. Octopus
26. Fleet
27. 8100-8399 City
28. 8100-8399 Test
29. 7000-7599 City
30. 7000-7599 Test
31. 8100-8399 Test
32. 7000-7599 City
33. 7000-7599 Mark
34. Nougat
35. Ghost
36. 6800-6999 City
37. 7000-7599 Test
38. 8100-8399 Mark
39. Pigeon
40. Webb
41. 7600-8099 City
42. 8100-8399 City
43. 8400-8699 Mark
44. Fleet
45. Vampire
46. 6800-6999 Test
47. 6800-6999 Mark
48. 7600-8099 Mark
49. Hammer
50. Yak
51. 8400-8699 City
52. 8400-8699 Test
53. 7600-8099 Test
54. Lever
55. Octopus
56. 7000-7599 Test
57. 7000-7599 Mark
58. 7000-7599 City
59. 8100-8399 Test
60. Vampire
61. 8100-8399 City
62. Hammer
63. 8100-8399 Mark
64. 7000-7599 Test
65. Ghost
66. Yak
67. 6800-6999 Mark
68. 7600-8099 City
69. Octopus
70. Fleet
71. 8400-8699 City
72. 7000-7599 Mark
73. 7600-8099 Test
74. 7600-8099 Mark
75. 6800-6999 City
76. 6800-6999 Test
77. Webb
78. Pigeon
79. Lever
80. 8400-8699 Test
81. 8400-8699 Mark
82. Nougat
83. 8400-8699 City
84. 7000-7599 City
85. 7000-7599 Test
86. Hammer
87. 6800-6999 Mark
88. Yak

PRACTICE ANSWER SHEET

PRACTICE III

1. Ⓐ Ⓑ Ⓒ Ⓓ Ⓔ
2. Ⓐ Ⓑ Ⓒ Ⓓ Ⓔ
3. Ⓐ Ⓑ Ⓒ Ⓓ Ⓔ
4. Ⓐ Ⓑ Ⓒ Ⓓ Ⓔ
5. Ⓐ Ⓑ Ⓒ Ⓓ Ⓔ
6. Ⓐ Ⓑ Ⓒ Ⓓ Ⓔ
7. Ⓐ Ⓑ Ⓒ Ⓓ Ⓔ
8. Ⓐ Ⓑ Ⓒ Ⓓ Ⓔ
9. Ⓐ Ⓑ Ⓒ Ⓓ Ⓔ
10. Ⓐ Ⓑ Ⓒ Ⓓ Ⓔ
11. Ⓐ Ⓑ Ⓒ Ⓓ Ⓔ
12. Ⓐ Ⓑ Ⓒ Ⓓ Ⓔ
13. Ⓐ Ⓑ Ⓒ Ⓓ Ⓔ
14. Ⓐ Ⓑ Ⓒ Ⓓ Ⓔ
15. Ⓐ Ⓑ Ⓒ Ⓓ Ⓔ
16. Ⓐ Ⓑ Ⓒ Ⓓ Ⓔ
17. Ⓐ Ⓑ Ⓒ Ⓓ Ⓔ
18. Ⓐ Ⓑ Ⓒ Ⓓ Ⓔ
19. Ⓐ Ⓑ Ⓒ Ⓓ Ⓔ
20. Ⓐ Ⓑ Ⓒ Ⓓ Ⓔ
21. Ⓐ Ⓑ Ⓒ Ⓓ Ⓔ
22. Ⓐ Ⓑ Ⓒ Ⓓ Ⓔ
23. Ⓐ Ⓑ Ⓒ Ⓓ Ⓔ
24. Ⓐ Ⓑ Ⓒ Ⓓ Ⓔ
25. Ⓐ Ⓑ Ⓒ Ⓓ Ⓔ
26. Ⓐ Ⓑ Ⓒ Ⓓ Ⓔ
27. Ⓐ Ⓑ Ⓒ Ⓓ Ⓔ
28. Ⓐ Ⓑ Ⓒ Ⓓ Ⓔ
29. Ⓐ Ⓑ Ⓒ Ⓓ Ⓔ
30. Ⓐ Ⓑ Ⓒ Ⓓ Ⓔ
31. Ⓐ Ⓑ Ⓒ Ⓓ Ⓔ
32. Ⓐ Ⓑ Ⓒ Ⓓ Ⓔ
33. Ⓐ Ⓑ Ⓒ Ⓓ Ⓔ
34. Ⓐ Ⓑ Ⓒ Ⓓ Ⓔ
35. Ⓐ Ⓑ Ⓒ Ⓓ Ⓔ
36. Ⓐ Ⓑ Ⓒ Ⓓ Ⓔ
37. Ⓐ Ⓑ Ⓒ Ⓓ Ⓔ
38. Ⓐ Ⓑ Ⓒ Ⓓ Ⓔ
39. Ⓐ Ⓑ Ⓒ Ⓓ Ⓔ
40. Ⓐ Ⓑ Ⓒ Ⓓ Ⓔ
41. Ⓐ Ⓑ Ⓒ Ⓓ Ⓔ
42. Ⓐ Ⓑ Ⓒ Ⓓ Ⓔ
43. Ⓐ Ⓑ Ⓒ Ⓓ Ⓔ
44. Ⓐ Ⓑ Ⓒ Ⓓ Ⓔ
45. Ⓐ Ⓑ Ⓒ Ⓓ Ⓔ
46. Ⓐ Ⓑ Ⓒ Ⓓ Ⓔ
47. Ⓐ Ⓑ Ⓒ Ⓓ Ⓔ
48. Ⓐ Ⓑ Ⓒ Ⓓ Ⓔ
49. Ⓐ Ⓑ Ⓒ Ⓓ Ⓔ
50. Ⓐ Ⓑ Ⓒ Ⓓ Ⓔ
51. Ⓐ Ⓑ Ⓒ Ⓓ Ⓔ
52. Ⓐ Ⓑ Ⓒ Ⓓ Ⓔ
53. Ⓐ Ⓑ Ⓒ Ⓓ Ⓔ
54. Ⓐ Ⓑ Ⓒ Ⓓ Ⓔ
55. Ⓐ Ⓑ Ⓒ Ⓓ Ⓔ
56. Ⓐ Ⓑ Ⓒ Ⓓ Ⓔ
57. Ⓐ Ⓑ Ⓒ Ⓓ Ⓔ
58. Ⓐ Ⓑ Ⓒ Ⓓ Ⓔ
59. Ⓐ Ⓑ Ⓒ Ⓓ Ⓔ
60. Ⓐ Ⓑ Ⓒ Ⓓ Ⓔ
61. Ⓐ Ⓑ Ⓒ Ⓓ Ⓔ
62. Ⓐ Ⓑ Ⓒ Ⓓ Ⓔ
63. Ⓐ Ⓑ Ⓒ Ⓓ Ⓔ
64. Ⓐ Ⓑ Ⓒ Ⓓ Ⓔ
65. Ⓐ Ⓑ Ⓒ Ⓓ Ⓔ
66. Ⓐ Ⓑ Ⓒ Ⓓ Ⓔ
67. Ⓐ Ⓑ Ⓒ Ⓓ Ⓔ
68. Ⓐ Ⓑ Ⓒ Ⓓ Ⓔ
69. Ⓐ Ⓑ Ⓒ Ⓓ Ⓔ
70. Ⓐ Ⓑ Ⓒ Ⓓ Ⓔ
71. Ⓐ Ⓑ Ⓒ Ⓓ Ⓔ
72. Ⓐ Ⓑ Ⓒ Ⓓ Ⓔ
73. Ⓐ Ⓑ Ⓒ Ⓓ Ⓔ
74. Ⓐ Ⓑ Ⓒ Ⓓ Ⓔ
75. Ⓐ Ⓑ Ⓒ Ⓓ Ⓔ
76. Ⓐ Ⓑ Ⓒ Ⓓ Ⓔ
77. Ⓐ Ⓑ Ⓒ Ⓓ Ⓔ
78. Ⓐ Ⓑ Ⓒ Ⓓ Ⓔ
79. Ⓐ Ⓑ Ⓒ Ⓓ Ⓔ
80. Ⓐ Ⓑ Ⓒ Ⓓ Ⓔ
81. Ⓐ Ⓑ Ⓒ Ⓓ Ⓔ
82. Ⓐ Ⓑ Ⓒ Ⓓ Ⓔ
83. Ⓐ Ⓑ Ⓒ Ⓓ Ⓔ
84. Ⓐ Ⓑ Ⓒ Ⓓ Ⓔ
85. Ⓐ Ⓑ Ⓒ Ⓓ Ⓔ
86. Ⓐ Ⓑ Ⓒ Ⓓ Ⓔ
87. Ⓐ Ⓑ Ⓒ Ⓓ Ⓔ
88. Ⓐ Ⓑ Ⓒ Ⓓ Ⓔ

PART B—MEMORY FOR ADDRESSES

5 Minutes—88 Questions

Directions: Darken your answers on the answer sheet in the section headed "MEMORY FOR ADDRESSES." This test will be scored. You are NOT permitted to look at the boxes. Work from memory, as quickly and as accurately as you can. Correct answers are on page 187.

1. 8400-8699 Test
2. 7000-7599 City
3. 8400-8699 Mark
4. Nougat
5. Pigeon
6. 6800-6999 Test
7. 8100-8399 Test
8. 8400-8699 City
9. 7000-7599 Mark
10. Ghost
11. Hammer
12. Vampire
13. 7600-8099 City
14. 7600-8099 Mark
15. 6800-6999 Mark
16. Octopus
17. Yak
18. 7600-8099 Test
19. 7000-7599 Test
20. 8400-8699 City
21. 8100-8399 Mark
22. Vampire
23. Lever
24. 7600-8099 Test
25. 7600-8099 City
26. 8100-8399 Mark
27. Webb
28. Ghost
29. 6800-6999 Mark
30. 7000-7599 Test
31. 8100-8399 City
32. 8400-8699 City
33. Pigeon
34. Yak
35. 7600-8099 Mark
36. 8400-8699 Mark
37. 8100-8399 Test
38. 6800-6999 City
39. Octopus
40. Hammer
41. Nougat
42. 7000-7599 City
43. 6800-6999 Test
44. 7600-8099 Mark
45. Nougat
46. 8400-8699 City
47. 6800-6999 Mark
48. 7600-8099 Test
49. 7000-7599 City
50. Ghost
51. Fleet
52. Yak
53. 7000-7599 Test
54. 8100-8399 City
55. 7600-8099 City
56. Pigeon
57. Octopus
58. 6800-6999 City
59. 8400-8699 Mark
60. 8100-8399 Mark
61. 8100-8399 Test
62. Webb
63. Hammer
64. 8400-8699 Test
65. 7000-7599 Mark
66. 8100-8399 City
67. Lever
68. Vampire
69. 8100-8399 Test
70. 8400-8699 City
71. 7000-7599 Test
72. 6800-6999 Mark
73. 8100-8399 City
74. 6800-6999 City
75. Yak
76. Nougat
77. Fleet
78. 6800-6999 Test
79. 7000-7599 Mark
80. 7000-7599 City
81. 8100-8399 Test
82. 8100-8399 Mark
83. Pigeon
84. Lever
85. Hammer
86. 8400-8699 Test
87. 8400-8699 Mark
88. 7600-8099 City

End of Memory For Addresses

PART C—NUMBER SERIES

SAMPLE QUESTIONS

The following sample questions show you the type of question that will be used in Part C. You will have three minutes to answer the sample questions and to study the explanations.

> **Directions:** Each number series question consists of a series of numbers that follows some definite order. The numbers progress from left to right according to some rule. One pair of numbers to the right of the series comprises the next two numbers in the series. Study each series to try to find a pattern to the series and to figure out the rule that governs the progression. Choose the answer pair that continues the series according to the pattern established and darken its letter on your answer sheet..

1. 75 75 72 72 69 69 66 .... (A) 66 66 (B) 66 68 (C) 63 63 (D) 66 63 (E) 63 60

The pattern established in this series is: repeat the number, −3; repeat the number, −3. . . . To continue the series, repeat 66, then subtract 3. The answer is (D).

2. 12 16 21 27 31 36 42 .... (A) 48 56 (B) 44 48 (C) 48 52 (D) 46 52 (E) 46 51

By marking the amount and direction of change from one number of the series to the next, you can see that the pattern is: +4, +5, +6; +4, +5, +6; +4, +5, +6. Continuing the series: 42 + 4 = 46 + 5 = 51. (E) is the correct answer.

3. 22 24 12 26 28 12 30 .... (A) 12 32 (B) 32 34 (C) 32 12 (D) 12 12 (E) 32 36

In this series the basic pattern is +2. The series may be read: 22 24 26 28 30 32. After each two numbers of the series we find the number 12, which serves no function except for repetition. To continue the series, add 2 to 30 to get 32. After 30 and 32, you must put in the number 12, so (C) is the correct answer.

4. 5 70 10 68 15 66 20 ..... (A) 25 64 (B) 64 25 (C) 24 63 (D) 25 30 (E) 64 62

In this problem there are two distinct series alternating with one another. The first series is going up by a factor of +5. It reads: 10 15 20. The alternating series is going down by a factor of −2. It reads: 70 68 66. At the point where you must continue the series, the next number must be a member of the descending series, so it must be 64. Following that number must come the next number of the ascending series, which is 25. (B) is the answer.

5. 13 22 32 43 55 68 82 .... (A) 97 113 (B) 100 115 (C) 96 110 (D) 95 105 (E) 99 112

The numbers are large, but the progression is simple. If you mark the differences between numbers, you can readily recognize: +9, +10, +11, +12, +13, +14. Continuing the series: 82 + 15 = 97 + 16 = 113. (A) is the correct answer.

Sample Answer Sheet

1. Ⓐ Ⓑ Ⓒ Ⓓ Ⓔ
2. Ⓐ Ⓑ Ⓒ Ⓓ Ⓔ
3. Ⓐ Ⓑ Ⓒ Ⓓ Ⓔ
4. Ⓐ Ⓑ Ⓒ Ⓓ Ⓔ
5. Ⓐ Ⓑ Ⓒ Ⓓ Ⓔ

Correct Answers

1. Ⓐ Ⓑ Ⓒ ● Ⓔ
2. Ⓐ Ⓑ Ⓒ Ⓓ ●
3. Ⓐ Ⓑ ● Ⓓ Ⓔ
4. Ⓐ ● Ⓒ Ⓓ Ⓔ
5. ● Ⓑ Ⓒ Ⓓ Ⓔ

PART C—NUMBER SERIES

20 Minutes—24 Questions.

> **Directions**: Each number series question consists of a series of numbers that follows some definite order. The numbers progress from left to right according to some rule. One lettered pair of numbers comprises the next two numbers in the series. Study each series to try to find a pattern to the series and to figure the rule that governs the progression. Choose the answer pair that continues the series according to the pattern established and darken the answer space on your answer sheet. Correct answers are on page 187.

1. 3 8 4 9 5 10 6 .... (A) 7 11 (B) 7 8 (C) 11 8 (D) 12 7 (E) 11 7

2. 18 14 19 17 20 20 21 .. (A) 22 24 (B) 14 19 (C) 24 21 (D) 21 23 (E) 23 22

3. 6 9 10 7 11 12 8 .... (A) 9 10 (B) 9 13 (C) 16 14 (D) 13 14 (E) 14 15

4. 7 5 3 9 7 5 11 .... (A) 13 12 (B) 7 5 (C) 9 7 (D) 13 7 (E) 9 9

5. 7 9 18 10 12 18 13 .... (A) 18 14 (B) 15 18 (C) 14 15 (D)15 14 (E) 14 18

6. 2 6 4 8 6 10 8 .... (A) 12 10 (B) 6 10 (C) 10 12 (D) 12 16 (E) 6 4

7. 7 9 12 14 17 19 22 .... (A) 25 27 (B) 23 24 (C) 23 25 (D) 24 27 (E) 26 27

8. 3 23 5 25 7 27 9 .... (A) 10 11 (B) 27 29 (C) 29 11 (D) 11 28 (E) 28 10

9. 1 2 2 3 4 12 5 6 .... (A) 7 8 (B) 117 (C) 1156 (D) 56 7 (E) 30 7

10. 1 2 3 6 4 5 6 6 7 ...... (A) 6 5 (B) 8 9 (C) 6 8 (D) 7 6 (E) 8 6

11. 1 3 40 5 7 37 9 .... (A) 11 39 (B) 9 11 (C) 34 11 (D) 11 34 (E) 1135

12. 25 27 29 31 33 35 37 .. (A) 39 41 (B) 38 39 (C) 37 39 (D) 37 38 (E) 39 40

13. 91 85 17 81 75 15 71 .. (A) 74 14 (B) 61 51 (C) 65 13 (D) 65 10 (E) 66 33

14. 41 37 46 42 51 47 56 .. (A) 5 170 (B) 52 61 (C) 41) 60 (D) 60 43 (E) 55 65

15. 6 6 6 18 18 18 54 ...... (A) 54 108 (B) 54 162 (C) 108 108 (D) 10 8 162 (F) 54 54

16. 13 23 14 22 15 21 16 .. (A) 17 20 (B) 20 17 (C) 17 18 (D) 20 19 (E) 16 20

17. 52 10 48 20 44 30 40 .. (A) 36 50 (B) 50 36 (C) 36 40 (D) 40 36 (E) 40 40

18. 94 84 75 67 60 54 49 .. (A) 45 42 (B) 49 45 (C) 44 40 (D) 46 42 (E) 45 40

19. 76 38 38 48 24 24 34 .. (A) 34 44 (B) 34 34 (C) 17 17 (D) 34 17 (E) 17 27

20. 83 38 84 48 85 58 86 .. (A) 86 68 (B) 87 78 (C) 59 95 (D) 68 88 (E) 68 87

21. 19 212124 24 24 28 ... (A) 28 31 (B) 28 33 (C) 32 36 (D) 28 28 (E) 28 32

22. 52 45 38 32 26 21 16 .. (A) 16 12 (B) 12 8 (C) 11 6 (D) 11 7 (E) 12 9

23. 100 81 64 49 36 25 16 . (A) 12 10 (B) 8 4 (C) 8 2 (D) 9 4 (E) 9 2

24. 4 40 44 5 50 55 6 ...... (A) 60 66 (B) 6 60 (C) 6 66 (D) 7 70 (E) 70 77

End of Number Series

PART D—FOLLOWING ORAL INSTRUCTIONS

DIRECTIONS AND SAMPLE QUESTIONS

Listening to Instructions: When you are ready to try these sample questions, give the following instructions to a friend and have the friend read them aloud to you at the rate of 80 words per minute. Do not read them to yourself. Your friend will need a watch with a second hand. Listen carefully and do exactly what your friend tells you to do with the worksheet and answer sheet. Your friend will tell you some things to do with each item on the worksheet. After each set of instructions, your friend will give you time to mark your answer by darkening the answer space on the sample answer sheet. Since B and D sound very much alike, your friend will say "B as in baker" when he or she means B and "D as in dog" when he or she means D.

Before proceeding further, tear out the worksheet on page 177. Then hand this book to your friend.

To The Person Who Is To Read The Instructions: The instructions are to be read at the rate of 80 words per minute. Do not read aloud the material that is in parentheses. Do not repeat any instructions.

READ ALOUD TO THE CANDIDATE

Look at line 1 on your worksheet. (Pause slightly.) Draw a line under the third letter in the line. (Pause 2 seconds.) Now, on your answer sheet, find the number that is 2 less than 17 and darken the space for the letter under which you drew a line. (Pause 10 seconds.)

Look at line 2 on your worksheet. (Pause slightly.) Locate the smallest number and draw a circle around it. (Pause 5 seconds.) Now, on your answer sheet, darken the space for the letter (C) for the number you have circled. (Pause 5 seconds.)

Look at line 3 on your worksheet. (Pause slightly.) There are 5 boxes. Each box has a number. In each box containing a number that can be found on a foot-long ruler, write the letter E. (Pause 10 seconds.) Now, on your answer sheet, darken the answer space for the number-letter combination that is in each box you wrote in. (Pause 10 seconds.)

Look at line 4 on your worksheet. (Pause slightly.) If in a week Wednesday comes before Thursday, write D as in dog in the box with the largest number. (Pause 5 seconds.) If it does not, write E in the box of the second-to-largest number. (Pause 5 seconds.) Now, on your answer sheet, darken the space for the number-letter combination that is in the box you just wrote in. (Pause 5 seconds.)

SAMPLE WORKSHEET

Directions: Listening carefully to each set of instructions, mark each item on this worksheet as directed. Then complete each question by darkening the answer space on the sample answer sheet below as directed. For each answer you will darken the answer for a number-letter combination. Should you fall behind and miss an instruction, don't become excited. Let that one go and listen for the next one. If, when you start to darken a space for a number, you find that you have already darkened another space for that number, either erase the first mark and darken the space for the new combination or let the first mark stay and do not darken a space for the new combination. Write with a pencil that has a clean eraser. When you finish, you should have no more than one space darkened for each number.

1. E C A D R

2. 6 3 12 14 5 8

3.

8 ___	30 ___	5 ___	27 ___	13 ___

4.

6 ___	13 ___	12 ___	9 ___

Sample Answer Sheet

1. Ⓐ Ⓑ Ⓒ Ⓓ Ⓔ	**6.** Ⓐ Ⓑ Ⓒ Ⓓ Ⓔ	**11.** Ⓐ Ⓑ Ⓒ Ⓓ Ⓔ
2. Ⓐ Ⓑ Ⓒ Ⓓ Ⓔ	**7.** Ⓐ Ⓑ Ⓒ Ⓓ Ⓔ	**12.** Ⓐ Ⓑ Ⓒ Ⓓ Ⓔ
3. Ⓐ Ⓑ Ⓒ Ⓓ Ⓔ	**8.** Ⓐ Ⓑ Ⓒ Ⓓ Ⓔ	**13.** Ⓐ Ⓑ Ⓒ Ⓓ Ⓔ
4. Ⓐ Ⓑ Ⓒ Ⓓ Ⓔ	**9.** Ⓐ Ⓑ Ⓒ Ⓓ Ⓔ	**14.** Ⓐ Ⓑ Ⓒ Ⓓ Ⓔ
5. Ⓐ Ⓑ Ⓒ Ⓓ Ⓔ	**10.** Ⓐ Ⓑ Ⓒ Ⓓ Ⓔ	**15.** Ⓐ Ⓑ Ⓒ Ⓓ Ⓔ

Correct Answers

1. Ⓐ Ⓑ Ⓒ Ⓓ Ⓔ	6. Ⓐ Ⓑ Ⓒ Ⓓ Ⓔ	11. Ⓐ Ⓑ Ⓒ Ⓓ Ⓔ
2. Ⓐ Ⓑ Ⓒ Ⓓ Ⓔ	7. Ⓐ Ⓑ Ⓒ Ⓓ Ⓔ	12. Ⓐ Ⓑ Ⓒ Ⓓ Ⓔ
3. Ⓐ Ⓑ ● Ⓓ Ⓔ	8. Ⓐ Ⓑ Ⓒ Ⓓ ●	13. Ⓐ Ⓑ Ⓒ ● Ⓔ
4. Ⓐ Ⓑ Ⓒ Ⓓ Ⓔ	9. Ⓐ Ⓑ Ⓒ Ⓓ Ⓔ	14. Ⓐ Ⓑ Ⓒ Ⓓ Ⓔ
5. Ⓐ Ⓑ Ⓒ Ⓓ ●	10. Ⓐ Ⓑ Ⓒ Ⓓ Ⓔ	15. ● Ⓑ Ⓒ Ⓓ Ⓔ

1. E C A D R

2. 6 3 12 14 5 8

3.

8 E	30 ___	5 E	27 ___	13 ___

4.

6 ___	13 D	12 ___	9 ___

PART D—FOLLOWING ORAL INSTRUCTIONS

Time: 25 Minutes.

LISTENING TO INSTRUCTIONS

Directions: When you are ready to try this test of the Model Exam, give the following instructions to a friend and have the friend read them aloud to you at the rate of 80 words per minute. Do NOT read them to yourself. Your friend will need a watch with a second hand. Listen carefully and do exactly what your friend tells you to do with the worksheet and with the answer sheet. Your friend will tell you some things to do with each item on the worksheet. After each set of instructions, your friend will give you time to darken the answer space on the answer sheet. Since B and D sound very much alike, your friend will say "B as in baker" when he or she means B and "D as in dog" when he or she means D.

Before proceeding further, tear out the worksheet on page 183 of this test. Then hand this book to your friend.

To The Person Who Is To Read The Instructions: The instructions are to be read at the rate of 80 words per minute. Do not read aloud the material that is in parentheses. Once you have begun the test itself, do not repeat any instructions. The next three paragraphs consist of approximately 120 words. Read these three paragraphs aloud to the candidate in about one and one-half minutes. You may reread these paragraphs as often as necessary to establish an 80-words-per-minute reading speed.

READ ALOUD TO THE CANDIDATE

On the job you will have to listen to directions and then do what you have been told to do. In this test, I will read instructions to you. Try to understand them as I read them; I cannot repeat them. Once we begin, you may not ask any questions until the end of the test.

On the job you won't have to deal with pictures, numbers, and letters like those in the test, but you will have to listen to instructions and follow them. We are using this test to see how well you can follow instructions.

You are to mark your test booklet according to the instructions that I'll read to you. After each set of instructions, I'll give you time to record your answers on the separate answer sheet.

THE ACTUAL TEST BEGINS NOW.

Look at line 1 on your worksheet. (Pause slightly.) Underline the fifth number on line 1. (Pause 2 seconds.) Now, on your answer sheet, find the number you have underlined and mark D as in dog. (Pause 5 seconds.)

Now look at line 2 on your worksheet. (Pause slightly.) In each box that contains a vowel, write that vowel next to the number in the box. (Pause 5 seconds.) Now, on your answer sheet, darken the answer spaces for the number-letter combinations in the box or boxes in which you just wrote. (Pause 10 seconds.)

Look at line 3 on your worksheet. (Pause slightly.) Find the smallest number on line 3 and multiply it by 2. Write the number at the end of line 3. (Pause 5 seconds.) Now, on your answer sheet, darken answer space (C) for that number. (Pause 5 seconds.)

Look at line 3 again. (Pause slightly.) Divide the third number by 10 and write that number at the end of the line. (Pause 2 seconds.) Now, on your answer sheet, darken answer space (A) for the number you just wrote. (Pause 5 seconds.)

Now look at line 4 on your worksheet. (Pause slightly.) Mail for Detroit and Hartford is to be put in box 3. (Pause slightly.) Mail for Cleveland and St. Louis is to be put in box 26. (Pause slightly.) Write C in the box in which you put mail for St. Louis. (Pause 2 seconds.) Now, on your answer sheet, darken the answer space for the number-letter combination that is in the box you just wrote in. (Pause 5 seconds.)

Look at line 5 on your worksheet. (Pause slightly.) Write B as in baker on the line next to the highest number. (Pause 2 seconds.) Now, on your answer sheet, darken the answer space for the number-letter combination in the circle in which you just wrote. (Pause 5 seconds.)

Look at line 5 again. (Pause slightly.) Write the letter C on the line next to the lowest number. (Pause 2 seconds.) Now, on your answer sheet, darken the answer space for the number-letter combination in the circle in which you just wrote. (Pause 5 seconds.)

Look at the boxes and words on line 6 of your worksheet. (Pause 2 seconds.) In Box 1, write the first letter of the third word. (Pause 5 seconds.) In Box 2, write the last letter of the first word. (Pause 5 seconds.) In Box 3, write the last letter of the second word. (Pause 5 seconds.) Now, on your answer sheet, darken answer spaces for the number-letter combinations in all three boxes. (Pause 15 seconds.)

Look at line 7 on your worksheet. (Pause slightly.) Write the number 33 next to the letter in the mid-size circle. (Pause 2 seconds.) Now, on your answer sheet, darken the answer space for the number-letter combination in the circle in which you just wrote. (Pause 5 seconds.)

Look at line 8 on your worksheet. (Pause slightly.) If July comes before June, write D as in dog on the line after the second number; if not, write A on the line after the first number. (Pause 10 seconds.) Now, on your answer sheet, darken the answer space for the number-letter combination you just wrote. (Pause 5 seconds.)

Look at line 9 on your worksheet. (Pause slightly.) The number on each sack represents the number of pieces of mail in that sack. Next to the letter, write the last two figures of the sack containing the most pieces of mail. (Pause 2 seconds.) On your answer sheet, darken the answer space for the number-letter combination in the sack you just wrote in. (Pause 5 seconds.)

Look at line 9 again. (Pause slightly.) Now, write next to the letter the first two figures in the sack containing the fewest pieces of mail. (Pause 2 seconds.) On your answer sheet, darken the answer space for the number-letter combination in the sack you just wrote in. (Pause 5 seconds.)

Look at line 10 on your worksheet. (Pause slightly.) Answer this question: What is the sum of 8 plus 13? (Pause 2 seconds.) If the answer is 25, write 25 in the second box; if not, write the correct answer in the fourth box. (Pause 2 seconds.) Now, on your answer sheet, darken the number-letter combination in the box you just wrote in. (Pause 5 seconds.)

Look at line 10 again. (Pause slightly.) In the fifth box, write the number of ounces in a pound. (Pause 2 seconds.) Now, on your answer sheet, draken the number-letter combination in the box you just wrote in. (Pause 5 seconds.)

Look at line 11 on your worksheet. (Pause slightly.) If the number in the circle is greater than the number in the star, write B as in baker in the triangle; if not, write E in the box. (Pause 5 seconds.) Now, on your answer sheet, darken the number-letter combination in the figure you just wrote in. (Pause 5 seconds.)

Look at line 12 on your worksheet. (Pause slightly.) Draw one line under each P in line 12. (Pause 5 seconds.) Draw two lines under each Q in line 12. (Pause 5 seconds.) Count the number of P's and the number of Q's. (Pause 5 seconds.) If there are more P's than Q's, darken 71 (A) on your answer sheet; if there are not more P's than Q's, darken 71 (C) on your answer sheet. (Pause 5 seconds.)

Look at line 13 on your worksheet. (Pause slightly.) Circle each odd number that falls between 65 and 85. (Pause 10 seconds.) Now, on your answer sheet, darken answer space (D) as in dog for each number that you circled. (Pause 10 seconds.)

Look at line 13 again. (Pause slightly.) Find the number that is divisible by 6 and underline it. (Pause 2 seconds.) Now, on your answer sheet, darken answer space (A) for that number. (Pause 5 seconds.)

Look at line 14 on your worksheet. (Pause slightly.) Each circled time represents a pickup time from a street letter box. Find the pickup time which is furthest from noon and write the last two figures of that time on the line in the circle. (Pause 2 seconds.) Now, on your answer sheet, darken the number-letter combination that is in the circle you just wrote in. (Pause 5 seconds.)

Look at line 14 again. (Pause slightly.) Find the pickup time that is closest to noon and write the last two figures of that time on the line in the circle. (Pause 2 seconds.) Now, on your answer sheet, darken the number-letter combination that is in the circle you just wrote in. (Pause 5 seconds.)

Look at line 15 on your worksheet. (Pause slightly.) Write the highest number in the small box. (Pause 2 seconds.) Write the lowest number in the large box. (Pause 2 seconds.) Now, on your answer sheet, darken the number-letter combinations in the boxes you just wrote in. (Pause 10 seconds.)

Look at line 16 on your worksheet. (Pause slightly.) If, in the alphabet, the fourth letter on line 16 comes before the first letter on line 16, draw a line under the fourth letter (pause 2 seconds); if not, draw a line under the first letter on line 16. (Pause 2 seconds.) Now, on your answer sheet, find number 39 and darken the answer space for the letter you underlined. (Pause 5 seconds.)

Look at line 17 on your worksheet. (Pause slightly.) Find the number that does not belong on line 17 and circle that number. (Pause 2 seconds.) Now, on your answer sheet, darken answer space (D) as in dog for the number you just circled. (Pause 5 seconds.)

Look at line 17 again. (Pause slightly.) Find the number that answers this question: 60 minus 20 equals . . . and draw two lines under that number. (Pause 2 seconds.) Now, on your answer sheet, darken answer space (C) for the number under which you just drew two lines. (Pause 5 seconds.)

Look at line 18 on your worksheet. (Pause slightly.) If 3 is less than 7 and 4 is more than 6, write the number 12 in the first box (pause 5 seconds); if not, write the number 48 in the third box. (Pause 5 seconds.) Now, on your answer sheet, darken the answer space for the number-letter combination in the box you just wrote in. (Pause 5 seconds.)

Look at line 19 on your worksheet. (Pause slightly.) Draw a circle around the number that represents the product of 5 x 6. (Pause 5 seconds.) Now, on your answer sheet, find the number that you just circled and darken answer space (A) for that number. (Pause 5 seconds.)

FOLLOWING ORAL INSTRUCTIONS

WORKSHEET

Directions: Listening carefully to each set of instructions, mark each item on this worksheet as directed. Then complete each question by marking the answer sheet as directed. For each answer you will darken the answer for a number-letter combination. Should you fall behind and miss an instruction, don't become excited. Let that one go and listen for the next one. If, when you start to darken an answer space for a number, you find that you have already darkened another answer space for that number, either erase the first mark and darken the answer space for the new combination, or let the first mark stay and do not darken an answer space for the new combination. Write with a pencil that has a clean eraser. When you finish, you should have no more than one answer space darkened for each number. Correct answers are on page 189.

1. 6 3 18 90 45 36 12

2.

B 25 ___	G 36 ___	E 5 ___	C 17 ___	A 82 ___	D 13 ___

3. 17 4 30 25 9 41

4.

3 DETROIT HARTFORD ________	26 ST. LOUIS CLEVELAND ________

5. (27 ___) (54 ___) (31 ___) (76 ___) (18 ___)

6.

12 ___	56 ___	87 ___	RED WHITE BLUE

7. (___ D) (___ E) (___ A)

8. 7 ___ 64 ___ 31 ___

9. 432 ___ D   863 ___ C   729 ___ A   366 ___ B

10. ___ C   ___ A   ___ D   ___ B   ___ E

11. 9   17   3   23

12. P P Q Q P QP Q Q P

13. 47 76 83 75 66 89

14. 12:49 _____A   12:22 _____B   12:42 _____C   12:38 _____D   12:53 _____E

15. 69 56 66 42 45

___ C   ___ A

16. C E A B D

17. 30 40 50 57 60 70

18. ___ C   ___ B   ___ E   ___ D

19. 45 50 30 11

End of Examination

CORRECT ANSWERS—U.S. POSTAL SERVICE CLERK, DISTRIBUTION CLERK (MACHINE) AND MARK-UP CLERK (AUTOMATED) EXAM

PART A—ADDRESS CHECKING

1. D	**17.** D	**33.** D	**49.** D	**65.** D	**81.** D
2. D	**18.** A	**34.** A	**50.** A	**66.** D	**82.** D
3. D	**19.** D	**35.** A	**51.** D	**67.** A	**83.** D
4. A	**20.** A	**36.** D	**52.** D	**68.** D	**84.** A
5. D	**21.** D	**37.** A	**53.** D	**69.** D	**85.** D
6. D	**22.** A	**38.** A	**54.** A	**70.** D	**86.** D
7. A	**23.** D	**39.** D	**55.** A	**71.** D	**87.** D
8. D	**24.** D	**40.** D	**56.** D	**72.** D	**88.** D
9. A	**25.** A	**41.** D	**57.** A	**73.** D	**89.** D
10. D	**26.** D	**42.** A	**58.** D	**74.** D	**90.** A
11. D	**27.** A	**43.** D	**59.** D	**75.** D	**91.** D
12. D	**28.** D	**44.** A	**60.** D	**76.** A	**92.** D
13. A	**29.** A	**45.** D	**61.** D	**77.** A	**93.** A
14. D	**30.** D	**46.** D	**62.** D	**78.** D	**94.** A
15. D	**31.** D	**47.** D	**63.** D	**79.** D	**95.** A
16. A	**32.** D	**48.** D	**64.** D	**80.** A	

ANALYZING YOUR ERRORS

This Address Checking Test contains 30 address pairs that are exactly alike and 65 address pairs that are different. The chart below shows what kind of difference occurs in each of the addresses that contains a difference. Check your answers against this chart to see which kind of difference you missed most often. Note also the questions in which you thought you saw a difference but in which there really was none. Becoming aware of your errors will help you to eliminate those errors on the actual exam.

Type of Difference	Question Numbers	Number of Questions You Missed
Difference in NUMBERS	2, 3, 10, 41, 45, 48, 59, 62, 63, 65, 66, 73, 79	
Difference in ABBREVIATIONS	8, 11, 12, 15, 17, 21, 26, 28, 30, 32, 47, 51, 52, 56, 61, 64, 72, 74, 83, 85, 86	
Difference in NAMES	1, 5, 6, 14, 19, 23, 24, 31, 33, 36, 39, 40, 43, 46, 49, 53, 58, 60, 68, 69, 70, 71, 75, 78, 81, 82, 87, 88, 89, 91, 92	
No Difference	4, 7, 9, 13, 16, 18, 20, 22, 25, 27, 29, 34, 35, 37, 38, 42, 44, 50, 54, 55, 57, 67, 76, 77, 80, 84, 90, 93, 94, 95	

PART B—MEMORY FOR ADDRESSES

PRACTICE I

1. B	**16.** A	**31.** E	**46.** B	**61.** C	**76.** B
2. B	**17.** B	**32.** A	**47.** D	**62.** D	**77.** C
3. E	**18.** E	**33.** E	**48.** C	**63.** A	**78.** D
4. C	**19.** D	**34.** E	**49.** B	**64.** D	**79.** E
5. A	**20.** A	**35.** B	**50.** B	**65.** A	**80.** A
6. E	**21.** C	**36.** D	**51.** E	**66.** D	**81.** C
7. E	**22.** E	**37.** C	**52.** E	**67.** D	**82.** E
8. D	**23.** B	**38.** A	**53.** A	**68.** B	**83.** E
9. B	**24.** A	**39.** D	**54.** D	**69.** C	**84.** B
10. C	**25.** C	**40.** E	**55.** C	**70.** A	**85.** C
11. D	**26.** D	**41.** C	**56.** A	**71.** E	**86.** A
12. C	**27.** C	**42.** D	**57.** C	**72.** C	**87.** A
13. A	**28.** B	**43.** C	**58.** B	**73.** E	**88.** E
14. D	**29.** A	**44.** C	**59.** E	**74.** B	
15. B	**30.** B	**45.** E	**60.** C	**75.** A	

PRACTICE II

1. C	**16.** A	**31.** E	**46.** D	**61.** A	**76.** A
2. D	**17.** C	**32.** B	**47.** D	**62.** E	**77.** A
3. B	**18.** E	**33.** E	**48.** D	**63.** A	**78.** E
4. A	**19.** A	**34.** C	**49.** E	**64.** E	**79.** A
5. E	**20.** C	**35.** A	**50.** E	**65.** B	**80.** D
6. D	**21.** E	**36.** B	**51.** D	**66.** A	**81.** B
7. B	**22.** B	**37.** B	**52.** C	**67.** B	**82.** D
8. A	**23.** A	**38.** A	**53.** E	**68.** D	**83.** B
9. D	**24.** E	**39.** C	**54.** D	**69.** E	**84.** C
10. D	**25.** B	**40.** C	**55.** A	**70.** B	**85.** E
11. A	**26.** C	**41.** C	**56.** B	**71.** D	**86.** C
12. E	**27.** B	**42.** E	**57.** C	**72.** C	**87.** A
13. D	**28.** D	**43.** A	**58.** A	**73.** C	**88.** A
14. C	**29.** A	**44.** D	**59.** B	**74.** D	
15. C	**30.** E	**45.** A	**60.** C	**75.** C	

PRACTICE III

1. C	**16.** B	**31.** A	**46.** B	**61.** C	**76.** B
2. E	**17.** D	**32.** B	**47.** A	**62.** D	**77.** A
3. D	**18.** A	**33.** C	**48.** D	**63.** E	**78.** A
4. B	**19.** D	**34.** E	**49.** D	**64.** E	**79.** E
5. A	**20.** E	**35.** D	**50.** B	**65.** D	**80.** D
6. B	**21.** B	**36.** D	**51.** E	**66.** B	**81.** B
7. A	**22.** E	**37.** E	**52.** D	**67.** A	**82.** E
8. A	**23.** D	**38.** E	**53.** C	**68.** A	**83.** E
9. E	**24.** C	**39.** A	**54.** E	**69.** C	**84.** B
10. E	**25.** C	**40.** A	**55.** C	**70.** C	**85.** E
11. C	**26.** C	**41.** A	**56.** E	**71.** E	**86.** D
12. C	**27.** C	**42.** C	**57.** C	**72.** C	**87.** A
13. D	**28.** A	**43.** B	**58.** B	**73.** C	**88.** B
14. B	**29.** B	**44.** C	**59.** A	**74.** D	
15. D	**30.** E	**45.** B	**60.** B	**75.** D	

MEMORY FOR ADDRESSES

1. D	**16.** C	**31.** C	**46.** E	**61.** A	**76.** E
2. B	**17.** B	**32.** E	**47.** A	**62.** A	**77.** C
3. B	**18.** C	**33.** A	**48.** C	**63.** D	**78.** B
4. E	**19.** E	**34.** B	**49.** B	**64.** D	**79.** C
5. A	**20.** E	**35.** D	**50.** D	**65.** C	**80.** B
6. B	**21.** E	**36.** B	**51.** C	**66.** C	**81.** A
7. A	**22.** B	**37.** A	**52.** B	**67.** E	**82.** E
8. E	**23.** E	**38.** D	**53.** E	**68.** B	**83.** A
9. C	**24.** C	**39.** C	**54.** C	**69.** A	**84.** E
10. D	**25.** A	**40.** D	**55.** A	**70.** C	**85.** D
11. D	**26.** E	**41.** E	**56.** A	**71.** E	**86.** D
12. B	**27.** A	**42.** B	**57.** C	**72.** A	**87.** B
13. A	**28.** D	**43.** B	**58.** D	**73.** C	**88.** A
14. D	**29.** A	**44.** D	**59.** B	**74.** D	
15. A	**30.** E	**45.** E	**60.** E	**75.** B	

PART C—NUMBER SERIES

1. E	**5.** B	**9.** E	**13.** C	**17.** D	**21.** D
2. E	**6.** A	**10.** B	**14.** B	**18.** A	**22.** B
3. D	**7.** D	**11.** D	**15.** E	**19.** C	**23.** D
4. C	**8.** C	**12.** A	**16.** B	**20.** E	**24.** A

EXPLANATIONS

1. **The correct answer is (E).** There are two alternating series, each ascending by +1. One series begins with 3, the other with S.
2. **The correct answer is (E).** The two alternating series progress at different rates. The first, beginning with 18, moves up one number at a time. The alternating series, beginning with 14, increases by +3.
3. **The correct answer is (D).** There are two alternating series, but this time two numbers of one series interpose between steps of the other series. Thus, one series reads 6 7 8 while the other reads 9 10 11 12 13 14.
4. **The correct answer is (C).** Here we have a series of mini-series. The pattern in each mini-series is −2, −2. Then the pattern repeats with the first number of the next mini-series two numbers higher than the first number of the preceding mini-series.
5. **The correct answer is (B).** The series really is +2, +1, with the number 18 appearing between the two numbers at the + 1 phase.
6. **The correct answer is (A).** Two series alternate, both ascending by +2.
7. **The correct answer is (D).** Here the progression is +2, +3; +2, +3; and so on.
8. **The correct answer is (C).** Both alternating series move up by +2.
9. **The correct answer is (E).** The series is essentially 1 2 3 4 5 6 7, but after each two numbers in the series we find the product of the multiplication of those two numbers: $1 \times 2 = 2$; $3 \times 4 = 12$; $5 \times 6 = 30$; 7. . . .
10. **The correct answer is (B).** The series is simply 1 2 3 4 5 6 7 8 9. After each three numbers of the series, we find the number 6.
11. **The correct answer is (D).** There are two series. The ascending series increases by +2. The descending series intervenes after every two members of the ascending series. The descending series moves in steps of −3.
12. **The correct answer is (A).** Weren't you ready for an easy one? There is no catch. The series moves by +2.

13. **The correct answer is (C).** You may feel the rhythm of this series and spot the pattern without playing around with the numbers. If you cannot solve the problem by inspection, then you might see three parallel series. The first series descends by –10 (91 81 71); the second series also descends by minus 10 (85 75 65); the third series descends by –2 (17 15 13). Or, you might see a series of mini-series. Each mini-series begins with a number 10 lower than the first number of the previous mini-series. Within each mini-series the pattern is –6 ÷ 5.
14. **The correct answer is (B).** The pattern is – 4, + 9; – 4, + 9 ... Or, there are two alternating series. The first series ascends at the rate of +5; the alternating series also ascends at the rate of +5.
15. **The correct answer is (E).** Each number appears three times, then is multiplied by 3.
16. **The correct answer is (B).** There are two alternating series. One starts at 13 and moves up by +1, and the other starts at 23 and moves down by –1.
17. **The correct answer is (D).** There are two alternating series. The first series begins with 52 and descends at the rate of –4. The alternating series begins with 10 and ascends at the rate of +10.
18. **The correct answer is (A).** The pattern is: –10, –9, –8, –7, –6, –5, –4, –3.
19. **The correct answer is (C).** The pattern is: ÷ 2, repeat the number, +10 ÷ 2, repeat the number, +10 ÷ 2, repeat the number, +10.
20. **The correct answer is (E).** You see a simple series, 83 84 85 86. . . . After each number in this series you see its mirror image, that is, the mirror image of 83 is 38; the mirror image of 84 is 48; and so forth. Or you might see a series that increases by +1 alternating with a series that increases by +10.
21. **The correct answer is (D).** The pattern is: +2, repeat the number 2 times; +3, repeat the number 3 times; +4, repeat the number 4 times.
22. **The correct answer is (B).**The pattern is –7, –7, –6, –6, –5, –5, –4, –4.
23. **The correct answer is (D).** The series consists of the squares of the whole numbers in descending order.
24. **The correct answer is (A).** You can probably get this one by inspection. If not, notice the series of mini-series. In each mini-series the pattern is 10 times the first number, 11 times the first number.

PART D—FOLLOWING ORAL INSTRUCTIONS

CORRECTLY FILLED-IN ANSWER GRID

1. Ⓐ Ⓑ Ⓒ Ⓓ Ⓔ	**23.** Ⓐ Ⓑ Ⓒ Ⓓ Ⓔ	**45.** Ⓐ Ⓑ Ⓒ ● Ⓔ	**67.** Ⓐ Ⓑ Ⓒ Ⓓ Ⓔ
2. Ⓐ Ⓑ Ⓒ Ⓓ Ⓔ	**24.** Ⓐ Ⓑ Ⓒ Ⓓ Ⓔ	**46.** Ⓐ Ⓑ Ⓒ Ⓓ Ⓔ	**68.** Ⓐ Ⓑ Ⓒ Ⓓ Ⓔ
3. ● Ⓑ Ⓒ Ⓓ Ⓔ	**25.** Ⓐ Ⓑ Ⓒ Ⓓ Ⓔ	**47.** Ⓐ Ⓑ Ⓒ Ⓓ Ⓔ	**69.** Ⓐ Ⓑ ● Ⓓ Ⓔ
4. Ⓐ Ⓑ Ⓒ Ⓓ ●	**26.** Ⓐ Ⓑ ● Ⓓ Ⓔ	**48.** Ⓐ Ⓑ Ⓒ Ⓓ ●	**70.** Ⓐ Ⓑ Ⓒ Ⓓ Ⓔ
5. Ⓐ Ⓑ Ⓒ Ⓓ Ⓔ	**27.** Ⓐ Ⓑ Ⓒ Ⓓ Ⓔ	**49.** Ⓐ Ⓑ Ⓒ Ⓓ Ⓔ	**71.** Ⓐ Ⓑ ● Ⓓ Ⓔ
6. Ⓐ Ⓑ Ⓒ Ⓓ Ⓔ	**28.** Ⓐ Ⓑ Ⓒ Ⓓ Ⓔ	**50.** Ⓐ Ⓑ Ⓒ Ⓓ Ⓔ	**72.** Ⓐ Ⓑ Ⓒ Ⓓ Ⓔ
7. ● Ⓑ Ⓒ Ⓓ Ⓔ	**29.** Ⓐ Ⓑ Ⓒ Ⓓ Ⓔ	**51.** Ⓐ Ⓑ Ⓒ Ⓓ Ⓔ	**73.** Ⓐ Ⓑ Ⓒ Ⓓ Ⓔ
8. Ⓐ Ⓑ ● Ⓓ Ⓔ	**30.** ● Ⓑ Ⓒ Ⓓ Ⓔ	**52.** Ⓐ Ⓑ Ⓒ Ⓓ Ⓔ	**74.** Ⓐ Ⓑ Ⓒ Ⓓ Ⓔ
9. Ⓐ Ⓑ Ⓒ Ⓓ ●	**31.** Ⓐ Ⓑ Ⓒ Ⓓ Ⓔ	**53.** Ⓐ Ⓑ Ⓒ Ⓓ ●	**75.** Ⓐ Ⓑ Ⓒ ● Ⓔ
10. Ⓐ Ⓑ Ⓒ Ⓓ Ⓔ	**32.** Ⓐ Ⓑ Ⓒ Ⓓ Ⓔ	**54.** Ⓐ Ⓑ Ⓒ Ⓓ Ⓔ	**76.** Ⓐ ● Ⓒ Ⓓ Ⓔ
11. Ⓐ Ⓑ Ⓒ Ⓓ Ⓔ	**33.** ● Ⓑ Ⓒ Ⓓ Ⓔ	**55.** Ⓐ Ⓑ Ⓒ Ⓓ Ⓔ	**77.** Ⓐ Ⓑ Ⓒ Ⓓ Ⓔ
12. Ⓐ ● Ⓒ Ⓓ Ⓔ	**34.** Ⓐ Ⓑ Ⓒ Ⓓ Ⓔ	**56.** Ⓐ Ⓑ Ⓒ ● Ⓔ	**78.** Ⓐ Ⓑ Ⓒ Ⓓ Ⓔ
13. Ⓐ Ⓑ Ⓒ Ⓓ Ⓔ	**35.** Ⓐ Ⓑ Ⓒ Ⓓ Ⓔ	**57.** Ⓐ Ⓑ Ⓒ ● Ⓔ	**79.** Ⓐ Ⓑ Ⓒ Ⓓ Ⓔ
14. Ⓐ Ⓑ Ⓒ Ⓓ Ⓔ	**36.** Ⓐ ● Ⓒ Ⓓ Ⓔ	**58.** Ⓐ Ⓑ Ⓒ Ⓓ Ⓔ	**80.** Ⓐ Ⓑ Ⓒ Ⓓ Ⓔ
15. Ⓐ Ⓑ Ⓒ Ⓓ Ⓔ	**37.** Ⓐ Ⓑ Ⓒ Ⓓ Ⓔ	**59.** Ⓐ Ⓑ Ⓒ Ⓓ Ⓔ	**81.** Ⓐ Ⓑ Ⓒ Ⓓ Ⓔ
16. Ⓐ Ⓑ Ⓒ Ⓓ ●	**38.** Ⓐ Ⓑ Ⓒ Ⓓ Ⓔ	**60.** Ⓐ Ⓑ Ⓒ Ⓓ Ⓔ	**82.** ● Ⓑ Ⓒ Ⓓ Ⓔ
17. Ⓐ Ⓑ Ⓒ Ⓓ Ⓔ	**39.** Ⓐ ● Ⓒ Ⓓ Ⓔ	**61.** Ⓐ Ⓑ Ⓒ Ⓓ Ⓔ	**83.** Ⓐ Ⓑ Ⓒ ● Ⓔ
18. Ⓐ Ⓑ ● Ⓓ Ⓔ	**40.** Ⓐ Ⓑ ● Ⓓ Ⓔ	**62.** Ⓐ Ⓑ Ⓒ Ⓓ Ⓔ	**84.** Ⓐ Ⓑ Ⓒ Ⓓ Ⓔ
19. Ⓐ Ⓑ Ⓒ Ⓓ Ⓔ	**41.** Ⓐ Ⓑ Ⓒ Ⓓ Ⓔ	**63.** Ⓐ Ⓑ ● Ⓓ Ⓔ	**85.** Ⓐ Ⓑ Ⓒ Ⓓ Ⓔ
20. Ⓐ Ⓑ Ⓒ Ⓓ Ⓔ	**42.** ● Ⓑ Ⓒ Ⓓ Ⓔ	**64.** Ⓐ Ⓑ Ⓒ Ⓓ Ⓔ	**86.** Ⓐ Ⓑ Ⓒ Ⓓ Ⓔ
21. Ⓐ ● Ⓒ Ⓓ Ⓔ	**43.** Ⓐ Ⓑ Ⓒ Ⓓ Ⓔ	**65.** Ⓐ Ⓑ Ⓒ Ⓓ Ⓔ	**87.** Ⓐ Ⓑ Ⓒ Ⓓ ●
22. Ⓐ ● Ⓒ Ⓓ Ⓔ	**44.** Ⓐ Ⓑ Ⓒ Ⓓ Ⓔ	**66.** ● Ⓑ Ⓒ Ⓓ Ⓔ	**88.** Ⓐ Ⓑ Ⓒ Ⓓ Ⓔ

CORRECTLY FILLED-IN WORKSHEET

1. 6 3 18 90 <u>45</u> 36 12

2. | B 25 ___ | G 36 ___ | E 5 ___ | C 17 ___ | A 82 A | D 13 ___ |

3. 17 4 30 25 9 41 8

4. | 3 DETROIT HARTFORD ___ | 26 ST. LOUIS CLEVELAND C |

5. (27 ___) (54 ___) (31 ___) (76 B) (18 C)

6. | 12 B | 56 D | 87 E | RED WHITE BLUE

7. (___ D) (___ E) (33 A)

8. 7 A 64 ___ 31 ___

9. 432 ___ D | 863 63 C | 729 ___ A | 366 36 B

10. ___ C | ___ A | ___ D | 21 B | 16 E

11. E 9 | 17 | 3 | 23

12. P P Q Q P Q P Q Q P

13. 47 76 83 75 66 89

14. 12:49 _____A | 12:22 22 B | 12:42 _____C | 12:38 _____D | 12:53 53 E

15. 69 56 66 42 45

69 C | 42 A

16. C E A B D

17. 30 40 50 57 60 70

18. ___ C | ___ B | 48 E | ___ D

19. 45 50 30 11

ANSWER SHEET

U.S. POSTAL SERVICE CLERK-TYPIST AND CLERK-STENOGRAPHER EXAMS

EXAM 710 PART A—CLERK-TYPIST

1. Ⓐ Ⓑ Ⓒ Ⓓ Ⓔ	23. Ⓐ Ⓑ Ⓒ Ⓓ Ⓔ	44. Ⓐ Ⓑ Ⓒ Ⓓ Ⓔ	65. Ⓐ Ⓑ Ⓒ Ⓓ Ⓔ
2. Ⓐ Ⓑ Ⓒ Ⓓ Ⓔ	24. Ⓐ Ⓑ Ⓒ Ⓓ Ⓔ	45. Ⓐ Ⓑ Ⓒ Ⓓ Ⓔ	66. Ⓐ Ⓑ Ⓒ Ⓓ Ⓔ
3. Ⓐ Ⓑ Ⓒ Ⓓ Ⓔ	25. Ⓐ Ⓑ Ⓒ Ⓓ Ⓔ	46. Ⓐ Ⓑ Ⓒ Ⓓ Ⓔ	67. Ⓐ Ⓑ Ⓒ Ⓓ Ⓔ
4. Ⓐ Ⓑ Ⓒ Ⓓ Ⓔ	26. Ⓐ Ⓑ Ⓒ Ⓓ Ⓔ	47. Ⓐ Ⓑ Ⓒ Ⓓ Ⓔ	68. Ⓐ Ⓑ Ⓒ Ⓓ Ⓔ
5. Ⓐ Ⓑ Ⓒ Ⓓ Ⓔ	27. Ⓐ Ⓑ Ⓒ Ⓓ Ⓔ	48. Ⓐ Ⓑ Ⓒ Ⓓ Ⓔ	69. Ⓐ Ⓑ Ⓒ Ⓓ Ⓔ
6. Ⓐ Ⓑ Ⓒ Ⓓ Ⓔ	28. Ⓐ Ⓑ Ⓒ Ⓓ Ⓔ	49. Ⓐ Ⓑ Ⓒ Ⓓ Ⓔ	70. Ⓐ Ⓑ Ⓒ Ⓓ Ⓔ
7. Ⓐ Ⓑ Ⓒ Ⓓ Ⓔ	29. Ⓐ Ⓑ Ⓒ Ⓓ Ⓔ	50. Ⓐ Ⓑ Ⓒ Ⓓ Ⓔ	71. Ⓐ Ⓑ Ⓒ Ⓓ Ⓔ
8. Ⓐ Ⓑ Ⓒ Ⓓ Ⓔ	30. Ⓐ Ⓑ Ⓒ Ⓓ Ⓔ	51. Ⓐ Ⓑ Ⓒ Ⓓ Ⓔ	72. Ⓐ Ⓑ Ⓒ Ⓓ Ⓔ
9. Ⓐ Ⓑ Ⓒ Ⓓ Ⓔ	31. Ⓐ Ⓑ Ⓒ Ⓓ Ⓔ	52. Ⓐ Ⓑ Ⓒ Ⓓ Ⓔ	73. Ⓐ Ⓑ Ⓒ Ⓓ Ⓔ
10. Ⓐ Ⓑ Ⓒ Ⓓ Ⓔ	32. Ⓐ Ⓑ Ⓒ Ⓓ Ⓔ	53. Ⓐ Ⓑ Ⓒ Ⓓ Ⓔ	74. Ⓐ Ⓑ Ⓒ Ⓓ Ⓔ
11. Ⓐ Ⓑ Ⓒ Ⓓ Ⓔ	33. Ⓐ Ⓑ Ⓒ Ⓓ Ⓔ	54. Ⓐ Ⓑ Ⓒ Ⓓ Ⓔ	75. Ⓐ Ⓑ Ⓒ Ⓓ Ⓔ
12. Ⓐ Ⓑ Ⓒ Ⓓ Ⓔ	34. Ⓐ Ⓑ Ⓒ Ⓓ Ⓔ	55. Ⓐ Ⓑ Ⓒ Ⓓ Ⓔ	76. Ⓐ Ⓑ Ⓒ Ⓓ Ⓔ
13. Ⓐ Ⓑ Ⓒ Ⓓ Ⓔ	35. Ⓐ Ⓑ Ⓒ Ⓓ Ⓔ	56. Ⓐ Ⓑ Ⓒ Ⓓ Ⓔ	77. Ⓐ Ⓑ Ⓒ Ⓓ Ⓔ
14. Ⓐ Ⓑ Ⓒ Ⓓ Ⓔ	36. Ⓐ Ⓑ Ⓒ Ⓓ Ⓔ	57. Ⓐ Ⓑ Ⓒ Ⓓ Ⓔ	78. Ⓐ Ⓑ Ⓒ Ⓓ Ⓔ
15. Ⓐ Ⓑ Ⓒ Ⓓ Ⓔ	37. Ⓐ Ⓑ Ⓒ Ⓓ Ⓔ	58. Ⓐ Ⓑ Ⓒ Ⓓ Ⓔ	79. Ⓐ Ⓑ Ⓒ Ⓓ Ⓔ
16. Ⓐ Ⓑ Ⓒ Ⓓ Ⓔ	38. Ⓐ Ⓑ Ⓒ Ⓓ Ⓔ	59. Ⓐ Ⓑ Ⓒ Ⓓ Ⓔ	80. Ⓐ Ⓑ Ⓒ Ⓓ Ⓔ
17. Ⓐ Ⓑ Ⓒ Ⓓ Ⓔ	39. Ⓐ Ⓑ Ⓒ Ⓓ Ⓔ	60. Ⓐ Ⓑ Ⓒ Ⓓ Ⓔ	81. Ⓐ Ⓑ Ⓒ Ⓓ Ⓔ
18. Ⓐ Ⓑ Ⓒ Ⓓ Ⓔ	40. Ⓐ Ⓑ Ⓒ Ⓓ Ⓔ	61. Ⓐ Ⓑ Ⓒ Ⓓ Ⓔ	82. Ⓐ Ⓑ Ⓒ Ⓓ Ⓔ
19. Ⓐ Ⓑ Ⓒ Ⓓ Ⓔ	41. Ⓐ Ⓑ Ⓒ Ⓓ Ⓔ	62. Ⓐ Ⓑ Ⓒ Ⓓ Ⓔ	83. Ⓐ Ⓑ Ⓒ Ⓓ Ⓔ
20. Ⓐ Ⓑ Ⓒ Ⓓ Ⓔ	42. Ⓐ Ⓑ Ⓒ Ⓓ Ⓔ	63. Ⓐ Ⓑ Ⓒ Ⓓ Ⓔ	84. Ⓐ Ⓑ Ⓒ Ⓓ Ⓔ
21. Ⓐ Ⓑ Ⓒ Ⓓ Ⓔ	43. Ⓐ Ⓑ Ⓒ Ⓓ Ⓔ	64. Ⓐ Ⓑ Ⓒ Ⓓ Ⓔ	85. Ⓐ Ⓑ Ⓒ Ⓓ Ⓔ
22. Ⓐ Ⓑ Ⓒ Ⓓ Ⓔ			

ANSWER SHEET

EXAM 710 PART B—CLERK-STENOGRAPHER

1. Ⓐ Ⓑ Ⓒ Ⓓ Ⓔ
2. Ⓐ Ⓑ Ⓒ Ⓓ Ⓔ
3. Ⓐ Ⓑ Ⓒ Ⓓ Ⓔ
4. Ⓐ Ⓑ Ⓒ Ⓓ Ⓔ
5. Ⓐ Ⓑ Ⓒ Ⓓ Ⓔ
6. Ⓐ Ⓑ Ⓒ Ⓓ Ⓔ
7. Ⓐ Ⓑ Ⓒ Ⓓ Ⓔ
8. Ⓐ Ⓑ Ⓒ Ⓓ Ⓔ
9. Ⓐ Ⓑ Ⓒ Ⓓ Ⓔ
10. Ⓐ Ⓑ Ⓒ Ⓓ Ⓔ
11. Ⓐ Ⓑ Ⓒ Ⓓ Ⓔ
12. Ⓐ Ⓑ Ⓒ Ⓓ Ⓔ
13. Ⓐ Ⓑ Ⓒ Ⓓ Ⓔ
14. Ⓐ Ⓑ Ⓒ Ⓓ Ⓔ
15. Ⓐ Ⓑ Ⓒ Ⓓ Ⓔ
16. Ⓐ Ⓑ Ⓒ Ⓓ Ⓔ
17. Ⓐ Ⓑ Ⓒ Ⓓ Ⓔ
18. Ⓐ Ⓑ Ⓒ Ⓓ Ⓔ
19. Ⓐ Ⓑ Ⓒ Ⓓ Ⓔ
20. Ⓐ Ⓑ Ⓒ Ⓓ Ⓔ
21. Ⓐ Ⓑ Ⓒ Ⓓ Ⓔ
22. Ⓐ Ⓑ Ⓒ Ⓓ Ⓔ
23. Ⓐ Ⓑ Ⓒ Ⓓ Ⓔ
24. Ⓐ Ⓑ Ⓒ Ⓓ Ⓔ
25. Ⓐ Ⓑ Ⓒ Ⓓ Ⓔ
26. Ⓐ Ⓑ Ⓒ Ⓓ Ⓔ
27. Ⓐ Ⓑ Ⓒ Ⓓ Ⓔ
28. Ⓐ Ⓑ Ⓒ Ⓓ Ⓔ
29. Ⓐ Ⓑ Ⓒ Ⓓ Ⓔ
30. Ⓐ Ⓑ Ⓒ Ⓓ Ⓔ
31. Ⓐ Ⓑ Ⓒ Ⓓ Ⓔ
32. Ⓐ Ⓑ Ⓒ Ⓓ Ⓔ
33. Ⓐ Ⓑ Ⓒ Ⓓ Ⓔ
34. Ⓐ Ⓑ Ⓒ Ⓓ Ⓔ
35. Ⓐ Ⓑ Ⓒ Ⓓ Ⓔ
36. Ⓐ Ⓑ Ⓒ Ⓓ Ⓔ
37. Ⓐ Ⓑ Ⓒ Ⓓ Ⓔ
38. Ⓐ Ⓑ Ⓒ Ⓓ Ⓔ
39. Ⓐ Ⓑ Ⓒ Ⓓ Ⓔ
40. Ⓐ Ⓑ Ⓒ Ⓓ Ⓔ
41. Ⓐ Ⓑ Ⓒ Ⓓ Ⓔ
42. Ⓐ Ⓑ Ⓒ Ⓓ Ⓔ
43. Ⓐ Ⓑ Ⓒ Ⓓ Ⓔ
44. Ⓐ Ⓑ Ⓒ Ⓓ Ⓔ
45. Ⓐ Ⓑ Ⓒ Ⓓ Ⓔ
46. Ⓐ Ⓑ Ⓒ Ⓓ Ⓔ
47. Ⓐ Ⓑ Ⓒ Ⓓ Ⓔ
48. Ⓐ Ⓑ Ⓒ Ⓓ Ⓔ
49. Ⓐ Ⓑ Ⓒ Ⓓ Ⓔ
50. Ⓐ Ⓑ Ⓒ Ⓓ Ⓔ
51. Ⓐ Ⓑ Ⓒ Ⓓ Ⓔ
52. Ⓐ Ⓑ Ⓒ Ⓓ Ⓔ
53. Ⓐ Ⓑ Ⓒ Ⓓ Ⓔ
54. Ⓐ Ⓑ Ⓒ Ⓓ Ⓔ
55. Ⓐ Ⓑ Ⓒ Ⓓ Ⓔ
56. Ⓐ Ⓑ Ⓒ Ⓓ Ⓔ
57. Ⓐ Ⓑ Ⓒ Ⓓ Ⓔ
58. Ⓐ Ⓑ Ⓒ Ⓓ Ⓔ
59. Ⓐ Ⓑ Ⓒ Ⓓ Ⓔ
60. Ⓐ Ⓑ Ⓒ Ⓓ Ⓔ
61. Ⓐ Ⓑ Ⓒ Ⓓ Ⓔ
62. Ⓐ Ⓑ Ⓒ Ⓓ Ⓔ
63. Ⓐ Ⓑ Ⓒ Ⓓ Ⓔ
64. Ⓐ Ⓑ Ⓒ Ⓓ Ⓔ
65. Ⓐ Ⓑ Ⓒ Ⓓ Ⓔ
66. Ⓐ Ⓑ Ⓒ Ⓓ Ⓔ
67. Ⓐ Ⓑ Ⓒ Ⓓ Ⓔ
68. Ⓐ Ⓑ Ⓒ Ⓓ Ⓔ
69. Ⓐ Ⓑ Ⓒ Ⓓ Ⓔ
70. Ⓐ Ⓑ Ⓒ Ⓓ Ⓔ
71. Ⓐ Ⓑ Ⓒ Ⓓ Ⓔ
72. Ⓐ Ⓑ Ⓒ Ⓓ Ⓔ
73. Ⓐ Ⓑ Ⓒ Ⓓ Ⓔ
74. Ⓐ Ⓑ Ⓒ Ⓓ Ⓔ
75. Ⓐ Ⓑ Ⓒ Ⓓ Ⓔ
76. Ⓐ Ⓑ Ⓒ Ⓓ Ⓔ
77. Ⓐ Ⓑ Ⓒ Ⓓ Ⓔ
78. Ⓐ Ⓑ Ⓒ Ⓓ Ⓔ
79. Ⓐ Ⓑ Ⓒ Ⓓ Ⓔ
80. Ⓐ Ⓑ Ⓒ Ⓓ Ⓔ
81. Ⓐ Ⓑ Ⓒ Ⓓ Ⓔ
82. Ⓐ Ⓑ Ⓒ Ⓓ Ⓔ
83. Ⓐ Ⓑ Ⓒ Ⓓ Ⓔ
84. Ⓐ Ⓑ Ⓒ Ⓓ Ⓔ
85. Ⓐ Ⓑ Ⓒ Ⓓ Ⓔ
86. Ⓐ Ⓑ Ⓒ Ⓓ Ⓔ
87. Ⓐ Ⓑ Ⓒ Ⓓ Ⓔ
89. Ⓐ Ⓑ Ⓒ Ⓓ Ⓔ
90. Ⓐ Ⓑ Ⓒ Ⓓ Ⓔ
91. Ⓐ Ⓑ Ⓒ Ⓓ Ⓔ
92. Ⓐ Ⓑ Ⓒ Ⓓ Ⓔ
93. Ⓐ Ⓑ Ⓒ Ⓓ Ⓔ
94. Ⓐ Ⓑ Ⓒ Ⓓ Ⓔ
95. Ⓐ Ⓑ Ⓒ Ⓓ Ⓔ
96. Ⓐ Ⓑ Ⓒ Ⓓ Ⓔ
97. Ⓐ Ⓑ Ⓒ Ⓓ Ⓔ
98. Ⓐ Ⓑ Ⓒ Ⓓ Ⓔ
99. Ⓐ Ⓑ Ⓒ Ⓓ Ⓔ
100. Ⓐ Ⓑ Ⓒ Ⓓ Ⓔ
101. Ⓐ Ⓑ Ⓒ Ⓓ Ⓔ
102. Ⓐ Ⓑ Ⓒ Ⓓ Ⓔ
103. Ⓐ Ⓑ Ⓒ Ⓓ Ⓔ
104. Ⓐ Ⓑ Ⓒ Ⓓ Ⓔ
105. Ⓐ Ⓑ Ⓒ Ⓓ Ⓔ
106. Ⓐ Ⓑ Ⓒ Ⓓ Ⓔ
107. Ⓐ Ⓑ Ⓒ Ⓓ Ⓔ
107. Ⓐ Ⓑ Ⓒ Ⓓ Ⓔ
109. Ⓐ Ⓑ Ⓒ Ⓓ Ⓔ
110. Ⓐ Ⓑ Ⓒ Ⓓ Ⓔ
111. Ⓐ Ⓑ Ⓒ Ⓓ Ⓔ
112. Ⓐ Ⓑ Ⓒ Ⓓ Ⓔ
113. Ⓐ Ⓑ Ⓒ Ⓓ Ⓔ
114. Ⓐ Ⓑ Ⓒ Ⓓ Ⓔ
115. Ⓐ Ⓑ Ⓒ Ⓓ Ⓔ
116. Ⓐ Ⓑ Ⓒ Ⓓ Ⓔ
117. Ⓐ Ⓑ Ⓒ Ⓓ Ⓔ
117. Ⓐ Ⓑ Ⓒ Ⓓ Ⓔ
119. Ⓐ Ⓑ Ⓒ Ⓓ Ⓔ
120. Ⓐ Ⓑ Ⓒ Ⓓ Ⓔ
121. Ⓐ Ⓑ Ⓒ Ⓓ Ⓔ
122. Ⓐ Ⓑ Ⓒ Ⓓ Ⓔ
123. Ⓐ Ⓑ Ⓒ Ⓓ Ⓔ
124. Ⓐ Ⓑ Ⓒ Ⓓ Ⓔ
125. Ⓐ Ⓑ Ⓒ Ⓓ Ⓔ

EXAM 711 PART C—CLERK-STENOGRAPHER

1. Ⓐ Ⓑ Ⓒ Ⓓ Ⓔ
2. Ⓐ Ⓑ Ⓒ Ⓓ Ⓔ
3. Ⓐ Ⓑ Ⓒ Ⓓ Ⓔ
4. Ⓐ Ⓑ Ⓒ Ⓓ Ⓔ
5. Ⓐ Ⓑ Ⓒ Ⓓ Ⓔ
6. Ⓐ Ⓑ Ⓒ Ⓓ Ⓔ
7. Ⓐ Ⓑ Ⓒ Ⓓ Ⓔ
8. Ⓐ Ⓑ Ⓒ Ⓓ Ⓔ
9. Ⓐ Ⓑ Ⓒ Ⓓ Ⓔ
10. Ⓐ Ⓑ Ⓒ Ⓓ Ⓔ
11. Ⓐ Ⓑ Ⓒ Ⓓ Ⓔ
12. Ⓐ Ⓑ Ⓒ Ⓓ Ⓔ
13. Ⓐ Ⓑ Ⓒ Ⓓ Ⓔ
14. Ⓐ Ⓑ Ⓒ Ⓓ Ⓔ
15. Ⓐ Ⓑ Ⓒ Ⓓ Ⓔ
16. Ⓐ Ⓑ Ⓒ Ⓓ Ⓔ
17. Ⓐ Ⓑ Ⓒ Ⓓ Ⓔ
18. Ⓐ Ⓑ Ⓒ Ⓓ Ⓔ
19. Ⓐ Ⓑ Ⓒ Ⓓ Ⓔ
20. Ⓐ Ⓑ Ⓒ Ⓓ Ⓔ
21. Ⓐ Ⓑ Ⓒ Ⓓ Ⓔ
22. Ⓐ Ⓑ Ⓒ Ⓓ Ⓔ
23. Ⓐ Ⓑ Ⓒ Ⓓ Ⓔ
24. Ⓐ Ⓑ Ⓒ Ⓓ Ⓔ
25. Ⓐ Ⓑ Ⓒ Ⓓ Ⓔ
26. Ⓐ Ⓑ Ⓒ Ⓓ Ⓔ
27. Ⓐ Ⓑ Ⓒ Ⓓ Ⓔ
28. Ⓐ Ⓑ Ⓒ Ⓓ Ⓔ
29. Ⓐ Ⓑ Ⓒ Ⓓ Ⓔ
30. Ⓐ Ⓑ Ⓒ Ⓓ Ⓔ
31. Ⓐ Ⓑ Ⓒ Ⓓ Ⓔ
32. Ⓐ Ⓑ Ⓒ Ⓓ Ⓔ
33. Ⓐ Ⓑ Ⓒ Ⓓ Ⓔ
34. Ⓐ Ⓑ Ⓒ Ⓓ Ⓔ
35. Ⓐ Ⓑ Ⓒ Ⓓ Ⓔ
36. Ⓐ Ⓑ Ⓒ Ⓓ Ⓔ
37. Ⓐ Ⓑ Ⓒ Ⓓ Ⓔ
38. Ⓐ Ⓑ Ⓒ Ⓓ Ⓔ
39. Ⓐ Ⓑ Ⓒ Ⓓ Ⓔ
40. Ⓐ Ⓑ Ⓒ Ⓓ Ⓔ
41. Ⓐ Ⓑ Ⓒ Ⓓ Ⓔ
42. Ⓐ Ⓑ Ⓒ Ⓓ Ⓔ
43. Ⓐ Ⓑ Ⓒ Ⓓ Ⓔ
44. Ⓐ Ⓑ Ⓒ Ⓓ Ⓔ
45. Ⓐ Ⓑ Ⓒ Ⓓ Ⓔ
46. Ⓐ Ⓑ Ⓒ Ⓓ Ⓔ
47. Ⓐ Ⓑ Ⓒ Ⓓ Ⓔ
48. Ⓐ Ⓑ Ⓒ Ⓓ Ⓔ
49. Ⓐ Ⓑ Ⓒ Ⓓ Ⓔ
50. Ⓐ Ⓑ Ⓒ Ⓓ Ⓔ
51. Ⓐ Ⓑ Ⓒ Ⓓ Ⓔ
52. Ⓐ Ⓑ Ⓒ Ⓓ Ⓔ
53. Ⓐ Ⓑ Ⓒ Ⓓ Ⓔ
54. Ⓐ Ⓑ Ⓒ Ⓓ Ⓔ
55. Ⓐ Ⓑ Ⓒ Ⓓ Ⓔ

SCORE SHEET

Your score on Part A and Part B of the examination for Clerk-Typist and Clerk-Stenographer is based only on the number of correct answers. Wrong answers have no effect on the score. Part A and Part B are timed and administered as two separate units, but they are not scored separately. There is no Clerical Ability score and no Verbal Ability score; there is only a single Exam 710 score.

To determine your raw score on this exam, count up all of your correct answers on the full exam.

Number Right = Raw Score

__________ = __________

Since there is only a single Exam 710 score, your performance on any single question type does not matter. In order to earn a high score, however, you must do well on all parts of the exam. Enter your scores below to chart your performance on each question type. Then concentrate your efforts toward improvement in the areas with whicH you had the most difficulty.

PART A—CLERICAL ABILITY

Sequencing, Questions 1–20. Number right __________ out of 20.
Comparisons, Questions 21–50. Number right __________ out of 30.
Spelling, Questions 51–70. Number right __________ out of 20.
Computations, Questions 71–85. Number right __________ out of 15.

PART B—VERBAL ABILITY

Following Written Instructions, Questions 1–20. Number right __________ out of 20.
Grammar/Punctuation, Questions 21–40. Number right __________ out of 20.
Vocabulary/Reading Comprehension, Questions 41–55. Number right __________ out of 15.

Now use the self evaluation chart below to see where your total score falls on a scale from Poor to Excellent.

SELF EVALUATION CHART

	Excellent	Good	Average	Fair	Poor
Exam 710	125–140	109–124	91–108	61–90	0–6

PART C—STENOGRAPHY

Your score on Part C, the stenography test, is based on your number of correct answers minus one fourth of your wrong answers. To determine your score, divide the number of answers you got wrong by 4 and subtract that number from the number of answers you got right.

Number Right – Number Wrong ÷ 4 = Raw Score

__________ – __________ = __________

Evaluate your performance on the stenography test by darkening the space in which your raw score falls in the chart below.

SELF EVALUATION CHART

	Excellent	Good	Average	Fair	Poor
Stenography	111–125	96–110	81–95	51–80	0–50

U.S. POSTAL SERVICE CLERK-TYPIST AND CLERK-STENOGRAPHER EXAM 710

PART A—CLERICAL ABILITY

SAMPLE QUESTIONS

There are four kinds of questions in Part A. Each kind of question has its own set of directions, and each portion of the part is timed separately. The four kinds of questions are:

Sequencing	3 minutes	20 questions
Comparisons	5 minutes	30 questions
Spelling	3 minutes	20 questions
Computations	8 minutes	15 questions

Directions for Sequencing Questions: For each question there is a name, number, or code in a box at the left and four other names or codes in alphabetical or numerical order at the right. Find the correct space for the boxed name or number so that it will be in alphabetical and/or numerical order with the others and darken the letter of that space on your answer sheet.

1. Sheppard, Gladys

(A) →
Shepard, Dwight
(B) →
Shepard, F.H.
(C) →
Shephard, Louise
(D) →
Shepperd, Stella
(E) →

2. 17643847

(A) →
17653821
(B) →
17654903
(C) →
17659115
(D) →
17720836
(E) →

3. GGG-2483

(A) →
GFH-3184
(B) →
GHF-3185
(C) →
HAG-2468
(D) →
HFC-1023
(E) →

Directions for Comparisons Questions: In each line across the page there are three names, addresses, or codes that are very much alike. Compare the three and decide which ones are EXACTLY alike. On your answer sheet, darken answer space:

(A) if **ALL THREE** names, addresses, or codes are exactly **ALIKE**
(B) if only the **FIRST** and **SECOND** names, addresses, or codes are exactly **ALIKE**
(C) if only the **FIRST** and **THIRD** names, addresses, or codes are exactly **ALIKE**
(D) if only the **SECOND** and **THIRD** names, addresses, or codes are exactly **ALIKE**
(E) if **ALL THREE** names, addresses, or codes are **DIFFERENT**

4.	H. Merritt Audubon	H. Merriott Audubon	H. Merritt Audubon
5.	2395890	2395890	2395890
6.	3418 W. 42nd St.	3418 W. 42nd Ave.	3148 W. 42nd Ave.

Directions for Spelling Questions: Find the correct spelling of the word and darken the appropriate answer space on the answer sheet. If none of the spellings is correct, darken space (D).

7. (A) exceed
(B) excede
(C) exseed
(D) none of these

8. (A) maneuver
(B) manuver
(C) manuever
(D) none of these

9. (A) corellation
(B) corrolation
(C) corralation
(D) none of these

Directions for Computations Questions: Perform the computation as indicated in the question and find the answer among the list of alternative responses. If the correct answer is not given among the choices, darken answer space (E).

10. $2\overline{)142}$

(A) 70
(B) 72
(C) 74
(D) 76
(E) none of these

11. $\begin{array}{r} 25 \\ -\ 10 \\ \hline \end{array}$

(A) 5
(B) 10
(C) 15
(D) 20
(E) none of these

12. $\begin{array}{r} 18 \\ \times\ 6 \\ \hline \end{array}$

(A) 108
(B) 7116
(C) 118
(D) 124
(E) none of these

Sample Answer Sheet

1. Ⓐ Ⓑ Ⓒ Ⓓ Ⓔ	**5.** Ⓐ Ⓑ Ⓒ Ⓓ Ⓔ	**9.** Ⓐ Ⓑ Ⓒ Ⓓ Ⓔ
2. Ⓐ Ⓑ Ⓒ Ⓓ Ⓔ	**6.** Ⓐ Ⓑ Ⓒ Ⓓ Ⓔ	**10.** Ⓐ Ⓑ Ⓒ Ⓓ Ⓔ
3. Ⓐ Ⓑ Ⓒ Ⓓ Ⓔ	**7.** Ⓐ Ⓑ Ⓒ Ⓓ Ⓔ	**11.** Ⓐ Ⓑ Ⓒ Ⓓ Ⓔ
4. Ⓐ Ⓑ Ⓒ Ⓓ Ⓔ	**8.** Ⓐ Ⓑ Ⓒ Ⓓ Ⓔ	**12.** Ⓐ Ⓑ Ⓒ Ⓓ Ⓔ

Corrected Answers

1. Ⓐ Ⓑ Ⓒ ● Ⓔ	**5.** ● Ⓑ Ⓒ Ⓓ Ⓔ	**9.** Ⓐ Ⓑ Ⓒ ● Ⓔ
2. ● Ⓑ Ⓒ Ⓓ Ⓔ	**6.** Ⓐ Ⓑ Ⓒ Ⓓ ●	**10.** Ⓐ Ⓑ Ⓒ Ⓓ ●
3. Ⓐ ● Ⓒ Ⓓ Ⓔ	**7.** ● Ⓑ Ⓒ Ⓓ Ⓔ	**11.** Ⓐ Ⓑ ● Ⓓ Ⓔ
4. Ⓐ Ⓑ ● Ⓓ Ⓔ	**8.** ● Ⓑ Ⓒ Ⓓ Ⓔ	**12.** ● Ⓑ Ⓒ Ⓓ Ⓔ

SEQUENCING

Time: 3 Minutes—20 Questions

Directions for Sequencing Questions: For each question there is a name, number, or code in a box at the left and four other names, numbers, or codes in alphabetical or numerical order at the right. Find the correct space for the boxed name or number so that it will be in alphabetical and/or numerical order with the others and darken the answer space of your choice on your answer sheet.

1. Hackett, Gerald

(A) →
Habert, James
(B) →
Hachett, J.J.
(C) →
Hachetts, K. Larson
(D) →
Hachettson, Leroy
(E) →

2. 159233362

(A) →
58146020
(B) →
59233162
(C) →
59233262
(D) →
59233662
(E) →

3. MYP-6734

(A) →
NYP-6733
(B) →
NYS-7412
(C) →
NZT-4899
(D) →
PYZ-3636
(E) →

4. Bobbitt, Olivier E.

(A) →
Bobbitt, D. Olivier
(B) →
Bobbitt, Olive B.
(C) →
Bobbitt, Olivia H.
(D) →
Bobbitt, R. Olivia
(E) →

5. 100102032

(A) →
00120312
(B) →
00120323
(C) →
00120324
(D) →
00200303
(E) →

6. LPD-6100

(A) →
LPD-5865
(B) →
LPD-6001
(C) →
LPD-6101
(D) →
LPD-6106
(E) →

7. Vanstory, George

(A) →
Vanover, Eva
(B) →
VanSwinderen, Floyd
(C) →
VanSyckle, Harry
(D) →
Vanture, Laurence
(E) →

8. Fitzsimmons, Hugh

(A) →
Fitts, Harold
(B) →
Fitzgerald, June
(C) →
FitzGibbon, Junius
(D) →
FitzSimons, Martin
(E) →

9. 01066010

(A) →
01006040
(B) →
01006051
(C) →
01016053
(D) →
01016060
(E) →

10. AAZ-2687

(A) →
AAA-2132
(B) →
AAS-4623
(C) →
ASA-3216
(D) →
ASZ-5490
(E) →

11. Pawlowicz, Ruth M.

(A) →
Pawalek, Edward
(B) →
Pawelek, Flora G.
(C) →
Pawlowski, Joan M.
(D) →
Pawtowski, Wanda
(E) →

12. NCD-7834

(A) →
NBJ-4682
(B) →
NBT-5066
(C) →
NCD-7710
(D) →
NCD-7868
(E) →

13. 36270013

(A) →
36260006
(B) →
36270000
(C) →
36270030
(D) →
36670012
(E) →

14. Freedinberg, Erma T.

(A) →
Freedenberg, Emerson
(B) →
Freedenberg, Erma
(C) →
Freedenburg, Erma E.
(D) →
Freedinburg, Erma F.
(E) →

15. Prouty, Martha

(A) →
Proutey, Margaret
(B) →
Proutey, Maude
(C) →
Prouty, Myra
(D) →
Prouty, Naomi
(E) →

16. 58006021

(A) →
58006130
(B) →
58097222
(C) →
59000599
(D) →
59909000
(E) →

17. EKK-1443

(A) →
EGK-1164
(B) →
EKG-1329
(C) →
EKK-1331
(D) →
EKK-1403
(E) →

18. D'Amato, Vincent

(A) →
Daly, Steven
(B) →
D'Amboise, S. Vincent
(C) →
Daniel, Vail
(D) →
DeAlba, Valentina
(E) →

19. Schaeffer, Roger D.

(A) →
Schaffert, Evelyn M.
(B) →
Schaffner, Margaret M.
(C) →
Schafhirt, Milton G.
(D) →
Shafer, Richard E.
(E) →

20. SPP-4856

(A) →
PPS-4838
(B) →
PSP-4921
(C) →
SPS-4906
(D) →
SSP-4911
(E) →

END OF SEQUENCING QUESTIONS

COMPARISONS

Time: 5 Minutes—30 Questions

Directions: In each line across the page there are three names, addresses, or codes that are very much alike. Compare the three and decide which ones are EXACTLY alike. On your answer sheet, darken answer space:

(A) if **ALL THREE** names, addresses, or codes are exactly **ALIKE**
(B) if only the **FIRST** and **SECOND** names, addresses, or codes are exactly **ALIKE**
(C) if only the **FIRST** and **THIRD** names, addresses, or codes are exactly **ALIKE**
(D) if only the **SECOND** and **THIRD** names, addresses, or codes are exactly **ALIKE**
(E) if **ALL THREE** names, addresses, or codes are **DIFFERENT**

21.	Drusilla S. Ridgeley	Drusilla S. Ridgeley	Drusilla S. Ridgeley
22.	Andrei I. Toumantzev	Andrei I. Tourmantzev	Andrei I. Toumantzov
23.	6-78912-e3e42	6-78912-3e3e42	6-78912-e3e42
24.	86529 Dunwoodie Drive	86529 Dunwoodie Drive	85629 Dunwoodie Drive
25.	1592514	1592574	1592574
26.	Ella Burk Newham	Ella Burk Newnham	Elena Burk Newnham
27.	5416R-1952TZ-op	5416R-1952TZ-op	5416R-1952TZ-op
28.	60646 West Touhy Avenue	60646 West Touhy Avenue	60646 West Touhey Avenue
29.	Mardikian & Moore, Inc.	Mardikian and Moore, Inc.	Mardikian & Moore, Inc.
30.	9670243	9670423	9670423
31.	Eduardo Ingles	Eduardo Inglese	Eduardo Inglese
32.	Roger T. DeAngelis	Roger T. D'Angelis	Roger T. DeAngeles
33.	7692138	7692138	7692138
34.	2695 East 3435 South	2695 East 3435 South	2695 East 3435 South
35.	63qs5-95YT3-001	63qs5-95YT3-001	63qs5-95YT3-001
36.	2789350	2789350	2798350
37.	Helmut V. Lochner	Helmut V. Lockner	Helmut W. Lochner
38.	2454803	2548403	2454803
39.	Lemberger, WA 28094-9182	Lemberger, VA 28094-9182	Lemberger, VA 28094-9182
40.	4168-GNP-78852	4168-GNP-78852	4168-GNP-78852
41.	Yoshihito Saito	Yoshihito Saito	Yoshihito Saito
42.	5927681	5927861	5927681
43.	O'Reilly Bay, LA 56212	O'Reillys Bay, LA 56212	O'Reilly Bay, LA 56212
44.	Francis Ransdell	Frances Ramsdell	Francis Ramsdell
45.	5634-OotV5a-16867	5634-Ootv5a-16867	5634-Ootv5a-16867
46.	Dolores Mollicone	Dolores Mollicone	Doloras Mollicone
47.	David C. Routzon	David E. Routzon	David C. Routzron
48.	8932 Shimabui Hwy.	8932 Shimabui Hwy.	8932 Shimabui Hwy.
49.	6177396	6177936	6177396
50.	A8987-B73245	A8987-B73245	A8987-B73245

END OF COMPARISONS QUESTIONS

SPELLING

Time: 3 Minutes—20 Questions

Directions: Find the correct spelling of the word and darken the appropriate space on your answer sheet. If none of the spellings is correct, darken answer space (D).

51. (A) anticipate
(B) antisipate
(C) anticapate
(D) none of these

52. (A) similiar
(B) simmilar
(C) similar
(D) none of these

53. (A) sufficiantly
(B) suficeintly
(C) sufficiently
(D) none of these

54. (A) intelligence
(B) inteligence
(C) intellegence
(D) none of these

55. (A) referance
(B) referrence
(C) referense
(D) none of these

56. (A) conscious
(B) consious
(C) conscius
(D) none of these

57. (A) paralell
(B) parellel
(C) parellell
(D) none of these

58. (A) abundence
(B) abundance
(C) abundants
(D) none of these

59. (A) corregated
(B) corrigated
(C) corrugated
(D) none of these

60. (A) accumalation
(B) accumulation
(C) accumullation
(D) none of these

61. (A) resonance
(B) resonence
(C) resonnance
(D) none of these

62. (A) benaficial
(B) benefitial
(C) beneficial
(D) none of these

63. (A) spesifically
(B) specificially
(C) specifically
(D) none of these

64. (A) elemanate
(B) elimenate
(C) elliminate
(D) none of these eliminate

65. (A) collosal
(B) colosal
(C) collossal
(D) none of these

66. (A) auxillary
(B) auxilliary
(C) auxiliary
(D) none of these

67. (A) inimitable
(B) inimitible
(C) inimatable
(D) none of these

68. (A) disapearance
(B) dissapearance
(C) disappearence
(D) none of these disappearance

69. (A) appelate
(B) appellate
(C) apellate
(D) none of these

70. (A) esential
(B) essential
(C) essencial
(D) none of these

END OF SPELLING QUESTIONS

COMPUTATIONS

Time: 8 Minutes—15 Questions

Directions: Perform the computation as indicated in the question and find the answer among the list of alternative responses. If the correct answer is not given among the choices, darken answer space (E).

71. $83 - 56$

(A) 23
(B) 29
(C) 33
(D) 37
(E) none of these

72. $15 + 17$

(A) 22
(B) 32
(C) 39
(D) 42
(E) none of these

73. 32×7

(A) 224
(B) 234
(C) 324
(D) 334
(E) none of these

74. 39×2

(A) 77
(B) 78
(C) 79
(D) 81
(E) none of these

75. $43 - 15$

(A) 23
(B) 32
(C) 33
(D) 35
(E) none of these

76. $50 + 49$

(A) 89
(B) 90
(C) 99
(D) 109
(E) none of these

77. $6\overline{)366}$

(A) 11
(B) 31
(C) 36
(D) 66
(E) none of these

78. $\begin{array}{r} 38 \\ \times\ 3 \\ \hline \end{array}$

(A) 111
(B) 113
(C) 115
(D) 117
(E) none of these

79. $\begin{array}{r} 19 \\ +\ 21 \\ \hline \end{array}$

(A) 20
(B) 30
(C) 40
(D) 50
(E) none of these

80. $\begin{array}{r} 13 \\ -\ 6 \\ \hline \end{array}$

(A) 5
(B) 7
(C) 9
(D) 11
(E) none of these

81. $6\overline{)180}$

(A) 29
(B) 31
(C) 33
(D) 39
(E) none of these

82. $\begin{array}{r} 10 \\ \times\ 1 \\ \hline \end{array}$

(A) 0
(B) 1
(C) 10
(D) 100
(E) none of these

83. $7\overline{)287}$

(A) 21
(B) 27
(C) 31
(D) 37
(E) none of these

84. $\begin{array}{r} 12 \\ +\ 11 \\ \hline \end{array}$

(A) 21
(B) 22
(C) 23
(D) 24
(E) none of these

85. $\begin{array}{r} 85 \\ -\ 64 \\ \hline \end{array}$

(A) 19
(B) 21
(C) 29
(D) 31
(E) none of these

END OF COMPUTATIONS QUESTIONS

END OF PART A

PART B—VERBAL ABILITY

SAMPLE QUESTIONS

There are four kinds of questions in Part B. Each kind of question has its own set of directions, but the portions containing the different kinds of questions are not separately timed. There are 55 questions in Part B, and candidates are allowed 50 minutes to complete the entire part. The four kinds of questions are:

Follwing Written Instructions	20 questions
Grammer Punctuation	20 questions
Vocabulary	15 questions (combined with Reading Comprehension)
Reading Comprehension	15 questions (combined with Vocabulary)

Directions for following written instructions: These questions test your ability to follow instructions. Each question directs you to darken a specific number and letter combination on your answer sheet. The questions require your total concentration because the answers that you are instructed to darken are, for the most part, NOT in numerical sequence (i.e., you would not use Number 1 on your answer sheet to answer Question 1; Number 2 for Question 2; etc.). Instead, you must darken the number and space specifically designated in each test question.

1. Look at the numbers below. Draw one line under the lowest number. Now, on your answer sheet, find that number and darken answer space (C) for that number.

4 2 3 6

2. Circle the middle letter in the line below. Now, on your answer sheet, find the number 3 and darken the answer space for the letter you just circled.

F A D B E

3. Subtract 8 from 9 and write your answer on the line below. Now, on your answer sheet, darken answer space (D) for the space of the number you wrote.

____

The remaining questions are to be answered on the answer sheet in numerical sequence: Question 4 is to be answered in Space 4, Question 5 in Space 5, and so forth.

Directions for Grammar/Punctuation Questions: Each question consists of a sentence written in four different ways. Choose the sentence that is most appropriate with respect to grammar, usage, and punctuation, so as to be suitable for a business letter or report, and darken its answer space on your answer sheet.

4. (A) Your pen is different from mine.
(B) Your pen is different to mine.
(C) Your pen is different than mine.
(D) Your pen is different with mine.

Directions for Vocabulary Questions: Each question consists of a sentence containing a word in **boldface** type. Choose the best meaning for the word in **boldface** type and darken its answer space on your answer sheet.

5. A passing grade on the special exam may **exempt** the applicant from the experience requirements for that job. **Exempt** most nearly means

(A) prohibit
(B) excuse
(C) subject
(D) specify

Directions for Reading Comprehension Questions: Read each paragraph and answer the question that follows it by darkening the answer space of your choice on your answer sheet.

6. The work goals of an agency can best be reached if the employees understand and agree with these goals. One way to gain such understanding and agreement is for management to encourage and seriously consider suggestions from employees in the setting of agency goals.

The paragraph best supports the statement that understanding and agreement with agency goals can be gained by

(A) allowing the employees to set agency goals
(B) reaching agency goals quickly
(C) legislative review of agency operations
(D) employee participation in setting agency goals

Sample Answer Sheet

1. Ⓐ Ⓑ Ⓒ Ⓓ Ⓔ	**4.** Ⓐ Ⓑ Ⓒ Ⓓ Ⓔ
2. Ⓐ Ⓑ Ⓒ Ⓓ Ⓔ	**5.** Ⓐ Ⓑ Ⓒ Ⓓ Ⓔ
3. Ⓐ Ⓑ Ⓒ Ⓓ Ⓔ	**6.** Ⓐ Ⓑ Ⓒ Ⓓ Ⓔ

Corrected Answers

1. Ⓐ Ⓑ Ⓒ ● Ⓔ	**4.** ● Ⓑ Ⓒ Ⓓ Ⓔ
2. Ⓐ Ⓑ ● Ⓓ Ⓔ	**5.** Ⓐ ● Ⓒ Ⓓ Ⓔ
3. Ⓐ Ⓑ Ⓒ ● Ⓔ	**6.** Ⓐ Ⓑ Ⓒ ● Ⓔ

PART B—VERBAL ABILITY

Time: 50 Minutes—55 Questions

> **Directions:** Questions 1–20 test your ability to follow instructions. Each question directs you to darken a specific number and letter combination on your answer sheet. The questions require your total concentration because the answers that you are instructed to darken are, for the most part, NOT in numerical sequence (i.e., you would not use Number 1 on your answer sheet to answer Question 1; Number 2 for Question 2; etc.). Instead, you must darken the number and space specifically designated in each test question.

1. Look at the letters below. Draw a circle around the letter that comes first in the alphabet. Now, on your answer sheet, find Number 12 and darken the answer space for the letter you just circled.

E G D Z (B) F B

2. Draw a line under the odd number below that is more than 5 but less than 10. Find this number on your answer sheet and darken space E.

8 10 5 6 11 <u>9</u> E

3. Divide the number 16 by 4 and write your answer on the line below. Now find this number on your answer sheet and darken answer space (A).

__3 A__

4. Write the letter C on the line next to the left-hand number below. Now, on your answer sheet, darken the answer space for the number-letter combination you see.

5 __C__ 19 ______ 7 ______

5. If in any week Wednesday comes before Tuesday, write the number 15 on the line below. If not, write the number 18. Now, on your answer sheet, darken answer space (A) for the number you just wrote.

__18 A__

6. Count the number of Bs in the line below and write that number at the end of the line. Now, on your answer sheet, darken answer space (D) for the number you wrote.

A D A E B D C A __1-D__

7. Write the letter B on the line with the highest number. Now, on your answer sheet, darken the number-letter combination that appears on that line.

16 ______ 9 ______ 20 __B__ 11 ______

8. If the product of 6 × 4 is greater than the product of 8 × 3, write the letter E on the line below. If not, write the letter C. Now, on your answer sheet find number 8 and darken the answer space for the letter you just wrote.

__24__

9. Write the number 2 in the largest circle below. Now, on your answer sheet, darken the answer space for the number-letter combination in that circle.

(__A) [__D] (2 C) [__B]

10. Write the letter D on the line next to the number that is the sum of 7 + 4 + 4. Now, on your answer sheet, darken the answer space for that number-letter combination.

13 ______ 14 ______ 15 ______ 16 ______ 17 ______

11. If 5 × 5 equals 25 and 5 + 5 equals 10, write the number 17 on the line below. If not, write the number 10. Now, on your answer sheet, darken answer space (E) for the number you just wrote.

______

12. Circle the second letter below. On the line beside that letter write the number that represents the number of days in a week. Now, on your answer sheet, darken the answer space for that number-letter combination.

______ C ______ D ______ B ______ E

13. If a triangle has more angles than a rectangle, write the number 13 in the circle below. If not, write the number 14 in the square. Now, on your answer sheet, darken the space for the number-letter combination in the figure that you just wrote in.

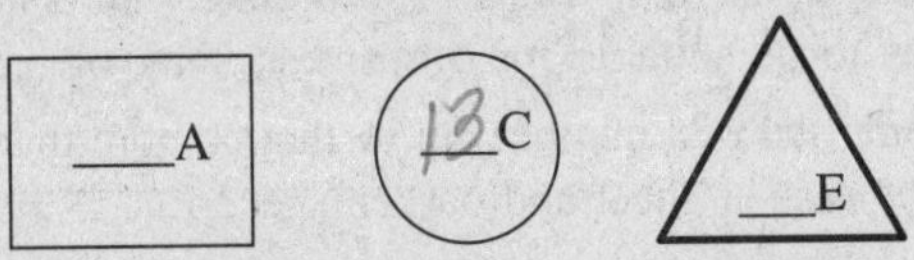

14. Count the number of Bs below and write that number at the end of the line. Subtract 2 from that number. Now, on your answer sheet, darken answer space (E) for the number that represents 2 less than the number of Bs in the line.

B E A D E C C B B B A E B D______

15. The numbers below represent morning pick-up times from neighborhood letter boxes. Draw a line under the number that represents the latest pick-up time. Now, on your answer sheet, darken answer space (D) for the number that is the same as the "minutes" of the time that you underlined.

9:19 10:16 10:10

16. If a person who is 6 feet tall is taller than a person who is 5 feet tall and if a pillow is softer than a rock, darken answer space 11 (A) on your answer sheet. If not, darken answer space 6 (B).

17. Write the fourth letter of the alphabet on the line next to the third number below. Now, on your answer sheet, darken that number-letter combination.

10 ______ 19 ______ 13 ______ 4 ______

18. Write the letter B in the box containing the next to smallest number. On your answer sheet, darken the answer space for that number-letter combination.

10____	19____	11____	6____

19. Directly below you will see three boxes and three words. Write the third letter of the first word on the line in the second box. Now, on your answer sheet, darken the answer space for that number-letter combination.

6____	19____	12____	BAD DRAB ALE

20. Count the number of points on the figure below. If there are five or more points, darken the answer space for 6 (E) on your answer sheet. If there are fewer than five points, darken answer space 6 (A).

Directions: Each question from 21–40 consists of a sentence written in four different ways. Choose the sentence that is most appropriate with respect to grammar, usage, and punctuation, so as to be suitable for a business letter or report, and darken its answer space on your answer sheet.

21. (A) Double parking is when you park your car alongside one that is already having been parked.
(B) When one double parks, you park your car alongside one that is already parked.
(C) Double parking is parking alongside a car already parked.
(D) To double park is alongside a car already parked.

22. (A) This is entirely among you and he.
(B) This is completely among him and you.
(C) This is between you and him.
(D) This is between he and you.

23. (A) As I said, "neither of them are guilty."
(B) As I said, "neither of them are guilty".
(C) As I said, "neither of them is guilty."
(D) As I said, neither of them is guilty.

24. (A) I think that they will promote whoever has the best record.
(B) The firm would have liked to have promoted all employees with good records.
(C) Such of them that have the best records have excellent prospects of promotion.
(D) I feel sure they will give the promotion to whomever has the best record.

25. (A) The receptionist must answer courteously the questions of all them callers.
(B) The receptionist must answer courteously the questions what are asked by the callers.
(C) There would have been no trouble if the receptionist had have always answered courteously.
(D) The receptionist should answer courteously the questions of all callers.

26. (A) Since the report lacked the needed information, it was of no use to them.
(B) This report was useless to them because there were no needed information in it.
(C) Since the report did not contain the needed information, it was not real useful to them.
(D) Being that the report lacked the needed information, they could not use it.

27. (A) The company had hardly declared the dividend till the notices were prepared for mailing.
(B) They had no sooner declared the dividend when they sent the notices to the stockholders.
(C) No sooner had the dividend been declared than the notices were prepared for mailing.
(D) Scarcely had the dividend been declared than the notices were sent out.

28. (A) The supervisors reprimanded the typists, whom she believed had made careless errors.
(B) The typists would have corrected the errors had they of known that the supervisor would see the report.
(C) The errors in the typed reports were so numerous that they could hardly be overlooked.
(D) Many errors were found in the reports which they typed and could not disregard them.

29. (A) "Are you absolutely certain, she asked, that you are right?"
(B) "Are you absolutely certain," she asked, "that you are right?"
(C) "Are you absolutely certain," she asked, "That you are right"?
(D) "Are you absolutely certain", she asked, "That you are right?"

30. (A) He goes only to church on Christmas and Easter.
(B) He only goes to church on Christmas and Easter.
(C) He goes to only church on Christmas and Easter.
(D) He goes to church only on Christmas and Easter.

31. (A) Most all these statements have been supported by persons who are reliable and can be depended upon.
(B) The persons which have guaranteed these statements are reliable.
(C) Reliable persons guarantee the facts with regards to the truth of these statements.
(D) These statements can be depended on, for their truth has been guaranteed by reliable persons.

32. (A) The success of the book pleased both the publisher and authors.
(B) Both the publisher and they was pleased with the success of the book.
(C) Neither they or their publisher was disappointed with the success of the book.
(D) Their publisher was as pleased as they with the success of the book.

33. (A) In reviewing the typists' work reports, the job analyst found records of unusual typing speeds.
(B) It says in the job analyst's report that some employees type with great speed.
(C) The job analyst found that, in reviewing the typists' work reports, that some unusual typing speeds had been made.
(D) In the reports of typists' speeds, the job analyst found some records that are kind of unusual.

34. (A) Every carrier should always have something to throw; not something to throw at the dog but something what will divert its attention.
(B) Every carrier should have something to throw—not something to throw at the dog but something to divert its attention.
(C) Every carrier should always carry something to throw not something to throw at the dog but something that will divert it's attention.
(D) Every carrier should always carry something to throw, not something to throw at the dog, but, something that will divert its' attention.

35. (A) Brown's & Company employees have recently received increases in salary.
(B) Brown & Company recently increased the salaries of all its employees.
(C) Recently Brown & Company has increased their employees' salaries.
(D) Brown & Company have recently increased the salaries of all its employees.

36. (A) If properly addressed, the letter will reach my mother and I.
(B) The letter had been addressed to myself and my mother.
(C) I believe the letter was addressed to either my mother or I.
(D) My mother's name, as well as mine, was on the letter.

37. (A) One of us have to make the reply before tomorrow.
(B) Making the reply before tomorrow will have to be done by one of us.
(C) One of us has to reply before tomorrow.
(D) Anyone has to reply before tomorrow.

38. (A) You have got to get rid of some of these people if you expect to have the quality of the work improve.
(B) The quality of the work would improve if they would leave fewer people do it.
(C) I believe it would be desirable to have fewer persons doing this work.
(D) If you had planned on employing fewer people than this to do the work, this situation would not have arose.

39. (A) The paper we use for this purpose must be light, glossy, and stand hard usage as well.
(B) Only a light and a glossy, but durable, paper must be used for this purpose.
(C) For this purpose, we want a paper that is light, glossy, but that will stand hard wear.
(D) For this purpose, paper that is light, glossy, and durable is essential.

40. (A) This letter, together with the reports, are to be sent to the postmaster.
(B) The reports, together with this letter, is to be sent to the postmaster.
(C) The reports and this letter is to be sent to the postmaster.
(D) This letter, together with the reports, is to be sent to the postmaster.

Directions: Each question from 41–48 consists of a sentence containing a word in **boldface** type. Choose the best meaning for the word in **boldface** type and darken its answer space on your answer sheet.

41. Please consult your office **manual** to learn the proper operation of our copying machine. **Manual** means most nearly
(A) labor
(B) handbook
(C) typewriter
(D) handle

42. There is a specified punishment for each **infraction** of the rules. **Infraction** means most nearly
(A) violation
(B) use
(C) interpretation
(D) part

43. The order was **rescinded** within the week. **Rescinded** means most nearly

(A) revised
(B) canceled
(C) misinterpreted
(D) confirmed

44. If you have a question, please raise your hand to **summon** the test proctor. **Summon** means most nearly

(A) ticket
(B) fine
(C) give
(D) call

45. We dared not prosecute the terrorist for fear of **reprisal**. **Reprisal** means most nearly

(A) retaliation
(B) advantage
(C) warning
(D) denial

46. The increased use of dictation machines has severely **reduced** the need for office stenographers. **Reduced** means most nearly

(A) enlarged
(B) cut out
(C) lessened
(D) expanded

47. Frequent use of marijuana may **impair** your judgment. **Impair** means most nearly

(A) weaken
(B) conceal
(C) improve
(D) expose

48. It is altogether **fitting** that the parent discipline the child. **Fitting** means most nearly

(A) illegal
(B) bad practice
(C) appropriate
(D) required

Directions: For questions 49–55, read each paragraph and answer the question that follows it by darkening the answer space of the correct answer on your answer sheet.

49. A survey to determine the subjects that have helped students most in their jobs shows that typewriting leads all other subjects in the business group. It also leads among the subjects college students consider most valuable and would take again if they were to return to high school.

The paragraph best supports the statement that

(A) the ability to type is an asset in business and in school
(B) students who return to night school take typing
(C) students with a knowledge of typing do superior work in college
(D) success in business is assured those who can type

50. Telegrams should be clear, concise, and brief. Omit all unnecessary words. The parts of speech most often used in telegrams are nouns, verbs, adjectives, and adverbs. If possible, do without pronouns, prepositions, articles, and copulative verbs. Use simple sentences, rather than complex and compound.

The paragraph best supports the statement that in writing telegrams one should always use

(A) common and simple words
(B) only nouns, verbs, adjectives, and adverbs
(C) incomplete sentences
(D) only words essential to the meaning

51. Since the government can spend only what it obtains from the people, and this amount is ultimately limited by their capacity and willingness to pay taxes, it is very important that the people be given full information about the work of the government.

The paragraph best supports the statement that

(A) governmental employees should be trained not only in their own work, but also in how to perform the duties of other employees in their agency
(B) taxation by the government rests upon the consent of the people
(C) the release of full information on the work of the government will increase the efficiency of governmental operations
(D) the work of the government, in recent years, has been restricted because of reduced tax collections

52. Both the high school and the college should take the responsibility for preparing the student to get a job. Since the ability to write a good application letter is one of the first steps toward this goal, every teacher should be willing to do what he can to help the student learn to write such letters.

The paragraph best supports the statement that

(A) inability to write a good letter often reduces one's job prospects
(B) the major responsibility of the school is to obtain jobs for its students
(C) success is largely a matter of the kind of work the student applies for first
(D) every teacher should teach a course in the writing of application letters

53. Direct lighting is the least satisfactory lighting arrangement. The desk or ceiling light with a reflector that diffuses all the rays downward is sure to cause a glare on the working surface.

The paragraph best supports the statement that direct lighting is least satisfactory as a method of lighting chiefly because

(A) the light is diffused, causing eye strain
(B) the shade on the individual desk lamp is not constructed along scientific lines
(C) the working surface is usually obscured by the glare
(D) direct lighting is injurious to the eyes

54. "White collar" is a term used to describe one of the largest groups of workers in American industry and trade. It distinguishes those who work with the pencil and the mind from those who depend on their hands and the machine. It suggests occupations in which physical exertion and handling of materials are not primary features of the job.

The paragraph best supports the statement that "white collar" workers are

(A) not so strong physically as those who work with their hands
(B) those who supervise workers handling materials
(C) all whose work is entirely indoors
(D) not likely to use machines as much as are other groups of workers

55. In large organizations some standardized, simple, inexpensive method of giving employees information about company policies and rules, as well as specific instructions regarding their duties, is practically essential. This is the purpose of all office manuals of whatever type.

The paragraph best supports the statement that office manuals

(A) are all about the same
(B) should be simple enough for the average employee to understand
(C) are necessary to large organizations
(D) act as constant reminders to the employee of his duties

END OF PART B

PART C—STENOGRAPHY

SAMPLE DICTATION

Have someone dictate the sample passage below to you. It should take 3 minutes. Take notes on your own paper.

Directions to person dictating: This practice dictation should be dictated at the rate of 80 words a minute. Do not dictate the punctuation except for periods, but dictate with the expression the punctuation indicates. Use a watch with a second hand to enable you to read the exercises at the proper speed.

Exactly on a minute start dictating. Finish reading each two lines at the number of seconds indicated below.

I realize that this practice dictation	
is not a part of the examination	10 sec.
proper and is not to be scored. (Period)	
The work of preventing and correcting	20 sec.
physical defects in children is becoming	
more effective as a result of change	30 sec.
in the attitude of many parents. (Period)	
In order to bring about this change,	40 sec.
parents have been invited to visit the	
schools when their children are being examined	50 sec.
and to discuss the treatment necessary	
for the correction of defects. (Period)	1 min.
There is a distinct value in having a	
parent see that his or her child is not the	10 sec.
only one who needs attention. (Period)	
Otherwise a few parents might feel that they	20 sec.
were being criticized by having the defects	
of their children singled out for medical	30 sec.
treatment. (Period) The special classes that	
have been set up have shown the value of	40 sec.
the scientific knowledge that has been	
applied in the treatment of children. (Period)	50 sec.
In these classes the children have been	
taught to exercise by a trained teacher	2 min.
under medical supervision. (Period) The	
hours of the school day have been divided	10 sec.
between school work and physical activity	
that helps not only to correct their defects	20 sec.
but also to improve their general physical	
condition. (Period) This method of treatment	30 sec.
has been found to be very effective	
except for those who have severe medical	40 sec.
defects. (Period) Most parents now see	
how desirable it is to have these classes	50 sec.
that have been set up in the regular	
school system to meet special needs. (Period)	3 min.

After dictating the practice, pause for 15 seconds to permit the competitor to complete notetaking. Then continue in accordance with the directions. After the sample dictation transcript has been completed, dictate the test on page 222.

SAMPLE DICTATION TRANSCRIPT SHEET

The transcript below is part of the material that was dictated to you for practice, except that many of the words have been left out. From your notes, you are to tell what the missing words are. Proceed as follows:

Compare your notes with the transcript and, when you come to a blank in the transcript, decide what word (or words) belongs there. For example, you will find that the word "practice" belongs in blank number 1. Look at the word list to see whether you can find the same word there. Notice what letter (A), (B), (C), or (D) is printed beside it, and write that letter in the blank. For example, the word "practice" is listed, followed by the letter (B). We have already written B in blank number 1 to show you how you are to record your choice. Now decide what belongs in each of the other blanks. (You may also write the word or words, or the shorthand for them, if you wish.) The same word may belong in more than one blank. If the exact answer is not listed, write E in the blank.

ALPHABETIC WORD LIST

Write (E) if the answer is not listed.

about — (B)
against — (C)
attitude — (A)
being — (D)
childhood — (B)
children — (A)
correcting — (C)
doctors — (B)
effective — (D)
efficient — (A)
examination — (A)
examining — (C)
for — (B)
health — (B)
mothers — (C)
never — (C)
not — (D)
paper — (B)
parents — (B)
part — (C)
physical — (D)
portion — (D)
practical — (A)
practice — (B)
preliminary — (D)
preventing — (B)
procedure — (A)
proper — (C)
reason for — (A)
result — (B)
result of — (C)
schools — (C)
to be — (C)
to prevent — (A)

TRANSCRIPT

I realize that this B (1) dictation is ___2___ a ___3___ of the ___4___ ___5___ and is ___6___ ___7___ scored.

The work ___8___ the ___9___ ___10___ defects in ___11___ is becoming more ___12___ as a ___13___ a change in the ___14___ of many ___15___.

ALPHABETIC WORD LIST

Write (E) if the answer is not listed.

all — (A)	reducing — (A)
at — (C)	satisfied — (D)
bring — (A)	say — (C)
collection — (B)	see — (B)
correction — (C)	soon — (C)
discuss — (C)	their — (D)
during — (D)	to discover
friend — (A)	to discuss
indicated — (C)	to endorse
insisted — (D)	to visit — (B)
is — (B)	treatments — (A)
is not — (A)	understand — (D)
know — (A)	undertake — (B)
knows — (D)	virtue — (D)
needed — (B)	visit — (A)
promote — (B)	volume — (B)
recognizing — (D)	young — (C)

TRANSCRIPT (Continued)

In order to ___16___ ___17___ this change, parents have been invited ___18___ the schools when ___19___ children are being examined and ___20___ the ___21___ necessary for the ___22___ of defects. There is a distinct ___23___ in having a parent ___24___ that his or her child ___25___ the only one who needs attention. . . . (The rest of the sample dictation is not transcribed here.)

Answer Sheet

1. Ⓐ Ⓑ Ⓒ Ⓓ Ⓔ	**8.** Ⓐ Ⓑ Ⓒ Ⓓ Ⓔ	**15.** Ⓐ Ⓑ Ⓒ Ⓓ Ⓔ	**22.** Ⓐ Ⓑ Ⓒ Ⓓ Ⓔ
2. Ⓐ Ⓑ Ⓒ Ⓓ Ⓔ	**9.** Ⓐ Ⓑ Ⓒ Ⓓ Ⓔ	**16.** Ⓐ Ⓑ Ⓒ Ⓓ Ⓔ	**23.** Ⓐ Ⓑ Ⓒ Ⓓ Ⓔ
3. Ⓐ Ⓑ Ⓒ Ⓓ Ⓔ	**10.** Ⓐ Ⓑ Ⓒ Ⓓ Ⓔ	**17.** Ⓐ Ⓑ Ⓒ Ⓓ Ⓔ	**24.** Ⓐ Ⓑ Ⓒ Ⓓ Ⓔ
4. Ⓐ Ⓑ Ⓒ Ⓓ Ⓔ	**11.** Ⓐ Ⓑ Ⓒ Ⓓ Ⓔ	**18.** Ⓐ Ⓑ Ⓒ Ⓓ Ⓔ	**25.** Ⓐ Ⓑ Ⓒ Ⓓ Ⓔ
5. Ⓐ Ⓑ Ⓒ Ⓓ Ⓔ	**12.** Ⓐ Ⓑ Ⓒ Ⓓ Ⓔ	**19.** Ⓐ Ⓑ Ⓒ Ⓓ Ⓔ	
6. Ⓐ Ⓑ Ⓒ Ⓓ Ⓔ	**13.** Ⓐ Ⓑ Ⓒ Ⓓ Ⓔ	**20.** Ⓐ Ⓑ Ⓒ Ⓓ Ⓔ	
7. Ⓐ Ⓑ Ⓒ Ⓓ Ⓔ	**14.** Ⓐ Ⓑ Ⓒ Ⓓ Ⓔ	**21.** Ⓐ Ⓑ Ⓒ Ⓓ Ⓔ	

The correct answers for the sample dictationare:

1. (B)	**6.** (D)	**10.** (D)	**14.** (A)	**18.** (B)	**22.** (C)
2. (D)	**7.** (C)	**11.** (A)	**15.** (B)	**19.** (D)	**23.** (E)
3. (C)	**8.** (B)	**12.** (D)	**16.** (A)	**20.** (D)	**24.** (B)
4. (A)	**9.** (C)	**13.** (C)	**17.** (E)	**21.** (E)	**25.** (A)
5. (C)					

Compare your answers with the correct ones. If one of your answers does not agree with the correct answer, again compare your notes with the samples and make certain you understand the instructions.

Your notes should show that the word "bring" goes in blank 16, and "about" in blank 17. But "about" is *not in the list*; so E should be your answer for question 17.

The two words, "to visit — (B)," are needed for 18, and the one word "visit — (A)," would be an incorrect answer.

For the actual test you will use a separate answer sheet. As scoring will be done by an electronic machine, it is important that you follow directions carefully. Use the special pencil if one is furnished by the examiner. If no pencil is furnished, use only a number 2 pencil, as directed. Make a heavy mark for each answer. If you have to change your mark for any question, be sure to erase the first mark completely (do not merely cross it out) before making another.

CORRECTLY FILLED-IN TRANSCRIPTS FOR SAMPLE DICTATION

Check your notes against the dictation; check your notes against the alphabetic list of words and the transcript sheet; check the transcript against your answer grid. Identify your errors.

I realize that this B dictation is D a C of the A C and is D
1 2 3 4 5
6 C scored. The work B the C D defects in A is becom-
7 8 9 10 11
ing more D as a C a change in the A of many B.
12 13 14 15

In order to A E this change, parents have been
16 17
invited B the schools when D children are being exam-
18 19
ined and D the E necessary for the C of defects. There
20 21 22
is a distinct E in having a parent B that his or her
23 24
child A the only one who needs attention. . . . (The
25
rest of the sample dictation is not transcribed here.)

PART C—DICTATION

Time: 3 Minutes

Exactly on a minute start dictating. Finish reading each two lines at the number of seconds indicated below.

In recent years there has been a great	
increase in the need for capable stenographers,	10 sec.
not only in business offices but also	
in public service agencies, both	20 sec.
governmental and private. (Period) The high	
schools and business schools in many parts of	30 sec.
the country have tried to meet this need by	
offering complete commercial courses. (Period)	40 sec.
The increase in the number of persons who	
are enrolled in these courses shows that	50 sec.
students have become aware of the great	
demand for stenographers. (Period) A person	1 min.
who wishes to secure employment in this	
field must be able to take dictation	10 sec.
and to transcribe the notes with both speed	
and accuracy. (Period) The rate of	20 sec.
speed at which dictation is given in most	
offices is somewhat less than that of	30 sec.
ordinary speech. (Period) Thus, one who has	
had a thorough training in shorthand	40 sec.
should have little trouble in taking complete	
notes. (Period) Skill in taking dictation	50 sec.
at a rapid rate is of slight value if	
the stenographer cannot also type the notes	2 min.
in proper form. (Period) A manager	
sometimes dictates a rough draft of the ideas	10 sec.
he/she wishes to have included in a letter,	
and leaves to the stenographer the task	20 sec.
of putting them in good form. (Period)	
For this reason, knowledge of the essentials	30 sec.
of grammar and of composition is as	
important as the ability to take	40 sec.
dictation. (Period) In addition, a stenographer	
should be familiar with the sources of	50 sec.
general information that are most likely	
to be used in office work. (Period)	3 min.

DICTATION TRANSCRIPT

Time: 30 Minutes—125 Questions

ALPHABETIC WORD LIST

Write (E) if the answer is not listed.

also — (A)
also in — (C)
business — (C)
busy — (D)
capable — (A)
commerce — (C)
commercial — (D)
county — (B)
culpable — (D)
decrease — (A)
governing — (D)
governmental — (C)
had been — (B)
has been — (D)
many — (A)
most — (D)
need — (C)
needy — (D)
offending — (A)
offering — (C)
officials — (D)
one — (C)
only — (B)
parts — (A)
private — (C)
public — (D)
recent — (B)
recurrent — (A)
school — (C)
schools — (B)
servant — (D)
stenographers — (D)
stenos — (A)
their — (D)
there — (B)
tied — (A)
to beat — (C)
tried — (B)

TRANSCRIPT

In ___1___ years ___2___ ___3___ a great ___4___ in the ___5___ for ___6___ ___7___, not ___8___ in ___9___ ___10___ but ___11___ in ___12___ ___13___ agencies, both ___14___ and ___15___. The high ___16___ and ___17___ schools in ___18___ ___19___ of the ___20___ have ___21___ ___22___ this ___23___ by ___24___ complete ___25___ courses.

ALPHABETIC WORD LIST

Write (E) if the answer is not listed.

awake — (C)
aware — (B)
be able — (A)
be able to — (C)
became — (B)
better — (A)
both — (D)
courses — (D)
curses — (C)
demand — (C)
demean — (A)
dictation — (B)
dictation notes — (C)
employing — (A)
employment — (D)
enrolled — (B)
enroute — (D)
feel — (A)
felt — (D)
grate — (D)
great — (A)
in a — (B)
in the — (A)
increase — (C)
increment — (A)
notations — (B)
notes — (C)
number — (C)
numbers — (D)
people — (A)
person — (C)
seclude — (C)
secure — (B)
speech — (C)
speed — (B)
students — (C)
studies — (D)
the — (C)
this — (A)
transcribe — (C)
transcript — (D)
who desires — (C)

TRANSCRIPT (Continued)

The ___26___ ___27___ ___28___ of ___29___ who are ___30___ in these ___31___ shows ___32___ ___33___ have ___34___ ___35___ of the ___36___ ___37___ for stenographers. A ___38___ ___39___ to ___40___ ___41___ in ___42___ ___43___ must ___44___ to take ___45___ and to ___46___ the ___47___ with ___48___ ___49___ and ___50___.

Continue on the next page.

ALPHABETIC WORD LIST

Write (E) if the answer is not listed.

also — (D)
also can — (B)
at a — (A)
at the — (C)
compete — B
complete — (D)
dictates — (B)
dictation — (D)
firm — (C)
form — (D)
gained — (A)
give — (D)
has — (C)
have — (B)
less — (B)
less than — (A)
many — (A)
most — (D)
note — (C)
notes — (B)
offices — (C)
orderly — (C)
ordinary — (D)
proffer — (C)
proper — (A)

rampant — (B)
rate — (C)
ratio — (D)
should — (D)
should not — (A)
sight — (C)
slight — (B)
somehow — (D)
speech — (A)
speed — (A)
stenographer — (C)
taking — (C)
that — (D)
thorough — (C)
through — (B)
treble — (D)
trial — (A)
typed — (D)
typewriter — (A)
valuate — (A)
value — (C)
what — (C)
which — (B)
who gets — (A)
who had — (C)

TRANSCRIPT (continued)

The ______ (51) of ______ (52) at ______ (53) dictation is ______ (54) in ______ (55) ______ (56) is ______ (57) ______ (58) than ______ (59) of ______ (60) ______ (61). Thus, one ______ (62) had a ______ (63) ______ (64) in shorthand ______ (65) ______ (66) little ______ (67) in ______ (68) ______ (69) ______ (70). Skill in ______ (71) ______ (72) ______ (73) ______ (74) ______ (75) is of ______ (76) ______ (77) if the ______ (78) cannot ______ (79) ______ (80) the ______ (81) in ______ (82) ______ (83).

Continue on the next page.

ALPHABETIC WORD LIST

Write (E) if the answer is not listed.

ability — (B)
adding — (C)
addition — (A)
are — (D)
as — (A)
composing — (A)
composition — (C)
dictates — (B)
essence — (B)
essentials — (C)
form — (A)
familial — (C)
familiar — (A)
general — (C)
generous — (A)
good — (C)
grammatical — (D)
great — (A)
had — (A)
have — (B)
ideals — (C)
ideas — (A)
included — (C)
inclusive — (A)
information — (D)
important — (B)
impotent — (A)
knowledge — (B)
knowledgeable — (C)
leaves — (B)
lets — (C)

letter — (D)
like — (A)
likely — (C)
manager — (A)
management — (B)
of the — (D)
of these — (A)
office — (A)
official — (B)
put in — (D)
putting — (C)
reasoning — (B)
rough — (A)
roughly — (D)
sauces — (A)
shall — (D)
should — (B)
some times — (A)
somethings — (D)
source — (D)
stenographic — (A)
take — (D)
task — (D)
this — (A)
to — (A)
to be — (B)
used — (C)
useful — (A)
wished — (D)
wishes — (A)
with the — (D)

TRANSCRIPT (Continued)

A ______ (84) ______ (85) ______ (86) a ______ (87) ______ (88)
______ (89) ______ (90) s/he ______ (91) to ______ (92) ______ (93)
in a ______ (94), and ______ (95) to the ______ (96) the
______ (97) of ______ (98) them in ______ (99) ______ (100). For
______ (101) ______ (102) ______ (103) ______ (104) ______ (105) of
______ (106) and of ______ (107) is ______ (108) ______ (109) ______ (110)
______ (111) to ______ (112) dictation. In ______ (113) ______ (114)
stenographer ______ (115) be ______ (116) ______ (117) ______ (118)
of ______ (119) ______ (120) that ______ (121) most ______ (122)
______ (123) ______ (124) in ______ (125) work.

You will now have ten minutes to transfer your answers to the Part C answer sheet.

END OF EXAM

CORRECT ANSWERS—U.S. POSTAL SERVICE CLERK-TYPIST AND CLERK-STENOGRAPHER EXAM

PART A—CLERICAL ABILITY

1. E	16. A	31. D	46. B	61. A	76. C
2. D	17. E	32. E	47. E	62. C	77. E
3. A	18. B	33. A	48. A	63. C	78. E
4. D	19. A	34. A	49. C	64. D	79. C
5. A	20. C	35. A	50. A	65. D	80. B
6. C	21. A	36. B	51. A	66. C	81. E
7. B	22. E	37. E	52. C	67. A	82. C
8. D	23. C	38. C	53. C	68. D	83. E
9. E	24. B	39. D	54. A	69. B	84. C
10. C	25. D	40. A	55. D	70. B	85. B
11. C	26. E	41. A	56. A	71. E	
12. D	27. A	42. C	57. D	72. B	
13. C	28. B	43. C	58. B	73. A	
14. D	29. C	44. E	59. C	74. B	
15. C	30. D	45. D	60. B	75. E	

EXPLANATIONS

1. **The correct answer is (E).** Hachettson; Hackett
2. **The correct answer is (D).** 59233262; 59233362
3. **The correct answer is (A).** MYP; NYP
4. **The correct answer is (D).** Olivia H.; Olivier E.; R. Olivia
5. **The correct answer is (A).** 0010; 0012
6. **The correct answer is (C).** 6001; 6100; 6101
7. **The correct answer is (B).** Vanover; Vanstory; VanSwinderen
8. **The correct answer is (D).** FitzGibbon; Fitzsimmons; FitzSimons
9. **The correct answer is (E).** 01016060; 01066010
10. **The correct answer is (C).** AAS; AAZ; ASA
11. **The correct answer is (C).** Pawelek; Pawlowicz; Pawlowski
12. **The correct answer is (D).** 7710; 7834; 7868
13. **The correct answer is (C).** 36270000; 36270013; 36270030
14. **The correct answer is (D).** Freedenberg; Freedenburg; Freedinberg; Freedinburg
15. **The correct answer is (C).** Proutey; Prouty, Martha; Prouty, Myra
16. **The correct answer is (A).** 58006021; 58006130
17. **The correct answer is (E).** EKK-1403; EKK-1443
18. **The correct answer is (B).** Daly; D'Amato; D'Amboise
19. **The correct answer is (A).** Schaeffer; Schaffert
20. **The correct answer is (C).** PSP; SPP; SPS
21. **The correct answer is (A).** Drusilla S. RidgeleyDrusilla S. RidgeleyDrusilla S. Ridgeley
22. **The correct answer is (E).** Andrei I. ToumantzevAndrei I. TourmantzevAndrei I. Toumantzov
23. **The correct answer is (C).** 6-78912-e3e426-78912-3e3e42678912-e3e42
24. **The correct answer is (B).** 86529 Dunwoodie Drive86529 Dunwoodie Drive85629 Dunwoodie Drive
25. **The correct answer is (D).** 1592514159257415925 74
26. **The correct answer is (E).** Ella Burk NewhamElla Burk NewnhamElena Burk Newnham
27. **The correct answer is (A).** 5416R-1952TZ-op5416R-1952TZ-op5416R-1952TZ-op
28. **The correct answer is (B).** 60646 West Touhy Avenue60646 West Touhy Avenue60646 West Touhey Avenue

29. **The correct answer is (C).** Mardikian & Moore, Inc.Mardikian and Moore, Inc-.Mardikian & Moore, Inc.
30. **The correct answer is (D).** 96702439670423967042 3
31. **The correct answer is (D).** Eduardo Ingles Eduardo IngleseEduardo Inglese
32. **The correct answer is (E).** Roger T. DeAngelisRoger T. D'AngelisRoger T. DeAngeles
33. **The correct answer is (A).** 769213876921387692138
34. **The correct answer is (A).** 2695 East 3435 South2695 East 3435 South2695 East 3435 South
35. **The correct answer is (A).** 63qs5-95YT3-00163qs5-95YT3-00163qs5-95YT3-001
36. **The correct answer is (B).** 278935027893502798350
37. **The correct answer is (E).** Helmut V. LochnerHelmut V. LocknerHelmut W. Lochner
38. **The correct answer is (C).** 245480325484032454803
39. **The correct answer is (D).** Lemberger, WA 28094-9182Lemberger, VA 28094-9182Lemberger, VA 28094-9182
40. **The correct answer is (A).** 4168-GNP-788524168-GNP-788524168-GNP-78852
41. **The correct answer is (A).** Yoshihito SaitoYoshihito SaitoYoshihito Saito
42. **The correct answer is (C).** 592768159278615927681
43. **The correct answer is (C).** O'Reilly Bay, LA 56212O'Reillys Bay, LA 56212O'Reilly Bay, LA 56212
44. **The correct answer is (E).** Francis RansdellFrances RamsdellFrancis Ramsdell
45. **The correct answer is (D).** 5634-OotV5a-168675634-Ootv5a-168675634-Ootv5a-16867
46. **The correct answer is (B).** Dolores MolliconeDolores MolliconeDoloras Mollicone
47. **The correct answer is (E).** David C. RoutzonDavid E. RoutzonDavid C. Routzron
48. **The correct answer is (A).** 8932 Shimabui Hwy.8932 Shimabui Hwy.8932 Shimabui Hwy.
49. **The correct answer is (C).** 617739661779366177396
50. **The correct answer is (A).** A8987-B373245A8987-B373245A8987-B373245
51. **The correct answer is (A).** anticipate
52. **The correct answer is (C).** similar
53. **The correct answer is (C).** sufficiently
54. **The correct answer is (A).** intelligence
55. **The correct answer is (D).** reference
56. **The correct answer is (A).** conscious
57. **The correct answer is (D).** parallel
58. **The correct answer is (B).** abundance
59. **The correct answer is (C).** corrugated
60. **The correct answer is (B).** accumulation
61. **The correct answer is (A).** resonance
62. **The correct answer is (C).** beneficial
63. **The correct answer is (C).** specifically
64. **The correct answer is (D).** eliminate
65. **The correct answer is (D).** colossal
66. **The correct answer is (C).** auxiliary
67. **The correct answer is (A).** inimitable
68. **The correct answer is (D).** disappearance
69. **The correct answer is (B).** appellate
70. **The correct answer is (B).** essential

71. The correct answer is (E).

$$\begin{array}{r} 83 \\ -\ 56 \\ \hline 27 \end{array}$$

72. The correct answer is (B).

$$\begin{array}{r} 15 \\ +\ 17 \\ \hline 32 \end{array}$$

73. The correct answer is (A).

$$\begin{array}{r} 32 \\ \times\ \ 7 \\ \hline 224 \end{array}$$

74. The correct answer is (B).

$$\begin{array}{r} 39 \\ \times\ 2 \\ \hline 78 \end{array}$$

75. The correct answer is (B).

$$\begin{array}{r} 43 \\ -\ 15 \\ \hline 28 \end{array}$$

76. The correct answer is (C).

$$\begin{array}{r} 50 \\ 49\ 49 \\ \hline 99 \end{array}$$

77. The correct answer is (E).

$$6\overline{)366}\ = 61$$

78. The correct answer is (E).

$$\begin{array}{r} 38 \\ \times\ \ 3 \\ \hline 114 \end{array}$$

79. The correct answer is (C).

$$\begin{array}{r} 19 \\ +\ 21 \\ \hline 40 \end{array}$$

80. The correct answer is (B).

$$\begin{array}{r} 13 \\ -\ \ 6 \\ \hline 7 \end{array}$$

81. The correct answer is (E).

$$6\overline{)180}\ = 30$$

82. The correct answer is (C).

$$\begin{array}{r} 10 \\ \times\ 1 \\ \hline 10 \end{array}$$

83. **The correct answer is (E).**

$$7\overline{)287} = 41$$

84. **The correct answer is (C).**

$$12 + 11 = 23$$

85. **The correct answer is (B).**

$$85 - 64 = 21$$

PART B—VERBAL ABILITY

1. D	12. B	23. D	34. B	45. A
2. C	13. D	24. A	35. B	46. C
3. E	14. A	25. D	36. D	47. A
4. A	15. D	26. A	37. C	48. C
5. C	16. D	27. C	38. C	49. A
6. E	17. E	28. C	39. D	50. D
7. D	18. A	29. B	40. D	51. B
8. C	19. D	30. D	41. B	52. A
9. E	20. B	31. D	42. A	53. C
10. B	21. C	32. D	43. B	54. D
11. A	22. C	33. A	44. D	55. C

EXPLANATIONS

Questions 1–20.2 If you made any errors in the *Following Written Instructions* portion, go back and reread those questions more carefully.

21. **The correct answer is (C).** Sentence (C) is the best expression of the idea. Sentence (A) has two grammatical errors: the use of *when* to introduce a definition and the unacceptable verb form *is already having been parked.* Sentence (B) incorrectly shifts subjects from *one* to *you.* Sentence (D) does not make sense.
22. **The correct answer is (C).** Choice (B) is incorrect because only two persons are involved in this statement. *Between* is used when there are only two, *among* is reserved for three or more. (A) makes a similar error. In addition, both (A) and (D) use the pronoun *he.* The object of a preposition, in this case *between,* must be in the objective case, hence *him.*
23. **The correct answer is (D).** Punctuation aside, both (A) and (B) incorrectly place the verb in the plural, *are. Neither* is a singular indefinite pronoun. It means *not one and not the other* and requires a singular verb. The choice between (C) and (D) is more difficult, but basically this is a simple statement and not a direct quote.
24. **The correct answer is (A).** Whoever is the subject of the phrase *whoever has the best record.* Hence (A) is the correct answer and (D) is wrong. Both (B) and (C) are wordy and awkward.
25. **The correct answer is (D).** All the other choices contain obvious errors.
26. **The correct answer is (A).** Choice (B) uses the plural verb *were* with the singular subject *report.* (C) and (D) are colloquial and incorrect even for informal speech. They have no place in business writing.
27. **The correct answer is (C).** Choices (A) and (B) use adverbs incorrectly; choice (B) is awkward and unidiomatic.
28. **The correct answer is (C).** Choices (B) and (D) are obviously incorrect. In (A), the pronoun *who* should be the subject of the phrase, *who had made careless errors.*

29. **The correct answer is (B).** Only the quoted material should appear enclosed by quotation marks, so (A) is incorrect. Only the first word of a sentence should begin with a capital letter, so both (C) and (D) are wrong. In addition, only the quoted material itself is a question; the entire sentence is a statement. Therefore, the question mark must be placed inside the quotes.
30. **The correct answer is (D).** Choices (A) and (B) imply that he stays in church all day on Christmas and Easter and goes nowhere else. Choice (C) makes the same implication and in addition splits the infinitive awkwardly. In (D) the modifier *only* is correctly placed to tell us that the only times he goes to church are on Christmas and Easter.
31. **The correct answer is (D).** Choice (A) might state either *most* or *all* but not both; choice (B) should read *persons who;* choice (C) should read *with regard to. . . .*
32. **The correct answer is (D).** Choice (A) is incorrect because *both* can refer to only two, but the publisher and authors implies at least three; choice (B) requires the plural verb *were;* choice (C) requires the correlative construction *neither . . . nor.*
33. **The correct answer is (A).** Choices (C) and (D) are glaringly poor. Choice (B) is not incorrect, but choice (A) is far better.
34. **The correct answer is (B).** Choice (A) incorrectly uses a semicolon to separate a complete clause from a sentence fragment. Additionally, (A) incorrectly uses *what* in place of *that.* Choice (C) is a run-on sentence that also misuses an apostrophe: *It's* is the contraction for *it is,* not the possessive of *it.* Choice (D) uses commas indiscriminately; it also misuses the apostrophe.
35. **The correct answer is (B).** In choice (A) the placement of the apostrophe is inappropriate; choices (C) and (D) use the plural, but there is only one company.
36. **The correct answer is (D).** Choices (A) and (C) are incorrect in use of the subject form *I* instead of the object of the preposition *me.* Choice (B) incorrectly uses the reflexive *myself.* Only I can address a letter to myself.
37. **The correct answer is (C).** Choice (A) incorrectly uses the plural verb form *have* with the singular subject *one.* (B) is awkward and wordy. (D) incorrectly changes the subject from *one of us* to *anyone.*
38. **The correct answer is (C).** (A) is wordy. In (B), the correct verb should be *have* in place of *leave.* In (D), the word *arose* should be *arisen.*
39. **The correct answer is (D).** The first three sentences lack parallel construction. All the words that modify *paper* must appear in the same form.
40. **The correct answer is (D).** The phrase, *together with . . .* is extra information and not a part of the subject; therefore, both (A) and (B) represent similar errors of agreement. Choice (C) also presents disagreement in number between subject and verb, but in this case the compound subject, indicated by the use of the conjunction, *and,* requires a plural verb.
41. **The correct answer is (B).** Even if you do not recognize the root *manu* meaning *hand* and relating directly to *handbook,* you should have no trouble getting this question right. If you substitute each of the choices in the sentence, you will readily see that only one makes sense.
42. **The correct answer is (A).** Within the context of the sentence, the thought of a specified punishment for use, interpretation, or an edition of the rules does not make too much sense. *Fraction* gives a hint of *part,* but you must also contend with the negative prefix *in.* Since it is reasonable to expect punishment for negative behavior with relation to the rules, *violation,* which is the meaning of INFRACTION, is the proper answer.
43. **The correct answer is (B).** The prefix should help you narrow your choices. The prefix *re* meaning *back* or *again* narrows the choices to (A) or (B). To RESCIND is to *take back* or to *cancel.*

44. **The correct answer is (D).** First eliminate (C) since it does not make sense in the sentence. Your experience with the word *summons* may be with relation to *tickets* and *fines,* but tickets and fines have nothing to do with asking questions while taking a test. Even if you are unfamiliar with the word SUMMON, you should be able to choose *call* as the best synonym in this context.
45. **The correct answer is (A).** REPRISAL means injury done for injury received or *retaliation.*
46. **The correct answer is (C).** To REDUCE is to *make smaller* or to *lessen.*
47. **The correct answer is (A).** To IMPAIR is to *make worse,* to *injure,* or to *weaken.*
48. **The correct answer is (C).** FITTING in this context means *suitable* or *appropriate.*
49. **The correct answer is (A).** The survey showed that of all subjects typing has helped most in business. It was also considered valuable by college students in their schoolwork.
50. **The correct answer is (D).** See the second sentence.
51. **The correct answer is (B).** According to the paragraph, the government can spend only what it obtains from the people. The government obtains money from the people by taxation. If the people are unwilling to pay taxes, the government has no source of funds.
52. **The correct answer is (A).** Step one in the job application process is often the application letter. If the letter is not effective, the applicant will not move on to the next step and job prospects will be greatly lessened.
53. **The correct answer is (C).** The second sentence states that direct lighting causes glare on the working surface.
54. **The correct answer is (D).** While all the answer choices are likely to be true, the answer suggested by the paragraph is that "white collar" workers work with their pencils and their minds rather than with their hands and machines.
55. **The correct answer is (C).** All the paragraph says is that office manuals are a necessity in large organizations.

PART C—STENOGRAPHY

1. B	26. C	51. C	76. B	101. A
2. B	27. A	52. A	77. C	102. E
3. D	28. C	53. B	78. C	103. B
4. E	29. E	54. E	79. D	104. D
5. C	30. B	55. D	80. E	105. C
6. A	31. D	56. C	81. B	106. E
7. D	32. E	57. E	82. A	107. C
8. B	33. C	58. B	83. D	108. A
9. C	34. E	59. D	84. A	109. B
10. E	35. B	60. D	85. E	110. E
11. A	36. A	61. A	86. B	111. B
12. D	37. C	62. E	87. A	112. D
13. E	38. C	63. C	88. E	113. A
14. C	39. E	64. E	89. D	114. E
15. C	40. B	65. D	90. A	115. B
16. B	41. D	66. B	91. A	116. A
17. C	42. A	67. E	92. B	117. D
18. A	43. E	68. C	93. C	118. E
19. A	44. A	69. D	94. D	119. C
20. E	45. B	70. C	95. B	120. D
21. E	46. C	71. B	96. E	121. D
22. E	47. C	72. D	97. D	122. C
23. C	48. D	73. A	98. C	123. B
24. C	49. B	74. E	99. C	124. C
25. D	50. E	75. C	100. A	125. A

CORRECTLY FILLED-IN TRANSCRIPT

In B years B D a great E in the C For A D,
1 2 3 4 5 6 7
not B in C E but A in D E agencies, both C
8 9 10 11 12 13 14
and C. The high B and D schools in A A of
15 16 17 18 19
the E have E E this C by C complete D
20 21 22 23 24 25
courses.

The C A C of E who are B In these D
26 27 28 29 30 31
shows E C have E B of the A C for
32 33 34 35 36
stenographers. A C E to B D in A E must A
37 38 39 40 41 42 43
to take B and to C the C with D B and E.
44 45 46 47 48 49

The C of A at B dictation is E in D C
50 51 52 53 54 55
is E B than D of D A. Thus, one E had
56 57 58 59 60 61
a C E in shorthand D B little E in C D B.
62 63 64 65 66 67 68 69
Skill in C D A E C is of B C if the C
70 71 72 73 74 75 76 77
cannot D E the B in A D. A A E B
78 79 80 81 82 83 84 85
a A E D A s/he A to B C in a D, and B
86 87 88 89 90 91 92 93 94
to the E the D of C them in C A.
95 96 97 98 99
For A E B D C of E and
100 101 102 103 104 105
of Cis A B E B to D dictation.
106 107 108 109 110 111
In A, E stenographer B be A D E
112 113 114 115 116 117
of C D that D most C B C in A work.
118 119 120 121 122 123 124

ANSWER SHEET

SENIOR OFFICE TYPIST EXAM (COURT SYSTEM)

1. Ⓐ Ⓑ Ⓒ Ⓓ Ⓔ	**26.** Ⓐ Ⓑ Ⓒ Ⓓ Ⓔ	**51.** Ⓐ Ⓑ Ⓒ Ⓓ Ⓔ	**76.** Ⓐ Ⓑ Ⓒ Ⓓ Ⓔ
2. Ⓐ Ⓑ Ⓒ Ⓓ Ⓔ	**27.** Ⓐ Ⓑ Ⓒ Ⓓ Ⓔ	**52.** Ⓐ Ⓑ Ⓒ Ⓓ Ⓔ	**77.** Ⓐ Ⓑ Ⓒ Ⓓ Ⓔ
3. Ⓐ Ⓑ Ⓒ Ⓓ Ⓔ	**28.** Ⓐ Ⓑ Ⓒ Ⓓ Ⓔ	**53.** Ⓐ Ⓑ Ⓒ Ⓓ Ⓔ	**78.** Ⓐ Ⓑ Ⓒ Ⓓ Ⓔ
4. Ⓐ Ⓑ Ⓒ Ⓓ Ⓔ	**29.** Ⓐ Ⓑ Ⓒ Ⓓ Ⓔ	**54.** Ⓐ Ⓑ Ⓒ Ⓓ Ⓔ	**79.** Ⓐ Ⓑ Ⓒ Ⓓ Ⓔ
5. Ⓐ Ⓑ Ⓒ Ⓓ Ⓔ	**30.** Ⓐ Ⓑ Ⓒ Ⓓ Ⓔ	**55.** Ⓐ Ⓑ Ⓒ Ⓓ Ⓔ	**80.** Ⓐ Ⓑ Ⓒ Ⓓ Ⓔ
6. Ⓐ Ⓑ Ⓒ Ⓓ Ⓔ	**31.** Ⓐ Ⓑ Ⓒ Ⓓ Ⓔ	**56.** Ⓐ Ⓑ Ⓒ Ⓓ Ⓔ	**81.** Ⓐ Ⓑ Ⓒ Ⓓ Ⓔ
7. Ⓐ Ⓑ Ⓒ Ⓓ Ⓔ	**32.** Ⓐ Ⓑ Ⓒ Ⓓ Ⓔ	**57.** Ⓐ Ⓑ Ⓒ Ⓓ Ⓔ	**82.** Ⓐ Ⓑ Ⓒ Ⓓ Ⓔ
8. Ⓐ Ⓑ Ⓒ Ⓓ Ⓔ	**33.** Ⓐ Ⓑ Ⓒ Ⓓ Ⓔ	**58.** Ⓐ Ⓑ Ⓒ Ⓓ Ⓔ	**83.** Ⓐ Ⓑ Ⓒ Ⓓ Ⓔ
9. Ⓐ Ⓑ Ⓒ Ⓓ Ⓔ	**34.** Ⓐ Ⓑ Ⓒ Ⓓ Ⓔ	**59.** Ⓐ Ⓑ Ⓒ Ⓓ Ⓔ	**84.** Ⓐ Ⓑ Ⓒ Ⓓ Ⓔ
10. Ⓐ Ⓑ Ⓒ Ⓓ Ⓔ	**35.** Ⓐ Ⓑ Ⓒ Ⓓ Ⓔ	**60.** Ⓐ Ⓑ Ⓒ Ⓓ Ⓔ	**85.** Ⓐ Ⓑ Ⓒ Ⓓ Ⓔ
11. Ⓐ Ⓑ Ⓒ Ⓓ Ⓔ	**36.** Ⓐ Ⓑ Ⓒ Ⓓ Ⓔ	**61.** Ⓐ Ⓑ Ⓒ Ⓓ Ⓔ	**86.** Ⓐ Ⓑ Ⓒ Ⓓ Ⓔ
12. Ⓐ Ⓑ Ⓒ Ⓓ Ⓔ	**37.** Ⓐ Ⓑ Ⓒ Ⓓ Ⓔ	**62.** Ⓐ Ⓑ Ⓒ Ⓓ Ⓔ	**87.** Ⓐ Ⓑ Ⓒ Ⓓ Ⓔ
13. Ⓐ Ⓑ Ⓒ Ⓓ Ⓔ	**38.** Ⓐ Ⓑ Ⓒ Ⓓ Ⓔ	**63.** Ⓐ Ⓑ Ⓒ Ⓓ Ⓔ	**88.** Ⓐ Ⓑ Ⓒ Ⓓ Ⓔ
14. Ⓐ Ⓑ Ⓒ Ⓓ Ⓔ	**39.** Ⓐ Ⓑ Ⓒ Ⓓ Ⓔ	**64.** Ⓐ Ⓑ Ⓒ Ⓓ Ⓔ	**89.** Ⓐ Ⓑ Ⓒ Ⓓ Ⓔ
15. Ⓐ Ⓑ Ⓒ Ⓓ Ⓔ	**40.** Ⓐ Ⓑ Ⓒ Ⓓ Ⓔ	**65.** Ⓐ Ⓑ Ⓒ Ⓓ Ⓔ	**90.** Ⓐ Ⓑ Ⓒ Ⓓ Ⓔ
16. Ⓐ Ⓑ Ⓒ Ⓓ Ⓔ	**41.** Ⓐ Ⓑ Ⓒ Ⓓ Ⓔ	**66.** Ⓐ Ⓑ Ⓒ Ⓓ Ⓔ	**91.** Ⓐ Ⓑ Ⓒ Ⓓ Ⓔ
17. Ⓐ Ⓑ Ⓒ Ⓓ Ⓔ	**42.** Ⓐ Ⓑ Ⓒ Ⓓ Ⓔ	**67.** Ⓐ Ⓑ Ⓒ Ⓓ Ⓔ	**92.** Ⓐ Ⓑ Ⓒ Ⓓ Ⓔ
18. Ⓐ Ⓑ Ⓒ Ⓓ Ⓔ	**43.** Ⓐ Ⓑ Ⓒ Ⓓ Ⓔ	**68.** Ⓐ Ⓑ Ⓒ Ⓓ Ⓔ	**93.** Ⓐ Ⓑ Ⓒ Ⓓ Ⓔ
19. Ⓐ Ⓑ Ⓒ Ⓓ Ⓔ	**44.** Ⓐ Ⓑ Ⓒ Ⓓ Ⓔ	**69.** Ⓐ Ⓑ Ⓒ Ⓓ Ⓔ	**94.** Ⓐ Ⓑ Ⓒ Ⓓ Ⓔ
20. Ⓐ Ⓑ Ⓒ Ⓓ Ⓔ	**45.** Ⓐ Ⓑ Ⓒ Ⓓ Ⓔ	**70.** Ⓐ Ⓑ Ⓒ Ⓓ Ⓔ	**95.** Ⓐ Ⓑ Ⓒ Ⓓ Ⓔ
21. Ⓐ Ⓑ Ⓒ Ⓓ Ⓔ	**46.** Ⓐ Ⓑ Ⓒ Ⓓ Ⓔ	**71.** Ⓐ Ⓑ Ⓒ Ⓓ Ⓔ	**96.** Ⓐ Ⓑ Ⓒ Ⓓ Ⓔ
22. Ⓐ Ⓑ Ⓒ Ⓓ Ⓔ	**47.** Ⓐ Ⓑ Ⓒ Ⓓ Ⓔ	**72.** Ⓐ Ⓑ Ⓒ Ⓓ Ⓔ	**97.** Ⓐ Ⓑ Ⓒ Ⓓ Ⓔ
23. Ⓐ Ⓑ Ⓒ Ⓓ Ⓔ	**48.** Ⓐ Ⓑ Ⓒ Ⓓ Ⓔ	**73.** Ⓐ Ⓑ Ⓒ Ⓓ Ⓔ	**98.** Ⓐ Ⓑ Ⓒ Ⓓ Ⓔ
24. Ⓐ Ⓑ Ⓒ Ⓓ Ⓔ	**49.** Ⓐ Ⓑ Ⓒ Ⓓ Ⓔ	**74.** Ⓐ Ⓑ Ⓒ Ⓓ Ⓔ	**99.** Ⓐ Ⓑ Ⓒ Ⓓ Ⓔ
25. Ⓐ Ⓑ Ⓒ Ⓓ Ⓔ	**50.** Ⓐ Ⓑ Ⓒ Ⓓ Ⓔ	**75.** Ⓐ Ⓑ Ⓒ Ⓓ Ⓔ	**100.** Ⓐ Ⓑ Ⓒ Ⓓ Ⓔ

SENIOR OFFICE TYPIST EXAM (COURT SYSTEM)

SECTION ONE: SPELLING

TIME: 3 Hours—95 Questions

Directions: Choose the word that is correctly spelled and darken its letter on your answer sheet.

1. (A) apellate
(B) appelate
(C) appeallate
(D) appellate

2. (A) presumption
(B) presoumption
(C) presumsion
(D) presumptsion

3. (A) litigiant
(B) litigent
(C) litigant
(D) litigint

4. (A) committment
(B) commitment
(C) comittment
(D) comitment

5. (A) affidavid
(B) afidavis
(C) affidavit
(D) afidavit

6. (A) arraign
(B) arrain
(C) arreign
(D) areign

7. (A) cumalative
(B) cummuletive
(C) cummalative
(D) cumulative

8. (A) sevarance
(B) severance
(C) severence
(D) severants

9. (A) adjurnment
(B) adjuornment
(C) ajournment
(D) adjournment

10. (A) comenced
(B) commentced
(C) commenced
(D) commensced

Directions: Each question consists of three sentences with one underlined word. One of the underlined words might be spelled incorrectly. On your answer sheet, darken the letter of the sentence which contains the incorrectly spelled word. If no sentence contains a misspelled word, darken answer space (D).

11. (A) Punishment must be a planned part of a comprehensive program of treating delinquency.
(B) It is easier to spot inexperienced check forjers than other criminals.
(C) Even young vandals and hooligans can be reformed if given adequate attention.
(D) No error.

12. (A) The court officer does not have authority to make exceptions.
(B) Usually the violations are the result of illegal and dangerous driving behavior.
(C) The safety division is required to investigate if the dispatcher files a complaint.
(D) No error.

13. (A) Comic books that glorify the criminal have a distinct influence in producing young criminals.
(B) Some of the people behind bars are innocent people who have been put there by mistake.
(C) Educational achievment is closely associated with delinquency.
(D) No error.

14. (A) Disciplinary action is most effective when it is taken promptly.
(B) Release on "personal recognizance" refers to release without bail.
(C) Parole violators forfeit their freedom.
(D) No error.

15. (A) Some responsibilities take precedence over preservation of evidence.
(B) Objects should not be touched unless there is some compelling reason.
(C) The detension system works unfairly against people who are single and unemployed.
(D) No error.

16. (A) Evidence is inmaterial if it does not prove the truth of a fact at issue.
(B) Without qualms the offender will lie and manipulate others.
(C) If spectators become disorderly, the court officer may threaten to cite them for contempt of court.
(D) No error.

17. (A) Under certain conditions, circumstantial evidence may be admissible.
(B) Just because evidence is circumstantial does not mean that it is irrelevant.
(C) An aggressive offender may appear to be very hostile.
(D) No error.

18. (A) A victim of assault may want to take revenge.
(B) The result of the trial was put in doubt when the prosecuter produced a surprise witness.
(C) The court officer must maintain order and decorum in the courtroom.
(D) No error.

19. (A) A person whose accident record can be explained by a correctable physical defect cannot be called "accident-prone."
(B) A litigant should not be permitted to invoke the aid of technical rules.
(C) Refusal to waive immunity automatically terminates employment.
(D) No error.

20. (A) Court employees may be fired for malfeasance.
(B) A common tactic used by defense lawyers is embarrassment of the witness.
(C) The criminal justice system may be called an "adversary system."
(D) No error.

SECTION TWO: GRAMMAR

Directions: Choose the sentence that is grammatically **incorrect** and darken its letter on your answer sheet.

21. (A) One of us has to reply before tomorrow.
(B) All employees who had served from 40 to 51 years were retired.
(C) The personnel office takes care of employment, dismissals, and etc.
(D) We often come across people with whom we disagree.

22. (A) The jurors have been instructed to deliver a sealed verdict.
(B) The court may direct the convict to be imprisoned in a county penitentiary instead of a state prison.
(C) Conveying self-confidence is displaying assurance.
(D) He devotes as much, if not more, time to his work than the rest of the employees.

23. (A) In comparison with that kind of pen, this kind is more preferable.
(B) The jurors may go to dinner only with the permission of the judge.
(C) There was neither any intention to commit a crime nor any injury incurred.
(D) It is the sociological view that all weight should be given to the history and development of the individual.

24. (A) The supervisor makes the suggestions for improvement, not the employee.
(B) Violations of traffic laws and illegal and dangerous driving behavior constitutes bad driving.
(C) Cynics take the position that the criminal is rarely or never reformed.
(D) The ultimate solution to the housing problem of the hardcore slum does not lie in code enforcement.

25. (A) No crime can occur unless there is a written law forbidding the act or omission in question.
(B) If one wants to prevent crime, we must deal with the possible criminals before they reach the prison.
(C) One could reasonably say that the same type of correctional institution is not desirable for the custody of all prisoners.
(D) When you have completed the report, you may give it to me or directly to the judge.

26. (A) The structure of an organization should be considered in determining the organization's goals.
(B) Complaints are welcomed because they frequently bring into the open conditions and faults in service that should be corrected.
(C) The defendant had a very unique alibi, so the judge dismissed the case.
(D) Court officers must direct witnesses to seats when the latter present themselves in court to testify.

27. (A) The clerk promptly notified the judge of the fire for which he was highly praised.
(B) There is justice among thieves; the three thieves divided the goods equally among themselves.
(C) If he had been notified promptly, he might have been here on time.
(D) Though doubt may exist about the mailability of some matter, the sender is fully liable for law violation if such matter should be nonmailable.

Directions: Choose the sentence that is grammatically **correct** and darken its letter on your answer sheet.

28. (A) In high-visibility crimes, it is apparent to all concerned that they are criminal acts at the time when they are committed.
(B) Statistics tell us that more people are killed by guns than by any kind of weapon.
(C) Reliable persons guarantee the facts with regards to the truth of these statements.
(D) The errors in the typed report were so numerous that they could hardly be overlooked.

29. (A) She suspects that the service is not so satisfactory as it should be.
(B) The court officer goes to the exhibit table and discovered that Exhibit B is an entirely different document.
(C) The jurors and alternates comprise a truly diverse group.
(D) Our aim should be not merely to reform law breakers but striking at the roots of crime.

30. (A) Close examination of traffic accident statistics reveal that traffic accidents are frequently the result of violations of traffic laws.
(B) If you had planned on employing fewer people than this to do the work, this situation would not have arose.
(C) As far as good looks and polite manners are concerned, they are both alike.
(D) If a murder has been committed with a bow and arrow, it is irrelevant to show that the defendant was well acquainted with firearms.

31. (A) An individual engages in criminal behavior if the number of criminal patterns which he or she has acquired exceeds the number of noncriminal patterns.
(B) Every person must be informed of the reason for their arrest unless arrested in the actual commission of a crime.
(C) The one of the following motorists to which it would be most desirable to issue a summons is the one which was late for an important business appointment.
(D) The officer should glance around quickly but with care to determine whether his entering the area will damage any evidence.

32. (A) The typist would of corrected the errors had she realized that the supervisor would see the report.
(B) If the budget allows, we are likely to reemploy anyone whose training fits them to do the work.
(C) Since the report lacked the needed information, it was of no value to me.
(D) There would have been no trouble if the receptionist would have always answered courteously.

33. (A) Due to the age of the defendant, the trial will be heard in Juvenile Court and the record will be sealed.
(B) Calculate the average amount stolen per incident by dividing the total value by the amount of offenses.
(C) The combination to the office safe is known only to the chief clerk and myself.
(D) Hearsay is evidence based on repeating the words told by another and not based on personal observation or knowledge.

34. (A) A court officer needs specific qualifications that are different than those required of police officers.
(B) Understanding how one's own work contributes to the effort of the entire agency indicates an appreciation for the importance of that job.
(C) If only one guard was assigned to the jury room, the chances of wrongdoing would be heightened.
(D) One should not use an improved method for performing a task until you have obtained approval of the supervisor.

SECTION THREE: CLERICAL CHECKING

Directions: For each question, compare the name/address/number listings in all three columns. Then darken answer space:

(A) if the listings in **ALL THREE** columns are exactly **ALIKE**
(B) if only the listings in **COLUMNS** 1 and 3 are exactly **ALIKE**
(C) if only the listings in **COLUMNS** 1 and 2 are exactly **ALIKE**
(D) if the listings in **ALL THREE** columns are **DIFFERENT**

	Column 1	Column 2	Column 3
35.	John H. Smith 238 N. Monroe Street Phila., PA 19147 176-54-326 5578-98765-33	John H. Smith 238 N. Monroe Street Phila, PA 19147 176-54-326 5578-98765-33	John H. Smith 238 N. Monroe Street Phila., PA 19147 176-54-326 5578-98765-33
36.	Evan A. McKinley 2872 Broadway East Amherst, NY 14051 212-883-5184 9803-115-6848	Evan A. McKinley 2872 Broadway East Amherst, NY 14051 212-883-5184 9083-115-6848	Evan A. McKinley 2872 Broadway East Amherst, NV 14051 212-883-5184 9083-115-6848
37.	Luigi Antonio Cruz, Jr. 2695 East 3435 South Salt Lake City, UT 84109 801-485-1563, x.233 013-5589734-9	Luigi Antonio Cruz, Jr. 2695 East 3435 South Salt, Lake City, UT 84109 801-485-1563, x.233 013-5589734-9	Luigi Antonio Cruz, Jr. 2695 East 3435 South Salt Lake City, UT 84109 801-485-1563, x.233 013-5589734-9
38.	Educational Records Inst. P.O. Box 44268a Atlanta, Georgia 30337 18624-40-9128 63qs5-95YT3-001	Educational Records Inst. P.O. Box 44268a Atlanta, Georgia 30337 18624-40-9128 63qs5-95YT3-001	Educational Records Inst. P.O. Box 44286a Atlanta, Georgia 30337 18624-40-9128 63qs5-95YT3-001
39.	Sr. Consultant, Labor Rel. Benner Mgmt. Group 86408 W. 3rd Ave. Trowbridge, MA 02178 617-980-1136	Sr. Consultant, Labor Rel. Banner Mgmt. Group 86408 W. 3rd Ave. Trowbridge, MA 02178 617-980-1136	Sr. Consultant, Labor Rel. Benner Mgmt. Group 84608 W. 3rd Ave. Trowbridge, MA 02178 617-980-1136
40.	Marina Angelika Salvis P.O.B. 11283 Gracie Sta. Newtown, PA 18940-0998 215-382-0628 4168-GNP-78852	Marina Angelika Salvis . P.O.B. 11283 Gracie Sta. Newtown, PA 18940-0998 215-382-0628 4168-GNP-78852	Marina Angelika Salvis PO.B. 11283 Gracie Sta. Newtown, PA 18940-0998 215-382-0628 4168-GNP-78852
41.	Durham Reichard, III 8298 Antigua Terrace Gaithersburg, MD 20879 301-176-9887-8 0-671-843576-X	Durham Reichard, III 8298 Antigua Terrace Gaithersburg, MD 20879 301-176-9887-8 0-671-843576-X	Durham Reichard, III 8298 Antigua Terrace Gaithersberg, MD 20879 301-176-9887-8 0-671-843576-X

	Column 1	Column 2	Column 3
42.	L. Chamberlain Smythe Mardikian & Moore, Inc. Cor. Mott Street at Pell San Francisco, Calif. 58312-398401-25	L. Chamberlain Smythe Mardikian and Moore, Inc. Cor. Mott Street at Pell San Francisco, Calif. 58312-398401-25	L. Chamberlain Smythe Mardikian & Moore, Inc. Cor. Mott Street at Pell San Francisco, Calif. 58312-398401-25
43.	Ramona Fleischer-Chris 60646 West Touhy Avenue Sebastopol, CA 95472 707-998-0104 0-06-408632-0	Ramona Fleisher-Chris 60646 West Touhy Avenue Sebastopol, CA 95472 707-998-0104 0-06-408632-0	Ramona Fleischer-Chris 60646 West Touhey Avenue Sebastopol, CA 95472 707-998-0104 0-06-408632-0
44.	George Sebastian Barnes Noble/Encore/Dalton 43216 M Street, NE Washington, DC 20036 202-222-1272	George Sebastian Barnes Noble/Encore/Dalton 43216 M. Street, NE Washington, DC 20036 202-222-1272	George Sebastian Barnes Noble/Encore/Dalton 43216 M Street, NE Washington, DC 20036 202-222-1272
45.	Baldwin Algonquin, III 2503 Bartholemew Way Lemberger, VA 28094-9182 9-1-303-558-8536 683-64-0828	Baldwin Algonquin, III 2503 Bartholemew Way Lemberger, VA 28094-9182 9-1-303-558-8536 683-64-0828	Baldwin Algonquin, III 2503 Bartholomew Way Lemberger, VA 28094-9182 9-l-303-558-8536 683-64-0828
46.	Huang Ho Cheung 612 Gallopade Gallery, E. Seattle, WA 98101-2614 001-206-283-7722 5416R-1952TZ-op	Huang Ho Cheung 612 Gallopade Gallery, E. Seattle, WA 98101-2614 001-206-283-7722 5416R-1952TZ-op	Huang Ho Cheung 612 Gallopade Gallery, E. Seattle, WA 98101-2614 001-206-283-7722 5416R-1952TZ-op
47.	Hilliard H. Hyacinth 86529 Dunwoodie Drive Kanakao, HI 91132 808-880-8080 6-78912-e3e42	Hilliard H. Hyacinth 86529 Dunwoodie Drive Kanakao, HI 91132 808-880-8080 6-78912-3e3e42	Hilliard H. Hyacinth 85629 Dunwoodie Drive Kanakao, HI 91132 808-880-8080 6-78912-e3e42
48.	Anoko Kawamoto 8932 Shimabui Hwy. O'Reilly Bay, LA 56212 713-864-7253-4984 5634-Ootv5a-16867	Anoko Kawamoto 8932 Shimabui Hwy. O'Reillys Bay, LA 56212 713-864-7253-4984 5634-Ootv5a-16867	Anoko, Kawamoto 8932 Shimabui Hwy. O'Reilly Bay, LA 56212 713-864-7253-4984 5634-Ootv5a-16867
49.	Michael Chrzanowski 312 Colonia del Valle 4132 ES, Mexico DF 001-45-67265 A8987-B73245	Michael Chrzanowski 312 Colonia del Valle 4132 ES, Mexico DF 001-45-67265 A8987-B73245	Michael Chrzanowski 312 Colonia del Valle 4132 ES, Mexico D.F 001-45-67265 A8987-B73245
50.	Leonard Wilson-Wood 6892 Grand Boulevard, W. St. Georges South, DE 302-333-4273 0-122365-3987	Leonard Wilson-Wood 6892 Grand Boulevard, W. St. Georges South, DE 302-333-4273 0-122365-3987	Leonard Wilson-Wood 6892 Grand Boulevard, W. St. Georges South, DE 302-333-4273 0-122365-3987

SECTION FOUR: OFFICE RECORD KEEPING

Directions: Study the information given in the tables and combine the information as indicated. Answer the multiple-choice questions in accordance with the information on the tables. You are NOT permitted to use a calculator to arrive at totals.

DAILY LOG OF CASES

Monday

Judge	*Date Filed*	*Sum at Issue*	*Disposition*	*Award*
Baron	6/5/98	$ 9,500	adjourned	X
Lee	4/2/99	20,000	dismissed	X
Conlon	12/8/97	12,000	settled	X
Ramos	3/31/99	5,500	settled	X
Lee	10/81/98	10,000	dismissed	X
Jones	1/5/99	14,000	found for plaintiff	$15,000
Baron	5/1/00	7,600	adjourned	X

Tuesday

Judge	*Date Filed*	*Sum at Issue*	*Disposition*	*Award*
Ramos	2/2/99	$ 3,000	found for plaintiff	$3,375
Amati	8/6/99	8,000	dismissed	X
Moro	4/8/98	11,500	found for plaintiff	9,000
Jones	11/17/97	12,000	adjourned	X
Conlon	12/4/97	4,500	adjourned	X
Amati	6/12/98	2,000	settled	X

Wednesday

Judge	*Date Filed*	*Sum at Issue*	*Disposition*	*Award*
Conlon	1/7/00	$10,000	dismissed	X
Baron	5/3/99	5,000	adjourned	X
Ramos	6/22/98	7,500	found for plaintiff	$ 6,000
Moro	2/15/00	22,000	settled	X
Lee	9/7/99	8,000	settled	X
Conlon	11/30/97	16,000	found for plaintiff	17,250
Amati	7/10/99	10,000	found for plaintiff	10,850

Thursday				
Judge	*Date Filed*	*Sum at Issue*	*Disposition*	*Award*
Jones	5/18/99	$ 7,500	found for plaintiff	$ 6,000
Amati	3/6/98	9,250	settled	X
Conlon	3/31/99	6,000	adjourned	X
Moro	8/28/98	12,000	adjourned	X
Conlon	10/30/97	4,600	found for plaintiff	5,000

Friday				
Judge	*Date Filed*	*Sum at Issue*	*Disposition*	*Award*
Lee	4/12/99	$ 6,000	adjourned	X
Baron	1/28/00	9,500	dismissed	X
Ramos	7/17/99	28,000	found for plaintiff	$20,000
Amati	12/2/98	15,000	settled	X
Lee	2/21/99	8,000	found for plaintiff	8,625
Moro	5/9/98	22,000	settled	X
Baron	8/25/98	11,000	dismissed	X
Jones	11/4/97	5,500	settled	X

DAILY BREAKDOWN OF CASES						
	Mon.	*Tue.*	*Wed.*	*Thurs.*	*Fri.*	*Total*
Case Status Dismissed	2	1	1	0	2	6
Adjourned						
Settled						
Found for Plaintiff						
Total Cases						
	Mon.	*Tue.*	*Wed.*	*Thurs.*	*Fri.*	*Total*
Cases Filed by Year	1	2	1	1	1	6
1997						
1998						
1999						
2000						
Total Cases						

SUMMARY OF CASES					
Judge	*Dismissed*	*Adjourned*	*Settled*	*Found for Plaintiff*	*Total*
Amati	1		3	1	5
Baron					
Conlon					
Jones					
Lee					
Moro					
Ramos					

51. The judge scheduled to hear the greatest number of cases in this week was
(A) Amati
(B) Lee
(C) Conlon
(D) Ramos

52. The judge who determined no cash awards in this week was
(A) Moro
(B) Jones
(C) Baron
(D) Lee

53. How many judges were assigned to hear more than one case in one day?
(A) 1
(B) 2
(C) 3
(D) 4

54. In how many cases was the sum finally awarded lower than the sum at issue?
(A) 2
(B) 3
(C) 4
(D) 5

55. How many of the cases filed in 1997 were dismissed?
(A) 0
(B) 1
(C) 2
(D) 3

56. Of the cases adjourned, the greatest number were filed in
(A) 1997
(B) 1998
(C) 1999
(D) 2000

57. Which two judges were scheduled to sit on only three days?
(A) Jones and Baron
(B) Baron and Lee
(C) Lee and Moro
(D) Ramos and Jones

58. In which month was the greatest number of cases filed?

(A) February
(B) May
(C) August
(D) November

59. The total amount of money awarded on Wednesday was

(A) $33,500
(B) $34,100
(C) $35,300
(D) $45,000

60. The total amount of money awarded by Jones was

(A) $39,000
(B) $21,500
(C) $21,000
(D) $17,500

61. The amount at issue in the cases that were adjourned on Thursday was

(A) $12,100
(B) $18,000
(C) $21,350
(D) $29,250

62. When the amount of an award is greater than the sum at issue, the higher award represents an additional sum meant to cover plaintiff's costs in the suit. The total amount awarded this week to cover costs was

(A) $ 4,500
(B) $ 4,850
(C) $ 9,000
(D) $13,500

63. If all the plaintiffs who filed cases in 2000 were awarded exactly the sums for which they sued, they would have received a total of

(A) $41,500
(B) $45,100
(C) $48,600
(D) $49,100

64. The total amount awarded to plaintiffs who filed their cases in 1997 was

(A) $ 1,650
(B) $20,600
(C) $22,250
(D) $22,650

65. Comparing cases filed in 1998 with cases filed in 1999,

(A) four more of the 1998 cases were settled than 1999 cases
(B) two fewer 1999 cases were settled than 1998 cases
(C) an equal number of cases was settled from the two years
(D) three more of the 1998 cases were settled than 1999 cases

SECTION FIVE: READING, UNDERSTANDING, AND INTERPRETING WRITTEN MATERIAL

Directions: Each passage below contains 15 numbered blanks. Read the passage once quickly to get the overall idea. Below each passage are listed sets of words numbered to match the blanks. Read the passage through a second time, more slowly, and choose the word from each set which makes the most sense both in the sentence and the total paragraph. Darken the letter of that word on your answer sheet.

A large proportion of people ______ (66) bars are ______ (67) convicted criminals, ______ (68) people who have been arrested and are being ______ (69) until ______ (70) trial in ______ (71). Experts have often pointed out that this ______ (72) system does not operate fairly. For instance, a person who can afford to pay bail usually will not get locked up. The theory of the bail system is that the person will make sure to show up in court when he or she is supposed to; ______ (73), bail will be forfeited—the person will ______ (74) the ______ (75) that was put up. Sometimes a person ______ (76) can show that he or she is a stable ______ (77) with a job and a family will be released on "Personal recognizance" (without bail). The result is that the well-to-do, the ______ (78), and the family men can often ______ (79) the detention system. The people who do wind up in detention tend to ______ (80) the poor, the unemployed, the single, and the young.

66. (A) under
(B) at
(C) tending
(D) behind

67. (A) always
(B) not
(C) hardened
(D) very

68. (A) but
(B) and
(C) also
(D) although

69. (A) hanged
(B) freed
(C) held
(D) judged

70. (A) your
(B) his
(C) daily
(D) their

71. (A) jail
(B) court
(C) fire
(D) judgment

72. (A) school
(B) court
(C) detention
(D) election

73. (A) otherwise
(B) therefore
(C) because
(D) then

74. (A) save
(B) spend
(C) lose
(D) count

75. (A) wall
(B) money
(C) front
(D) pretense

76. (A) whom
(B) which
(C) what
(D) who

77. (A) citizen
(B) horse
(C) cleaner
(D) clown

78. (A) handsome
(B) athletic
(C) employed
(D) alcoholic

79. (A) survive
(B) avoid
(C) provide
(D) institute

80. (A) become
(B) help
(C) be
(D) harm

______ (81) acts are classified according to ______ (82) standards. One is whether the ______ (83) is major or minor. A major offense, such as murder, would be ______ (84) a felony, ______ (85) a minor offense, such as reckless driving, would be considered a misdemeanor. ______ (86) standard of classification is the specific kind of crime committed. Examples are burglary and robbery, which are ______ (87) often used incorrectly by individuals who are ______ (88) aware of the actual ______ (89) as defined by law. A person who breaks ______ (90) a building to commit a ______ (91) or other major crime is ______ (92) of burglary, while robbery is the felonious taking of an individual's ______ (93) from his person or ______ (94) his immediate ______ (95) by the use of violence or threat.

81. (A) People's
(B) Criminal
(C) Felonious
(D) Numerous

82. (A) decent
(B) published
(C) community
(D) several

83. (A) crime
(B) act
(C) offender
(D) standard

84. (A) labeled
(B) convicted
(C) executed
(D) tried

85. (A) moreover
(B) because
(C) whereas
(D) hence

86. (A) Gold
(B) Juried
(C) Another
(D) My

87. (A) crimes
(B) terms
(C) verdicts
(D) sentences

88. (A) sometimes
(B) very
(C) not
(D) angrily

89. (A) difference
(B) definitions
(C) crimes
(D) victims

90. (A) down
(B) into
(C) apart
(D) from

91. (A) felony
(B) burglary
(C) robbery
(D) theft

92. (A) accused
(B) convicted
(C) freed
(D) guilty

93. (A) life
(B) liberty
(C) property
(D) weapon

94. (A) throughout
(B) in
(C) by
(D) for

95. (A) lifetime
(B) home
(C) presence
(D) concern

CORRECT ANSWERS—SENIOR OFFICE TYPIST EXAM

1. D	21. C	41. C	61. B	81. B
2. A	22. D	42. B	62. A	82. D
3. C	23. A	43. D	63. D	83. A
4. B	24. B	44. B	64. C	84. A
5. C	25. B	45. C	65. D	85. C
6. A	26. C	46. A	66. B	86. C
7. D	27. A	47. D	67. B	87. B
8. B	28. D	48. B	68. A	88. C
9. D	29. C	49. C	69. C	89. A
10. C	30. D	50. A	70. D	90. B
11. B	31. A	51. C	71. B	91. D
12. D	32. C	52. C	72. C	92. D
13. C	33. D	53. D	73. A	93. C
14. D	34. B	54. C	74. C	94. B
15. C	35. B	55. A	75. B	95. C
16. A	36. D	56. C	76. D	
17. D	37. A	57. B	77. A	
18. B	38. C	58. B	78. C	
19. A	39. D	59. B	79. B	
20. D	40. A	60. C	80. C	

ANSWERS AND EXPLANATIONS

SECTION ONE: SPELLING

1. **The correct answer is (D).** appellate
2. **The correct answer is (A).** presumption
3. **The correct answer is (C).** litigant
4. **The correct answer is (B).** commitment
5. **The correct answer is (C).** affidavit
6. **The correct answer is (A).** arraign
7. **The correct answer is (D).** cumulative
8. **The correct answer is (B).** severance
9. **The correct answer is (D).** adjournment
10. **The correct answer is (C).** commenced
11. **The correct answer is (B).** forgers
12. **The correct answer is (D).** no error
13. **The correct answer is (C).** achievement
14. **The correct answer is (D).** no error
15. **The correct answer is (C).** detention
16. **The correct answer is (A).** immaterial
17. **The correct answer is (D).** no error
18. **The correct answer is (B).** prosecutor
19. **The correct answer is (A).** correctible
20. **The correct answer is (D).** no error

SECTION TWO: GRAMMAR

21. **The correct answer is (C).** There should be no "and" before the "etc." at the end of a series of words.
22. **The correct answer is (D).** This is an incomplete comparison. It should read: "He devotes as much *as*, if not more, time to his work than do the rest of the employees."
23. **The correct answer is (A).** (A) "More preferable" is a redundancy. "Preferable" alone is quite adequate.
24. **The correct answer is (B).** The compound subject requires the plural form of the verb—constitute.
25. **The correct answer is (B).** This sentence shifts point of view midstream. It could read either "If one wants to prevent crime, one must deal . . ." or "If we want to prevent crime, we must deal . . ."
26. **The correct answer is (C).** "Unique" means that there is only one; therefore, the word can take no qualifier.
27. **The correct answer is (A).** This is an ambiguous statement. Was the judge praised for the fire? Was the clerk praised for the fire? It would be better to say, "The clerk was highly praised for promptly notifying the judge of the fire."
28. **The correct answer is (D).** (A) reads as if all concerned are criminal acts. Since guns are a kind of weapon, (B) would have to read . . . than any *other* kind of weapon." In (C), "regards" is the wrong word. The word required is "regard."
29. **The correct answer is (C).** In (A) the idiomatic form is "*as* satistactory." (B) confuses two tenses in the same sentence. It would be correct to say the court officer *went* and discovered. (D) requires a parallel construction, either "reforming and striking" or "to reform and to strike."
30. **The correct answer is (D).** In (A) "examination" being singular requires the singular verb, "reveals." In (B) we need "would not have *arisen.*" As for (C), the word "alike" obviously includes "both," so the word "both" is redundant.
31. **The correct answer is (A).** In (B) every person is singular and therefore must be informed for the reason for *his* (or *her)* arrest. In (C), a motorist is a person, not a thing, so use *who* and *to whom* rather than *which.* In (D) we need the parallelism of "quickly but carefully."
32. **The correct answer is (C).** In (A) we need the auxiliary verb have in place of the incorrect of. In (B) "anyone" is singular so the referrent pronoun must also be singular. In (D), the construction is awkward. ". . . if the receptionist had always answered . . ." is sufficient and accurate.
33. **The correct answer is (D).** (A) is incorrect because it is poor form to begin a sentence with "due to." In (B) what is meant is the *number* of offenses. In (C) we need a simple objective case pronoun, ". . . is known only to the chief clerk and *me*."
34. **The correct answer is (B).** In (A) the correct idiomatic form is "different *from*." (C) requires a subjunctive form because the statement is contrary to fact. "If only one guard *were* . . . ." (D) shifts point of view. For consistency the pronoun throughout may be either "one" or "you."

SECTION THREE: CLERICAL CHEKCING

35. **The correct answer is (B).** In Column 2, Phila, PA 19147 differs from Phila., PA 19147.
36. **The correct answer is (D).** In Column 3, East Amherst, NV 14051 differs from East Amherst, NY 14051. In Column 2, 9083-115-6848 differs from 9803-115-6848.
37. **The correct answer is (A).** All columns are alike.
38. **The correct answer is (C).** In Column 3, P.O. Box 44286a differs from P.O. Box 44268a.
39. **The correct answer is (D).** In Column 2, Banner differs from Benner. In Column 3, 84608 differs from 86408.
40. **The correct answer is (A).** All columns are alike.
41. **The correct answer is (C).** In Column 3, Gaithersberg differs from Gaithersburg.

42. **The correct answer is (B).** In Column 2, the word *and* is spelled out; in Column 1, the same effect is gained with &.
43. **The correct answer is (D).** In Column 2, Fleisher differs from Fleischer. In Column 3, Touhey differs from Touhy.
44. **The correct answer is (B).** In Column 2, 43216 M. Street, NE differs from 43216 M Street, NE.
45. **The correct answer is (C).** In Column 3, Bartholomew differs from Bartholemew.
46. **The correct answer is (A).** All columns are alike.
47. **The correct answer is (D).** In Column 3, 85629 Dunwoodie Drive differs from 86529 Dunwoodie Drive. In Column 2, 6-78912-3e3e42 differs from 6-78912-e3e42.
48. **The correct answer is (B).** In Column 2, O'Reillys Bay differs from O'Reilly Bay.
49. **The correct answer is (C).** In Column 3, Mexico D.F. differs from Mexico DF.
50. **The correct answer is (A).** All columns are alike.

SECTION FOUR: OFFICE RECORD KEEPING

51. **The correct answer is (C).** Conlon was scheduled to hear six cases, Amati and Lee were scheduled for five apiece, and Ramos was scheduled for four.
52. **The correct answer is (C).** Of the cases Baron was scheduled to hear, three were adjourned and two were dismissed. Jones gave cash awards in two cases, and Moro and Lee gave cash awards in one each.
53. **The correct answer is (D).** Lee and Baron were both scheduled for two trials on Monday and Friday, Amati was scheduled for two on Tuesday, and Conlon was scheduled for two on Wednesday and Thursday.
54. **The correct answer is (C).** On Tuesday, Moro awarded $9,000 in a suit for $11,500; on Wednesday, Ramos awarded $6,000 in a suit for $7,500; on Thursday, Jones awarded $6,000 in a suit for $7,500; and on Friday, Ramos awarded $20,000 in a suit for $28,000.
55. **The correct answer is (A).** Of the six cases filed in 1997, two were settled, two were adjourned, and two were adjudicated. None was dismissed.
56. **The correct answer is (C).** Three of the 1999 cases were adjourned, one 2000 case was adjourned, and two each of 1997 and 1998 cases were adjourned.
57. **The correct answer is (B).** Lee and Baron each sat on Monday, Wednesday, and Friday. Jones sat on Monday, Tuesday, Thursday, and Friday. Moro sat on Tuesday, Wednesday, Thursday, and Friday. Ramos sat on Monday, Tuesday, Wednesday, and Friday.
58. **The correct answer is (B).** Four cases were filed in May. Three cases were filed in each of February, August, and November.
59. **The correct answer is (B).** $6,000 + $17,250 + $10,850 $34,100
60. **The correct answer is (C).** $15,000 + $6,000 = $21,000
61. **The correct answer is (B).** $6,000 + $12,000 = $18,000
62. **The correct answer is (A).**

$15,000	– $14,000 =	$1,000	(Jones on Monday)
$3,375	– $3,000 =	$375	(Ramos on Tuesday)
$17,250	– $16,000 =	$1,250	(Conlon on Wednesday)
$10,850	– $10,000 =	$850	(Amati on Wednesday)
$5,000	– $4,600 =	$400	(Conlon on Thursday)
$8,625	– $8,000 =	$625	(Lee on Friday)
		$4,500	

63. **The correct answer is (D).**

5/1/00	$ 7,600
1/7/00	10,000
2/15/00	22,000
+1/28/00	9,500
	$49,100

64. The correct answer is (C).

On Wednesday, Conlon awarded $17,250 in a 11/30/97 case.
On Thursday, Conlon awarded 5,000 in a 10/30/97 case.
$22,250

65. The correct answer is (B). Four 1998 cases were settled; only two 1999 cases were settled.

SECTION FIVE: READING, UNDERSTANDING, AND INTERPRETING WRITTEN MATERIAL

Correct answers for questions 66–80, completed paragraph:

A large proportion of people behind (96) bars are not (97) convicted criminals, but (98) people who have been arrested and are being held (99) until their (100) trial in court (101). Experts have often pointed out that this detention (102) system does not operate fairly. For instance, a person who can afford to pay bail usually will not get locked up. The theory of the bail system is that the person will make sure to show up in court when he or she is supposed to; otherwise (103), bail will be forfeited—the person will (104) lose the money (105) that was put up. Sometimes a person who (106) can show that he or she is a stable citizen (107) with a job and a family will be released on "personal recognizance" (without bail). The result is that the well-to-do, the employed (108), and the family men can often avoid (109) the detention system. The people who do wind up in detention tend to be (110) the poor, the unemployed, the single, and the young.

Correct answers for questions 81–95, completed paragraph:

Criminal (111) acts are classified according to several (112) standards. One is whether the crime (113) is major or minor. A major offense, such as murder, would be labeled (114) a felony, whereas (115) a minor offense, such as reckless driving, would be considered a misdemeanor. Another (116) standard of classification is the specific kind of crime committed. Examples are burglary and robbery, which are terms (117) often used incorrectly by individuals who are not (118) aware of the actual difference (119) as defined by law. A person who breaks into (120) a building to commit a theft (121) or other major crime is guilty (122) of burglary, while robbery is the felonious taking of an individual's property (123) from his person or in (124) his immediate presence (125) by the use of violence or threat.

ANSWER SHEET

MUNICIPAL OFFICE AIDE EXAM

1. Ⓐ Ⓑ Ⓒ Ⓓ Ⓔ	21. Ⓐ Ⓑ Ⓒ Ⓓ Ⓔ	41. Ⓐ Ⓑ Ⓒ Ⓓ Ⓔ	61. Ⓐ Ⓑ Ⓒ Ⓓ Ⓔ
2. Ⓐ Ⓑ Ⓒ Ⓓ Ⓔ	22. Ⓐ Ⓑ Ⓒ Ⓓ Ⓔ	42. Ⓐ Ⓑ Ⓒ Ⓓ Ⓔ	62. Ⓐ Ⓑ Ⓒ Ⓓ Ⓔ
3. Ⓐ Ⓑ Ⓒ Ⓓ Ⓔ	23. Ⓐ Ⓑ Ⓒ Ⓓ Ⓔ	43. Ⓐ Ⓑ Ⓒ Ⓓ Ⓔ	63. Ⓐ Ⓑ Ⓒ Ⓓ Ⓔ
4. Ⓐ Ⓑ Ⓒ Ⓓ Ⓔ	24. Ⓐ Ⓑ Ⓒ Ⓓ Ⓔ	44. Ⓐ Ⓑ Ⓒ Ⓓ Ⓔ	64. Ⓐ Ⓑ Ⓒ Ⓓ Ⓔ
5. Ⓐ Ⓑ Ⓒ Ⓓ Ⓔ	25. Ⓐ Ⓑ Ⓒ Ⓓ Ⓔ	45. Ⓐ Ⓑ Ⓒ Ⓓ Ⓔ	65. Ⓐ Ⓑ Ⓒ Ⓓ Ⓔ
6. Ⓐ Ⓑ Ⓒ Ⓓ Ⓔ	26. Ⓐ Ⓑ Ⓒ Ⓓ Ⓔ	46. Ⓐ Ⓑ Ⓒ Ⓓ Ⓔ	66. Ⓐ Ⓑ Ⓒ Ⓓ Ⓔ
7. Ⓐ Ⓑ Ⓒ Ⓓ Ⓔ	27. Ⓐ Ⓑ Ⓒ Ⓓ Ⓔ	47. Ⓐ Ⓑ Ⓒ Ⓓ Ⓔ	67. Ⓐ Ⓑ Ⓒ Ⓓ Ⓔ
8. Ⓐ Ⓑ Ⓒ Ⓓ Ⓔ	28. Ⓐ Ⓑ Ⓒ Ⓓ Ⓔ	48. Ⓐ Ⓑ Ⓒ Ⓓ Ⓔ	68. Ⓐ Ⓑ Ⓒ Ⓓ Ⓔ
9. Ⓐ Ⓑ Ⓒ Ⓓ Ⓔ	29. Ⓐ Ⓑ Ⓒ Ⓓ Ⓔ	49. Ⓐ Ⓑ Ⓒ Ⓓ Ⓔ	69. Ⓐ Ⓑ Ⓒ Ⓓ Ⓔ
10. Ⓐ Ⓑ Ⓒ Ⓓ Ⓔ	30. Ⓐ Ⓑ Ⓒ Ⓓ Ⓔ	50. Ⓐ Ⓑ Ⓒ Ⓓ Ⓔ	70. Ⓐ Ⓑ Ⓒ Ⓓ Ⓔ
11. Ⓐ Ⓑ Ⓒ Ⓓ Ⓔ	31. Ⓐ Ⓑ Ⓒ Ⓓ Ⓔ	51. Ⓐ Ⓑ Ⓒ Ⓓ Ⓔ	71. Ⓐ Ⓑ Ⓒ Ⓓ Ⓔ
12. Ⓐ Ⓑ Ⓒ Ⓓ Ⓔ	32. Ⓐ Ⓑ Ⓒ Ⓓ Ⓔ	52. Ⓐ Ⓑ Ⓒ Ⓓ Ⓔ	72. Ⓐ Ⓑ Ⓒ Ⓓ Ⓔ
13. Ⓐ Ⓑ Ⓒ Ⓓ Ⓔ	33. Ⓐ Ⓑ Ⓒ Ⓓ Ⓔ	53. Ⓐ Ⓑ Ⓒ Ⓓ Ⓔ	73. Ⓐ Ⓑ Ⓒ Ⓓ Ⓔ
14. Ⓐ Ⓑ Ⓒ Ⓓ Ⓔ	34. Ⓐ Ⓑ Ⓒ Ⓓ Ⓔ	54. Ⓐ Ⓑ Ⓒ Ⓓ Ⓔ	74. Ⓐ Ⓑ Ⓒ Ⓓ Ⓔ
15. Ⓐ Ⓑ Ⓒ Ⓓ Ⓔ	35. Ⓐ Ⓑ Ⓒ Ⓓ Ⓔ	55. Ⓐ Ⓑ Ⓒ Ⓓ Ⓔ	75. Ⓐ Ⓑ Ⓒ Ⓓ Ⓔ
16. Ⓐ Ⓑ Ⓒ Ⓓ Ⓔ	36. Ⓐ Ⓑ Ⓒ Ⓓ Ⓔ	56. Ⓐ Ⓑ Ⓒ Ⓓ Ⓔ	76. Ⓐ Ⓑ Ⓒ Ⓓ Ⓔ
17. Ⓐ Ⓑ Ⓒ Ⓓ Ⓔ	37. Ⓐ Ⓑ Ⓒ Ⓓ Ⓔ	57. Ⓐ Ⓑ Ⓒ Ⓓ Ⓔ	77. Ⓐ Ⓑ Ⓒ Ⓓ Ⓔ
18. Ⓐ Ⓑ Ⓒ Ⓓ Ⓔ	38. Ⓐ Ⓑ Ⓒ Ⓓ Ⓔ	58. Ⓐ Ⓑ Ⓒ Ⓓ Ⓔ	78. Ⓐ Ⓑ Ⓒ Ⓓ Ⓔ
19. Ⓐ Ⓑ Ⓒ Ⓓ Ⓔ	39. Ⓐ Ⓑ Ⓒ Ⓓ Ⓔ	59. Ⓐ Ⓑ Ⓒ Ⓓ Ⓔ	79. Ⓐ Ⓑ Ⓒ Ⓓ Ⓔ
20. Ⓐ Ⓑ Ⓒ Ⓓ Ⓔ	40. Ⓐ Ⓑ Ⓒ Ⓓ Ⓔ	60. Ⓐ Ⓑ Ⓒ Ⓓ Ⓔ	80. Ⓐ Ⓑ Ⓒ Ⓓ Ⓔ

Raw score = number right ____________

MUNICIPAL OFFICE AIDE EXAM

Time: 3½ Hours—80 Questions, all of equal weight

Directions: Choose the best answer to each question and darken its letter on the answer sheet. Correct answers are on page 269.

1. Assume that a few co-workers meet near your desk and talk about personal matters during working hours. Lately, this practice has interfered with your work. In order to stop this practice, the best action for you to take *first* is to

   (A) ask your supervisor to put a stop to the co-workers' meeting near your desk.
   (B) discontinue any friendship with this group.
   (C) ask your co-workers not to meet near your desk.
   (D) request that your desk be moved to another location.

2. In order to maintain office coverage during working hours, your supervisor has scheduled your lunch hour from 1 P.M. to 2 P.M. and your co-worker's lunch hour from 12 P.M. to 1 P.M. Lately, your co-worker has been returning late from lunch each day. As a result you don't get a full hour, since you must return to the office by 2 P.M. Of the following, the best action for you to take *first* is to

   (A) explain to your co-worker in a courteous manner that his or her lateness is interfering with your right to a full hour for lunch.
   (B) tell your co-worker that his lateness must stop or you will report him to your supervisor.
   (C) report your co-worker's lateness to your supervisor.
   (D) leave at 1 P.M. for lunch, whether your co-worker has returned or not.

3. Assume that, as an office worker, one of your jobs is to open mail sent to your unit, read the mail for content, and send the mail to the appropriate person for handling. You accidentally open and begin to read a letter marked "personal" addressed to a co-worker. Of the following, the best action for you to take is to

   (A) report to your supervisor that your co-worker is receiving personal mail at the office.
   (B) destroy the letter so that your co-worker doesn't know you saw it.
   (C) reseal the letter and place it on the co-worker's desk without saying anything.
   (D) bring the letter to your co-worker and explain that you opened it by accident.

4. Suppose that in evaluating your work your supervisor gives you an overall good rating, but states that you sometimes turn in work with careless errors. The best action for you to take would be to

   (A) ask a co-worker who is good at details to proofread your work.
   (B) take time to do a careful job, paying more attention to detail.
   (C) continue working as usual since occasional errors are to be expected.
   (D) ask your supervisor if he or she would mind correcting your errors.

5. Assume that you are taking a telephone message for a co-worker who is not in the office at the time. Of the following, the least important item to write on the message is the

   (A) length of the call.
   (B) name of the caller.
   (C) time of the call.
   (D) telephone number of the caller.

Questions 6–13 each consists of a sentence which may or may not be an example of good English. The underlined parts of each sentence may be correct or incorrect. Examine each sentence considering grammar, punctuation, spelling, and capitalization. If the English usage in the underlined parts of the sentence given is better than any of the changes in the underlined words suggested in choice (B), (C), or (D), choose choice (A). If the changes in the underlined words suggested in choice (B), (C), or (D) would make the sentence correct, choose the correct choice. Do not select a choice that will change the meaning of the sentence.

6. This Fall the office will be closed on Columbus Day, October 9th.

(A) Correct as is
(B) fall . . . Columbus Day, October
(C) Fall . . . columbus day, October
(D) fall . . . Columbus Day, october

7. This manual discribes the duties performed by an office aide.

(A) Correct as is
(B) describe the duties performed
(C) discribe the duties performed
(D) describes the duties performed

8. There weren't no paper in the supply closet.

(A) Correct as is
(B) weren't any
(C) wasn't any
(D) wasn't no

9. The new employees left there office to attend a meeting.

(A) Correct as is
(B) they're
(C) their
(D) thier

10. The office worker started working at 8;30 A.M.

(A) Correct as is
(B) 8:30 A.M.
(C) 8;30 A,M.
(D) 8;30 AM.

11. The alphabet, or A to Z sequence are the basis of most filing systems.

(A) Correct as is
(B) alphabet, or A to Z sequence, is
(C) alphabet, or A to Z, sequence are
(D) alphabet, or A too Z sequence, is

12. Those file cabinets are five feet tall.

(A) Correct as is
(B) Them . . . feet
(C) Those . . . foot
(D) Them . . . foot

13. The office aide checked the register and finding the date of the meeting.

(A) Correct as is
(B) regaster and finding
(C) register and found
(D) regaster and found

Questions 14–21 have two lists of numbers. Each list contains three sets of numbers. Check each of the three sets in the list on the right to see if they are the same as the corresponding set in the list on the left. Darken answer space:

(A) if **NONE** of the sets in the right list are the SAME as those in the left list
(B) if **ONLY ONE** of the sets in the right list is the **SAME** as those in the left list
(C) if **ONLY TWO** of the sets in the right list are the **SAME** as those in the left list
(D) if ALL **THREE** sets in the right list are the **SAME** as those in the left list

14.	7354183476 4474747744 57914302311	7354983476 4474747774 57914302311
15.	7143592185 8344517699 9178531263	7143892185 8344518699 9178531263
16.	2572114731 8806835476 8255831246	257214731 8806835476 8255831246
17.	331476853821 6976658532996 3766042113715	331476858621 6976655832996 3766042113745
18.	8806663315 74477138449 211756663666	8806663315 74477138449 211756663666
19.	990006966996 53022219743 4171171117717	99000696996 53022219843 4171171177717
20.	24400222433004 5300030055000355 20000075532002022	24400222433004 5300030055500355 20000075532002022
21.	611166640660001116 7111300117001100733 26666446664476518	61116664066001116 7111300117001100733 26666446664476518

Questions 22–25 have two lists of names and addresses. Each list contains three sets of names and addresses. Check each of the three sets in the list on the right to see if they are the same as the corresponding set in the list on the left. Darken answer space:

(A) if **NONE** of the sets in the right list are the **SAME** as those in the left list
(B) if **ONLY ONE** of the sets in the right list is the **SAME** as those in the left list
(C) if **ONLY TWO** of the sets in the right list are the **SAME** as those in the left list
(D) if ALL **THREE** sets in the right list are the **SAME** as those in the left list

22.	Mary T. Berlinger 2351 Hampton St. Monsey, N.Y. 20117	Mary T. Berlinger 2351 Hampton St. Monsey, N.Y. 20117
	Eduardo Benes 473 Kingston Avenue Central Islip, N.Y. 11734	Eduardo Benes 473 Kingston Avenue Central Islip, N.Y. 11734
	Alan Carrington Fuchs 17 Gnarled Hollow Road Los Angeles, California 91635	Alan Carrington Fuchs 17 Gnarled Hollow Road Los Angeles, California 91685
23.	David John Jacobson 178 35 St. Apt. 4C New York, N.Y. 00927	David John Jacobson 178 53 St. Apt. 4C New York, N.Y. 00927
	Ann-Marie Calonella 7243 South Ridge Blvd. Bakersfield, California 96714	Ann-Marie Calonella 7243 South Ridge Blvd. Bakersfield, California 96714
	Pauline M. Thompson 872 Linden Ave. Houston, Texas 70321	Pauline M. Thomson 872 Linden Ave. Houston, Texas 70321
24.	Chester LeRoy Masterton 152 Lacy Rd. Kankakee, Ill. 54532	Chester LeRoy Masterson 152 Lacy Rd. Kankakee, Ill. 54532
	William Maloney S. LaCrosse Pla. Wausau, Wisconsin 52146	William Maloney S. LaCross Pla. Wausau, Wisconsin 52146
	Cynthia V. Barnes 16 Pines Rd. Greenpoint, Mississippi 20376	Cynthia V. Barnes 16 Pines Rd. Greenpoint, Mississippi 20376
25.	Marcel Jean Frontenac 6 Burton On The Water Calender, Me. 01471	Marcel Jean Frontenac 6 Burton On The Water Calender, Me. 01471
	J. Scott Marsden 174 S. Tipton St. Cleveland, Ohio	J. Scott Marsden 174 Tipton St. Cleveland, Ohio
	Lawrence T. Haney 171 McDonough St. Decatur, Ga. 31304	Lawrence T. Haney 171 McDonough St. Decatur, Ga. 31304

Questions 26–31 are to be answered solely on the basis of the information contained in the following passage:

Duplicating is the process of making a number of identical copies of letters, documents, etc., from an original. Some duplicating processes make copies directly from the original document. Other duplicating processes require the preparation of a special master, and copies are then made from the master. Four of the most common duplicating processes are stencil, fluid, offset, and Xerox.

In the stencil process, the typewriter is used to cut the words into a master, called a stencil. Drawings, charts, or graphs can be cut into the stencil using a stylus. As many as 3,500 good-quality copies can be reproduced from one stencil. Various grades of finished paper from inexpensive mimeograph to expensive bond can be used.

The fluid process is a good method of copying from 50 to 125 good-quality copies from a master which is prepared with a special dye. The master is placed on the duplicator, and special paper with a hard finish is moistened and then passed through the duplicator. Some of the dye on the master is dissolved, creating an impression on the paper. The impression becomes lighter as more copies are made, and once the dye on the master is used up, a new master must be made.

The offset process is the most adaptable office duplicating process because this process can be used for making a few copies or many copies. Masters can be made on paper or plastic for a few hundred copies or on metal plates for as many as 75,000 copies. By using a special technique called photo-offset, charts, photographs, illustrations, or graphs can be reproduced on the master plate. The offset process is capable of producing large quantities of fine, top-quality copies on all types of finished paper.

The Xerox process reproduces an exact duplicate from an original. It is the fastest duplicating method because the original material is placed directly on the duplicator, eliminating the need to make a special master. Any kind of paper can be used. The Xerox process is the most expensive duplicating process; however, it is the best method of reproducing small quantities of good-quality copies of reports, letters, official documents, memos, or contracts.

26. Of the following, the most efficient method of reproducing 5,000 copies of a graph is

(A) stencil
(B) fluid
(C) offset
(D) Xerox

27. The offset process is the most adaptable office duplicating process because

(A) it is the quickest duplicating method.
(B) it is the least expensive duplicating method.
(C) it can produce a small number or large number of copies.
(D) a softer master can be used over and over again.

28. Which one of the following duplicating processes uses moistened paper?

(A) stencil
(B) fluid
(C) offset
(D) Xerox

29. The fluid process would be the best process to use for reproducing

(A) five copies of a school transcript.
(B) 50 copies of a memo.
(C) 500 copies of a form letter.
(D) 5,000 copies of a chart.

30. Which one of the following duplicating processes does not require a special master?

(A) fluid
(B) Xerox
(C) offset
(D) stencil

31. Xerox is not used for all duplicating jobs because

(A) it produces poor-quality copies.
(B) the process is too expensive.
(C) preparing the master is too time-consuming.
(D) it cannot produce written reports.

Questions 32–35: select the choice that is closest in meaning to the underlined word.

SAMPLE QUESTION

This division reviews the fiscal reports of the agency. In this sentence the word fiscal most nearly means

(A) financial
(B) critical
(C) basic
(D) personnel

The correct answer is (A). Choose "financial," because "financial" is closest to "fiscal."

32. A central file eliminates the need to retain duplicate material. The word retain most nearly means

(A) keep
(B) change
(C) locate
(D) process

33. Filing is a routine office task. Routine most nearly means

(A) proper
(B) regular
(C) simple
(D) difficult

34. Sometimes a word, phrase, or sentence must be deleted to correct an error. Deleted most nearly means

(A) removed
(B) added
(C) expanded
(D) improved

35. Your supervisor will evaluate your work. Evaluate most nearly means

(A) judge
(B) list
(C) assign
(D) explain

Code Table

T	M	V	D	S	P	R	G	B	H
1	2	3	4	5	6	7	8	9	0

Questions 36–43. The code table above shows 10 letters with matching numbers. For each question there are three sets of letters. Each set of letters is followed by a set of numbers which may or may not match their correct letter according to the code table. For each question, check all three sets of letters and numbers and darken answer space:

(A) if **NO PAIRS** are **CORRECTLY MATCHED**
(B) if only **ONE PAIR** is **CORRECTLY MATCHED**
(C) if only **TWO PAIRS** are **CORRECTLY MATCHED**
(D) if **ALL THREE PAIRS** are **CORRECTLY MATCHED**

SAMPLE QUESTION

TMVDSP — 123456
RGBHTM — 789011
DSPRGB — 256789

The correct answer is (B). In the sample question above, the first set of numbers correctly matches its set of letters. But the second and third pairs contain mistakes. In the second pair, M is incorrectly matched with number 1. According to the code table, the letter M should be correctly matched with number 2. In the third pair, the letter D is incorrectly matched with number 2. According to the code table, the letter D should be correctly matched with number 4. Since only one of the pairs is correctly matched, the answer to this sample question is (B).

36. RSBMRM — 759262
GDSRVH — 845730
VDBRTM — 349713

37. TGVSDR — 183247
SMHRDP — 520647
TRMHSR — 172057

38. DSPRGM — 456782
MVDBHT — 234902
HPMDBT — 062491

39. BVPTRD — 936184
GDPHMB — 807029
GMRHMV — 827032

40. MGVRSH — 283750
TRDMBS — 174295
SPRMGV — 567283

41. SGBSDM — 489542
MGHPTM — 290612
MPBMHT — 269301

42. TDPBHM — 146902
VPBMRS — 369275
GDMBHM — 842902

43. MVPTBV — 236194
PDRTMB — 647128
BGTMSM — 981232

Questions 44–49. In each of the questions the names of four people are given. For each question, choose as your answer the one of the four names given which should be filed first according to the usual system of alphabetical filing of names, as described in the paragraph below.

In filing names, you must start with the last name. Names are filed in order of the first letter of the last name, then the second letter, etc. Therefore BAILY would be filed before BROWN, which would be filed before COLT. A name with fewer letters of the same type comes first, i.e., Smith before Smithe. If the last names are the same, the names are filed alphabetically by the first name. If the first name is an initial, a name with an initial would come before a first name that starts with the same letter as the initial. Therefore, I. BROWN would come before IRA BROWN. Finally, if both last name and first name are the same, the name would be filed alphabetically by the middle name, once again an initial coming before a middle name that starts with the same letter as the initial. If there is no middle name at all, the name would come before those with middle initials or names.

SAMPLE QUESTION

(A) Lester Daniels
(B) William Dancer
(C) Nathan Danzig
(D) Dan Lester

The correct answer is (B). The last names beginning with D are filed before the last name beginning with L. Since DANIELS, DANCER, and DANZIG all begin with the same three letters, you must look at the fourth letter of the last name to determine which name should be filed first. C comes before I or Z in the alphabet, so DANCER is filed before DANIELS or DANZIG. Therefore, the correct answer to the above sample question is (B).

44. (A) Scott Biala
(B) Mary Byala
(C) Martin Baylor
(D) Francis Bauer

45. (A) Howard J. Black
(B) Howard Black
(C) J. Howard Black
(D) John H. Black

46. (A) Theodora Garth Kingston
(B) Theadore Barth Kingston
(C) Thomas Kingston
(D) Thomas T. Kingston

47. (A) Paulette Mary Huerta
(B) Paul M. Huerta
(C) Paulette L. Huerta
(D) Peter A. Huerta

48. (A) Martha Hunt Morgan
(B) Martin Hunt Morgan
(C) Mary H. Morgan
(D) Martine H. Morgan

49. (A) James T. Meerschaum
(B) James M. Mershum
(C) James F. Mearshaum
(D) James N. Meshum

50. Which one of the following statements about proper telephone usage is *not* always correct? When answering the telephone, you should

(A) know who you are speaking to.
(B) give the caller your undivided attention.
(C) identify yourself to the caller.
(D) obtain the information the caller wishes before you do your other work.

51. Assume that, as a member of a Worker's Safety Committee in your agency, you are responsible for encouraging other employees to follow correct safety practices. While you are working on your regular assignment, you observe an employee violating a safety rule. Of the following, the best action for you to take *first* is to

(A) speak to the employee about safety practices and order him or her to stop violating the safety rule.
(B) speak to the employee about safety practices and point out the safety rule he or she is violating.
(C) bring the matter up in the next committee meeting.
(D) report this violation of the safety rule to the employee's supervisor.

52. Assume that you have been temporarily assigned by your supervisor to do a job which you do not want to do. The best action for you to take is to

(A) discuss the job with your supervisor explaining why you don't want to do it.
(B) discuss the job with your supervisor and tell him or her that you will not do it.
(C) ask a co-worker to take your place on this job.
(D) do some other job that you like; your supervisor may give the job you don't like to someone else.

53. Assume that you keep the confidential personnel files of employees in your unit. A friend asks you to obtain some information from the file of one of your co-workers. The best action to take is to

(A) ask the co-worker if you can give the information to your friend.
(B) ask your supervisor if you can give the information to your friend.
(C) give the information to your friend.
(D) refuse to give the information to your friend.

Questions 54–75. You are to answer the questions *solely* on the basis of the information contained in the following passage:

The city government is committed to providing a safe and healthy work environment for all city employees. An effective agency safety program reduces accidents by educating employees about the types of careless acts that can cause accidents Even in an office, accidents can happen. If each employee is aware of possible safety hazards, the number of accidents on the job can be reduced.

Careless use of office equipment can cause accidents and injuries. For example, file cabinet drawers which are filled with papers can be so heavy that the entire cabinet could tip over from the weight of one open drawer.

The bottom drawers of desks and file cabinets should never be left open, since employees could easily trip over open drawers and injure themselves.

When reaching for objects on a high shelf, an employee should use a strong, sturdy object such as a stepstool to stand on. Makeshift platforms made out of books, papers, or boxes can easily collapse. Even chairs can slide out from underfoot, causing serious injury.

Even at an employee's desk, safety hazards can occur. Frayed or cut wires should be repaired or replaced immediately. Typewriters which are not firmly anchored to the desk or table could fall, causing injury.

Smoking is one of the major causes of fires in the office. A lighted match or improperly extinguished cigarette thrown into a wastebasket filled with paper could cause a major fire with possible loss of life. Where smoking is permitted, ashtrays should be used. Smoking is particularly dangerous in offices where flammable chemicals are used.

54. The goal of an effective safety program is to

(A) reduce office accidents.
(B) stop employees from smoking on the job.
(C) encourage employees to continue their education.
(D) eliminate high shelves in offices.

55. Desks and file cabinets can become safety hazards when

(A) their drawers are left open.
(B) they are used as wastebaskets.
(C) they are makeshift.
(D) they are not anchored securely to the floor.

56. Smoking is especially hazardous when it occurs

(A) near exposed wires.
(B) in a crowded office.
(C) in an area where flammable chemicals are used.
(D) where books and papers are stored.

57. Accidents are likely to occur when

(A) employees' desks are cluttered with books and papers.
(B) employees are not aware of safety hazards.
(C) employees close desk drawers.
(D) stepstools are used to reach high objects.

58. Assume that part of your job as a worker in the accounting division of a city agency is to answer the telephone. When you first answer the telephone, it is *least* important to tell the caller

(A) your title.
(B) your name.
(C) the name of your unit.
(D) the name of your agency.

59. Assume that you are assigned to work as a receptionist and your duties are to answer phones, greet visitors, and do other general office work. You are busy with a routine job when several visitors approach your desk. The best action to take is to

(A) ask the visitors to have a seat and assist them after your work is completed.
(B) tell the visitors that you are busy and they should return at a more convenient time.
(C) stop working long enough to assist the visitors.
(D) continue working and wait for the visitors to ask you for assistance.

60. Assume that your supervisor has chosen you to take a special course during working hours to learn a new payroll procedure. Although you know that you were chosen because of your good work record, a co-worker, who feels that he or she should have been chosen, has been telling everyone in your unit that the choice was unfair. Of the following, the best way to handle this situation *first* is to

(A) suggest to the co-worker that everything in life is unfair.
(B) contact your union representative in case your co-worker presents a formal grievance.
(C) tell your supervisor about your co-worker's complaints and let him or her handle the situation.
(D) tell the co-worker that you were chosen because of your superior work record.

61. Assume that while you are working on an assignment that must be completed quickly, a supervisor from another unit asks you to obtain information for her. Of the following, the best way to respond to her request is to

(A) tell her to return in an hour, since you are busy.
(B) give her the names of some people in her own unit who could help her.
(C) tell her you are busy and refer her to a co-worker.
(D) tell her that you are busy, and ask her if she could wait until you finish your assignment.

62. A co-worker in your unit is often off from work because of illness. Your supervisor assigns the co-worker's work to you when she is not there. Lately, doing her work has interfered with your own job. The best action for you to take first is to

(A) discuss the problem with your supervisor.
(B) complete your own work before starting your co-worker's work.
(C) ask other workers in your unit to assist you.
(D) work late in order to get the jobs done.

63. During the month of June, 40,587 people attended a city-owned swimming pool. In July, 13,014 more people attended the swimming pool than the number that had attended in June. In August, 39,655 people attended the swimming pool. The total number of people who attended the swimming pool during the months of June, July, and August was

(A) 80,242.
(B) 93,256.
(C) 133,843.
(D) 210,382.

64. Assume a city agency has 775 office workers. If 2 out of 25 office workers were absent on a particular day, how many office workers reported to work on that day?

(A) 713
(B) 744
(C) 750
(D) 773

Questions 65–72 test how well you understand what you read. It will be necessary for you to read carefully because your answers to these questions must be based only on the information in the following paragraphs.

The telephone directory is made up of two books. The first book consists of the introductory section and the alphabetical listing of names section. The second book is the classified directory (also known as the Yellow Pages). Many people who are familiar with one book do not realize how useful the other can be. The efficient office worker should become familiar with both books in order to make the best use of this important source of information.

The introductory section gives general instructions for finding numbers in the alphabetical listing and classified directory. This section also explains how to use the telephone company's many services, including the operator and information services; gives examples of charges for local and long-distance calls; and lists area codes for the entire country. In addition, this section provides a useful postal ZIP code map.

The alphabetical listing of names section lists the names, addresses, and telephone numbers of subscribers in an area. Guide names, or "telltales," are on the top corner of each page. These guide names indicate the first and last name to be found on that page. "Telltales" help locate any particular name quickly. A cross-reference spelling is also given to help locate names which are spelled several different ways.

City, State, and Federal Government agencies are listed in the blue pages of the alphabetical book under the major government heading, For example, an agency of the Federal Government would be listed under "United States Government."

The classified directory, or Yellow Pages, is a separate book. In this section are advertising services, public transportation line maps, shopping guides, and listings of businesses arranged by the type of product or services they offer. This book is most useful when looking for the name or phone number of a business when all that is known is the type of product offered and the address, or when trying to locate a particular type of business in an area. Businesses listed in the classified directory can usually be found in the alphabetical listing of names section. When the name of the business is known, you will find the address or phone number more quickly in the alphabetical listing of names section.

65. The introductory section provides
(A) shopping guides.
(B) government listings.
(C) business listings.
(D) information services.

66. Advertising services would be found in the
(A) introductory section.
(B) alphabetical listing of names section.
(C) classified directory.
(D) information services.

67. According to the information in the passage for locating government agencies, the Information Office of the Department of Consumer Affairs of New York City government would be alphabetically listed first under
(A) "I" for Information Office.
(B) "D" for Department of Consumer Affairs.
(C) "N" for New York City.
(D) "G" for government.

68. When the name of a business is known, the quickest way to find the phone number is to look in the

(A) classified directory.
(B) introductory section.
(C) alphabetical listing of names section.
(D) advertising service section.

69. The quickest way to find the phone number of a business when the type of service a business offers and its address is known, is to look in the

(A) classified directory.
(B) alphabetical listing of names section.
(C) introductory section.
(D) information service.

70. What is a "telltale"?

(A) An alphabetical listing
(B) A guide name
(C) A map
(D) A cross-reference listing

71. The best way to find a postal ZIP code is to look in the

(A) classified directory.
(B) introductory section.
(C) alphabetical listing of names section.
(D) government heading.

72. To help find names that have several different spellings, the telephone directory provides

(A) cross-reference spelling.
(B) "telltales."
(C) spelling guides.
(D) advertising services.

73. Assume that your agency has been given $2,025 to purchase file cabinets. If each file cabinet costs $135, how many file cabinets can your agency purchase?

(A) 8
(B) 10
(C) 15
(D) 16

74. Assume that your unit ordered 14 staplers at a total cost of $30.20 and each stapler costs the same amount. The cost of one stapler was most nearly

(A) $1.02.
(B) $1.61.
(C) $2.16.
(D) $2.26.

75. Assume that you are responsible for counting and recording licensing fees collected by your department. On a particular day your department collected in fees 40 checks in the amount of $6 each; 80 checks in the amount of $4 each; 45 $20 bills; 30 $10 bills; 42 $5 bills; and 186 $1 bills. The total amount in fees collected on that day was

(A) $1,406.
(B) $1,706.
(C) $2,156.
(D) $2,356.

76. Assume that you are responsible for your agency's petty cash fund. During the month of February you pay out 7 subway fares at $1.25 each and one taxi fare for $7.30; you pay out nothing else from the fund. At the end of February, you count the money left in the fund and find 3 $1 bills, 4 quarters, 5 dimes, and 4 nickels. The amount of money you had available in the petty cash fund at the *beginning* of February was

(A) $4.70.
(B) $11.35.
(C) $16.05.
(D) $20.75.

77. You overhear your supervisor criticize a co-worker for handling equipment in an unsafe way. You feel that the criticism may be unfair. Of the following, it would be best for you to

(A) take your co-worker aside and tell him or her how you feel about your supervisor's comments.
(B) interrupt the discussion and defend your co-worker to your supervisor.
(C) continue working as if you had not overheard the discussion.
(D) make a list of other workers who have violated safety rules and give it to your supervisor.

78. Assume that you have been assigned to work on a long-term project with an employee who is known for being uncooperative. In beginning to work with this employee, it would be *least* desirable for you to

(A) understand why the person is uncooperative.
(B) act in a calm manner rather than an emotional manner.
(C) be appreciative of the co-worker's work.
(D) report the co-worker's lack of cooperation to your supervisor.

79. Assume that you are assigned to sell tickets at a city-owned ice skating rink. An adult ticket costs $3.75 and a children's ticket costs $2.00. At the end of a day, you find that you have sold 36 adult tickets and 80 children's tickets. The total amount of money you collected for that day was

(A) $285.50.
(B) $295.00.
(C) $298.75.
(D) $301.00.

80. If each office worker files 487 index cards in one hour, how many cards can 26 office workers file in one hour?

(A) 10,662
(B) 12,175
(C) 12,662
(D) 14,266

CORRECT ANSWERS—MUNICIPAL OFFICE AIDE EXAM

MUNICIPAL OFFICE AIDE EXAM

1. C	11. B	21. C	31. B	41. A	51. B	61. D	71. B
2. A	12. A	22. C	32. A	42. D	52. A	62. A	72. A
3. D	13. C	23. B	33. B	43. A	53. D	63. C	73. C
4. B	14. B	24. B	34. A	44. D	54. A	64. A	74. C
5. A	15. B	25. C	35. A	45. B	55. A	65. D	75. C
6. B	16. C	26. C	36. B	46. B	56. C	66. C	76. D
7. D	17. A	27. C	37. B	47. B	57. B	67. C	77. C
8. C	18. D	28. B	38. C	48. A	58. A	68. C	78. D
9. C	19. A	29. B	39. A	49. C	59. C	69. A	79. B
10. B	20. C	30. B	40. D	50. D	60. C	70. B	80. C

ANSWERS AND EXPLANATIONS

Questions 1–5 rely on your common sense and good judgment in interpersonal relations.

6. **The correct answer is (B).** The seasons are not capitalized, but names of holidays and months are.
7. **The correct answer is (D).** The subject of the sentence, the manual, is singular, so the verb must be singular as well. The correct spelling is *describes.*
8. **The correct answer is (C).** "Paper" is a singular noun taking the singular verb "was." The construction ". . . n't no" constitutes an unacceptable double negative.
9. **The correct answer is (C).** "Their" is the possessive. "They're" is the contraction for "they are." "There" refers to a place. Choice (D) is a misspelling.
10. **The correct answer is (B).** The correct way to express time is 8:30 A.M.
11. **The correct answer is (B).** The "alphabet," singular, "is." The phrase "or A to Z sequence" is extra information about the alphabet, so it is enclosed by commas. "Too" means "also" or "excessive" and is the incorrect spelling of *to.*
12. **The correct answer is (A).** "Five" is plural, so use the plural "feet."
13. **The correct answer is (C).** "Checked and found"—both verbs must be in the past tense. The correct spelling is *register.*

For questions 14–25, we have circled the areas of difference.

14. **The correct answer is (B).** The numbers are alike in only one set.

7354(1)83476	7354(9)83476
44747477(4)4	44747477(7)4
57914302311	57914302311

15. **The correct answer is (B).** The numbers are alike in only one set.

7143(5)92185	7143(8)92185
834451(7)699	834451(8)699
9178531263	9178531263

16. **The correct answer is (C).** The numbers are alike in two sets.

2572(114)731	2572(14)731
8806835476	8806835476
8255831246	8255831246

17. **The correct answer is (A).** None of the sets are alike.

33147685(38)21	33147685(86)21
69766(585)32996	69766(558)32996
39660421137(1)5	37660421137(4)5

18. **The correct answer is (D).** All of the sets are exactly alike.

19. **The correct answer is (A).** None of the sets are alike

9900069(669)96	9900069(69)96
53022219(7)43	53022219(8)43
417117(1117)717	417117(117)7717

20. **The correct answer is (C).** The numbers are alike in two sets.

24400222433004	24400222433004
530003005(500)0355	530003005(550)0355
20000075532002022	20000075532002022

21. **The correct answer is (C).** The numbers are alike in two sets.

611166640660(001)116	611166640660(01)116
7111300117001100733	7111300117001100733
26666446664476518	26666446664476518

22. **The correct answer is (C).**The names and addresses are exactly alike in two sets.

Mary T. Berlinger 2351 Hampton St. Monsey, N.Y. 20117	Mary T. Berlinger 2351 Hampton St. Monsey, N.Y. 20117
Eduardo Benes 473 Kingston Avenue Central Islip, N.Y. 11734	Eduardo Benes 473 Kingston Avenue Central Islip, N.Y. 11734
Alan Carrington Fuchs 17 Gnarled Hollow Road Los Angeles, California 916(35)	Alan Carrington Fuchs 17 Gnarled Hollow Road Los Angeles, California 91611(85)

23. **The correct answer is (B).** The names and addresses are alike in only one set.

David John Jacobson 178(35) St. Apt. 4C New York, N.Y. 00927	David John Jacobson 178(53) St. Apt. 4C New York, N.Y. 00927
Ann-Marie Calonella 7243 South Ridge Blvd. Bakersfield, California 96714	Ann-Marie Calonella 7243 South Ridge Blvd. Bakersfield, California 96714
Pauline M. Tho(mps)on 872 Linden Ave. Houston, Texas 70321	Pauline A Tho(ms)on 872 Linden Ave. Houston, Texas 70321

24. **The correct answer is (B).** The names and addresses are alike in only one set.

Chester LeRoy Master(t)on 152 Lacy Rd. Kankakee, Ill. 54532	Chester LeRoy Master(s)on 152 Lacy Rd. Kankakee, Ill. 54532
William Maloney S. LaCros(se) Pla. Wausau, Wisconsin 52146	William Maloney S. LaCros(s) Pla. Wausau, Wisconsin 52146
Cynthia V. Barnes 16 Pines Rd. Greenpoint, Mississippi 20376	Cynthia V. Barnes 16 Pines Rd. Greenpoint, Mississippi 20376

25. The correct answer is (C). The names and addresses are exactly alike in two sets.

Marcel Jean Frontenac 6 Burton On The Water Calender, Me. 01471	Marcel Jean Frontenac 6 Burton On The Water Calender, Me. 01471
J. Scott Marsden 174 S. Tipton St. Cleveland, Ohio	J. Scott Marsden 174 ( ) Tipton St. Cleveland, Ohio
Lawrence T. Haney 171 McDonough St. Decatur, Ga. 31304	Lawrence T. Haney 171 McDonough St. Decatur, Ga. 31304

26. The correct answer is (C). The offset process can produce up to 75,000 good copies. Stencil is good for up to 3,500 and fluid process for only up to 125. Xerox is very expensive for that many copies.

27. The correct answer is (C). See the first sentence of the fourth paragraph.

28. The correct answer is (B). See the second sentence of the third paragraph.

29. The correct answer is (B). In choices (C) and (D) the numbers are too high for the fluid process. Five copies would be most efficiently reproduced by the Xerox process without preparing a master.

30. The correct answer is (B). See the last paragraph.

31. The correct answer is (B). Again, refer to the last paragraph.

If you made errors in questions 32 through 35, consult a dictionary. For questions 36 through 43, the areas of miscoding are marked.

636. The correct answer is (B). Only one set is correctly coded.

RSBMRM — 759262
GDSRVH — 845730
VDBRTM — 349713

37. The correct answer is (B). Only one set is correctly coded.

TGVSDR — 183247
SMHRDP — 520647
TRMHSR — 172057

38. The correct answer is (C). Two sets are correctly coded.

DSPRGM — 456782
MVDBHT — 234902
HPMDBT — 062491

39. The correct answer is (A). No sets are correctly coded.

BVPTRD — 936184
GDPHMB — 8070029
GMRHMV — 827032

40. The correct answer is (D). All three sets are correctly coded.

41. The correct answer is (A). No sets are correctly coded.

SGBSDM — 489542
MGHPTM — 290612
MPBMHT — 269301

42. The correct answer is (D). All three sets are correctly coded.

43. **The correct answer is (A).** No sets are correctly coded.

MVPTB(V)	—	23619(4)
PDRTM(B)	—	64712(8)
BGTM(S)M	—	9812(3)2

44. **The correct answer is (D).** Bauer—Baylor—Biala—Byala
45. **The correct answer is (B).** Howard—Howard J—J. Howard—John H.
46. **The correct answer is (B).** Theadore—Theodora—Thomas—Thomas T.
47. **The correct answer is (B).** Paul M.—Paulette L.—Paulette Mary—Peter A.
48. **The correct answer is (A).** Martha—Martin—Martine—Mary
49. **The correct answer is (C).** Mearshaum—Meerschaum—Mershum—Meshum
50. **The correct answer is (D).** You must always identify yourself, find out to whom you are speaking, and be courteous to the caller, but sometimes a return call could give information at a later hour or date.
51. **The correct answer is (B).** The first thing to do is speak to the employee who may not even be aware of the rule.
52. **The correct answer is (A).** Be "up front" with your supervisor. Refusing to do a distasteful task or trying to hand it off to someone else is not proper business procedure.
53. **The correct answer is (D).** Confidential means "private."
54. **The correct answer is (A).** See the first paragraph.
55. **The correct answer is (A).** See the third paragraph.
56. **The correct answer is (C).** See the last paragraph.
57. **The correct answer is (B).** See the first paragraph.
58. **The correct answer is (A).** Think of what the caller needs to know. He or she needs to know what agency has been reached and to whom he or she is speaking. Your title is irrelevant.
59. **The correct answer is (C).** A receptionist receives visitors.
60. **The correct answer is (C).** No matter how you approach the co-worker, you are likely to create ill-feeling. Let your supervisor handle this tricky office morale problem.
61. **The correct answer is (D).** Your own work comes first, but you do want to be helpful. Tactfully offer to help out when your own work is completed, and let the supervisor ask for a referral if she needs the information more quickly.'
62. **The correct answer is (A).** The supervisor does the assigning and is responsible for having the work done. Let the supervisor know what the problem is.
63. **The correct answer is (C).**

June		40,587
July	40,587+13,014 =	53,601
+ August		39,655
Total		133,842

64. **The correct answer is (A).**

$775 \div 25 =$ 31 groups of 25 workers in the agency.
$31 \times 2 =$ 62 absent that day (2 from each group of 25)
$775 - 62 = 713$ present

65. **The correct answer is (D).** See the second paragraph.
66. **The correct answer is (C).** See the last paragraph.
67. **The correct answer is (C).** See the fourth paragraph.
68. **The correct answer is (C).** See the third paragraph.
69. **The correct answer is (A).** See the last paragraph.
70. **The correct answer is (B).** See the second sentence of the third paragraph.
71. **The correct answer is (B).** See the second paragraph.
72. **The correct answer is (A).** See the last sentence of the third paragraph.
73. **The correct answer is (C).** $2,025 ÷ $135 = $15
74. **The correct answer is (C).** $30.20 ÷ 14 = $2.157 = $2.16

75. The correct answer is (C).

40 checks	@ $6 =	$240
80 checks	@ 4 =	320
45 bills	@ 20 =	900
30 bills	@ 10 =	300
42 bills	@ 5 =	210
+ 186 bills	@ 1 =	186
	Total	$2,156

76. The correct answer is (D).

7 fares	@ = $1.25 =	$8.75
+ 1 fare	@ = 7.30 =	7.30
	Total spent	$16.05

3 dollar bills =	$3.00
4 quarters =	1.00
5 dimes =	.50
+ 4 nickels =	.20
Amount left	$4.70

Amount spent	$16.05
+ Amount left	4.70
Amount to begin	$20.75

77. The correct answer is (C). The remarks were not meant for your ears. Do your own work and mind your own business.

78. The correct answer is (D). You've just begun to work, and the co-worker has not had a chance to prove cooperative or uncooperative. There is nothing to report.

79. The correct answer is (B).

36 adults	@ $3.75 =	$135
+ 80 children	@ 2.00 =	160
	Total	$295

80. The correct answer is (C). 487 x 26 = 12,662

PRIVATE SECTOR CLERICAL EXAMINATION

SECTION A—FILING

Directions: Arrange the names in each question in proper alphabetical order for filing.

1. Adam Dunn
   E. Dunn
   A. Duncan
   Edward Robert Dunn

   1. ____________________
   ____
   ____
   ____

2. Paul Moore
   William Moore
   Paul A. Moore
   William Allen Moore

   2. ____________________
   ____
   ____
   ____

3. William Carver
   Howard Cambell
   Arthur Chambers
   Charles Banner

   3. ____________________
   ____
   ____
   ____

4. George Peters
   Eric Petersen
   G. Peters
   E. Petersen

   4. ____________________
   ____
   ____
   ____

5. Edward Hallam
   Jos. Frank Hamilton
   Edward A. Hallam
   Joseph F. Hamilton

   5. ____________________
   ____
   ____
   ____

6. William O'Hara
   Arthur Gordon
   James DeGraff
   Anne von Glatin

   6. ____________________
   ____
   ____
   ____

7. Theodore Madison
   Timothy McGill
   Thomas MacLane
   Thomas A. Madison

   7. ____________________
   ____
   ____
   ____

8. Dr. Chas. D. Peterson
   Miss Irene F. Petersen
   Lawrence E. Peterson
   Prof. N. A. Petersen

   8. ____________________
   ____
   ____
   ____

9. Edward La Gabriel
   Marie Doris Gabriel
   Marjorie N. Gabriel
   Mrs Marian Gabriel

   9. ____________________
   ____
   ____
   ____

10. Herbert Restman
H. Restman
Harry Restmore
H. Restmore

10. ____________ ____________ ____________ ____________

11. Timothy Macalan
Fred McAlden
Thomas MacAllister
Mrs. Frank McAllen

11. ____________ ____________ ____________ ____________

12. Peter La Vance
George Van Meer
Wallace De Vance
Leonard Vance

12. ____________ ____________ ____________ ____________

13. Devine, Sarah
Devine, S.
Devine, Sara H.
Devin, Sarah

13. ____________ ____________ ____________ ____________

14. Bennet, C.,
Benett, Chuck
Bennet, Chas.
Bennett, Charles

14. ____________ ____________ ____________ ____________

15. Rivera, Ilena
Riviera, Ilene
Rivere, I.
Riviera Ilana

15. ____________ ____________ ____________ ____________

16. Corral, Dr. Robert
Carrale, Prof Robert
Corren, R.
Corret, Ron

16. ____________ ____________ ____________ ____________

17. Chas. A. Levine
Kurt Levene
Charles Levine
Kurt E. Levene

17. ____________ ____________ ____________ ____________

18. Prof. Geo. Kinkaid
Mr. Alan Kinkaid
Dr. Albert A. Kinkade
Kincade, Lillian

18. ____________ ____________ ____________ ____________

19. Charles Green
Chas. T. Greene
Charles Thomas Greene
Wm. A. Greene

19. ____________ ____________ ____________ ____________

20. Doris MacAllister
D. McAllen
Lewis T. MacBride
Lewis McBride

20. ____________
____
____
____

21. Robert B. Pierce
R. Bruce Pierce
Ronald Pierce
Robert Bruce Pierce

21. ____________
____
____
____

22. Charlotte Stair
C. B. Stare
Charles B. Stare
Elaine La Stella

22. ____________
____
____
____

23. James Borenstein
Frieda Albrecht
Samuel Brown
George Appelman

23. ____________
____
____
____

24. James McCormack
Ruth MacNamara
Kathryn McGillicuddy
Frances Mason

24. ____________
____
____
____

25. A. S. Martinson
Albert Martinson
Albert S. Martinson
M. Martanson

25. ____________
____
____
____

SECTION B—SPELLING

Directions: In the following list, some words are spelled correctly and some words are misspelled. On the line to the right, write the correct spelling of each misspelled word. If a word is spelled correctly, write the letter "Correct as written."

1.	professor	1. ________
2.	sabbatical	2. ________
3.	associate	3. ________
4.	dictater	4. ________
5.	accidently	5. ________
6.	bureau	6. ________
7.	auxilary	7. ________
8.	synthesis	8. ________
9.	receiveable	9. ________
10.	facsimile	10. ________
11.	proxey	11. ________
12.	negotiable	12. ________
13.	confidential	13. ________
14.	pertainent	14. ________
15.	corrective	15. ________
16.	satisfactorally	16. ________
17.	accomplishment	17. ________
18.	bookeeping	18. ________
19.	beforhand	19. ________
20.	supervisor	20. ________
21.	manifest	21. ________
22.	machinary	22. ________
23.	harassment	23. ________
24.	bankrupcy	24. ________
25.	requisition	25. ________
26.	pollish	26. ________
27.	acknowledgment	27. ________
28.	typograpfical	28. ________
29.	codify	29. ________
30.	performence	30. ________
31.	weight	31. ________
32.	occasionally	32. ________
33.	carefuly	33. ________
34.	deceit	34. ________
35.	efficiently	35. ________
36.	scheduling	36. ________
37.	distorsion	37. ________
38.	exemplify	38. ________
39.	chronological	39. ________
40.	liability	40. ________
41.	courtesy	41. ________
42.	notarary	42. ________
43.	memmoranda	43. ________

44.	ellimination	44.	________
45.	clogging	45.	________
46.	refered	46.	________
47.	aggressive	47.	________
48.	shelfs	48.	________
49.	personnel	49.	________
50.	initiative	50.	________
51.	occurance	51.	________
52.	guage	52.	________
53.	resources	53.	________
54.	appearence	54.	________
55.	rehearsal	55.	________
56.	departmental	56.	________
57.	sacrilegious	57.	________
58.	subdivision	58.	________
59.	self-evident	59.	________
60.	over-charge	60.	________
61.	primery	61.	________
62.	cessation	62.	________
63.	obediance	63.	________
64.	employees	64.	________
65.	conspicuous	65.	________
66.	assinement	66.	________
67.	thier	67.	________
68.	effectual	68.	________
69.	acreage	69.	________
70.	frequently	70.	________
71.	commisioner	71.	________
72.	alien	72.	________
73.	embarassment	73.	________
74.	conference	74.	________
75.	have'nt	75.	________
76.	admissible	76.	________
77.	allowance	77.	________
78.	wellcome	78.	________
79.	salarys	79.	________
80.	proffitable	80.	________
81.	engineerred	81.	________
82.	interview	82.	________
83.	procedure	83.	________
84.	nineth	84.	________
85.	simultanous	85.	________
86.	handicaped	86.	________
87.	foriegner	87.	________
88.	italicize	88.	________
89.	overhear	89.	________
90.	evaluation	90.	________

SECTION C—GRAMMAR, PUNCTUATION, AND CAPITALIZATION

Directions: Some of the following sentences are correct as written. Others contain an error of grammar, punctuation, or capitalization. On the lines beside each sentence, rewrite the sentence correctly. If the sentence contains no error, write "Correct as written."

1. He was not informed, that he would have to work overtime. **1.** ____________

2. The wind blew several papers off of his desk. **2.** ____________

3. Charles Dole, who is a member of the committee, was asked to confer with commissioner Wilson. **3.** ____________

4. Miss Bell will issue a copy to whomever asks for one. **4.** ____________

5. Most employees, and he is no exception do not like to work overtime. **5.** ____________

6. This is the man whom you interviewed last week. **6.** ____________

7. Of the two cities visited, White Plains is the cleanest. **7.** ____________

8. Although he was willing to work on other holidays, he refused to work on labor day. **8.** ____________

9. If an employee wishes to attend the conference, he should fill out the necessary forms. **9.** ____________

10. The division chief reports that an engineer and an inspector is needed for this special survey. **10.** ____________

11. The work was assigned to Miss Green and me. **11.** ____________

12. The staff regulations state that an employee,who is frequently tardy, may receive a negative evaluation. 12. ____________

13. He is the kind of person who is always willing to undertake difficult assignments. 13. ____________

14. Mr. Wright's request cannot be granted under no conditions. 14. ____________

15. George Colt a new employee was asked to deliver the report to the Domestic Relations Court. 15. ____________

16. The supervisor entered the room and said, "The work must be completed today." 16. ____________

17. The employees were given their assignments and, they were asked to begin work immediately. 17. ____________

18. The letter will be sent to the United States senate this week. 18. ____________

19. When the supervisor entered the room, he noticed that the book was laying on the desk. 19. ____________

20. All the clerks, including those who have been appointed recently are required to work on the new assignment. 20. ____________

21. One of our clerks were promoted yesterday. 21. ____________

22. Between you and me, I would prefer not going there. 22. ____________

23. The National alliance of Businessmen is trying to persuade private businesses to hire youth in the summertime. 23. ____________

24. The supervisor who is on vacation, is in charge of processing vouchers. 24. ____________

25. The activity of the committee at its conferences is always stimulating. 25. ______

26. After checking the addresses again, the letters went to the mailroom. 26. ______

27. The director, as well as the employees, are interested in sharing the dividends. 27. ______

28. Mrs. Black the supervisor of the unit, has many important duties. 28. ______

29. We spoke to the man whom you saw yesterday. 29. ______

30. When a holiday falls on sunday, it is officially celebrated on monday. 30. ______

31. Neither Mr. Smith nor Mr. Jones was able to finish his assignment on time. 31. ______

32. The task of filing these cards is to be divided equally between you and he. 32. ______

33. He is an employee whom we consider to be efficient. 33. ______

34. I believe that the new employees are not as punctual as us. 35. ______

35. The employees, working in this office, are to be congratulated for their work. 36. ______

SECTION D—PROOFREADING

Directions: The letter which follows contains far more errors than you are likely to encounter in anything which you must proofread. Read through the letter and make your corrections directly on the page, between the lines and in the margins. Then type the letter, incorporating all of your corrections.

january 24th, 2001

Mr Steven p Anderson
Alacon Manufacturin Comp. Inc
387 Bramson Bullevard
Waltham, MA., 02154

Re: Red worsted wool
Die lot no 68423

My Dear Mr. Andreson,

My knitting store Wooly crafts of 12 Myrtle Ln., Beloit, Wisconsin, tole me to right to you to tell you, about my disappointtion with you're wool. I bought sevin skeins of wool to make a sweater in decembr of 2000. After a few month's i put the work a side. last week i buyed another skien of the same die lot 64823 to finnish the the sweater. The red does'nt match, it is not the same.

Mrs Browne the store Manager said that "The yarn is two old. That may be so, but i read on the rapper that you offer a garantee. The garante says this wool will not fade." Be sure to match die lots. satisfaction is garanteed. "

The hole sweater is know good. I am non satisfied. You could:

1. send me a refund for all nine skeins of wool
2. send me new wool

I am wait for you'r reply as to how you plan to handel my complain?

Very Truly Yours:
Mollie Jones Customer

CORRECT ANSWERS—PRIVATE SECTOR CLERICAL EXAMINATION

SECTION A—FILING

Correct alphabetical filing is made much easier when all names are placed in reverse order, that is, with last name first.

1. Duncan, A.
   Dunn, Adam
   Dunn, E.
   Dunn, Edward Robert
2. Moore, Paul
   Moore, Paul A.
   Moore, William
   Moore, William Allen
3. Banner, Charles
   Cambell, Howard
   Carver, William
   Chambers, Arthur
4. Peters, G.
   Peters, George
   Petersen, E.
   Petersen, Eric
5. Hallam, Edward
   Hallam, Edward A.
   Hamilton, Joseph F.
   Hamilton, Jos. Frank
6. DeGraff, James
   Gordon, Arthur
   O'Hara, William
   von Glatin, Anne
7. MacLane, Thomas
   Madison, Theodore
   Madison, Thomas A.
   McGill, Timothy
8. Petersen, Irene F., Miss
   Petersen, N. A., Prof.
   Peterson, Chas. D., Dr.
   Peterson, Lawrence E.
9. Gabriel, Marian, Mrs.
   Gabriel, Marie Doris
   Gabriel, Marjorie N.
   La Gabriel, Edward
10. Restman, H.
    Restman, Herbert
    Restmore, H.
    Restmore, Harry
11. Macalan, Timothy
    MacAllister, Tomas
    McAlden, Fred
    McAllen, Frank, Mrs.
12. De Vance, Wallace
    La Vance, Peter
    Vance, Leonard
    Van Meer, George
13. Devin, Sarah
    Devine, S.
    Devine, Sara H.
    Devine, Sarah
14. Benett, Chuck
    Bennet, C.
    Bennet, Chas.
    Bennett, Charles
15. Rivera, Ilena
    Rivere, I.
    Riviera, Ilana
    Riviera, Ilene
16. Carrale, Robert, Prof.
    Corral, Robert, Dr.
    Corren, R.
    Corret, Ron
17. Levene, Kurt
    Levene, Kurt E.
    Levine, Charles
    Levine, Chas. A.
18. Kincade, Lillian
    Kinkade, Albert A., Dr.
    Kinkaid, Alan, Mr.
    Kinkaid, Geo., Prof.
19. Green, Charles
    Greene, Chas. T.
    Greene, Charles Thomas
    Greene, Wm. A.
20. MacAllister, Doris
    MacBride, Lewis T.
    McAllen, D.
    McBride, Lewis
21. Pierce, R. Bruce
    Pierce, Robert B.
    Pierce, Robert Bruce
    Pierce, Ronald
22. La Stella, Elaine
    Stair, Charlotte
    Stare, C. B.
    Stare, Charles B.

23. Albrecht, Frieda
Appelman, George
Borenstein, James
Brown, Samuel

24. MacNamara, Ruth
Mason, Frances
McCormack, James
McGillicudy, Kathryn

25. Martanson, M.
Martinson, A. S.
Martinson, Albert
Martinson, Albert S.

SECTION B—SPELLING

1. **Correct as written.**
2. **Correct as written.**
3. **Correct as written.**
4. **The correct spelling is:** dictator
5. **The correct spelling is:** accidentally
6. **Correct as written.**
7. **The correct spelling is:** auxiliary
8. **Correct as written.**
9. **The correct spelling is:** receivable
10. **Correct as written.**
11. **The correct spelling is:** proxy
12. **Correct as written.**
13. **Correct as written.**
14. **The correct spelling is:** pertinent
15. **Correct as written.**
16. **The correct spelling is:** satisfactorily
17. **Correct as written.**
18. **The correct spelling is:** bookkeeping
19. **The correct spelling is:** beforehand
20. **Correct as written.**
21. **Correct as written.**
22. **The correct spelling is:** machinery
23. **Correct as written.**
24. **The correct spelling is:** bankruptcy
25. **Correct as written.**
26. **The correct spelling is:** polish
27. **Correct as written.**
28. **The correct spelling is:** typographical
29. **Correct as written.**
30. **The correct spelling is:** performance
31. **Correct as written.**
32. **Correct as written.**
33. **The correct spelling is:** carefully
34. **Correct as written.**
35. **Correct as written.**
36. **Correct as written.**
37. **The correct spelling is:** distortion
38. **Correct as written.**
39. **Correct as written.**
40. **Correct as written.**
41. **Correct as written.**
42. **The correct spelling is:** notary
43. **The correct spelling is:** memoranda
44. **The correct spelling is:** elimination

45. Correct as written.
46. The correct spelling is: referred
47. Correct as written.
48. The correct spelling is: shelves
49. Correct as written.
50. Correct as written.
51. The correct spelling is: occurrence
52. The correct spelling is: gauge
53. Correct as written.
54. The correct spelling is: appearance
55. Correct as written.
56. Correct as written.
57. Correct as written.
58. Correct as written.
59. Correct as written.
60. The correct spelling is: overcharge
61. The correct spelling is: primary
62. Correct as written.
63. The correct spelling is: obedience
64. Correct as written.
65. Correct as written.
66. The correct spelling is: assignment
67. The correct spelling is: their
68. Correct as written.
69. Correct as written.
70. Correct as written.
71. The correct spelling is: commissioner
72. Correct as written.
73. The correct spelling is: embarrassment
74. Correct as written.
75. The correct spelling is: haven't
76. Correct as written.
77. Correct as written.
78. The correct spelling is: welcome
79. The correct spelling is: salaries
80. The correct spelling is: profitable
81. The correct spelling is: engineered
82. Correct as written.
83. Correct as written.
84. The correct spelling is: ninth
85. The correct spelling is: simultaneous
86. The correct spelling is: handicapped
87. The correct spelling is: foreigner
88. Correct as written.
89. Correct as written.
90. Correct as written.

SECTION C—GRAMMAR, PUNCTUATION, AND CAPITALIZATION

1. He was not informed that he would have to work overtime. There is no reason for a comma between the verb and its object.
2. The wind blew several papers off his desk. Off of is unacceptable usage.
3. Charles Dole, who is a member of the committee, was asked to confer with Commissioner Wilson. *Commissioner Wilson* is a specific commissioner, so the *C* must be capitalized.
4. Miss Bell will issue a copy to whoever asks for one. *Whoever* is the subject of the verb asks.
5. Most employees, and he is no exception, do not like to work overtime. A parenthetical expression must *always* be enclosed by commas.
6. This sentence is correct.
7. Of the two cities visited, White Plains is the cleaner. The comparative *er* is used when only two items are being compared. *Est* requires three or more items.
8. Although he was willing to work on other holidays, he refused to work on Labor Day. *Labor Day* is *a proper name; it must have initial caps.*
9. This sentence is correct.
10. The division chief reports that an engineer and an inspector are needed for this special survey. A plural subject requires a plural verb.
11. This sentence is correct.
12. The staff regulations state that an employee who is frequently tardy may receive a negative evaluation. A restrictive clause, that is, a clause that is vital to the meaning of a sentence, should not be set off by commas.
13. This sentence is correct.
14. Mr. Wright's request cannot be granted under any conditions. Use of a double negative is not permitted.
15. George Colt, a new employee, was asked to deliver the report to the Domestic Relations Court. "*A new employee*" is an appositive and must be set off by commas.
16. This sentence is correct.
17. The employees were given their assignments, and they were asked to begin work immediately. Two independent clauses connected by *and* must be separated by a comma placed before the *and.*
18. The letter will be sent to the United States Senate this week. This very specific *Senate* must begin with a capital letter.
19. When the supervisor entered the room, he noticed that the book was lying on the desk. The verb *to lay* should be used only when it could be replaced with the verb *to put*. At all other times use a form of the verb *to lie.*
20. All the clerks, including those who have been appointed recently, are required to work on the new assignment. Omitting the clause *"including those who have been appointed recently"* does not change the meaning of the remaining words. Therefore, this is a nonrestrictive clause and should be set off by commas.
21. One of our clerks *was* promoted yesterday. The subject of the sentence is *one,* which takes a singular verb.
22. This sentence is correct.
23. The National Alliance of Businessmen is trying to persuade private businesses to hire youth in the summertime. Each important word in the name of the organization must begin with a capital letter.

24. The supervisor, who is on vacation, is in charge of processing vouchers, OR The supervisor who is on vacation is in charge of processing vouchers. The first version indicates that there is only one supervisor and that supervisor happens to be on vacation. In this case, "who is on vacation" is a nonrestrictive clause and is set off by commas. The second version indicates that there are several supervisors, but the one in charge of processing vouchers is on vacation. In this case, "who is on vacation" is a restrictive clause and should not be set off by commas. The sentence is correct with either two commas or with no commas, depending on the meaning intended, but one comma is definitely wrong.
25. The sentence is correct.
26. After the addresses were checked again, the letters went to the mailroom. As the sentence was originally written, the letters did the checking of the addresses.
27. The director, as well as the employees, is interested in sharing the dividends. The *director* is the subject of the sentence and requires a singular verb.
28. Mrs. Black, the supervisor of the unit, has many important duties. *The supervisor of the unit*is an appositive and must be set off by commas.
29. This sentence is correct.
30. When a holiday falls on Sunday, it is officially celebrated on Monday. Days of the week must be capitalized.
31. This sentence is correct.
32. The task of filing these cards is to be divided equally between you and him. *Him* is an object of the preposition *between.*
33. This sentence is correct.
34. I believe that the new employees are not as punctual as we. *As* is an adverb and so does not take an object. You can check your answer in such an instance by silently finishing off the sentence ". . . *as we are.*"
35. The employees working in this office are to be congratulated for their work. *Working in this office* is a restrictive clause so must not be set off by commas.

SECTION D—PROOFREADING

THE CORRECTLY TYPED LETTER

January 24, 2001
1 2

Mr. Steven P. Anderson
3 4 5
Alacon Manufacturing Co. Inc.
6 7 8
387 Bramson Boulevard
9
Waltham, MA_02154
10,11

Re: Red worsted wool

Dye lot no. 68423
12 13

My dear Mr. Anderson:
14 15 16

My knitting store, Wooly Crafts , of 12 Myrtle Lane, Beloit, Wisconsin, told me to
17 18 19 20 21
write to you to tell you about my disappointment with your wool. ______ I bought seven
22 23 24 25 26
27 skeins of wool to make a sweater in December of 2000. After a few months I put
28 29 30
the work aside. Last week I bought another skein of the same dye lot 68423 to finish
31 32 33 34 35 36 37 38
the sweater. The red doesn't match; it is not the same.
39 40 41

Mrs. Browne, the store manager, said that the yarn is too old. That may be so,
42 43 44 45 46 47
but I read on the wrapper that you offer a guarantee. The guarantee says, " This
48 49 50 51 52 53 54
wool will not fade. Be sure to match dye lots. Satisfaction is guaranteed."59
55 56 57 58 59

The whole sweater is no good. I am not satisfied. You could:
60 61 62

1. send me a refund for all eight skeins of wool
63
2. send me new wool.
64

I am waiting for your reply as to how you plan to handle my complaint.
65 66 67 68 69

Very truly yours ,
70 71 72
Mollie Jones, Customer
73

EXPLANATIONS TO THE CORRECTLY TYPED LETTER

1. Capitalize days of the week, months of the year, and holidays.
2. When typing a full date, do not use *th* or *rd.*
3. Use a period after an abbreviation.
4. Capitalize all proper names. The initial stands for the name.
5. Use a period after the initial in a person's name.
6. Spelling error.
7. The abbreviation of *Company* is *Co.* There may or may not be a comma between *Co.* and *Inc.,* depending upon the actual company name. An error cannot be assumed.
8. Use a period after an abbreviation.
9. Spelling error.
10. Do not use a period after official Postal Service two-letter state name designations.
11. Do not use a comma between Postal Service two-letter state name designation and ZIP code.
12. Incorrect word choice. The word referring to color is "dye."
13. Use a period after an abbreviation.
14. Capitalize only first and last words, titles, and proper names in the salutation.
15. Spelling error. See inside address, above.
16. Use a colon after the salutation in a business letter.
17. An appositive must be set off by commas.
18. Capitalize all proper names, including, but not limited to, names of people.
19. An appositive must be set off by commas. (See #17)
20. Abbreviate *street, road, lane,* etc., only on the envelope and the inside address.
21. Spelling error.
22. Wrong word choice.
23. Comma is not needed here.
24. The word, as written, does not exist.
25. *You're* is the contraction for *you are*. The correct possessive of *you* is *your.*
26. Begin a new paragraph for a new thought.
27. Spelling error.
28. Capitalize days of the week and months of the year. Also spelling error here.
29. This should not be a possessive. The plural of *month* is *months.*
30. Capitalize the letter *I* when it stands alone.
31. One word.
32. Capitalize the first word of a complete sentence.
33. Capitalize the letter *I* when it stands alone.
34. The past tense of *buy* is *bought.*
35. Spelling error.
36. Incorrect word choice. (See #12)
37. Typographical error. Check against dye lot number in reference line.
38. Spelling error.
39. Repeated word.
40. In a contraction, insert an apostrophe in place of the omitted letter or letters. Here, does + not = doesn't.
41. A semicolon may be used to join two short, related independent clauses. As originally written, this is a comma splice.
42. Use a period after an abbreviation.
43. An appositive must be set off by commas.
44. A nonspecific title should not be capitalized.
45. An appositive must be set off by commas. (See #43)
46. The word "that" introduces an indirect quote. An indirect quote must not be enclosed by quotation marks.
47. Wrong word choice. The word meaning "excessively" is *too.*
48. Capitalize the letter *I* when it stands alone.

49. Spelling error.
50. Spelling error.
51. Spelling error.
52. A comma separates a short direct quotation from the speaker.
53. All directly quoted material must be enclosed by quotation marks.
54. Capitalize the first word of a complete sentence.
55. The quotation does not end here.
56. Word choice. (See #12 and #36)
57. Capitalize the first word of a complete sentence.
58. Spelling error.
59. A period always goes inside the quotation marks, whether the quotation marks are used to denote quoted material, to set off titles, or to isolate words used in a special sense.
60. Wrong word choice. The word meaning "entire" is *whole.*
61. Wrong word choice. The negative is *no*.
62. Spelling error.
63. Look back at the letter to be sure all facts are accurate and internally consistent. 7 + 1 = 8.
64. Internal style must be consistent too. The figure *1)* must be followed by *2)*; *a)* and *b)* would be equally acceptable.
65. Word ending omitted.
66. The correct possessive form of *you* is *your.*
67. Spelling error.
68. Spelling error.
69. Do not use a question mark after an indirect question; use a period.
70. Capitalize only the first word in a complimentary closing.
71. Capitalize only the first word in a complimentary closing.
72. The complimentary close of a letter is followed by a comma.
73. Use a comma to separate a name from a title.

PART FIVE

Civil Service Career Information Resources

HOW TO FIND A GOVERNMENT JOB

Very often finding a job is a matter of luck. However, we'd like to take some of the luck out of it, and make it more directive. Below are a variety of sources you can contact in your search for employment.

THE PRIVATE SECTOR

Most jobs in the private sector can be found in two ways—employment agencies or newspaper classified advertisements. Wherever you live there is certainly a local employment agency. Call to make an appointment, and bring your resume. Keep in mind that they're the first interview that you will have in the line for employment, so you should dress appropriately, and be somewhat informed about the types of jobs in which you would be interested. Reading through the section on various careers in this book will help you. Then, go to your local newspaper, or, if you live in a small town, perhaps you can pick up a newspaper from a larger city near you. In many cases, you will be directed toward an employment agency to apply for a job. In others, you may be asked to call the company directly, write a letter or send your resume to the company. Remember that just like an interview, your telephone call, letter, and/or resume are the first impressions someone makes of you, so be on your best behavior.

There are also dozens of career-oriented Web sites that will be helpful to you. One excellent site is America's Job Bank at http://www.ajb.dni.us/. You can post your resume online, as well as search for jobs on a state-by-state basis.

FEDERAL JOBS

The office of Personnel Management (OPM) is the place to start. It has a list of job openings that is updated daily. In addition, the office also publishes the *Federal Exam Announcement* each quarter during the year. Although staff members at the OPM are not responsible for hiring for jobs, they will provide you with access to each hiring agency, and there you can get the specific details about each job. You can reach the OPM's telephone line at 912-757-3000. Since it's an automated number, it's available 7 days a week, 24 hours a day.

If you are connected to the Internet, you will find the OPM site easier to use than the telephone line, and a lot less expensive. It can be found at http://www.usajobs.opm.gov/. You can find here a complete application for federal employment along with instructions on how to fill it out. It also provides explanations of federal job categories and specific job descriptions. You can then search geographically and alphabetically to find out which jobs have current openings and exactly where the openings are located. The listings, in turn, refer you to full vacancy announcements, including qualifications requirements and application procedures and deadlines. With adequate equipment you can download the announcement. Or you can then take notes from the information on your screen. Likewise, you can download application forms or even apply electronically using your computer. You can also follow instructions for getting the proper forms by telephone or mail.

Another excellent source is the *Federal Jobs Digest*, a bi-weekly newspaper that lists thousands of government jobs, both in the United States and in foreign countries. Its Web site features thousands of job listings at any one time. It can be reached at

http://www.jobsfed.com
email: webmaster@jobsfed.com
voice: 1-800-824-5000
fax: 914-366-0059.

You might also look under the heading "U.S. Government" in the blue pages of your telephone directory for a listing for Office of Personnel Management or Federal Job Information Center. A telephone call to this number may give you automated information pertinent to your own area or may direct you to a location at which you can pick up printed materials or conduct a search on a computer touch screen.

STATE EMPLOYMENT

Almost every state has its own Web site. In order to access the state systems via the Internet, there's a very simple way to find each state, although it may take some searching once you're online.

To find the state Internet site, enter the following: www.state.____.us. In the blank, enter the two-letter abbreviation for that state. For Arizona, for example, you would enter www.state.az.us. For Wisconsin, enter www.state.wi.us. See the list of the latest URLs for the state sites. Be aware, however, that the sites may change from time to time.

If that state also has a Job Bank, you can also find that the same way. This time you would enter www.abj.org/____, and enter the state's two-letter abbreviation in the blank space.

STATE INTERNET SITES

Alabama	www.state.al.us/	Missouri	www.state.mo.us/
Alaska	www.state.ak.us/	Montana	www.mt.gov/
Arizona	www.state.az.us/	Nebraska	www.state.ne.us/
Arkansas	www.state.ar.us/	Nevada	www.state.nv.us/
California	www.state.ca.us/	New Hampshire	www.state.nh.us/
Colorado	www.state.co.us/	New Jersey	www.state.nj.us/
Connecticut	www.state.ct.us/	New Mexico	www.state.nm.us/
Delaware	www.state.de.us/	New York	www.state.ny.us/
District of Columbia	www.dchomepage.net/	North Carolina	www.state.nc.us/
		North Dakota	www.state.nd.us/
Florida	www.state.fl.us/	Ohio	www.state.oh.us/
Georgia	www:state.ga.us/	Oklahoma	www.state.ok.us/
Hawaii	www.state.hi.us/	Oregon	www.state.or.us/
Idaho	www.state.id.us/	Pennsylvania	www:state.pa.us/
Illinois	www.state.il.us/	Rhode Island	www.state.ri.us/
Indiana	www.state.in.us/	South Carolina	www:state.sc.us/
Iowa	www.state.ia.us/	South Dakota	www.state.sd.us/
Kansas	www.state.ks.us/	Tennessee	www.state.tn.us/
Kentucky	www.state:ky.us/	Texas	www.state.tx.us/
Louisiana	www.state.la.us/	Utah	www.state.ut.us/
Maine	www.state.me.us/	Vermont	www.state.vt.us/
Maryland	www.state.md.us/	Virginia	www.state.va.us/
Massachusetts	www.state.ma.us/	Washington	www.wa.gov/
Michigan	www.state.mi.us/	West Virginia	www.state.wv.us/
Minnesota	www.state.mn.us/	Wisconsin	www.state.wi.us/
Mississippi	www.state.ms.us/	Wyoming	www.state.wy.us/

LOCAL EMPLOYMENT

You may find city and county employment information on the Internet through your state's home page. Or, if you're in a large city, it is likely that the city has it's own Web site. Use some of the popular search vehicles such as Yahoo.com, Ask.com, Altavista.com, and so on, to locate other job-related sites. Use search terms such as *jobs*, *employment*, *labor*, *business*, *help-wanted*, and so on. Add that to the specific city or state, and you'll be surprised at the number of suggested sites you'll get. You might enter into the search box something like *Miami+jobs*. The plus sign (+) indicates that you want both Miami and jobs to be in the same suggested sites.

You should also investigate to see if there is a local city Civil Service publication that would list upcoming job announcements. For example, in New York City, *The Chief-Leader* is the primary source for upcoming Civil Service jobs. (You can write to them at 277 Broadway, New York, NY 10007 to order a subscription.) You will also find information about state and federal jobs in the paper.

HOW TO GET A GOVERNMENT JOB

Now that you know where to look for a job, it's important to understand the procedure. The procedure you must follow to get a government job varies little from job to job and from one level of government to another. There are variations in details, of course, but certain steps are common to all.

Once you have found a *Notice of Examination* (it may be called an Announcement) read it very carefully. If you can get a copy for yourself all the better. If not, then take lots of time to take notes. Make sure, you have written down all of the details. The *Notice of Examination* will give a brief job description. It will tell the title of the job and describe some of the job duties and responsibilities. On the basis of the job description, you will decide whether or not you want to try for this job. If the job appeals to you, you must concentrate on:

- **Education and experience requirements.** If you cannot meet these requirements, do not bother to apply. Government service is very popular; many people apply. The government has more than enough applicants from whom to choose. It will not waive requirements for you.
- **Age requirements.** Discrimination on the basis of age is illegal, but a number of jobs demand so much sustained physical effort that they require retirement at an early age. For these positions there is an entry age limit. If you are already beyond that age, do not apply. If you are still too young, inquire about the time lag until hiring. It may be that you will reach the minimum age by the time the position is to be filled.
- **Citizenship requirements.** Many jobs are open to all people who are eligible to work in the United States, but all law enforcement jobs and most federal jobs are limited to citizens. If you are well along the way toward citizenship and expect to be naturalized soon, inquire as to your exact status with respect to the job.
- **Residency requirements.** If there is a residency requirement, you must live within the prescribed limits or be willing to move. If you are not willing to live in the area, do not waste time applying.
- **What forms must be filed.** The Announcement of the position for which you are applying will specify the form of application requested. For most federal jobs, you may submit either the Optional Application for Federal Employment (OF 612) or a resume which fulfills the requirements set forth in the pamphlet, *Applying for a Federal Job* (OF 510). For other than federal jobs, the Notice of Examination may tell you where you must go or write to get the necessary form or forms. Be sure you secure them all. The application might be a simple form asking nothing more than name, address, citizenship, and social security number or it may be a complex Experience Paper. An Experience Paper, as its title implies, asks a great deal about

education, job training, job experience, and life experience. Typically, the Experience Paper permits no identification by name, sex, or race; the only identifying mark is your social security number. The purpose of this procedure is to avoid permitting bias of any sort to enter into the weighting of responses. The Experience Paper generally follows a short form of application which does include a name. When the rating process is completed, the forms are coordinated by means of the social security number

- **Filing dates, place, and fee.** There is great variation in this area. For some positions you can file your application at any time. Others have a first day and last day for filing. If you file too early or too late, your application will not be considered. Sometimes it is sufficient to have your application postmarked by the last day for filing. More often, your application must be received by the last date. If you are mailing your application, allow five full business days for it to get there on time. Place of filing will be stated right on the Notice. Get the address right! Most applications may be filed by mail, but occasionally in-person filing is specified. Follow directions. Federal and postal positions require no filing fee. Most, but not all, other government jobs do charge a fee for processing your application. The fee is not always the same. Be sure to check this out. If the Notice specifies "money order only," plan to purchase a money order. Be sure the money order is made out properly. If you send or present a personal check, your application will be rejected without consideration. If the announcement specifies "money order only," you cannot submit cash, even in person.
- **How to qualify.** This portion of the Notice will tell you the basis on which the candidate will be chosen. Some examination scores consist of a totaling up of weighted education and experience factors. This type, of examination, called "an unassembled exam" because you do not come to one place to take the exam, is based upon your responses on the application and supplementary forms. Obviously, these must be very complete for you to get full credit for all you have learned and accomplished. The Notice may tell you of a qualifying exam, an exam which you must pass in addition to scoring high on an unassembled, written, or performance test. Or, the Notice may tell you of a competitive exam, written performance, or both. The competitive exam may be described in very general terms or in detail. It is even possible that a few sample questions will be attached. If the date of the exam has been set, that date will appear on the Notice. Write it down.

When you have the application forms in hand, photocopy them. Fill out the photocopies first. This way you can correct mistakes, change the order of information, add or delete. You can work at fitting what you have to say into the space allowed. Do not exaggerate, but be sure to give yourself credit for responsibilities you took on, cost saving ideas you gave your prior employer, or any accomplishments. Be clear and thorough in telling what you have learned and what you can do.

When you are satisfied with your draft, copy over the application onto the form(s). Be sure to include any backup material that is requested; by the same token, do not send more "evidence" than is truly needed to support your claims of qualification. Your application must be complete according to the requirements of the announcement, but must not be overwhelming. You want to command hiring attention by conforming exactly to requirements.

Check over all forms for neatness and completeness. Sign wherever indicated. Attach the fee, if required. Then mail or personally file the application on time.

If you are currently employed, *do not* give your notice now. Stay at your present job. If you are job hunting, continue your search. The time lag between application for a government job and actual employment is always many months; it may even be a year or two. Most people cannot afford to sit back and wait for the job.

If the Notice of Examination told you that there will be a competitive exam and told you about subjects of the examination, you can begin to study now. If not, just continue working and await notice of next steps.

When the Civil Service commission or personnel office to which you submitted your application receives it, the office will date, stamp, log, and open your file. The office may acknowledge receipt with more forms, sample exam questions, or a simple receipt slip. You may hear nothing at all for months.

Eventually you will receive a testing date or an interview appointment. Write these on your calendar in red so that you don't let the dates slip by. Write the address to which you are to report in the same place. If you receive an admission ticket for an exam, be sure to put it in a safe place; but keep it in sight so that you will not forget to take it with you to the exam. With an exam date, you should get information about the exam. Time may be short. Begin to study and prepare right away if you have not already done so.

If the next step is an exam, that exam might be either a paper and pencil exam or a performance exam. The exam depends on the nature of the job. The applicant for a locksmith's position might be asked to cut some complicated keys and to repair a broken lock; the track maintainer hopeful might have to replace ties or reset switches. The applicant for a position as a clerk-stenographer might have to take dictation and a typing test, along with a multiple-choice test of general clerical abilities. Applicants for most jobs will take only a written test. The written test is most frequently a multiple-choice test, one in which the test-taker chooses the best of four or five answer choices and marks its number on a separate answer sheet. Multiple-choice tests are machine scored. Machine scoring insures accuracy and objectivity. No one can misinterpret your answers. Machine scoring also allows for many applicants to be rated at the same time. It speeds up the process, though if you are waiting to hear about your job, you may doubt this fact.

Occasionally, the written test will consist of an essay portion along with or instead of the multiple-choice section. Essays usually appear at levels above initial entry level where there are fewer applicants and fewer papers to score. On an essay, the examiners are looking for indications that you can organize your thoughts and can express them effectively in writing.

If you are called for an exam, arrive promptly and dress appropriately. Neatness is always appropriate; however, you do not need to dress up for a performance exam nor for a written exam. If you will do manual work for your performance exam, wear clean work clothes. For a written exam, neat, casual clothing is fine.

THE INTERVIEW

If there is no exam and you are called directly to an interview, what you wear is more important. Take special care to look businesslike and professional. You must not appear to be too casual, and certainly not sloppy. Overdressing is also inappropriate. A neat dress or skirted suit is fine for women; men should wear a shirt and tie with suit or slacks and a jacket. And do pay attention to your grooming.

Interviews take up an interviewer's time. If you are called for an interview, you are under serious consideration. There may still be competition for the job; someone else may be more suited than you, but you are qualified and your skills and background have appealed to someone in the hiring office. The interview may be aimed at getting information about:

- **Your knowledge.** The interviewer wants to know what you know about the area in which you will work. For instance, if you will be doing data entry in a budget office, what do you know about the budget process? Are you at all interested in this area of financial planning? You may also be asked questions probing your knowledge of the agency for which you are interviewing. Do you care enough to have educated yourself about the functions and role of the agency, whether it's child welfare, pollution control, or international trade?
- **Your judgment.** You may be faced with hypothetical situations, job-related or in interpersonal relations, and be asked "What would you do if . . . ?" questions. Think carefully before answering. You must be decisive but diplomatic. There are no "right answers." The interviewer is aware that you are being put on the spot. How well you can handle this type of question is an indication of your flexibility and maturity.

- **Your personality.** You will have to be trained and supervised. You will have to work with others. What is your attitude? How will you fit in? The interviewer will be trying to make judgments in these areas on the basis of general conversation with you and from your responses to specific lines of questioning. Be pleasant, polite, and open with your answers, but do not volunteer a great deal of extra information. Stick to the subjects introduced by the interviewer Answer fully, but resist the temptation to ramble on.
- **Your attitude towards work conditions.** These are practical concerns: If the job will require frequent travel for extended periods, how do you feel about it? What is your family's attitude? If you will be very unhappy about the travel, you may leave the job and your training will have been a waste of the taxpayers' money. The interviewer also wants to know how you will react to overtime or irregular shifts.

Remember, working for the government is working for the people. Government revenues come from taxes. The hiring officers have a responsibility to put the right people into the right jobs in order to spend the taxpayers' money most effectively. And, as a government employee, you have a responsibility to give the people (including yourself) their money's worth.

Other steps along the hiring route may be a medical examination, physical performance testing, and psychological interviewing. If there is a written test, these steps do not occur until the written tests are scored and ranked. Steps that require the time of one examiner with one applicant are taken only when there is reasonable expectation of hiring.

MEDICAL EXAMINATION

A medical exam is self-explanatory. If there are eyesight or hearing requirements for the position, these must be checked against agency standards. If the job requires standing, lifting, or running, the applicant must be medically able to withstand the rigors. Since all government employers afford some sort of health coverage, there must be assurance of the general health of the employee or at least full awareness of current or potential problems. Drug testing is often included. Drug testing is legal if applied routinely and equally to all applicants and if notice of it is given beforehand.

PHYSICAL EXAMINATION

Physical performance testing is limited to applicants for physically demanding jobs. Police officers, firefighters, and correction officers, for example, must be able to run, climb, and carry, often under stress of personal danger as well as under the pressures of the immediate situation. Mail handlers and sanitation workers must be able to lift and carry many heavy loads, one after the other. Usually the physical performance test is a qualifying test-either you can do it or you can't. Sometimes, especially where speed may be a crucial element, the physical test is competitively scored and enters into the rating the candidate earns for placement on the certification list.

PSYCHOLOGICAL INTERVIEW

Finally, there is the psychological interview. This interview differs from the general information interview or the final hiring and placement interview in that it tries to assess your behavior under stress. Not all applicants for government jobs must be subjected to a psychological interview. It is limited to persons who will carry guns, to people who must make very quick decisions at moments of danger, and to people who might find themselves under interrogation by hostile forces. In other words, police officers, firefighters, CIA agents and DEA (Drug Enforcement Agency) agents, to name just a few, must be able to do their jobs without "cracking" under the strain.

Reading all the applications and weeding out the unqualified ones takes time. Weighing education and experience factors takes time. Administering and scoring of exams takes time. Interviews, medical exams, and physical performance tests take time. Verifying references takes time. And, finally, the vacancies must occur, and the government agency must have the funds to fill the vacancies.

All of this clarifies why you must not leave a job or a job search at any step along the way. Wait until you are offered your government job before you cut other ties. But when you finally do get that job, you will have a good income, many benefits, and job security.

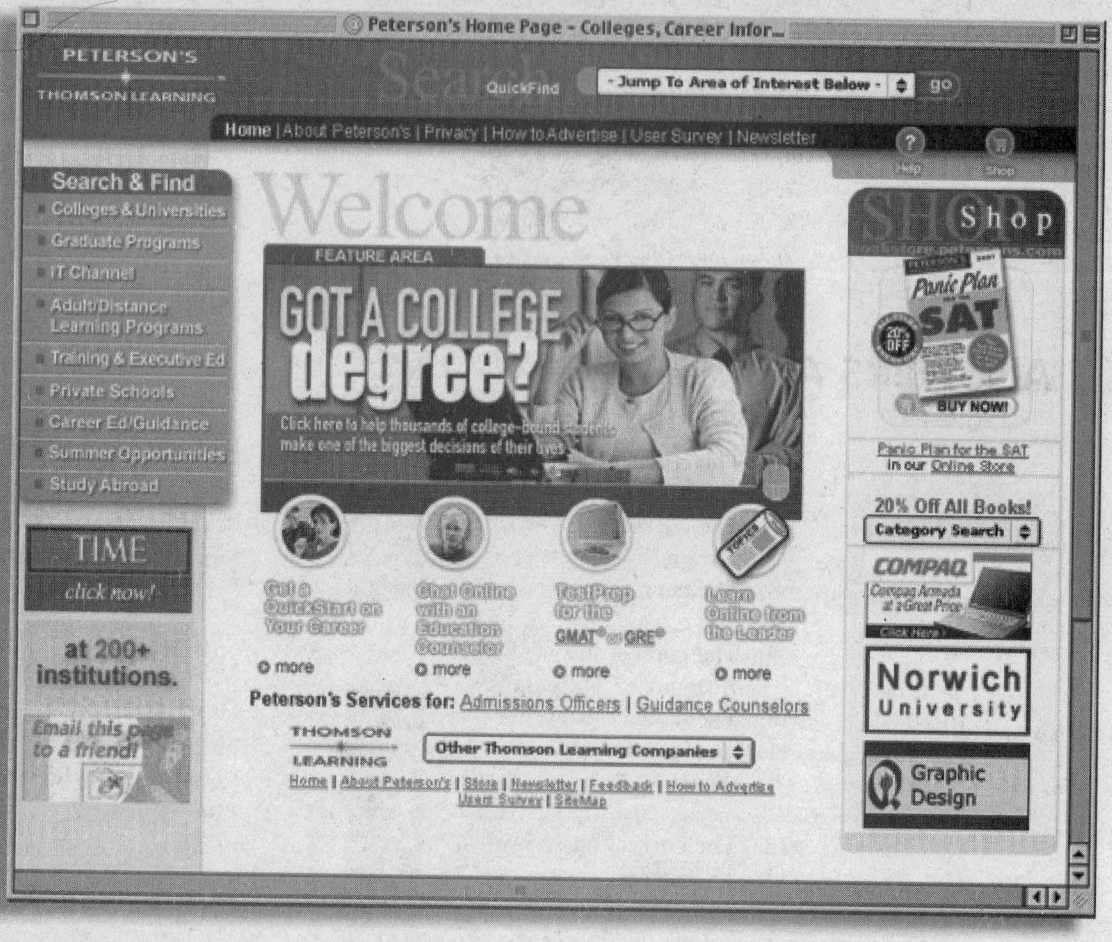

Peterson's Home Page - Colleges, Career Infor...
PETERSON'S
THOMSON LEARNING
Search
QuickFind
- Jump To Area of Interest Below -
go
Home | About Peterson's | Privacy | How to Advertise | User Survey | Newsletter
Help
Shop
Search & Find
Colleges & Universities
Graduate Programs
IT Channel
Adult/Distance Learning Programs
Training & Executive Ed
Private Schools
Career Ed/Guidance
Summer Opportunities
Study Abroad
TIME
click now!
at 200+ institutions.
Email this page to a friend!
Welcome
FEATURE AREA
GOT A COLLEGE degree?
Click here to help thousands of college-bound students make one of the biggest decisions of their lives.
Got a QuickStart on Your Career
Chat Online with an Education Counselor
TestPrep for the GMAT® or GRE®
Learn Online from the Leader
more
more
more
more
Peterson's Services for: Admissions Officers | Guidance Counselors
THOMSON LEARNING
Other Thomson Learning Companies
Home | About Peterson's | Store | Newsletter | Feedback | How to Advertise
Users Survey | SiteMap
Shop
Panic Plan for the SAT
20% OFF
BUY NOW!
Panic Plan for the SAT in our Online Store
20% Off All Books!
Category Search
COMPAQ
Compaq Armada at a Great Price
Norwich University
Graphic Design